MURDER BY CROWS

Hot Crimes in California

Steve Cassady

All rights reserved
Copyright 2017
Steve Cassady

ISBN: 0988192160
ISBN 13: 9780988192164
Library of Congress Control Number: 2016921387
Literacy, Ink, Atwater, CALIFORNIA

TABLE OF CONTENTS

Prologue	Alisal	1
Chapter 1	Burbank: Barbara Graham	19
Chapter 2	Wildwood: Burton W. Abbott	64
Chapter 3	Willow Springs: Spade Cooley	112
Chapter 4	Bel Air: The Manson Family	162
Chapter 5	Santa Cruz: Frazier, Mullin, and Kemper	211
Chapter 6	Berkeley: The SLA/Patty Hearst	262
Chapter 7	Brentwood: O. J. Simpson	317
Epilogue	Merced	371

PROLOGUE
ALISAL

East Salinas, California, a.k.a. Alisal, Spanish for "alder grove". Never a garden spot, unincorporated until 1963, Alisal draws its heritage from Dust Bowl Okies, Mexican braceros, and GIs mustering out of Fort Ord. Windswept Alisal is hemmed in on three sides, north, south, and east, by vast acres of furrowed row crops—sugar beets to celery to iceberg lettuce. It is separated from the Salinas city limits by convenient segregators—SP tracks, State Highway 101, and a backwater slough.

Post-WWII Alisal: profuse with two- and three-bedroom one-bath cracker boxes jerry-built on cramped lots with dirt yards. The houses clustered in neighborhoods with motor courts, trailer parks, and tent camps on streets without sidewalks, forming a town with limited public services. Alisal was home base for low-strata farmworkers from the produce fields and packing sheds of the Salinas Valley—upward mobility capped at foreman and/or tractor driver. Alisal, always bad, evolved worse. After annexation into Salinas, it still was Alisal. It has grown to a population of plus sixty thousand, transitioned from 75/25 Caucasian/Hispanic to 25/75 the other way.

Garner Avenue and Sanborn Road, the heart of Alisal, once was a neighborhood of farmworkers and families. Now it is ground zero for prison-bred blue-bandana Sureno blood spilling—among the most notorious zones in America for gangbang murders, assaults, drug deals, prostitution, and property crimes. Sixteen murders were committed in East Salinas in the first half of 2013, to pick one year, ten of them on summer nights between July 24 and August 11. Abatement is nowhere in sight. The stats horrify: twenty-nine kills in 2014, escalating past thirty in 2015.

Badass symbols all around, evocative of East LA barrios: cinder-block *llanterias* painted garish yellow; metal security grates bolted to windows; razor wire coiling over building and fence tops; spray-can graffiti tagging walls; pit bulls and Rottweilers snarling through chain-link fences; dark-eyed *carnales* on the prowl in sagging denims and oversized T-shirts, necks and arms sleeved in jailhouse ink.

December 2012: New K–6 campus under construction, opening scheduled for the 2013/14 academic year. It would become the sixteenth elementary school in the district. Alisal Unified Elementary School Board (AUESB) reached for a name to radiate positive Hispanic associations. Precedents: Alisal branch of the Salinas Public Library on Williams Road, named after iconic farm-labor activist Cesar Chavez; and Alisal's second high school, christened Everett Alvarez High.

June 1956: Everett Alvarez Jr. graduated from Salinas High School. He went to Santa Clara University on an academic scholarship. In June 1960, he earned his bachelors degree, joined the Navy, and was trained as a fighter pilot. He shipped out to Southeast Asia right after hostilities broke out.

August 1964: Lieutenant Everett Alvarez launched from the USS *Ticonderoga*, piloting an A-4 Skyhawk. He red-buttoned North Vietnamese Swatows (patrol boats), retaliating for attacks on American destroyers in the Gulf of Tonkin. His plane caught flak. Smoke billowed from the fuselage. He thumbed "eject," blew back the canopy, and catapulted into Charlie's front yard—the first

American prisoner of the war. He endured eight-plus years of torture—second-longest POW stretch in the Vietnam conflict.

Lt. Commander Everett Alvarez Jr. retired from the service highly decorated. He coauthored books about his Hanoi Hilton ordeal. He earned masters and JD degrees. Ronald Reagan appointed him deputy director of the Peace Corps. He has made a career in Washington, DC, as an executive and a member of multiple acronymic boards administering health services to veterans.

Cesar Chavez defined nonviolent nobility in the farmworker struggle for living wages. Everett Alvarez Jr. embodies the words *hero* and *distinguished*. With these men as background, the AUESB voted in 2013 to name the new school after Tiburcio Vasquez, nineteenth-century Monterey County desperado, hanged for murder in 1875.

The selection sparked animated debate along ethnic lines. Defenders, mostly Hispanic, cited dispossession. They said fourth-generation *californio* Tiburcio Vasquez had merely stood his ground against Anglo encroachment. They cited the tradition of social outlaws—Emiliano Zapata, Frank and Jesse James, Billy the Kid—all raging against injustice wielded by corrupt authority. AUESD superintendent John Ramirez, typical: "Tiburcio Vasquez…was a revolutionary…He was not OK with oppression."

Opponents, predominantly Caucasian, argued literal history. Regardless of motive, Tiburcio Vasquez had rustled livestock, robbed stagecoaches, looted towns, and murdered innocents. His backstory, abridged…

Hernando Cortes and five hundred *conquistadores* overwhelmed the Aztec Empire in the sixteenth century, claiming territory and riches for Spain. They came on horseback armed with the latest in European cannonry and tactics, but their best weapon was airborne pathogens. The Spaniards were largely immune to their own diseases, and the natives were not. Epidemic smallpox introduced by the Spaniards wiped out between three and fifteen million Aztecs, inspiring the primitives to believe the Spaniards' Christian God superior. Double dip: doomed Aztecs defeated by Spanish military might and spiritual rule of Roman Catholicism.

Spanish suzerainty in Mexico City camped on. With government sanction, Franciscan friar Junipero Serra forged the Mission Trail from San Diego to Sonoma, for the putative purpose of civilizing the simple Alta California savages, training them in agricultural trades, and saving their pagan souls through the grace of their omnipotent Catholic God. Father Serra led humble penitents on foot and the backs of burros, wearing sandals and brown robes, featuring perhaps history's worst haircuts. Poorly emphasized sidebar: the missionaries didn't come alone.

Mexico City had strategic designs on Alta California. Mexico City wanted California for itself and needed population to ward off colonization by England, France, Germany, and Russia. Mexico City sent legions of the poor behind Padre Serra, offering rations, horses, cattle, land, and money for establishing pueblos contiguous to the missions. Colonel Juan Bautista de Anza, the last of the *conquistadores,* for one, blazed a twelve-hundred-mile trail from the northern Sonoran Desert to various Alta California points along the Pacific.

In late March 1775, Anza led an expedition of 240 men, women, and children; 340 horses; 320 head of cattle; and 165 pack mules from San Miguel de Casitas, capital of Sonora, through what is now southern Arizona. Anza's pilgrims pushed across the desert, moving ten to twenty miles a day. They crossed the Gila and Colorado Rivers and by January had found their way to the present site of Los Angeles. They rested six weeks at Mission San Gabriel before setting off to Monterey, arriving a year after their original departure, in March 1776.

Among the group, forty-five-year-old *campesino* Juan Atanasio Vasquez; his wife, Maria; and three sons and a daughter-in-law.

Anza pushed north with his lieutenant, Jose Joaquin Moraga, and twenty soldiers plus a contingent of settlers including the Vasquez family, stopping on the shores of a natural bay.

June 26, 1776: Six days before the signing of the Declaration of Independence in Philadelphia, Anza's group broke ground on the settlement of San Francisco.

Juan Atanasio Vasquez stayed put, but within a year, one of his sons, Jose Tiburcio, along with his wife and infant daughter, joined sixty-three soldiers and settlers to form a pueblo on the south end of the Bay, the eventual San Jose. Jose Tiburcio de Vasquez was rare among *campesinos*—he was literate. He rose to prominence as an *alcalde* (mayor and judge) in San Jose. He fathered thirteen children, four of whom died in childhood. He grandfathered myriad more, including the *bandido* Tiburcio Vasquez, youngest son of Jose Tiburcio's fifth-born, Jose Hermengildo.

Jose Hermengildo Vasquez, literate like his father, served as a Spanish soldier, garrisoned at the presidio of Monterey. He met and married Maria Guadalupe Cantua. He was thirty-six. She was sixteen. Monterey was governed by home rule. Colonists from Sonora kept out Europeans. Mexico had achieved independence from Spain in 1821. Mexico City was too distant to establish effective government. Monterey built itself around ranching, farming, shipping, and trading in and out of Monterey Bay. Colonists considered themselves *californios*—independent citizens of their region, owners and operators of their own lives. Prosperous *rancheros* grew around cattle herds, farming, and horsemanship. *Vaqueros* skilled in riding and roping achieved elite stature.

America was moving across by then. The Louisiana Purchase; the Gadsden Purchase; the Alamo—Manifest Destiny inexorably on the move by rail, hoof, and wagon wheel, often at gunpoint. General Sam Houston and his undermanned rebel forces defeated Mexican general Santa Anna at San Jacinto in 1836, and Texas became a US republic. The Mexican-American War in 1846 and 1847 led to the

Treaty of Guadalupe-Hidalgo. Terms: for $15 million, Mexico ceded all lands north of a horizontal line along the Rio Grande, the Gila River, and the port of San Diego—a border strung between future Brownsville, Texas, and Tijuana—including all of Alta California.

Bad timing for the Mexicans. Guadalupe-Hidalgo was signed February 2, 1848. Gold had been discovered at Sutter's Mill eight days earlier, on January 24, but news hadn't traveled. The United States had gained priceless Western lands plus impossibly rich veins of precious metals. Population blew up. Fortune seekers rode the hurricane into El Dorado, overwhelming existent culture. California demography before Sutter's Mill: fourteen thousand *californios* and a hundred thousand Indians. One year later, 1849: 380,000, most of them Anglos from across the nation. *Californios* now the minority. American rules now in play.

Almost overnight, *californios* became second-class citizens in their own country. Apologists ascribe Tiburcio Vasquez's outlaw inclinations to noble outrage over Yankee imperialism. The facts don't concur. He was a child during the Mexican-American War, thirteen at the signing of Guadalupe-Hidalgo. Of his nine siblings and countless uncles and cousins, he was the only one of Juan Atanasio de Vasquez's progeny to turn sour.

In 2010, the University of Oklahoma Press released *Bandido: The Life and Times of Tiburcio Vasquez*, by John Boessenecker, a scholarly text, exhaustively researched, tightly documented. Boessenecker acknowledges Tiburcio Vasquez wasn't enamored of Anglos, but uncovered no evidence that he pillaged for motive other than profit and thrill. The book is dense with accounts of Tiburcio Vasquez terrorizing the state, the bio-drama of a paleo-gangbanger. Episodes paraphrased from *Bandido* bracket insight.

Tiburcio Vasquez turned rogue at nineteen. Indisposed toward *campesino* sunburn and calluses, he fell into an idle life, running with Monterey County hoodlum Anastacio Garcia, eleven years older, married to one of his first cousins. He embraced low virtue: gambling, stealing, drinking, chasing loose women.

Anastacio Garcia and his gang sported fine clothes, fast horses, fancy tack, and deadly weapons. They solicited wild times and violent incident. They crashed a *fandango* in downtown Monterey one Saturday night in 1854. Tequila flowed. Testosterone surged. Fist fights broke out. A sheriff's deputy arrived. Hand guns cleared leather. One from Anastacio Garcia's crew shot the deputy dead. Witnesses identified the shooter, Alejandro Ramos. Town vigilantes lynched Ramos the next day. Tiburcio Vasquez hit the saddle, swirling dust ahead of the posse, sealing his destiny.

Joaquin Murrieta was a mythic gold-rush marauder. Bronze plaques on commemorative rocks all over Northern California claim proximity to yet another Joaquin Murrieta outrage. He initiated his notorious but short-lived spree in 1849. By 1853, Joaquin Murrieta's head was brining in a jar of formaldehyde. Three and a half years to terrorize half the state on horseback? If the infamous Murrieta accomplished even a fraction of his own legend, he would have to have been a dozen *bandidos*. Tiburcio Vasquez, lesser known to history, surpassed him. Vasquez rode the outlaw trail for two decades from Mendocino to San Gabriel, Sonora to Hollister, pausing only for two separate stretches in San Quentin.

Tiburcio Vasquez never denied brandishing weapons or pulling triggers, but he maintained that he never killed anyone himself. A spurious contention at best, contrary to researched accounts in Boessenecker's *Bandido*. Even if technically true, fatalities dogged his path. Too many victims, alive at first encounter with Tiburcio Vasquez's gang, were corpses soon thereafter.

His range was epic, the stuff of legends, tempting to romanticize. He committed crimes in hometown Monterey, the Salinas Valley, and the roads and towns in contiguous San Benito County. He crossed the Diablo into the San Joaquin Valley, robbing stages, stores, and citizens from Los Banos to Bakersfield. He found his way north into Sonoma and Mendocino Counties and back down through the gold-rush camps in the low Sierra from Columbia to Mariposa.

He crisscrossed a felonious course between the Sierra foothills and the San Joaquin Valley floor. He scaled the Tehachapi into the desert of northern Los Angeles County. He established a hideout between the Santa Clarita and Antelope Valleys near the village of Agua Dulce among nine hundred acres of sandstone outcrops jutting up from the desert floor, since designated Vasquez Rocks Natural Area Park.

Hollywood would discover Vasquez Rocks in the 1930s as a stand-in for Tibet in *The Werewolf of London*. Television camped on, filming on-location episodes for more than seventy-five series from *Rin Tin Tin* to *Star Trek*. Mel Brooks chose it as background for the set of *Blazing Saddles*. In his time, Tiburcio Vasquez used the rocks and caves as a citadel. He nested in ahead of Northern California posses before working his way into Los Angeles. He holed up ahead of Southern California trackers before scaling the mountains on his returns north. The local high school—in Acton across Highway 14 from the village of Agua Dulce—carries his name: Vasquez High, nicknamed "Trailer Trash High" because of its architecture—a compound of double-wide relocatables, all perimeters fenced and gated with chain link.

1857, age twenty-three: Tiburcio Vasquez arrested for horse theft in Los Angeles, sentenced to five years in San Quentin, operated then by private contract not state commission. Profit ruled policy. Contractors cut costs by hiring few guards and paying them poorly. They leased out convicts as cheap labor for brick making, wood chopping, and ship lading. Food was bad, hygiene poor, and health care nonexistent. Prisoners were crammed inside stone cellblocks, four to a six-by-ten space. Ill-treated convicts obsessed over escape; 547 broke out in the ten years between 1851 and 1861. Less than half were captured and returned. The unforuntate few were tied to a ladder leaning against a cellblock and bullwhipped, though no time was added to their sentences.

Tiburcio Vasquez and another convict escaped in June 1859, an action that took the lives of two prisoners and wounded three more. They escaped on foot into Amador County, stole horses, and rode toward Stockton. The sheriff of Amador County caught up with them along the San Joaquin River. They took 150 lashes on the ladder (prison medics treated the wounds with salt water). Vasquez attempted a shipboard breakout three months later. Eight convicts died in that attempt. He was sent back and flogged again. He joined sixteen others for an attempt in January 1861. Three prisoners were killed, eleven more, including Vasquez, wounded.

Upon recovery, the ladder, sixty lashes, and more salt in his wounds. In 1862, with a year left in his sentence, he tried again with more ambitious scope and predictable results. Mass crash out. Chaos. Gunfire. Recapture. Ten convicts dead, more than thirty wounded. Tiburcio Vasquez had had enough by then. He attempted no more escapes. He rode out his last year with a reputation secured by ugly statistics: four attempted escapes in five years behind bars. Twenty dead, fifty-odd wounded.

Tiburcio Vasquez left San Quentin on August 13, 1863. He returned to Monterey and San Benito Counties, hiring on as a *vaquero*, a calling that couldn't sustain him as well as banditry. Less than a year later in the cantina of a Santa Clara mining camp, New Almaden, the camp butcher, an Italian named Pellegrini, entered drunk, flashing money. Witnesses said Vasquez and his cousin Faustina Lorenza pushed through the batwing doors just after Pellegrini stumbled out. Pellegrini was found later, pockets empty, stabbed to death in the bedroom adjacent to his butcher shop.

Tiburcio Vasquez felt the heat in San Benito and Santa Clara Counties. He moved north toward Sonoma. In Petaluma in 1865, somebody broke one of Tiburcio Vasquez's bandit comrades out of the town jail. Authorities routinely attributed strong-arm Sonoma County crime to Vasquez. As usual, he claimed innocence. He had free time; he could afford fine horses, clothes, and weapons while leading a debauched social life, but he was innocent. Eventually, in exchange for leniency, two confederates informed on him for burglary and larceny. He was tried, convicted, and sent back to prison for two years on each charge, terms to run concurrently.

San Quentin had updated its policies since his last stay five years earlier. Convicts were credited two months for each one served. Vasquez reestablished criminal contacts in San Quentin but served his time without notable incident. He was released on June 4, 1870. He claimed he tried honest occupation but was hounded by reputation. He said he gave into the inevitable and went full bore on banditry.

August 26, 1873, daybreak: Tiburcio Vasquez rode with four other outlaws into Tres Pinos, four miles south of Hollister, to rob Snyder's store. Chaos followed. Patrons inside the store. Citizens out on the street. Tiburcio Vasquez carrying a fifteen-round Henry repeater, a Navy Colt Dragoon revolver, and a large knife. The other bandits also fully armed. Inside Snyder's, two gang members, Abdon Leiva and Romulo Gonzales, pulled pistols and cocked them. They ordered two storekeepers and two customers to the ground and hog-tied them. Outside, Tiburcio Vasquez, Clodoveo Chavez, and Teodoro Moreno approached the store with a pack mule. Townspeople milled around.

Vasquez ordered them to "Halt and lie down." A sheepherder broke for the back of the barn. Teodoro Moreno shot him in the mouth. Romulo Gonzalez finished him off. Tiburcio Vasquez pistol-whipped a fifteen-year-old boy who responded slowly to his commands. A deaf teamster with a wagonload of wire pulled up to the store. He saw the guns but couldn't hear the commands. He bolted for the cover of a nearby barn. Tiburcio Vasquez cut him down with his Henry .44. A hotel keeper, Leander Davidson, and his wife on the hotel porch reached simultaneously for the front doorknob, seeking cover inside. Tiburcio Vasquez fired through the glass, killing Davidson.

Vasquez's gang looted the Snyder store while citizens cowered. They extracted money and jewelry from trussed-up patrons.

Vasquez prodded Andrew Snyder at rifle point to the hotel, stepping over the corpse of the innkeeper Davidson. He forced Snyder's wife to retrieve $220 dollars in gold dust from their room. They robbed another teamster of four dollars. They went back to the store and helped themselves to new wardrobes. They scarfed cheese, crackers, tinned sardines, and oysters. They tapped into a keg of beer. On the way out of town, two and a half hours later, they stole eight horses, two with saddles. The take: $2,200 in cash and goods plus livestock, at the cost of three lives. Hard to locate revolutionary nobility in the plunder of a town, of an unarmed man dying in his wife's arms, regardless who fired the fatal bullets.

Four months later, December 26: Tiburcio Vasquez and twelve gangsters hit the settlement of Kingston in Tulare County, located on the south bank of the Kings River, across the water from what would become the town of Laton. Main Street of Kingston featured the Pioneer Store, owned and operated by merchants Elias Jacob and Louis Einstein. The Pioneer Store was first in a line of three businesses, the other two adjacent to the east: Simon Sweet's general store and Reichart's hotel.

The gang hid horses in the woods near the river. Some wore masks; others, including Tiburcio Vasquez, did not. He carried four Colt Dragoons. They walked across the toll bridge and encountered bridge owner Oliver Bliss. They bound and gagged Bliss, robbing him of nine dollars. They lifted $180 from two more citizens walking on the street. They posted sentries and split up. Vasquez and one group entered the hotel saloon. They ordered patrons to flatten and threatened them with death should any of the gang suffer injury. Vasquez pistol-whipped a recalcitrant.

More outlaws burst into the hotel dining room with demands to hit the floor. The clerk, Ed Erlanger, rushed out the back door into Simon Sweet's store and yelled a warning. A black cook fled through the door in the rear of the kitchen. Vasquez finished sacking the saloon. He entered the Pioneer Store and forced a clerk to open the safe. He pulled out $800. He left twelve patrons on the floor bound and gagged. The Vasquez gang moved into Sweet's store, trussed more citizens, and looted more money from the safe and till: a measly twenty-five dollars. The day before, Simon Sweet had transported $3,000 cash to a bank in Visalia.

The cook had alerted the town's most prominent businessman, rancher/livery owner John Sutherland. Sutherland grabbed his own Henry repeater. He collected three hard men with revolvers. They set up across from the Main Street businesses, on the high bank of the Kings. John Sutherland sighted in on a sentry patrolling the boardwalk in front of Simon Sweet's store, an erstwhile sheepshearer named Ramon Molina. He squeezed off a shot into Ramon Molina's upper torso. Ramon Molina screamed, "I am shot."

Tiburcio Vasquez yelled, "Vamonos!" The gang rushed into the street. Rifle and revolver rounds cross-fired. Vasquez's crew ran for the bridge, dragging the wounded Ramon Molina. Their sentry with the horses opened fire at Sutherland and his men. The *bandidos* reached the *remuda*. Three of them carried bullet wounds. The posse ran dry of shells. The gang quirted horse flanks. They fled with $2,500 worth of cash and jewelry, leaving thirty-five townspeople tied up on the floors of Kingston's businesses.

The sheepshearer Molina died of his wounds. The posse captured one of the other lookouts. News spread. More posses were formed. Tiburcio Vasquez hid out in the Mexican settlement of Panama, three miles south of Bakersfield on the banks of a branch of the Kern River. Panama provided refuge, cantinas, and fandango houses. Tiburcio Vasquez tipped tequila bottles and trifled with senoritas until the hunt was abandoned.

Tiburcio Vasquez was a relentless womanizer. Literate like his father and grandfather, he read and wrote poetry. He was dashing with charm. He played the guitar. Balladeers wrote *corridos*—rap music in charro pants—about his hair-raising adventures. Women swooned. Tiburcio Vasquez accepted their adoration without imposition of moral limits. In March 1873, Vasquez hid out with his brother Chico's family in high-desert Elizabeth Lake, in the Antelope Valley. Chico worked long days in the copper mines of Soledad Canyon. Tiburcio lazed around, taking up with Chico's impressionable seventeen-year-old daughter, Felicita.

Chico wasn't especially proud of his younger brother. He harbored him out of blood loyalty alone. Nobody had bothered to tell Felicita that Tiburcio was her uncle. Tiburcio didn't broadcast it either, for reasons of his own. Felicita turned pregnant. Tiburcio rode on, oblivious to the disgrace he left behind.

Tiburcio Vasquez established values with his crotch. One of his henchmen for the Tres Pinos raid, another sheepman named Abdon Leiva, was married to a woman named Rosario. Abdon Leiva was a reluctant *bandido*, but Rosario, enamored of Vasquez and thrilled by desperado daring, prodded her husband to join the gang. She eventually had her way with a willing Vasquez and missed her period. The most likely father was the outlaw lover (she later would miscarry).

Running from the law after Tres Pinos, Tiburcio Vasquez contrived escape routes that took Rosario (and her three children by Abdon Leiva) with him on one path, sending the cuckold confederate along another. Abdon Leiva was caught and jailed in San Jose. The charm of outlaw existence wore thin for Rosario. Tiburcio sent her to live with friends near Milpitas.

Women were his downfall. Things were closing in. Santa Clara County sheriff John H. Adams led a posse as far north as Fort Tejon at the peak of the Tehachapi. Alameda County sheriff Harry Morse, the best man hunter in the territory, joined with San Joaquin County sheriff Tom Cunningham and an eight-man posse. They covered twenty-seven-hundred miles over a period of sixty-one days between March and May 1874. Los Angeles County sheriff William R. "Billy" Rowland had been pushing from Los Angeles as far as the Mojave Desert. For a time, Vasquez dodged them all.

In Los Angeles, he headquartered in Rancho La Brea (present-day Melrose Place) in an adobe residence of Yiorgos "Greek George" Xaralampo (anglicized to Georgios Caralamba). Greek George had come to the United States from Smyrna, Turkey, in 1856. He was stationed in Ft. Tejon, at the crest of the Techapi, one of eight drivers that the US government enlisted to herd camels (technically dromedaries). The camels were projected for use in shipping construction supplies for the Butterfield Overland Stage route from Saint Louis to Los Angeles.

Greek George (he later changed his name to George Allen) met pioneer LA surveyor/landowner Henry Hancock. Hancock envisioned the dromedaries carrying mail along the Butterfield route, a one-hump Pony Express. Henry Hancock was a Harvard-trained attorney who owned all of Rancho La Brea (now West Hollywood). He allowed Greek George to build an adobe farmhouse on rancho property, including stabling for the dromedaries. Hancock's Camel Express mail service never materialized. Greek George released his herd into the Mojave wilds. He stayed in La Brea to manage Henry Hancock's livestock holdings.

Greek George worked the fringes. He mixed with a diverse crowd. He numbered among his circle politicians, newsmen, lawyers, criminals, and lawmen. He married a *californio* noble, Cornelia Lopez, a cousin to both Felicita Vasquez's mother and a young *vaquero* in love with Felicita, Jose Jesus Lopez.

Tiburcio Vasquez visited Greek George frequently, mostly while evading the law. He grew fond of Cornelia Lopez's twenty-eight-year-old sister Modesta. Modesta didn't resist. When Tiburcio's niece Felicita bore his child, the scandal spread through Greek George's in-law sorority, so did rumors that Tiburcio was keeping company with a notorious Los Angeles *puta* nicknamed *La Coneja* ("The Rabbit"). The strong-minded women in Greek George's life grew ill-disposed toward the amorous *bandido*.

May 13, 1874: Reward money for the capture of Tiburcio Vasquez inflated to $8,000. Greek George saw a way to profit while maintaining harmony in his home. He contacted sheriff Billy Rowland and sold him Tiburcio Vasquez. A posse of Southern California lawmen—including undersheriff Albert Johnson and police chief Frank Hartley—converged on Rancho La Brea. Vasquez was in the company of Modesta Lopez at 8:30 a.m. when deputies rushed Greek George's adobe. He tried to run but was shot in the arm and surrendered. In the room where he was staying, lawmen found the spoils from raids in Northern California: stolen jewelry, knives, guns, and tack. They found a white horse, taken a year earlier from a prominent Los Angeles attorney.

In LA County jail, Tiburcio Vasquez freely granted interviews with local newsmen until he was well enough from his gunshot wound to travel. Sheriff Rowland, undersheriff Johnson, and a deputy, Walter Rogers, took him shackled hand and foot in a wagon to the railroad depot. They escorted him by train to LA Harbor in San Pedro. They boarded a steamship for a rough-seas three-day voyage to Monterey Bay. They rode by horseback to county seat Salinas and delivered him to Monterey County jail.

The district court in Salinas served both Monterey and Santa Clara Counties. Authorities reckoned that insecure hoosegows in Salinas or scene-of-the-crime Hollister couldn't hold such a dangerous defendant. For security, Judge Belden ordered him taken by train to the Santa Clara County jail in San Jose, where ninety-eight years earlier, Tiburcio Vasquez's grandfather had helped settle a new community.

A Spanish-language newspaper in San Francisco hired attorney Ben Darwin to defend Tiburcio Vasquez. Ben Darwin argued the impossibility of a fair trial in San Benito County. Judge Belden gaveled a change of venue to San Jose. In the end, it didn't matter. Tiburcio Vasquez's notoriety overwhelmed his claims of innocence. Tiburcio Vasquez had flaunted authority for two well-publicized decades. He pandered to all forms of pretrial publicity. He allowed interviews promiscuously. He sat for sepia photo shots. He cooperated with pulp biographers. No venue in California could have produced an untainted jury pool.

With nineteenth-century jurisprudence, he was a dead man anyway. A century later, on two points alone, he would have found a mistrial, hung jury, or outright acquittal. Two days before the trial began, January 4, 1875, Ben Darwin resigned, claiming he hadn't been paid. He left with all his defense documents, including the transcript of the trial of Tres Pinos codefendant Teodoro Moreno, useful for impeaching witnesses who might testify differently in the Vasquez proceedings.

In late November 1874, in Salinas, Teodoro Moreno, defended by Ben Darwin's cocounsel Bob Tully, had been found guilty for his part in the Tres Pinos raid but had escaped the gallows. Judge Belden sentenced Moreno to life in prison. In the Vasquez trial two months later, he saw no relevance to the Moreno trial transcripts. He denied Bob Tully's request for continuance. The trial proceeded on schedule.

The trial was a carnival. People poured in by the trainload. Newspapers around the state and the country sent reporters. Photographers and biographers flocked with common citizen voyeurs. Forty to fifty Northern California lawmen rode in. Tiburcio Vasquez racked up constant visitations. Swooning musicians strummed *corridos*.

The trial took five days and included witnesses from Tres Pinos eyeballing the killer of their friends. It included corroboration from coconspirator Abdon Leiva, wronged husband of Tiburcio Vasquez's lover Rosario Leiva. Abdon Leiva testified that Tiburcio Vasquez shot and killed two Tres Pinos citizens. Without the transcript from Teodoro's Moreno's trial to impeach Leiva, Bob Tully was forced to call Tiburcio Vasquez in his own defense. Vasquez stumbled over his lines. Attorneys had him speak through an interpreter, but often he answered in English before the interpreter could begin. At one point, he claimed he was sitting under a tree outside town until the shooting stopped. At another, he said he had planned the robbery and entered town with the others but didn't shoot anybody. Jurors found his accounts disingenuous.

Deliberation: three hours. Verdict: guilty. Sentence: death. Only hope: appeal and/or clemency from the governor. The appeal was perfunctory and denied—in fact didn't even include legal points that surely would spring future defendants: mention of lawyer Ben Darwin's abrupt resignation and the missing Moreno trial transcript. The Vasquez camp held out for executive clemency. A month earlier, governor Newton Booth had left office to serve in the US Senate. He was replaced by lieutenant governor Romualdo Pacheco, a *californio* from Santa Barbara, five years older than Tiburcio Vasquez.

Governor Pacheco was a contemporary. He endured the same conditions in the same time frame as Tiburcio Vasquez. He faced the same indignities from Anglo overtake but bootstrapped himself into the new order as a prominent politician. He symbolized possibilities available for spirited, ambitious *californios*. Living testimony the outlaw life was not foreordained by Anglo usurpation.

Pacheco was twice a state senator. He was a brigadier general during the Civil War, charged by governor Leland Stanford with disarming military companies in and around Los Angeles disloyal to the Union. From 1863 to 1867, he was state treasurer. He was a three-term member of the US House of Representatives and lieutenant governor of California. From February 27 to December 9, 1875, he governed California after Newton Booth's departure for Washington, until the newly elected governor, William Irwin, elected in September, could be inaugurated.

March 16, 1875: Romualdo Pacheco heard Bob Tulley's plea for clemency but saw no merit and felt no sympathy. Petition denied. March 19: Execution in the 19th century was entertainment, a spectator sport. San Jose and surrounding hotels, all booked. Streets, saloons, and restaurants, jammed. San Jose commerce hopped on a Mardi Gras scale. Hookers, pimps, grifters, and dips mixed with throngs of the morbidly curious.

Main event by invitation only; 250 ticketed citizens crowded into the county jail's courtyard. A little after 1:30 p.m., Sheriff John H. Adams nodded. The hangman draped the prisoner with a black hood, set the noose, and levered the trap. Tiburcio Vasquez dropped hard. The fall snapped his neck clean. He swung in the spring breeze, on full display for his deliberate life of crime…

Alisal, 2013. Opponents' argument paraphrased: K–6 districts in Clay County, Missouri, or Lincoln County, New Mexico, weren't naming elementary schools after Jesse and Frank James and William Bonny, no matter how sympathetic their motives or how glamorous their legends. Legend, after all, is insufficient motive. Murder crosses lines and damns the legends. Murder dishonors, regardless of what rationalizes the act—the ultimate arrogance of ego unchecked by conscience: *my life is more important than yours.* Barely a stretch parallel: Bonnie and Clyde Elementary in their hometowns of Rowena or Telico, Texas. Unthinkable, except perhaps in California.

In California, capital criminals tend to linger in myth and lore long beyond their time, blurring lines between truth and fiction, between justice and law. They tend to gain perverse celebrity. Revisionists tend to romance infamy in California, confusing ignominy with purity, sponsoring sympathy where none is warranted.

Legend over fact: Epidemic throughout California's history of 20th century capital offense. The accounts that follow reverse the inclination, calling it straight—*Murder by Crows.* True tales of bad people committing rash acts and generating bold notice.

CHAPTER 1
BURBANK: BARBARA GRAHAM

Los Angeles, post-WWII, pre-freeway, pre-skyscraper: Different then. By code, 150-foot height limits were enforced on downtown buildings. LA city fathers decreed that nothing should surpass majestic City Hall. Located downtown, 200 N. Spring, the City Hall rises thirty-two stories, a 454-foot bright-white obelisk atop a broad rectangular base. The tower itself, a classic LA identifier, a world-famous law-and-order logo. Its image is embossed on the LAPD shield that once backdropped opening credits of *Dragnet*, the 1950s and 60s weekly TV police procedural starring wooden Jack Webb as detective sergeant Joe Friday, badge 714.

LA County in the '50s: Ten thousand square miles of suburbs, communities, districts, and neighborhoods fast overtaking farmlands, spiraling from downtown, ringed by mountains, desert, and ocean; 4.5 million inhabitants spread under sun, smog, and palm trees from Northridge to Long Beach, from the foot of Mount Baldy to the Anaheim orange groves, from the snows of San Gorgonio to the shores of Santa Monica.

Concentrated within, the city of Los Angeles itself. Two-million-plus population in 1953 crammed between the San Fernando Valley and Long Beach, between Santa Monica and Rosemead. Then and now, traffic in the city never abates. Trolley cars, metro buses, cars, cabs, and trucks all traverse busy boulevards and crowded cross streets. Then and now, epic diversity—racketeers, hoodlums, and punks melting into the civic pot with entitled old money, nouveau Hollywood glitz, dense ethnic enclaves, transplanted Dust Bowl Okies, and standard white-bread middle class.

Then and now a volatile mix—anything possible.

I

Monday, May 4, 1953, Los Angeles, 3:00 p.m.: Real-life noir setting up in a shithole apartment on E. Imperial Highway, Lynwood, a three-room flop slapped together with plywood siding and hollow-core doors inside a National Tire Retreading franchise.

LAPD had dispatched a fourteen-man squad of hard case cops and patrolmen representing the notorious robbery-homicide (R-H) division and Burbank PD. Eight patrolmen formed a perimeter cordon around the tire shop. Chief of detectives Thad Brown and sergeant Dick Ruble approached the flimsy rear door flanked by two R-H dicks. Homicide commander Captain R. A. Lohrman at the front leading two patrolmen. Front and back, they drew weapons. Inside, unaware: three unrepentant hoods minutes from headline arrest.

Thad Brown and Dick Ruble shouldered through, splintering wood panels and exploding hinge screws. Captain Lohrman and two others punched through the front. They saw Emmett Raymond Perkins, forty-four, standing in the frame of the bedroom door; John Albert Santo, fifty-two, pants down, flat on his back, receptive, on a living room mattress; Barbara Diane Graham, twenty-nine, nude, bending over Santo, liquid eyes in a dreamy stare.

Outlaw tableau: ferret-faced Emmett Perkins, thinning hair, jittery eyes, sunken cheeks, protuberant ears; bosomy Barbara Graham, gorgeous, chestnut hair dyed blond, red welts inside her left elbow; big Jack Santo, dark wavy hair, Mr. Potato Head features offset by a hardened scowl—horned-rim glasses, lounge-lizard '50s pencil moustache under a big honker.

Tableau shattered by police intrusion. Santo shriveled. Twelve-gauge riot guns pointed at vitals: surefire boner kill. Perkins backed up against a wall. Graham frantically trying to cover three body parts with two hands. Thad Brown, boring his Remington pump at Jack Santo, daring retaliation, barking terse orders: "Get them dressed, cuff them, haul them downtown, and sift this dump for evidence." Santo, Perkins, and Graham: "We give up. Don't shoot." Thad Brown didn't mention obtaining counsel or remaining silent. Pre-Miranda: nobody gave a rat's ass about suspect rights.

The three were taken on suspicion of kidnapping one Baxter Shorter, Bunker Hill ex-con, three weeks missing, presumed dead, and for questioning in the murder of Mable Monohan, widowed sixty-four-year-old resident of Burbank, fatally bludgeoned in her home two months earlier on the evening of March 9. Three low-grade hoods graduated by rash acts into the big time, now riding to police headquarters in the backseats of three separate unmarked LAPD sedans twenty-seven minutes along eleven boulevard miles—Imperial via Century over to Alameda, eight more miles to R-H headquarters at City Hall for marathon interrogation. Heavy hitters in on the grill: chief William H. Parker himself, in rotation with Burbank police chief Rex Andrews, chief of Ds Thad Brown, Captain Lohrman, detective Dick Ruble, and Burbank homicide lieutenant Robert Coveney.

City Hall tower visible through front windshields all the way up Alameda. One car had diverted Babs to Georgia Street Receiving Hospital. Babs told a tale about serious heart trouble. Said arm welts were caused from medicinal injections for a cardiac condition that would kill her in five months. ER doctors dispelled her story: welts the result of heroin skin pops. Babs had the heart of a healthy horse. Babs: a habitual liar. She joined the party at City Hall. For long hours, the three of them stonewalled inquiry over the disappearance of Baxter Shorter and the murder of Mable Monohan.

May 5, early morning: LAPD brass ordered the trio into shackles and squad cars for a ride west up Temple Street to North Broadway, across the LA River on a bridge overlooking Union Station to the city jail in Lincoln Heights.

The Mable Monohan murder on the surface, a gruesome beating of a crippled widow for no apparent motive. Underneath, an all-time LA story destined for Hollywood treatment, twisting around ironic subplots running subsurface deep to gnarled civic roots.

Roll back history. Through Prohibition, repeal, and the Depression, LA was a cesspool of corruption: strong-arm extortion on both sides of the law; kickbacks; police protection for prostitution, narcotics, and gambling; police commissioners and politicians in bed with local racketeers. Eastern and Midwestern Mafia families ran organized crime through LA crime boss Jack Dragna but never managed a total tentacle overtake. They couldn't squeeze LA like eastern towns or Las Vegas. Transcontintental distances mitigated direct oversight. LAPD, particularly during W.H. Parker's gangster squad regime, 1950-1966, met incoming hoods at Union Station or LAX with leather saps and knuckle dusters, discouraging a long stay. In Los Angeles, organized crime was more regional and diffuse—local power brokers combining with cops and crooks to corner the action. Famous LA mobster Bugsy Siegel began with the New York families under Mafiosi Lucky Luciano, Frank Costello, and Meyer Lansky, but Siegel operated in LA more or less as an indie, seizing only shares of illicit So-Cal opportunities.

In an exponential LA episode in 1938, intelligence division captain Earl Kynette and one police henchman were sentenced to ten years in San Quentin for attempted murder and assault after a bomb detonated in the car of a reform movement informant who survived the attempt. The informant, PI Harry Raymond, was himself a double turncoat—a vice cop twice fired by the department who delivered incriminating evidence to reform leaders only after failing to blackmail the department with the same information. (Earle Kynette's crew in fact car-bombed him *because* of the blackmail.)

Reform momentum escalated in the late '30s and early '40s. Straight-arrow citizen, cafeteria magnate Clifford Clinton, son of Salvation Army parents, steered an acronym group, CIVIC (Citizens Independent Vice Investigating Committee), and CIVIC prevailed. Mayor Frank Shaw, who had openly protected bootleggers and bordellos, was recalled in 1938 in favor of Fletcher Bowron. Frank Shaw's fixer, his brother Joe, was convicted on sixty-three counts of patronage and graft. Police chief James Davis jumped ahead of the push and resigned.

Without sanction from City Hall, local vice lords crossed the state line toward Las Vegas, an overheated railroad stop morphing via Mafia money into an oasis for sin. One of them, Luther B. "Tutor" Scherer, emigrated to the desert and purchased points in the Pioneer Club on Fremont Street. Scherer was a bootlegger during Prohibition. He transitioned to gambling after repeal. Before Vegas, Tutor Scherer ran a Venice boardwalk nightclub, Ships, featuring entertainment of all kinds, some legal.

In the early 1930s, a singer named Iris Monohan auditioned for the floor show at Ships. Scherer liked her act. He liked her even better. Decades older than Iris, he married her in 1936, and they settled in Burbank, 1718 Parkside, a tree-shaded residence across Riverside Boulevard from the horse trails of Griffith Park. Tutor Scherer secured the house with door and window locks; he installed perimeter floodlights and built a six-foot plaster wall surrounding a large backyard.

Iris's father, George, died in 1940 at age seventy-one. She moved her mother, Mable, widowed at fifty-two, into the Parkside property as a live-in housekeeper. In 1942 Tutor and Iris moved to the desert, where Tutor leveraged his legal gambling interests with stakes in the El Rancho Vegas, the Las Vegas Club, the Sahara, and the Thunderbird. Mable stayed in Burbank. By 1949, the Iris-Tutor marriage had disintegrated. In 1950, Iris married New York importer Robert Sowder and moved to Park Avenue. In her divorce settlement, Iris received the Parkside house, jewelry, and $100,000 cash. Iris had married up; she didn't need the Burbank property or the money. She gave the house to her mother plus $40,000 cash. Frugal Mable banked the gift.

LA underworld as the wartime '40s turned to the Red Scare '50s: Overrun with end-of-the-line grifters chasing the elusive bigtime caper, losers with ex-con pedigrees and felony tendencies mingling among their own. LA after World War II was a breeding ground for criminal assembly. Grid-work boulevards trailed through contiguous towns profuse with shabby walk-up hotels, transient motor courts, all of them proximate to seedy bars, gambling dens, pool halls, and all-night diners.

Crime was rampant. Criminals assembled and conspired. Rumors passed through the grapevine in smoky dives and returned as established fact. Losers are losers among other causes because they aren't long-range planners, critical thinkers, or documented researchers. They believe the bullshit legends they invent.

Tutor Scherer's name found its way into underworld urban legend in the late 1940s/early 1950s in one or both of two forms: Iris Monohan's divorce settlement sitting liquid for the taking in Mable Monahan's house and Tutor Scherer ferrying casino skim from Las Vegas, stashing it in a floor safe at 1718 Parkside, Burbank.

December 1951: Five men gathered to spec a home invasion at 1718 Parkside, coincidental with Mable Monahan visiting her daughter in New York. The five: George Washington Allen (nicknamed "Indian George"), Baxter Shorter, William Alvin Upshaw, John Paul Wilds, and Solly Davis. They scrubbed the thought of heisting Sherer's stash, fearing underworld retribution if the take was tied to Vegas proceeds.

The example of the "Two Tonys" reverberated. Tony Brancato and Tony Trombino were contract killers imported to LA in the 1940s from Kansas City by local rackets boss Mickey Cohen.

Post-WWII episode: Benjamin "Bugsy" Siegel, franchising crime in Los Angeles, opened shop in mob-controlled Las Vegas with construction of the Flamingo Hotel. Bugsy was brilliant—way ahead of his time—but volatile and impulsive, his finances an intolerable mess. He overran construction costs by millions; his shady girlfriend, Virginia Hill, palmed a percentage of the Flamingo stake, which she fed into a numbered Swiss account. Las Vegas would prove a gold mine, but Ben Siegel outlived his purpose. Meyer Lansky, partner of Lucky Luciano, and Siegel's sponsor, ordered a hit.

June 20, 1947, evening: Bugsy lounging on the chintz sofa in the living room of Virginia Hill's Beverly Hills mansion, reading the morning *LA Times*, front window drapes wide open. Unknown snipers fired through the window, planting four .30 caliber slugs into Bugsy Siegel's head.

Mickey Cohen, originally from Brooklyn, grew up in the Boyle Heights section of East LA, above Union Station. Cohen had been conscripted from the Cleveland mob in 1939 to sidekick Ben Siegel when Siegel was running his piece of LA. With Siegel down, Cohen stepped into the top spot until 1961, when he was imprisoned the second time for tax evasion. At his criminal peak in the 50s, Myer Harris Cohen was pure hoodlum color—dapper, vicious, and quotable. Five foot five, in two-toned wing-tip lifts and a tall fedora, he strutted his mob-boss act across a real-life stage set.

Mickey headquartered in his Sunset Strip clothing store, Michael's Haberdashery. The Strip runs through West Hollywood, unincorporated at the time—meaning it was LA sheriff's department turf, not LAPD. Mickey Cohen paid big bag to LASD brass. LAPD, with ethical issues of its own, seethed over Mickey C.'s flaunting of protected criminal extortion, vice, and strong-arm operations.

LAPD went extracurricular. Intelligence units black-bagged Mickey's Brentwood house. They ran a wire through the television console in his den and gathered enough dirt to take down Cohen henchmen. Mickey returned the gesture. He doubled LAPD's wire man, Jimmy Vaus, and greedy Vaus tapped a payoff-for-protection exchange between notorious Hollywood madam Brenda Allen and LAPD administrative vice sergeant Elmer Jackson. Mickey leaked the incriminating tape to the grand jury. Scandal reverberated. Interagency resentments grew virulant.

Tony and Tony were suspected of multiple murders in LA in the 1940s, including Bugsy Siegel's assassination. Freelancing

Tonys stupidly robbed the Flamingo sports book in 1951; they earned a mob hit ordered from New York. The contract was assigned through Mickey Cohen to Jimmy "the Weasel" Frattiano. The Weasel blasted the Tonys in the backs of their skulls on a side street off the Strip.

LA in the '40s and '50s: Corrupt criminal stew.

II

Burbank PD was puzzled by the dead Mable Monohan. No evidence of break-in. Evidence in every room of animal rage: drawers pulled out, contents dumped; carpets ripped up; furniture upended; mattresses ripped off beds. Evidence in every room of deranged brutality. Mable Monohan's blood splattered floors and walls throughout the house while her killer or killers dragged her from room to room.

Mable Monohan was murdered in the evening of March 9, 1953, but wasn't discovered until noon on March 11, by her gardener. She was lying facedown on a hallway carpet, lower body half in a closet, her head beaten to a pulp but covered with a pillowcase, her hands bound by a torn strip of bedsheet. Another strip, cut in half under her neck, matched purple marks around her throat. Burbank PD concluded only what evidence supported. Time of death: thirty-six hours earlier. Cause of death: asphyxiation via bedsheet garrote, though multiple blunt blows to the head—probably twelve, probably from pistol-whipping—ultimately would have proved fatal. Cops were stumped by who or why. If robbery, the killer(s) left behind a purse hanging from a closet hook that contained $474 in cash and $10,000 in jewelry—diamond-in-gold rings, watches, brooches, earrings, and clasps. If not robbery, what? Mable Monohan was an old lady by 1953 measures. Sixty-four, gray-haired. She wore floral dresses and block-heeled shoes with toe-point perforations. She walked with a limp and used a cane from knee and pelvic injuries suffered in a car accident years before.

Iris was notified in New York. Lieutenant Coveney contacted Tutor Scherer in Vegas. Tutor Scherer didn't favor the company of Burbank dicks in Las Vegas. He agreed to meet the detectives in Palm Springs for an interview that led nowhere. Tutor Scherer knew nothing. He commented how dumb it would be to leave large amounts of money lying around a residence, double dumb to believe he would be dumb enough to do so. Tutor Scherer said Mable had little worth stealing. He said he never had a safe installed at 1718 Parkside. He said he was fond of his mother-in-law and remained in touch after divorcing Iris. He was seventy-three, nearly a decade older than Mable, and visited often. Said she nursed him when he was ill, newspapers said from "cirrhosis." Burbank PD discounted rush-to-judgment gambling-tie headlines. Cops scratched Tutor Scherer as a suspect.

Iris flew west and offered a $5,000 reward for information leading to arrest and conviction. One week after the murder, "Indian George" Allen, thirty-seven, contacted Burbank Police Chief Andrews. Andrews arranged a meet. George Allen outlined his 1951 conversations between Baxter Shorter, Willie Upshaw, John Wild, and Solly Davis. Under chief William H. Parker and intelligence division captain James Hamilton, LAPD equaled the FBI in the sophistication of its local criminal information network. Burbank PD contacted Captain Hamilton on the names. Four hits.

William Upshaw, thirty-four, known burglar, bookie, and box man (safecracker) with a long string of arrests and convictions, once affiliated with Mickey Cohen in Burbank gambling operations; Baxter Shorter, forty-three, ex-con, San Quentin, convicted in 1938 of hotel burglaries from San Francisco to Los Angeles, known for strong-arm, safe-cracking, and bunco; John Paul Wild, fifty, gambler formerly with ownership interest in Mickey Cohen clip joints in Los Angeles and Burbank; Solly Davis, forty-eight, one of Cohen's original minions in a group nicknamed the Seven Dwarfs. Solly Davis footnote: on Mickey's orders, he abetted the beating of a wiretapper, the fallout from which produced the recorded liaison between busy Brenda Allen and amoral Elmer Jackson. From New York, Davis was an alumnus of the infamous Murder, Inc.

Television was still a novelty in 1953. Big news came via the print medium. Five daily papers targeted a color-spectrum demographic at seven cents a copy through multiple editions. White-collar citizens read the morning *Times* for gray facts. Blue-collar grunts, the Hearst morning *Examiner* for yellow-journalistic takes on lurid blue and gory red insight into the City of Angels. The *Times* hedged with the afternoon tabloid *Mirror*. Hearst doubled its coverage with the hyperbolic evening *Herald Express*.

LA Times page-one headline on March 12, 1953, the day after Mable Monohan's gardener found her body: NEW MYSTERY IN SLAYING AT BURBANK. No subhead. Story lead: "Burbank police disclosed early today they were ruling out burglary as a prime motive in the slaying of Mrs. Mable Monohan, about 62, who was found brutally beaten to death in her home at 1718 W. Parkside Ave. Burbank…"

LA Examiner that morning: LONE WIDOW SLAIN IN HOME AS SHE READS 'Whodunit.' Subhead: RICH BURBANK WOMAN'S HANDS TIED, HOUSE RANSACKED. Page-one lead: "Brutally murdered with her hands lashed behind her back, the body of a wealthy crippled widow was found today in a closet amid the ransacked shambles of her fashionable Burbank home…"

LA Herald Express the same afternoon: FIENDISH SLAYING OF WIDOW. Subhead: BRUTAL MURDER OF BURBANK WIDOW LINKED TO GAMBLING CZAR.

No traction until Indian George named names.

LA Times on Thursday, March 27: THREE EX-COHEN HENCHMEN HELD IN SLAYING OF WIDOW. Subhead: FIVE IN BURBANK JAIL ALL KNEW MURDER VICTIM. Burbank detectives detained all five as material witnesses, interrogated them for eight hours. Lieutenant Coveney, the next day: "The key to the situation is among them." He told reporters the five all knew details of the Tutor/Iris divorce settlement. He said the men had planned to rob the Monohan residence. He didn't distinguish between 1951 and 1953. He referred to the $40,000 cash and said, "There can be no doubt. The murder motive was robbery."

Detectives pressed on and clicked.

Solly Davis said he'd talk about the 1951 plot but only with police protection. He alluded to deadly retribution if he said more. Indian George eyed Iris Sowder's $5,000 reward offer. He asked to be wired and put in the same cell as Baxter Shorter and Willie Upshaw. Detectives read Allen's offer as Upshaw and Baxter separate from the rest. Cops countered with immunity on the 1951 plot. They said black box on the murder only. Anyone admitting 1951 but cleared on Monohan would be eliminated as a suspect. Allen and Wild jumped on it. They passed the polygraph and were released by noon on Saturday, March 28. Davis followed later that day. Willie Upshaw and Baxter Shorter went halfway: admitted 1951 but flatly refused a polygraph on Monahan. Big-time hink.

Detectives bore in on both. Upshaw cracked first. He admitted that Baxter Shorter could name the Monohan killer(s) but never would, no matter what pressure the police could exert. Upshaw said he couldn't name names himself but feared polygraph results would reveal knowledge of the murder despite the fact that he didn't participate. He said with two days of freedom, he might convince Baxter Shorter to spill. Chief Andrews and Lieutenant Coveney bought in. They released Upshaw and Shorter that same Saturday at midnight. They gave Upshaw forty-eight hours to produce.

With a two-day deadline, Upshaw worked Shorter hard. Upshaw possessed insider knowledge in a capital crime. He was facing criminal conspiracy and more prison time. His only hope: wedge Shorter into an immunity deal. He promoted same via an attorney in Beverly Hills. His price for brokering the deal—omission of his name from any confession. Shorter was looking at bad options. He talks, and he gains immunity from a gas chamber rap. He talks, and he loses immunity from accomplice retribution. He doesn't talk, and he risks the San Quentin green room. Rock and a hard place. He fretted through his forty-eight hours. He drank.

He sweated. He unburdened himself to his wife. She said he cried while retelling the facts of the March 9 bloodbath.

John Paul Wilds ran an airplane-parts operation from an office in Beverly Hills. Monday, March 30: Baxter Shorter called Upshaw at John Wilds's office and asked for the name of the lawyer. That afternoon, Shorter met with attorney Thomas Mercola. Shorter unloaded under privilege. Mercola phoned LA County district attorney Ernest Roll. Mercola dealt full immunity for full disclosure, excepting one name (Upshaw).

That night Shorter and Mercola drove to the Miramar Hotel in Santa Monica for a clandestine 9:00 p.m. session with Ernest Roll; Roll's chief deputy DA, Adolph Alexander; Burbank chief Rex Andrews; Burbank detective lieutenant Robert Coveney; and a stenographer. Baxter Shorter divulged criminal secrets for two-and-a-half hours. He coughed up all details of the Monahan caper but only first names for the accomplices, four of them: Jack, John, Emmett, and Mary. He said it had started with a telephone call to his Bunker Hill rooms, a voice saying, "You don't know me, but my name is Emmett. I have something that might be to your advantage..."

Shorter's tale:

Emmett arranged a meeting the next day, Saturday, March 7, at the La Bonita Motel on Garvey Boulevard in El Monte, a Dust Bowl/Baja California destination town, dense with rundown bungalows housing Okies and green cards, located thirteen miles east of LA out Valley Boulevard. Baxter Shorter elided the presence of Willie Upshaw. (Upshaw attended the March 7 meeting.) Baxter Shorter (and Upshaw) met with two men: John, who had rented the room, and Jack, obviously in charge. John spoke when spoken to. Jack prompted. John told of a trip across the desert with Tutor Scherer. He said Tutor Scherer was carrying a shoe box full of money.

Jack said they were planning to hit the Monohan house. Baxter Shorter wondered about his part. Jack said he needed a lookout familiar with the residence. He said he had a full crew for the inside operation: three men (including himself) and a woman. He said they already had mapped out the steps. Baxter Shorter could sit in the car for 10 percent. Baxter Shorter saw dollar signs. Ten grand for fingering the house and watching for cops. Baxter Shorter failed to register implications: he already knew too much, he could be pulled inside as a backup box man, and he was expendable afterward (whether the job succeeded or failed). He didn't know: Jack had told John to invent the Tutor Scherer shoe-box/skim legend to rope in his (Shorter's) involvement.

Jack met Baxter Shorter (and Willie Upshaw) at a drive-in hamburger joint on Ventura Boulevard in Burbank the afternoon of March 9. The invasion crew (including Upshaw) cased 1718 Parkside and saw Mrs. Monohan standing on the porch talking with a Fuller Brush man. Jack arranged a rendezvous that evening for the parking lot across from the Smoke House restaurant off Riverside Boulevard, itself across from Warner Brothers Studio. Willie Upshaw opted out; he said with his record, he'd be the first one the cops picked up on suspicion.

That night near dusk, Baxter Shorter drove into the vicinity of two cars. Emmett entered Baxter Shorter's car. Jack, John, and a woman followed in a late-model two-tone Oldsmobile. Jack drove the Olds. Shorter led them to Parkside. It took five minutes. The woman exited Jack's car. She walked to the Monohan door hiding a .38 revolver under her forearm. The woman rang the bell. Peephole conversation; the woman convincing: car stalled in an intersection; she needed to telephone a garage. Tall irony—hard-case Mary afraid, a woman alone in the dark. Mable disengaged the burglar chain.

Baxter Shorter heard a scream then silence. Five minutes passed. John strolled from the Oldsmobile through Mable Monohan's unlocked front door. Six to eight minutes later, Emmett said, "John was supposed to have her tied up with sheets and pillowcases by now." He rushed to the Olds to talk to Jack. Jack to Emmett: "Take my gun and see what's wrong." Emmett inside and back:

"She's finally tied up. Come in and help us look." Jack and Emmett back inside. Four minutes later, Jack returned. To Baxter Shorter: "Come in, there's nothing here." Baxter Shorter walked through the door and saw a bloody mess, a lady on the floor with her head in a pillowcase, moaning. Mary to Emmett: "Knock her out—she won't shut up."

Mayhem. Emmett striking Monohan with a nickel-plated sidearm. Emmett and Jack tying her hands with strips of bedsheet. Jack tying a strip around her neck. Mary placing a pillowcase over her head. Emmett and Jack tearing up the house. Mable Monohan lying in a pool of blood; John kneeling down, holding her. Baxter Shorter to John: "You came down here with Tutor Scherer, and he brought the box full of money."

John: "It's not here." Baxter Shorter begged for medical attention for the woman. Jack and Emmett looked at him like he was a Martian.

Jack: "Let's go. Nothing here."

They returned to the Smoke House. En route, Baxter Shorter to Jack: "That woman looked awful bad. I'm awful worried about her."

Pause. Jack: "She stopped breathing five minutes ago."

Baxter Shorter: "Jesus Christ, that's murder."

Jack: "So what? Give us a ring in a day or two."

Baxter Shorter: "You can't call me."

Jack: "I will know how to get in touch with you."

Baxter Shorter drove out W. Alameda to San Fernando Road and south toward downtown LA. He turned right on Los Feliz Boulevard to a Standard filling station and a phone booth. He dialed 116, LA's 911 forerunner, and asked for an ambulance to be sent to 1718 Parkside but forget to add, "Burbank." Help never arrived.

Baxter Shorter ended his deposition with shallow answers to questions about Jack, Emmett, and Mary. Emmett was an old-timer; Jack may have pulled jobs in San Francisco but was from someplace way north of the city. Jack had mentioned a robbery in Oregon. Said he could handle a safe but Emmett was better. Beyond first name and description, nothing about Mary.

Earnest Roll relayed the four first names to Captain Hamilton. Captain Hamilton contacted San Francisco chief of police Thomas Cahill. ID's came fast. Cahill found Emmett's file through an Oakland detective: Emmett R. Perkins. Perkins had an LA record and aliases: Emmett Green and Roy Bradley. Cahill knew Perkins's girlfriend: Barbara Graham, a.k.a. Barbara Kielhammer and Barbara Radcliff. He ID'ed Jack as Jack Santo, a.k.a. James A. Mahoney and John as John Lawson True from Grass Valley, a mining town above Sacramento. LAPD had the names within twenty-four hours of Baxter Shorter's deposition, and they all fit.

Perkins had spent most of his adult life in stir: Folsom or San Quentin for safe burglary, auto theft, bank robbery, and violation of the weapons act while on parole. In 1931, he was suspected of murdering a payroll messenger, but the only witness suddenly died. Santo's rap sheet dated back to Prohibition: robbery, suspicion of kidnapping, intent to commit murder, violation of the federal Dyer Act (transporting stolen cars across any state line). Barbara Graham had an SFPD sheet that included arrests for perjury, narcotics, prostitution, and multiple pops for vagrancy.

III

Burbank detectives drove back to Palm Springs looking for confirmation/refutation of John True's Tutor Scherer shoe-box fable. Tutor Scherer never heard of John True. He called skim a fairy tale. One day later, chief W. H. Parker convened a Monohan murder summit comprised of LAPD and Burbank homicide detectives plus Thad Brown, James Hamilton, and Dick Ruble. The reason: that morning, Dick Ruble had sketched Monohan murder details to homicide detectives. Dick Ruble's account paralleled Baxter Shorter's top-secret deposition. Dick Ruble also named Jack Santo, John True, Baxter Shorter, Emmett Perkins, and Barbara Graham as likely suspects.

Dick Ruble knew where Perkins and Graham were living—a bungalow in El Monte, 4172 La Madera, where Barbara Graham shilled for crooked gambling games operated by Emmett Perkins. He had Jack Santo's address in Auburn, where Santo lived with a common-law wife, Harriet Henson. He had John True's address in Grass Valley. Up to that morning, Dick Ruble was not connected to the case. He worked burglary and safe, headquartered around the corner from City Hall at 314 First Street. Ruble said he heard the story early in April from an Emmett Perkins aquaintance who wanted to deal information for immunity if anything back-splattered. Dick Ruble cleared it with Thad Brown and Adolph Alexander. Dick Ruble told the informant's tale at the City Hall summit after Baxter Shorter's deposition.

Dick Ruble wouldn't divulge his snitch beyond the meeting, but the snitch cross-referred Monohan murder facts with accomplice IDs. He knew where Santo and True lived, where Perkins and Graham were staying. Figure John True, Jack Santo, and Emmett Perkins weren't blabbing. Figure Baxter Shorter a nervous wreck, talking to his wife and Miramar interrogators. Shorter could answer the March 10 question, "How did it go yesterday?" in depth to the only one who would ask. Dick Ruble would know every LA box man with a record. Figure Willie Upshaw the source.

John True's best friend, Seth Terry, lived in Grass Valley. Burbank detectives flipped a girlfriend who informed them when John True was expected at Seth Terry's house. They dressed in rual khaki pants and plaid wool Pendleton shirts for a stakeout. John True arrived on schedule, Saturday, April 11. The detectives arrested him while he was taking a bath and transported him south.

Snitch information had Jack Santo scheduled to fly out of the Reno airport. Perkins and Graham were under surveillance in El Monte. Too many Nevada County locals knew of John True's arrest. One notified a stringer for the *San Francisco Chronicle*. News broke. A headline story sizzled across newswires to Reno and Los Angeles: John True nabbed in connection with Monohan. Burbank

PD, furious with intrusive media, sensed their suspects slipping away. Jack Santo no-showed his Reno flight. Emmett Perkins and Barbara Graham slipped their surveillance in El Monte.

Detectives booked John True into Burbank jail Sunday, April 12, after an overnight stay in Stockton. He admitted nothing during hours of interrogation. Dicks flashed mugs of Shorter, Perkins, Upshaw, and Santo. He recognized only Santo. He said Santo transacted mother-lode gold deals. He said Santo was a nice guy. He said he himself was a deep-sea diver.

He said he had driven to LA with Santo on March 7 in a two-tone Oldsmobile belonging to Santo's girlfriend in Grass Valley, Bernadine Pearney—distinct from his common-law wife, Harriet Henson, in Auburn. He said Santo had business in LA. He—True—was seeing his brother-in-law in Costa Mesa about a potential diving deal. He admitted to signing the register at the La Bonita in El Monte on March 7 for himself and Jack Santo.

He said Santo had a visitor, and Santo told him—True—to take a walk during the visit. He said he called his nephew but could drum up no business. He said Santo dropped him at the Greyhound bus depot that night, March 8. He said he was back in Grass Valley by 9:00 p.m. the night of March 9. Detectives put him on the box. At the mention of Monohan, True asked for an attorney.

On Monday, April 13, True's Grass Valley lawyer, Harold Berliner, filed a writ of habeas corpus with Nevada County superior court Judge James Snell, claiming True was kidnapped by out-of-jurisdiction authorities. Judge Snell signed it. Berliner telegraphed the writ demands to Chief Andrews. The terms: delivery of John Lawson True to Judge Snell's court by 1:30 p.m. on Friday, April 17. Berliner expedited the matter via LA attorney Patrick J. Cooney, a shyster acolyte of Clarence Darrow with Mickey Cohen ties. Cooney passed through City Hall beat reporters. He was known to be chatty. John True's release writ made local news that evening.

Ernest Roll smelled votes. Monohan too hot to suppress. He couldn't resist. He leaked progress to sniffing newshounds. He denied it later, but no one else could have. The Monday, April 13, *Examiner* bulldog featured a front-page scoop: police had positively ID'd the Monohan suspects. The story cited a suspect not in custody; referred to a man named "Emmett," his "wife," and an ex-con named "Jack." Included: police mugs of big-beaked Jack Santo and ugly Emmett Perkins. Tuesday, April 14, the early edition claimed Monohan was slain by four men and a woman.

Burbank PD was irate. Perkins, Santo, Graham burrowed deeper into hiding. Baxter Shorter feared for his life. Monohan fugitives could read and calculate. They knew Willie Upshaw had fled to Mexico. They knew the unnamed witness was free, and John True was in custody until his writ would be executed three days hence. They plus True equaled three men and a woman. Only squealer possible—Baxter Shorter.

Baxter Shorter lived on the second floor of a three-story residential hotel on Bunker Hill, four units to a floor, the Lancaster at 121 N. Flower. Shorter was trapped. A police guard would peg him as the source. Unguarded, he'd be on his own. He kept a .30-06 propped against the wall behind the drapes. He drank. He frequented Sunset Strip dives. He returned home nights. On Tuesday night, April 14, LAPD robbery-homicide received a frantic 116 call regarding a snatch. Squad cars rolled to 121 N. Flower. Officers found Shorter's wife, Olivia, hysterical, sitting on a living room couch next to a loaded deer rifle. She told the tale through gasps and sobs.

Two hallway entry doors to Shorter's second-story flat—living room and kitchen, twenty feet apart. Knock on the living room door, Baxter pulling it open. Man in the frame with a sidearm. Olivia Shorter grabbing the rifle and entering the hall through the kitchen door, pointing. The gunman saying put it down or everyone gets it. Baxter Shorter ordering her back inside. She zipped back inside to the bay window. She saw the gunman at the curb shoving Baxter Shorter into the front seat of a '50 or '51 Dodge Coupe, light gray or beige, another man in back, a woman behind the wheel.

The cops transported Olivia Shorter downtown. She told them: "This all has to do with that awful Burbank murder." She picked big-eared Emmett Perkins out of a mug book and signed a complaint against him for kidnapping. LAPD now fully vested in Monohan. The Shorter abduction brought the murder case tangentially inside LAPD jurisdiction. Chief Parker ordered an APB on Perkins, Santo, and Graham, an all-units dragnet to scour the bottom of the LA underworld until all three were hauled in. Strict orders: Don't move on one or two. Take them all.

LAPD detective Dick Ruble had dealt with Emmett Perkins for years. They had an understanding. Perkins never capered in Dick Ruble's territory. Emmett Perkins met Ruble for snitch confabs now and then. Four nights after the kidnapping, March 18, Dick Ruble answered his doorbell in robe and slippers. On the porch, Emmett Perkins asking for a sitdown in a car at the curb, a two-tone green/cream Olds, '51 or '52, Barbara Graham behind the wheel. Ruble followed him off the porch.

Perkins demanded to know why the heat was on. Dick Ruble told him: for Monohan. Perkins told him the old lady wouldn't shut up. He implicated Babs in the beating. Babs: "They'll never prove we did it." Babs conversant with underworld code—no living witnesses means the same as innocence. Certainty: Baxter Shorter already dead. Dick Ruble, under orders to take in all three suspects or none, implored Perkins to give himself up. Perkins mentioned clearing up a few things. He mentioned needing a hundred grand to "square the beef." He promised he'd turn himself in on Monday, April 20.

Monday the 20th came and went.

IV

May 5 headline in the *Times*: TRAP NETS 3 SUSPECTS IN SLAYING AT BURBANK. In the *Examiner*: GIRL, 2 MEN SEIZED AS MURDER CASE SUSPECTS. Subhead: TRAIL WOMAN TO HIDEOUT. Babs had led them to Lynwood. The trio had moved around since the news of John True's arrest in Grass Valley. Santo and True had left the La Bonita late the night of the Monohan murder. Perkins and Graham returned to his card room/bungalow on La Madera. Perkins had another residence in El Monte, occupied by his wife and son. Jack Santo drove to LA in the Olds following John True's arrest, rejoining Perkins and Graham. They contacted Patrick J. Cooney. Cooney secured them a room in a fireproof motel on the 7600 block of Figueroa in South Central LA, the Ambassador, an L-shaped two-floor stucco dump near Cooney's office on West Manchester.

They reloed to the Sunset Motel in Seal Beach for a few days while Cooney arranged new quarters with a man named Willis Carter, a San Quentin ex-con who worked here and there for Cooney. Carter managed the National Tire Retread shop in Lynwood. Cooney pointed Santo, Perkins, and Graham to Carter's office in a tire-molding equipment warehouse five blocks from the retread shop/flophouse apartment.

The fugitives told Carter they didn't have alibis for the night of the Monohan murders. Establishing same might be too tough to rig. Next-best option: alibi for the Baxter Shorter kidnapping. Without Shorter, the DA had no case. Zero direct evidence at 1718 Parkside. Only eyewitness testimony could tie Santo, Perkins, and Graham to Mable Monohan's murder. If they were elsewhere the day Shorter was snatched, the three would walk on Shorter, hence on Monohan. Emmett Perkins told Dick Ruble it would take 100k to "square the beef." Figure100k Patrick Cooney's retainer to kick Shorter and Monohan. Willis Carter stashed them in the retread apartment.

They had the Oldsmobile slap-painted gray—probably through a Willis Carter chop-shop connection—changed it out to Washington plates, and parked it several blocks from their Lynwood hideout. The Olds, an escape vehicle only if needed. They sent Babs for food and supplies. She paid with forged checks. For ten days, she flitted around on foot or by metro bus, eluding the dragnet she never spotted. Women cops had marked her downtown on multiple occasions but lost her in crowds.

Three fugitives close-quartered in a Lynwood shack. Nerve ends twitching; pressures building; Babs craving junk. She arranged a buy for early afternoon, May 4, at a bus depot in Huntington Park, four miles up Atlantic Boulevard. Babs chose badly. The pusher doubled as a vice snitch. He dealt a dime bag to Babs and Babs to the cops. Babs carried a spike, matches, and bent spoon in her shoulder bag. She fixed in a ladies' room stall. She exited with a tail of three plainclothes policewomen of various ages.

One followed her onto the Atlantic Boulevard bus headed south to Lynwood. Unmarked sedans in three-way radio contact bracketed the bus. Babs stepped off on the corner of Imperial. She crossed at the light and turned east. She disappeared into the tire shop. Hop high, she settled in for a romp with Perkins and Santo when R-H and Burbank cops smashed through the doors.

Following the interrogation at City Hall, Babs was booked on seven counts of forgery—$266 in hot checks passed over the past two weeks—bail set at $25,000. LA couldn't hold Santo. They released him, but Burbank rearrested him at city jail for suspicion of the Monohan murder. Emmett Perkins was held without bail for kidnapping and assault with a deadly weapon on eyewitness testimony after Olivia Shorter picked him out of a lineup. Murderers were safe in stir—for now—but the DA still had no direct evidence for Monohan. No fingerprints; no eyewitness account; no weapons. Baxter Shorter's deposition was worthless—uncorroborated accomplice statement with said accomplice unavailable. Patrick J. Cooney appeared as counsel for all three.

Cops needed to make a case. Santo, Perkins, and Graham denied involvement and stuck to it. Cops zeroed on weak link Willis Carter. Carter had prepped a story: Santo, Perkins, and Graham said they were in Las Vegas when Baxter Shorter was abducted. Carter had arranged it by letter. A doctored repair ticket would say that Santo's car had been towed from Gene, Nevada, twenty-five miles out. A suborned mechanic would claim Santo was humping Graham in the backseat while he was turning a wrench under the hood. A bribed cabdriver would claim he picked up Santo, Perkins, and Graham from the repair shop and ferried them to the Desert Inn.

R-H dicks flew to Las Vegas. They talked to the garage operator, Royal Holmes, president of National Tire Retreaders, legal owner of the Lynwood building where the fugitives were nabbed. Royal Holmes flubbed his lines. Detectives found repair tickets from April 12 through 18 missing or out of sequence. The mechanic recited on cue. Detectives showed him mugs; he pointed to Baxter Shorter as one of the three in question. The cabbie made the same identification. Braced with backfire, Willis Carter admitted cooking the story on Cooney's orders.

The police flipped Carter under threat of prosecution, but the DA needed more. The cops wanted Patrick Cooney jailed on harboring. Patrick Cooney was a Catholic who tithed large. Catholics vote as a bloc. The ranking monsignor phoned Ernest Roll. Ernest Roll was zealous but not to the point of losing the LA County Catholic vote. Cooney was wired into LA's Democratic Party machine. More phone calls from fat cats. Cooney skated on charges. The cops freed Willis Carter but kept him on ice.

They still had Emmett Perkins on a no-bail hold in the Hall of Justice jail (HOJJ) at Temple and Broadway for Baxter Shorter. They still had Babs on $25,000 bail for bad checks. Burbank had Santo on suspicion for Monohan but not for long. Patrick Cooney cited no direct evidence; no witness testimony. He filed a successful writ of habeas corpus. Willie Upshaw returned from Mexico and worked an immunity deal between Ernest Roll and attorney Thomas Mercola that included twenty-four-hour police protection. He agreed to testify even though he had bailed on the Monohan job. His contribution: foreknowledge of the plan and hearsay corroboration of the Baxter Shorter deposition. Baxter Shorter had told him the whole story the day after the murder.

Still not enough. Santo was free on Cooney's writ. The cops had found Bernadine Pearney's Olds in a neighborhood sweep of the Lynwood apartment. Santo was rearrested for fake plates. The

Olds tantalized. It held no actual evidence, but trunk mats were missing. Scientific Investigation Division technicians detected foliage on the undercarriage indigenous to a location in the San Bernardino Mountains. No proof, but cops figured Baxter Shorter was fertilizing wildflowers in the foothills near Big Bear. Santo scraped up the $1,000 bond for the Compton justice court.

Jack Santo thought he was smarter than he was. The day before Emmett Perkins's May 26 preliminary hearing for Shorter's kidnapping, Santo went to San Diego and sent a telegram to Baxter Shorter's mother, Mary, and signed it "Baxter." The message: "Alive and well. Stop. See you soon. Stop. Caution to Olivia to be careful and not make any mistakes. Stop." Mary Shorter passed the wire to LAPD detectives, who drove to San Diego. Detectives flashed Santo's mug to a ticket clerk and waitress at the bus terminal. Both identified Jack Santo as the sender. Cops showed both women a Baxter Shorter mug. Neither recognized him. The cops phoned it in. The team surveilling Santo pulled him in on a felony warrant for telegram forgery, bail set at 50k. Santo couldn't make the 5k bond.

June 1, 1953: LAPD and Burbank PD brass met in secret with Ernest Roll and Adolph Alexander at the police academy in Elysian Park overlooking Chavez Ravine. They reached consensus—time to press the next-weakest link up the chain, John True. Since his April 17 release on Judge Snell's Grass Valley writ, True had been working in a San Francisco shipyard under a local police shadow. LAPD placed a pick-up order with SFPD chief Thomas Cahill.

Homicide commander Frank Ahearn and inspector George Murray brought True to the San Francisco Hall of Justice. True held tight for two days. Police brought in close friends, including Seth Terry, and told them to convince True he would earn a pass with a confession and a gas chamber ticket without. By June 4, the message seeped in. Frank Ahearn called LA. Adolph Alexander flew to San Francisco and offered immunity on Monohan with complete police protection.

John L. True told the same tale as Baxter Shorter: Babs gaining sob-story entry; Babs pistol-whipping Monohan; Perkins taking over with his nickel-plated sidearm when Babs said she wouldn't shut up; Santo and Perkins gagging her, Babs pillow-casing her head, Santo binding her hands and neck with strips from a bedsheet; Perkins, Santo, and Babs trashing the house, dragging inert Mable Monohan through the house. True diverged on details of his own complicity. He said he knelt to hold Mable Monohan's head, her blood staining his trousers. He said he implored her not to cry out. He said he pulled a knife to cut air holes in the pillowcase. He said he sliced the strip of sheeting around her neck. John True, angel of mercy.

Adolph Alexander returned to Los Angeles. The DA's file was building. It had defendants without alibis, Upshaw's testimony supporting Baxter Shorter's deposition, John True's accomplice account, Willis Carter's harboring account, and Olivia Shorter's eyewitness accusation of Emmett Perkins's gunpoint kidnapping. John True was interrogated in Burbank for crime-scene reenactment then transferred to HOJJ.

June 9: Ernest Roll wouldn't lose another witness. He whisked John True under guard to the HOJ grand jury room. True testified for all of twenty minutes.

June 12: The GJ returned murder, burglary, and robbery indictments for all four defendants. John True was placed into protective custody at the Wayside Honor Rancho, the LA sheriff's county jail farm in Castaic.

July 6: Superior court judge Clement D. Nye overruled Patrick Cooney's challenge of the legality of the indictments and denied his request for dismissal. Judge Nye transferred the case to Department 43 for trial on August 14, superior court judge Charles Fricke presiding. Charles Fricke was LA's leading judicial authority on criminal law and evidence, a recognized expert on forensics, ballistics, medicine, psychiatry, chemistry, and photography. Patrick Cooney forecast failure. Charles Fricke was a hanging judge. He had condemned red-light bandit Caryl Chessman five years earlier. During trials, he positioned a small ceramic skull on the edge of his bench. He had sent more defendants to execution than any judge in LA history: fourteen. Cooney clients on the docket as numbers fifteen, sixteen, and seventeen.

1953 timeline for capital crimes: Eighteen months from opening arguments to cyanide fumes. Patrick Cooney imagined five LA dailies competing to headline the case of the losing lawyer. Defendants were destitute—they derived income from committing crimes. In HOJJ without bail, they couldn't earn the outsize cash for a maximum defense. They'd fall to a public defender. Patrick Cooney told Judge Frye that his "...health would prevent him from giving full attention to the grueling task of a major trial."

V

The trial spanned five weeks, from paneling the jury on August 14, 1953, to verdicts on September 22. Deputy DAs Adolph Alexander and J. Miller Leavy prosecuted. The court appointed attorneys for indigent defendants: Jack Hardy and Benjamin Wolfe for Babs, Ward Sullivan for Santo and Perkins. Babs was media-labeled right away. Newspeople loved Babs. She was headline fodder: knockout siren in a red-hot capital crime. Santo and Perkins were dull sidebars at best—mean, unengaging hoods. The evening tabloid the *LA Mirror* headlined her "Bloody Babs," a reference pulled from Adolph Alexander's dramatic depiction of crime-scene gore. The label stuck.

The prosecution presented eyewitness (if accomplice) testimony in John True. It presented Olivia Shorter. It presented crime-scene photos. It reenacted the murder, documenting assault on a bludgeoned widow. It timelined the case and charted it in sequence on a big cork board propped on an easel. J. Miller Leavy ticked it off step by step with a long wooden pointer—the planning, the murder, the arrest, the accumulation of incriminating evidence. He and Adolph Alexander presented Willie Upshaw supporting Baxter Shorter's deposition and Willis Carter admitting to fabricating Las Vegas cover stories. The defense, in turn, presented nothing exculpatory, especially nothing to offset the crucial matter of alibis.

On the morning of September 4, Ward Sullivan called Emmett Perkins's witnesses. A dental nurse from El Monte said Perkins had an appointment for extensive work at nine thirty the morning of March 10. A neighbor of Perkins's sister, Thelma Sustrick, testified that she was hanging wash next door and saw Perkins and his brother-in-law John Sustrick planting a nectarine tree in the Sustricks' backyard in Alhambra the afternoon of March 9. On cross from J. Miller Leavy, the neighbor, Gladys Jones, waffled on the date and time or any other date and time she might have seen him.

John Sustrick corroborated the nectarine story. On cross, both Sustricks were vague about every date and time they encountered Emmett Perkins *except* March 9. Perkins's wife, Eleanor, said Emmett was home on March 9, and she had accompanied him to the dentist the next day. She conceded her husband was seldom home and that he left the first week of April and never returned. General sentiment of Emmett Perkins's alibi: serial perjury, a lineup of Okie cronies lying to save his ass.

Jack Santo's common-law wife, Harriet Henson, took the stand that afternoon. Henson claimed Santo was home in Auburn on March 9. She said that on the morning of March 10, he drove south and stopped for car repairs at a garage in Modesto run by a man named Jack Furnaux.

Harriet Henson had bought the story from Jack Furnaux. Adolph Alexander broke her down on cross. Henson had negotiated the deal in the front seat of Jack Furnaux's car at his repair shop. Furnaux was wearing a Minifone wire at the time, working undercover with the state department of justice regarding gold-country crimes. Adolph Alexander played the scratchy recording for the court. Ward Sullivan didn't bother to cross-examine. He didn't bother to put either of his clients on the stand. He rested his case.

Babs's alibi prefaced Perkins's and Santo's by a week. Hers was even worse, entered into the record on August 27. Her initial story to Jack Hardy: she couldn't exactly remember. At the time, Babs was living around, legally married to her fourth husband, Henry Graham, a shaky union at best. Hank was a bartender, 1950s-slimy: dirty blond duck's-ass haircut and weak chin.

Hank skin-popped skag and lost jobs. Babs took up heroin herself when married to Hank. Hank brokered her current occupation. Babs trolled downtown lounges, cozying up to saps in search of action. The saps ran tabs for booze she nursed, and they swilled. She escorted them to crooked dice and card games run by Emmett Perkins out of his bungalow in El Monte. Babs and Hank fought over drugs and money. They had an eighteen-month-old baby, Tommy.

March 1953: Babs shuttled between home life with husband and baby and shilling suckers toward Emmett Perkins's card parlor.

She told Jack Hardy that the night of the murder, she probably was fighting with Hank at home, 1231½ Inness Avenue, a craftsman duplex east of the Strip off Sunset in the Angelino Heights section of Echo Park, over the hill south of Chavez Ravine. Both sides had subpoenaed Hank Graham for the alibi question, but neither could find him. Jack Hardy had pressed the need with Babs.

He pored over court documents and police reports. He tracked witnesses, examined evidence, assessed the opposition. He wasn't sanguine. He said without a credible alibi, Babs was doomed. He said she had to tell him the truth. He stressed the truth demand three times, twice in person and one via registered letter to HOJJ. Babs half heard the message. She registered the irony—tell the truth *and* provide an alibi?

Twenty-year-old Donna Prow was serving a year of county time for vehicular manslaughter. Flying on barbiturates one night in Burbank, Donna Prow had clipped a car full of Illinois tourists, killing the female driver and injuring the husband and a niece. Detective lieutenant Robert Coveney knew her as a waitress in a local diner. He approached her at women's wing of HOJJ. They worked through captain James Hamilton's intelligence division.

They enlisted LAPD undercover cop Sam Sirianni. Donna Prow sold out Babs for an early release.

Love-starved Babs was not always gender-particular. In jail, she and Donna became "Mommy" and "Candy Pants." They stole downtime for intimate exchange. They wrote mushy letters. Donna Prow sympathized with Babs's predicament. Babs let down. She exuded desperation. Prow paraphrasing Babs: "If some things come to light, I'll be smelling cyanide. I need an alibi." Prow offered an acquaintance, "Sam," via a friend, "Vince." Babs promised money: $500 at first, $25,000 later. She conjured a code, a verse from Omar Khayyam: "I came like water/and like the wind I go." Sam recited the code his first visit, August 7. He visited twice more, the tenth and the twelfth.

Sam wore a wire on August 12 while selling his pitch. He wanted guarantees from perjury possibilities. Sam demanded assurances that Baxter Shorter would not emerge from hiding. Babs repeated: Baxter Shorter wouldn't appear anywhere as anything. He bullied Babs as to her whereabouts on March 9—he claimed he couldn't afford a blindside witness eyeballing her elsewhere. Sam concocted a previous lover fiction as the alibi—he and Babs reconnecting on March 9 at an Encino motel registered as Mr. and Mrs. J. Clark. They rehearsed the play until the fabricated lines fell smoothly into sync.

Discovery—an evolving concept in American jurisprudence—worked by different rules in 1953. Exclusion and Miranda still were a decade-plus into the future. Witness stashing was common; surprise witnesses, routine. Babs told Jack Hardy about Sam. She promised Sam would contact Jack Hardy, but Sam dropped from sight, SO Jack Hardy never could prep him.

August 27: The prosecution called "Sam Sirianni." Babs looked to the rear of department 43. Her Sam walked through the double doors up the aisle. She grabbed Jack Hardy's suit sleeve. Babs: "That's Sam. That's my witness."

The bailiff swore in Sirianni. J. Miller Leavy asked him to state his name and occupation. His answers drained the defendants:

"Sam Sirianni, officer, Los Angeles Police Department." Emmett Perkins skittered his eyes in Babs's direction. Jack Santo glared straight ahead. Jack Hardy bolted to the bench, asking Charles Frye for permission to withdraw. Judge Frye denied Hardy's request, ruling that no one else competent was available at this late date. Hardy returned to the table. He sat transfixed while Sam Sirianni's Miniphone transcription took his client down.

Excerpts:

On Baxter Shorter:

Sam: Okay. How about Bax? That's one thing you'll have to assure me about...
Babs: I can assure you he'll not be here.
Sam: He won't be here? Do you know personally what happened to him?
Babs: If I wasn't sure he wouldn't show up; I wouldn't say this. So you can use your imagination.

On fighting with Hank the night of March 9:

Babs: I haven't seen him since the 7th [of March].
Sam: Then your husband left the 7th of March?
Babs: Better not mention my husband at all.

On Perkins/Santo, March 9:

Sam: You were with those four guys on the night of March 9 when everything took place...
Babs: I was with them.

Total disaster for the defense. Sam was an undercover cop, "Vince": Burbank detective lieutenant Robert Coveney; Donna Prow, a double-dealer unavailable, already set free on a commuted sentence and relocated. Sam had Babs on Minifone tape. J. Miller Leavy played Babs's own voice for the jury.

Babs took the stand to mitigate. J. Miller Leavy was relentless. He maintained criminal complicity was contained in jailhouse love notes to "Candy Pants" Donna Prow. Jack Hardy objected. Charles Frye overruled. J. Miller Leavy humiliated Babs by making her read pillow-talk smut. He made her admit to misleading Jack Hardy. He branded her a liar, a lesbian lover, inferentially a murderess.

His trump card: Babs had skipped probation, moving to LA in 1951. In 1947, at age twenty-four, demonstrating compulsively poor judgment, she had agreed to alibi two goons charged with assault during an attempted robbery of San Francisco society madam Sally Stanford. Babs did no homework. Without much effort, the prosecution produced a motel card from Chicago in her handwriting for the night the crime was committed in San Francisco. She was sentenced to a year in Tehachapi but was allowed to serve it in SF County jail. J. Miller Leavy snapped the sequence as Babs was scrambling about the Minifone, claiming she was desperate, begging to be believed. J. Miller Leavy asked about probation in San Francisco. Babs affirmed. He asked her about the charge. Babs, for all of department 43 to hear: "Perjury."

September 3, 1953: J. Miller Leavy asked Judge Fricke for permission to bring in a new witness. Permission granted. Through the double doors: Henry Graham. Gallery stir. Both sides announced immediate service of subpoenas. Graham was available because he was in custody at at the Hall of Justice jail on a heroin-possession charge. He was represented by local attorney Al Matthews.

Hank was a low-life weasel. He "stayed in the background because he didn't want to get mixed up in the case." He admitted receiving a letter from Babs after she was arrested. He told his mother to tell Babs he was out of town. On direct examination from Adolph Alexander, Hank testified he left the duplex on Innes on March 7, eliminating himself as an alibi witness. He recalled the date because it was one day after he received his next-to-last unemployment check. On redirect,

Jack Hardy finished him off for either side. Jack Hardy grilled Hank until he was babbling. Hank was a junky. He couldn't remember specifics of much of anything on any date from March 7 through 11.

Hank's mother visited Babs and Hank after Hank's botched testimony. On Babs's behalf, she implored Hank to recant.

September 8: Hank said he remembered: He said his unemployment ticket was stamped March 11—that was the day he moved out of 1231½ Innes. He stammered that he was home on March 9—he and Babs arguing all night. Too little, too late. Sam Sirianni's transcripted testimony swamped the seesawing words of a strung-out husband already discredited by both sides.

The jury received the case at 2:30 p.m. on September 22. The foreman read the verdict at 2:30 p.m. the next day. Clock time for deliberation: five hours, twenty minutes Adolph Alexander's closing sentiment to the panel: "Where in this case can you find a single mitigating circumstance for any one of these defendants?" No juror comeback for his rhetorical question. Jury foreman Robert Dodson read the verdict three times, once each for Graham, Santo, and Perkins: "...We the jury in the above and entitled action find the defendant guilty of murder...and find it murder in the first degree." No recommendation for mercy followed.

Charles Fricke was on vacation. Judge Clement Nye substituted. Ward Sullivan, attorney for Santo and Perkins, moved for a new trial and was granted a hearing. Jack Hardy didn't bother. He was court appointed and had been deceived. He wanted out. Charles Fricke interrupted his vacation to hear and deny Ward Sullivan's motion. Babs's new attorney: Henry Graham's counsel, Al Matthews. Al Matthews asked for additional time to review the transcript. Fricke granted him a week and pronounced the death sentence on Santo and Perkins. Numbers fifteen and sixteen.

October 13: Al Matthews filed for a new trial. He wanted to subpoena Colleen Perez, eighteen, wheelchair-bound duplex neighbor on Innes, who claimed she had overheard Babs fighting with Hank all evening on March 9; a Mr. Pitts, a.k.a. Armando Duran, from whom Babs allegedly had bought marijuana the night in question; and an unnamed witness from Iowa who allegedly overheard the March 9 domestic disturbance. Al Matthews was taking cues from Babs. Babs was wishful thinking—throwing out names she hoped would stick. Matthews couldn't locate Pitts/Duran or the Iowa witness. Adolph Alexander countered Colleen Perez.

Judge Frye requested a statement read into the record. The DA's office had taken it from Perez's mother, Aurora. The statement said her daughter had told her about overhearing the fight, but that she could not verify the precise date—it could have happened any time from March 6 to March 11. Aurora Perez also stated her daughter had gone to a movie on March 9 and hadn't returned until after midnight. Al Matthews's last chance: discrediting lieutenant Robert Coveney's/Sam Sirianni's trickery. Judge Fricke said, "I see no grounds for criticism." He denied the new trial motion.

Al Matthews escorted Babs to bench to hear Charles Frye read:

> It is the judgment and sentence of this court that the defendant Barbara Graham suffer the extreme penalty, to wit: the death penalty...And that said penalty be inflicted within the walls of the State Penitentiary at San Quentin, California in the manner prescribed by law, to wit: the administration of lethal gas until said defendant is dead, at a time to be fixed by this court in the warrant for execution.

Babs on the clock, number seventeen from Charles Fricke's court—cyanide and sulphuric acid upon exhaustion of appeals.

VI

San Francisco Examiner reporter and Pulitzer winner Ed Montgomery is prominently associated with a 1958 movie about Barbara Graham titled *I Want to Live!* Enduring assumption since release of the movie: Ed Montgomery covered the case from inception in LA, changed his mind on Babs, and led a crusade to prove her innocent. Implication: Ed Montgomery slammed a series of exculpatory byline articles designed to reveal justice for the wrongly convicted. Not quite the case. Big shock: Hollywood took liberties. Ed Montgomery didn't cover the crime, the capture, or the trial, nor did he write stories from San Francisco afterward. He sidekicked Al Matthews during the appeals phase.

Monahan was an LA story; the local dailies had it blanketed. Babs was old news from sentencing in October 1953. Unlikely Hearst SF would send a reporter to LA to recover already trampled ground. San Francisco had prior items cooking—the war in Korea; Soviet Russia's H-bomb capabilities; nuclear testing in Utah and Nevada; Ike's golf game; the trial of Artie Samish, the three-hundred-pound statehouse lobbyist for California vice interests—Babs wouldn't hit the headlines again until execution neared in early June 1955. An *Examiner* reporter named George Draper bylined that story (not Ed Montgomery) because he was following cases involving Santo and Perkins.

Santo and Perkins were shackled and taken by train with a sixteen-man guard detail to San Quentin in October 1953. Babs was housed in Corona—no appropriate quarters in men-only death row. (Rumors of a breakout at Corona prompted officials to move her for seven months to a hospital ward in San Quentin between November 1953 and June 1954.) When the final headlines hit San Francisco in June 1955, they focused on the "Santo Mob," the "Santo Trio," and the "Santo Gang." Babs made it above the fold after her last ride from Corona, and then adjunctively: SANTO MOLL IN QUENTIN; TRIO TO DIE TODAY. Santo and Perkins were the Nor-Cal focal points for violent acts in Plumas and Nevada Counties. Familiar pattern in both: big-money mirage; brutal slayings; convictions on accomplice testimony.

Before Monohan, Jack Santo included among his felonious résumé the robbery of high-grading miners. ("High-grading": Sourdough form of skimming—miners pocketing quality nuggets until gathering enough to make an underworld sale.) Jack Santo enlarged the concept. He could make peanuts middle-manning the sales. Or, thinking as he did, he could make more by boosting the high grade. In December 1951, he heard that a miner named Ed Hansen was holding $40,000 worth of gold. Santo masterminded. Emmett Perkins and a recruit named George Boles, who worked odd jobs at a sanitarium in Weimar near Colfax, would rob Ed Hansen at gunpoint. Harriet Henson would drive.

As they often did in a Santo scheme, plans fell apart. Ed Hanson had no gold on hand and wouldn't divulge where it was hidden. Emmett Perkins and George Boles shot him in frustration. Ed Hansen lived long enough to ID Perkins and Boles. He died within two weeks of a heart attack brought on by gunshot wounds, making it murder. Nevada County sheriff Wayne Brown camped at the LA County Hall of Justice during the Monohan murder trial, waiting his turn.

September 4, 1953: Harriet Henson walked out of department 43 after perjuring an alibi for Jack Santo. Wayne Brown slapped on handcuffs. He arrested her on a Nevada County warrant signed by the ubiquitous judge James Snell. Harriet Henson and George Boles confessed to the murder of Ed Hansen. They implicated Santo and Perkins. Nevada County borrowed Santo and Perkins from death row on October 17. Judge Snell sentenced them to life after a short trial in Nevada City.

Chester, California, is a logging town on the shore of Lake Almanor. Chester's population in 1952 was one-to-four inverse to elevation: one thousand residents to 4,121 feet. The town was pretty much hidden among the peaks of the Lassen National Forest, camoed by tall conifers banked in red dirt, a nothing town in a nowhere place. Chester supported two stores but no bank. Loggers were paid twice a month by check. An accommodating grocer named Gard Young cashed their paychecks.

Early mornings on the tenth and the twenty-fifth, Gard Young would traverse thirteen wilderness miles thirty minutes along the serpentine Ten Road to the company town of Westwood (owned by Red River Lumber). Gard Young would pick up payroll cash and return to his store in Chester. A housepainter named Lawrence Shay observed the routine and told Jack Santo. Santo cut in Shay for 10 percent, even though Shay didn't figure in the actual crime. Santo speculated a 70k score.

October 10, 1952: Gard Young was winding back from Westwood. He was traveling with his three young children and a neighbor kid. A car driven by Harriet Henson and containing Emmett Perkins and Jack Santo intercepted Young, forcing him to screech to a stop in the dirt on the shoulder. Santo and Perkins attacked Young and the children. Young's three-and-a-half-year-old daughter was bludgeoned but survived. Young and the others didn't. Santo and Perkins piled the four bodies into the trunk of Gard Young's car. They sped off well short of inflated expectations—with $7,000.

Santo and Perkins were transported from death row to Quincy for trial in the spring of 1954. A high-country jury heard testimony from Lawrence Shay and Harriet Henson and delivered a guilty verdict: first-degree murder, another death sentence. Lawrence Shay walked on immunity; Harriet Henson, dealt down to life. When he was in custody, John True told interrogators that Jack Santo once said: "Me and that little man [Emmett Perkins] have put a lot of people in the ground." Santo's and Perkins's body count in the seventeen months from Ed Hanson's murder in December 1951 to the arrest in Lynwood in May 1953 was seven (Ed Hansen, Gard Young and the three children in Chester, Mable Monahan, and Baxter Shorter), for a combined cash payout of $7,000 and a legal reckoning of two death penalties and one life sentence each.

Al Matthews had been dismissed as counsel when Babs was sentenced. He was reappointed by the state supreme court to handle the automatic appeal. Al Matthews was a natural choice. By experience and temperament, he would confront what Patrick Cooney and Jack Hardy would flee: a lost cause. Al Matthews crusaded against the death penalty. Perry Mason's creator, Erle Stanley Gardner, figures in. Gardner wrote prolifically, often under pseudonyms. His Perry Mason series originated with *The Velvet Claw* in 1933, which began a long, eighty-four-book series with a single underlying theme: bungling police and overeager DAs railroading the wrongly accused, their efforts ultimately overturned by a relentless and brilliant Perry Mason.

In 1946, with the help of Los Angeles attorney Al Matthews, Erle Stanley Gardener discovered that guilty evidence had been manufactured by police in the case of an accused sexual slayer named William Marvin Lindley. Gardner appealed to the governor. Lindley was extricated from death row on the eve of execution, his sentence commuted to life until new evidence proved his innocence. From that episode, Gardener recruited a panel of seven professionals (including himself), experts in law, forensic medicine, polygraph testing, crime scene investigation, and handwriting. He called it the "Court of Last Resort," CLR undertook no-hope cases beginning in 1948. In 1957/58, the court became the basis of a twenty-six-episode TV program of the same name.

Al Matthews brought Babs's case to the Court of Last Resort. Ed Montgomery signed on as legman. Montgomery was a hotshot investigative reporter in San Francisco, a former marine with a hearing aid who talked out of the side of his mouth, a *Front Page* throwback. He had won his Pulitzer, not for anything related to Babs, but for local reporting in 1951 for exposing a kickback scam inside the Bureau of Internal Revenue. In 1955, in the Trinity Alps, along with an upcountry tracker, two blue-tick bloodhounds, and a SF *Examiner* photographer, he would unearth the buried body of Berkeley kidnap victim fourteen-year-old Stephanie Bryan. UC student Burton W. Abbott was convicted for the crime in 1955, executed in 1957.

The state had housed Babs in her San Quentin hospital quarters between November 1953 and July 1954. Matthews greased access for Ed Montgomery and a sickly thirty-three-year-old criminal psychologist, Carl Palmberg. Palmberg professed clinical interest in Babs's case in spite of his threatening health issues.

Al Matthews based his appeal along three lines: (1) sensational/prejudicial news coverage tainting jury perspective, (2) egregious entrapment by law-enforcement authorities in violation of defendants' rights, and (3) the legality of accomplice testimony without corroboration from sources extraneous to the crime in question. He could handle the briefs. He assigned Carl Palmberg and Ed Montgomery the task of investigating new grounds for proving Barbara Graham innocent.

Palmberg was empathetic but didn't make the finish. He died of cancer in the spring of 1955. No way of knowing what he might have contributed, but his early returns were tenuous. He pointed to forensic evidence—Mable Monohan assaulted by someone right-handed—and John's True's account: Babs had Mable Monohan's hair in her left hand while striking her with her right. Babs, Carl Palmberg said, was left-handed. Forget the law: Babs was guilty if present, even if she didn't deal the fatal blows. Forget the coroner ruling asphyxiation the cause of death, not the beating. Forget John True testifying and Baxter Shorter deposing that Mable Monohan was beaten by Babs first *and* the right-handed Emmett Perkins later.

Look to Babs herself. In 1951, she was arrested on a narcotics charge. She filled out a Lincoln Heights handwriting sample card listing herself as right-handed. She filled out another card upon arrest in May 1953. Line 14 ("Left or Right-handed"), she entered "right." Line 10 ("In case of Emergency, notify"), she wrote: "Jack Santo and Emmett Perkins." For their address: "Biltmore Hotel." Loveless Babs, murderous cohorts her closest ties; their residence pure fiction.

Palmberg's other point: his examination determined that Babs was amoral but averse to violence. Palmberg no doubt believed his opinion, but shrinks' opinions don't and shouldn't constitute legal proof. Psychiatry is inexact. Shrinks don't prove, they hypothesize, which is to say guess. Adolph Alexander and J. Miller Leavy could flip the Rolodex to *P* and dial up any number of rebuttal psychiatric guessers.

Another reputable expert could hypothesize that Babs's deprivation of mother love drove *everything*. Babs had Mable Monohan by the hair bun. Mable Monohan wouldn't give up the goods. Not a long leap: Babs rushed with adrenaline, maybe hopped on heroin, snapping at Momma Mable's resistance, punishing a stand-in mother, churning into frenzy all her accumulated pain.

For his part, Ed Montgomery was predisposed. Ed Montgomery was an investigative reporter but a person first. If he extricates Babs, he bylines a front-page exclusive and maybe scores a best-selling book. Babs guilty: business as usual, no story, no scoop. Babs was yesterday's news after conviction. Ed Montgomery's true motive, probably mixed. He said at the time, "The more I talk to that gal, the more I became convinced she wasn't the gal." Possibilities: (1) she was framed, and he truly believed her; (2) she used him.

Babs shook her ass for a living. She had manipulated men since childhood. She was desperate. She could have sensed Ed Montgomery's investigation on her behalf as a ticket out of death row and spun him around her thumb. He needed her innocence to break a career story. Whatever his reason(s), he uncovered only grounds for pity.

Highlights from her past:

Born Barbara Diane Wood in 1923 into shantytown poverty in west Oakland near the tracks. Father Joe Wood checked out early. Mother, Hortense Ford, an unwed delinquent teen stuck with a child she resented. Hortense was sent to reform school when Babs was two, the Ventura School for Girls. Babs was handed to a spate of uncaring or abusive relatives. Babs was bright and wanted to read but couldn't find help even in obtaining a library card. She was pretty but poor, loved by no one. She acted out. She discovered sex and went out of control. Hortense conceded. Babs was made a ward of the court at fourteen. The court placed her in the Convent of the Good Shepherd in Oakland where she resisted nunnery constraints.

1937: Babs remanded to Hortense's alma mater, Ventura School for Girls, a Brownie-troop version of the big house. In VSG, Babs grew a hard jailhouse shell.

She was released in 1939. Parole officers tagged her as impossible to manage. Stacked and sixteen, glib and promiscuous, she worked the streets with no moral base or impulse control. She lived in cheap hotels and took jobs that mixed her inevitably into the company of bad men: cocktail waitress, gambling shill, and hooker. World War II on the horizon; deep-water Navy port of Oakland mobilizing. Babs became a "seagull," a female flitting around sailors and ships, sometimes for sex, sometimes not, always for money. With other seagulls, she flew off to San Diego and graduated to B-girl status, traveling on a whim to places including Chicago.

She returned to San Francisco. Pre-pill; pre–women's lib. Pregnancy the price for sleeping around. Needy, streetwise Babs embarked on a wrong-place search for love. She married Harry Kielhammer in 1940, had two children, and dumped him with custody of the kids. She married Aloyse Puechel in 1944 and divorced him a year later. She built a rap sheet with vagrancy arrests in 1941, 1943, and 1944. She was popped for perjury in 1947 under the name Barbara Kielhammer. Released on five years' probation in 1948, she longed for square-john stability. She jumped probation, married Charles Newman, moved to Reno, then Tonapah, Nevada, working as a waitress and in a nursing care unit. Boredom set in. Marriage failed.

She bused to LA and worked the shadows. She frequented downtown dives. She met bartender Henry Graham. She was busted for narcotics in 1951. Through Hank, she reunited with a gambler/felon ex-con she had known in San Francisco, Emmett Perkins. She shilled for Perkins. She fell for weak-ass Hank. She married him, took up heroin, and gave birth to Tommy.

March 1953: She split with Hank over hype-habit pressures. She moved to El Monte with her benefactor, Emmett Perkins and hung with his partner, Jack Santo.

VII

Ed Montgomery dug up Babs's bathetic backstory but found nothing that would free her. He tried visiting Santo and Perkins to convince them to recant on Babs's complicity. They wouldn't talk. Legend has Santo/Perkins using Babs as a shield, hoping the state wouldn't execute a woman and mother. Odds in their favor. Before Babs, California had ever only executed two women, both of them unsympathetic harridans. No reason for Santo/Perkins to hold the play after Chester convictions in 1954. They were facing additional gas chamber death/LWOP verdicts even if sprung on Monohan. Saving Babs wouldn't alter their fate, but they were resistant to the end.

Al Matthews fared no better. The Court of Last Resort went moot when all stages of the appeal concurred: no legal errors. The trial record for appeal was listed as *People v. Santo, 43 Cal. 2nd 319*. On August 11, 1954, the argument was ruled without merit. Al Matthews ran his case through district, state, and federal courts and was rebuffed. In the end, the higher courts agreed with Charles Frye. They found that prejudicial publicity had not been originated by the district attorney, and the jury was properly instructed to disregard same. They ruled Sam Sirianni's Minifone transcripts as underhanded but not unlawful entrapment. They judged John True's testimony as corroborated by nonaccomplice Willie Upshaw and by the defendants' own fugitive flight.

Al Matthews was assiduous if not successful. He gained stays up to the last minute, including two on execution day that extended Babs's life by a combined hour and forty-two minutes, causing her to cry out after the second one, "Why do they torture me? I was ready at ten o'clock." In the end, he was left holding a bag of overturned writs. Babs was strapped into Chair B at 11:36 a.m. on June 4, 1955, and was pronounced dead six minutes later, at 11:42 a.m.; Jack Santo and Emmett Perkins went in at 2:30 p.m. In Chairs A and B they sucked fumes and died within seven minutes.

Two years after the execution, Ed Montgomery pitched a treatment of the Barbara Graham story to Hollywood producer

Walter Wanger—a deal brokered by Al Matthews. Wanger bought the idea and assigned Don Mankiewicz and Nelson Giddings to write the screenplay. The film was released in 1958, produced by Wanger, directed by Robert Wise, and starring Susan Hayward as Babs. Beginning credits open with a graphic, a printed statement undersigned by Pulitzer Prize winner and *San Francisco Examiner* reporter Edward S. Montgomery: "You are about to see a FACTUAL STORY. It is based on the articles I wrote, other newspaper and magazine stories, legal and private correspondence, investigative reports, personal interviews—and the letters of Barbara Graham." Ending credits repeat the same graphic with one first-line change: "You have just seen a FACTUAL STORY..."

Implication: the film is documentary. Implication translated: most names were changed (except for dead defendants and those who signed releases for money—Henry Graham, Al Matthews, and Ed Montgomery); characters compressed and real events distorted. Literacy license liberally applied. Facts bent to fit a theme. Babs's rough edges filed down. Drug use, child abandonment, multiple marriages, guilt on Monohan—all elided or denied to suggest wrongful execution.

1958: Signet Books published pulp novel called *I Want to Live: Analysis of a Murder*, by Tabor Rawson, adapted from the *I Want to Live* screenplay, retailing its premise. Front-cover blurb: "The story of Barbara Graham...a 'bad girl' who was tried for murder and convicted...by her past." The name Tabor Rawson sounds fake and is. According to women's-crime scholar Kathleen Cairns in *Proof of Guilt*, the book was written by Budd Schulberg with an informational assist from Ed Montgomery. The book was published to coincide with the 1958 release of *I Want to Live*, the movie, part of the PR flack package publicizing the film.

At the beginning of the book, the actual end of the story, minutes after the execution, Al Matthews approaches Montgomery outside the prison gates:

"I'm going to keep digging," Matthews said...
Montgomery looked at him bleakly. "Why?"
"To get at the truth—That's why."

Revisionist pipe dream. Ed Montgomery hadn't exonerated Barbara Graham, so he transformed a presumption of innocence into fiction. The Al Matthews exit line: their shared obsession. Ed Montgomery's daughter claims he never wavered. "He was against capital punishment from that time on," says Diana Lavagnino. "He said it was better guilty people go free than one innocent women like Barbara Graham be put to death."

Walter Wanger apprenticed in the Army with WWI propaganda films. He had a social conscience. He was opposed to capital punishment. Walter Wanger was married to actress Joan Bennett. LA story. Joan Bennett's movie career was managed by MCA agent Jennings Lang. Walter Wanger owned a gun and was inclined toward jealousy: never a healthy combination.

One day in December 1951, Walter Wanger drove past the MCA office on Santa Monica and Rexford in Beverly Hills, across the street from the Beverly Hills PD. He saw Joan Bennett's Cadillac convertible in the parking lot. He swung by later with his gun and saw Joan Bennett exiting Jennings Lang's car, walking with Lang toward her own parked convertible. Walter Wanger screeched into the parking lot. He bolted from the car, approaching his wife and her agent. He fired on Jennings Lang twice, one slug hitting him near the hip, the other in the crotch. Lang survived.

Celebrity attorney Jerry Geisler pled temporary insanity. Walter Wanger waived a jury trial. The judge sentenced him to four months at Wayside.

Jail affected Walter Wanger. He produced *Riot in Cell Block 11* in 1954, directed by Don Siegel and starring film-noir heavies Neville Brand and Leo Gordon. In 1958, he hit a grand slam with *I Want to Live.* The movie has become a noir classic, documentary in tone and mood (if not in fact), haunted by Johnny Mandel's modern jazz score, featuring Gerry Mulligan's trombone accompanying femme fatale Babs on her path to perdition. Susan Hayward scintillates as Babs. Character actors carry the periphery: Theodore Bikel as Carl Palmberg; Simon Oakland as Ed Montgomery; Phillip Coolidge and Lou Krugman as cold, creepy killers Perkins and Santo.

I Want to Live swept awards. Susan Hayward won the best actress Oscar, New York Film Critics, and Golden Globes awards for 1958. The Directors Guild of America nominated Robert Wise best director. More Oscar nominations—for best cinematography, best director, best film editing, best sound, best writing. Robert Wise was nominated for Golden Globes best director; Johnny Mandel for a best souundtrack Grammy. Nelson Gidding and Don Mankiewicz were nominated from the Writers Guild of America for best-written American drama. Fifty-four years later, the movie still evokes critical favor. In 2012, it was rated near perfect by Rotten Tomatoes: eleven fresh out of twelve reviews.

I Want to Live's singular flaw: It is a movie.

June 4, 1955, *LA Times* page-one headline, Babs spotlighted, Gene Blake byline: BABS, SANTO, PERKINS GASSED AFTER DELAYS. Subhead: LAST-MINUTE APPEALS FAIL DOOMED WOMAN; TWO MEN DIE LATER. Story lead: "Barbara Graham, 32, died in the gas chamber with a prayer on her lips at 11:42 a.m. today after her execution twice was delayed by last-minute appeals..." *SF Examiner* page-one headline the same day, Babs subordinated, George Draper byline: SANTO MURDER TRIO EXECUTED; DELAYS TORTURE BARBARA. Big NorCal news. Triple execution of Gold Country killers and Mable Monohan murderers. Story lead: "Ruthless, hulking Jack Santo and his jug-eared triggerman, Perkins..."

Final scene of *I Want to Live* shows a slump-shouldered Simon Oakland playing Ed Montgomery fiddling with his hearing aid, tuning out the honking horns of spontaneous execution revelry. He passes through the San Quentin gates in his Chevy hardtop lamenting Babs's demise, Gerry Mulligan's jazz sax playing an exit dirge.

Fade to black. The end. Roll the lie: You have just seen a 'FACTUAL STORY".

Generations of filmgoers have accepted *I Want to Live* as viewed. Those closest to the case consider it revisionist Hollywood horseshit. Gene Blake covered the trial for the *LA Times* and witnessed the execution. He penned an editorial column in response to the movie in 1958, calling the movie "an insult to…those jurors…discharging a distasteful but necessary duty."

He labeled *I Want to Live* "an eloquent piece of propaganda for the abolition of the death penalty. Too bad it is not frankly labeled as such, instead of with glowing words 'true,' 'factual,' and 'documentary.'" He said, "…the movie was inspired by a Los Angeles criminal attorney known as a crusader against the death penalty…[who] had no part in the trial [and a] San Francisco reporter [who] likewise did not cover the Southern California investigation or the trial…"

Burbank detective lieutenant Robert Coveney, also an execution witness, remarked: "She died an easier death than Mrs. Monohan." Reporter Bill Walker covered the case and execution for the Hearst *LA Herald-Examiner*. He voted with Gene Blake and Robert Coveney. Post-execution and film, he accessed insider documents in collaboration with case prosecutor deputy DA J. Miller Leavy. In 1961, Ballantine Books published Walker's treatment, *The Case of Barbara Graham,* a potboiler subheaded *The Ruthless Deals between Informers and Cops in a Heinous Trial for Murder.*

Mable Monohan's murder was ultimately an LA story spotlighting Babs. Babs alone has compelled the case through history. John True was a tool. Perkins and Santo were dime-a-dozen LA hoods absent childhood sob stories—criminals synonymous with their crimes, not movie-legend material. Perkins: no more than a lop-eared rap sheet. Santo: Mr. Potato Head look-alike on a serial-murder spree. They had no sex appeal, or appeal of any kind. The public didn't hunger after Santo's and Perkins's soap opera bio-facts. Nobody wrote about them, cared about them, investigated to justify their lives, or lamented their deaths—merely dismissed them as vicious, murderous bastards.

I Want to Live achieves factual fidelity only in the June 4, 1955, gas chamber frames. Babs is blindfolded at her own insistence—she doesn't want outsiders gloating over her undignified torment. She is escorted by empathetic guards into the octagonal chamber, where they strap her in, seal the hatch door, and watch with thirty-seven witnesses as the prison executioner cranks cyanide eggs wrapped in cheesecloth into a vat of sulfuric acid.

Audible plop; poisonous fumes ascending. Witnesses behold: Babs gulps, squirming/thrashing six minutes, before her masked face slumps in agony upon her chest. Walter Wanger and Robert Wise accomplish their propaganda purpose: re-creating state-sanctioned killing as a protest against capital punishment. They spool gas chamber details with chilling verisimilitude and direct them to unsettle the audience. Viewers since have agreed: images of horror linger and disturb…

The rest of the flick is invented, told in a way that withholds essential facts and shies from inevitable conclusions. The truth, in short? Stated offhand by deputy DA Adolph Alexander, captured by the *LA Mirror*'s alliterative headline writers, conferring her enduring nickname: "Bloody Babs."

The truth? On March 9, 1953, Barbara Graham held Mable Monohan's bludgeoned head in her hands, her destiny ratified by two immutable facts: she consorted with killers by choice, and when her life depended on it, she couldn't establish that she was elsewhere at the time.

CHAPTER 2

WILDWOOD: BURTON W. ABBOTT

Trinity County—remote beyond flatlander imagination. Two million acres of high-altitude forests. Zero freeways, stoplights, or parking meters in four unincorporated evergreen towns. County population barely thirteen thousand, thirty-five hundred of it confined to Weaverville, the county seat. Nearest civilization two hours drive time east or west via car-sickening hairpin routes between I-5 and Highway 101—State Route 36 between Red Bluff and Fortuna and SR 299 from Redding to Eureka.

Wildwood (technically a "population place") sits in a short decline off SR 36, sixty miles west of Red Bluff, twenty-one miles from Hayfork (on 299), accessible through a one-lane bridge over Hayfork Creek, a Trinity River tributary. Green sign on a bend in the Hayfork road reads: WILDWOOD/POP   ELEV 3300. Translation: insufficient number of residents to count as even as a "census-designated place" (CDP); elevation well above the snow line, deep into the tall and the uncut.

Two businesses only for miles around. The Wildwood Store on SR 36: general goods and gas. The Wildwood Inn, just north of the creek, a plank-sided dive, home away from home for rustic barflies, serving ranchhouse food and backwoods drinks—domestic beer and bottle shots. The inn caters to ranchers, farmers, campers, hikers, fishermen, hunters, trackers plus the local labor force—loggers and millers (once); marijuana growers and trimmers (now).

Wildwood, in the middle of nowhere, dense with old-growth conifers, thick with pines towering from red-dirt hillsides, carpeted with needle mulch and manzanita brush. Habitat for blacktail deer, black bear, native trout, mountain lions, and spotted owls.

The high lonesome, as distant as the grave.

I

Across the Bay from San Francisco, the city of Berkeley rises east from the mudflats of the Bay to the foothills of Oakland Canyon. Berkeley spreads through neighborhoods into the prestigious University of California. Bronze entry arches, oxidized green, open to walking paths lined by sycamore shade trees winding through a hilly complex of monolithic Beaux-Arts stone buildings roofed with terra-cotta tiles. At the campus center, the 307-foot Campanile—formally Sather Tower—stands as the tallest bell-and-clock tower in the world, pealing carillon concerts on the hour. Classic old-school old school, Cal—178 urban acres, thirty-six thousand students, a city and tradition of its own.

A mile south of campus, Ashby Avenue runs from the Emeryville mud flats east through town as a two-lane bottleneck. Ashby becomes Tunnel Road at the corner of Domingo Avenue and winds through the Oakland Hills into the half-mile-long Caldecott (formerly Broadway) Tunnel. It becomes Monte Diablo Boulevard (State Route 24), ferrying commuters to/from Contra Costa County.

Up from the Ashby/Domingo intersection at 41 Tunnel Road, the majestic Claremont Hotel rises six stories across twenty-two acres of forested grounds. It features 279 rooms, a twenty-thousand-square-foot spa, and a fenced-in ten-court tennis complex available to guests but operating also as the Berkeley Tennis Club.

In business since 1915, the Claremont notches into a wooded hillside. It was constructed for opulence in the style of Mediterranean royalty: a white-stone castle with expansive verandas, lighted roof gables and dormers, tall palms swaying in front of an illuminated domed tower, flag-festooned at the carriage entrance.

Above the hotel, residential streets shaded with oak, laurel, spruce, and buckeye trees braid through ridgelines and empty onto Tunnel Road. A family named Bryan, two years removed from Massachusetts in 1955, lived in the Berkeley Hills at 131 Alvarado Road, in a thirty-seven-hundred-square-foot, six-bedroom, two-story (three, counting a street-level garage) Moroccan stucco with a tiled roof and tall, arched windows offering a priceless view of the Bay, the city, and both bridges.

The father, Charles, was a radiologist at Peralta Hospital in Oakland; the mother, Mary, a stay-at-home. Five Bryan children: Stephanie, age fourteen; Cheryl, twelve; Rutledge ("Sam"), ten; Estelle, eight; and Beatrice, three. Stephanie and Cheryl attended ninth and seventh grades at Willard Junior High on Telegraph Avenue, 1.6 miles downhill from the Alvarado/Tunnel intersection, past the Claremont Hotel, across Domingo, down Ashby seven blocks to Telegraph, and right two and a half blocks to the corner of Stuart Street.

In the mornings, Dr. Bryan drove Stephanie and Cheryl to school. Afternoons, the girls made their own way home, though seldom together. They had their own friends and walked at different paces, Cheryl slower. Mary, initially concerned about the girls walking alone, was reassured by liberal parents of classmates. She acceded to insular halls-of-ivy assumptions. She had come from Dartmouth, Massachusetts. She felt safe in a college town. Pre-1960s Berkeley was de facto segregated—coloreds lived south of Grove Street. Her family resided in the hills, well north of Grove.

Mary posted strict rules. School let out at three fifteen; Stephanie and Cheryl were expected through the front door by four. Figure junior-high girls before students rolled backpacks: armloads of books, binders, and papers, trekking uphill along heavy traffic on Tunnel Road. Shortcuts imperative. Mary and the girls mapped out approved detours through the Claremont grounds.

From Willard Junior High, they strolled through residential streets on diagonal paths to Ashby. They crossed trolley tracks behind the tennis courts on Domingo, on the western edge of the hotel property. From there, they took a tree-shaded dirt path a hundred feet to a turnout on Alvarado Place, 150 flat-ground paces to Alvarado Road, and another 150 steps home.

Thursday, April 28, 1955, 3:15 p.m.: Stephanie Bryan and a girlfriend, Mary Ann Stewart, exited Willard JH at the south entrance onto Stuart Street. They walked east two blocks to Benvenue Avenue (just south of the shingle-sided fourplex from which newspaper heiress Patricia Campbell Hearst would be abducted nineteen years later) and turned right another two blocks.

They crossed Ashby to the Claremont branch of the Berkeley Public Library. Stephanie checked out *Sue Barton, Staff Nurse* and *Two's Company*. They walked east again on Ashby to College and stepped a half-block north to Elmwood Pet Supply. Stephanie bought a twenty-five-cent booklet, *Everything about Parakeets*; she was planning to buy a pet bird.

They walked back to Ashby and backtracked west a few storefronts to a brick building with a green awning, Dream Fluff Donuts, for takeout crullers—Stephanie's idea of rebellion. She was dealing with upper-lip eczema. Her mother warned her against sugary foods. They exited Dream Fluff east and crossed Claremont and Domingo with the lights. Mary Ann Stewart parted for a four-thirty lesson at the tennis club. Stephanie dressed in the Betty-and-Veronica fashions of the day: turquoise pleated skirt, white Orlon pullover, navy-blue cardigan, bobby socks, and brown-and-white saddle oxfords. She walked to the dirt path toward home with her binder and books, consumed with fourteen-year-old schoolgirl thoughts…

Mary Bryan sensed something wrong by four fifteen. Cheryl, the slow walker, already was home. Mary called three of Stephanie's schoolmates. Nothing. She dialed the school. No answer at the switchboard. Friends were supposed to pick up Mary and meet Charles at Peralta Hospital before six for a planned outing to a garden show at the Oakland Auditorium. Different era: one-car family; mother didn't drive; rotary-dial phones; few ways to connect. Mary left the other children with her mother. She had her friends take her to Willard JH instead of the hospital.

Dr. Bryan called home when Mary failed to show by six. Mary's mother told him Stephanie was missing. Mary arrived at his office at six-thirty, dropped off by the other couple. Charles and Mary rationalized—she stopped at a girlfriend's house, forgot to call; stayed at school and was walking home while Mary was driving around—but they couldn't chase the fear. Charles called the Berkeley police at 6:43 p.m. He told responding officer Wilbur H. Plantz, "She's never been this late…"

Berkeley PD might have disregarded the call. Nervous parents panicked over nothing. A teenager late after school without checking in—big deal. An era before cellphones, texts, and tweets: contact not always possible, even likely. Statistics said worst case she was a runaway who would reappear within hours, at most in a day or two. Except Berkeley PD had been fielding phone calls from the city editor of the *Berkeley Gazette* since four thirty: eyewitness reports of a car, a torpedo-back Chevrolet or Pontiac, 1949 or 1950, veering onto the shoulder just east of the Broadway Tunnel while a grown man on the driver's side struggled with a young woman.

Willard Junior High was conducting an open house the night of April 28. The Bryans met detective Willard Hutchins at the school. Hutchins opened case file J-22219, with the Bryans searching every room at the school and backtracking Stephanie's normal path home though the Claremont path to Alvarado Place. Berkeley police canvassed the neighborhood that night. Nothing turned up. Long, sleepless night for the Bryans. Long night of logistics for Berkeley PD. Press conference at noon the next day, Friday. Four San Francisco dailies—the *Chronicle,* the *Examiner,* the *Call-Bulletin,* and the *News*—competing with the *Oakland Tribune,* the *Berkeley Gazette,* and the *San Jose Mercury,* all running page-one stories above the fold.

Typical: *Oakland Tribune,* headline and lead paragraph, Saturday, April 30, 1955:

BERKELEY GIRL DISAPPEARS;
KIDNAP FEARED

All available East Bay police were thrown into a hunt for the 14-year old daughter of a prominent Berkeley radiologist who disappeared Thursday afternoon while on her way home from school...

Naval ROTC instructor at UC Berkeley Allen Hill read the morning paper. He notified BPD that afternoon. He said the day before he was driving west with his wife, Jacqueline, at about 4:15 p.m. on SR 24 just east of the tunnel. The Hills said they saw an eastbound car raising dust, slewing off the road. In the time it took Allen Hill to pass at slowing speeds, both the Hills claimed, they saw a girl in the open left rear window, ten or twelve years old, mouthing the word *No*.

Two days later, a groundsman with the Berkeley parks department named Percy Dappen said he left work at 4:10 p.m. on April 28, driving on Ashby en route home to Lafayette on SR 24. He said a gray/green '49 Chevy tore out of the Claremont grounds behind him. Percy Dappen said he had a look at the driver. Dappen said he was frail and slender with a "vicious, mean look on his face." He said he had a young female passenger. He said the man in the Chevy swerved into the westbound lane to pass, a near-suicidal maneuver on Tunnel Road. He said the Chevy skittered onto the shoulder just clear of the tunnel. He said it looked like the man was attacking the girl. His quote: "I recall seeing him with both hands raised, as with some small club in his hands, swinging down with terrific speed."

At least a dozen witnesses corroborated...with customary eye-witness reliability. Everyone verified the roadside struggle. No one recalled a license number, except Jacqueline Hill, who only caught the letter *Y* or *V*. The incident occurred at different times through a ninety-minute time span...from three thirty to past five. The car was a Pontiac and a Chevrolet. It was gray, green, and black. The girl was ten, twelve, and twenty. She had short hair and long. She was sitting in the right-front and left-rear seats. Her window was open and closed. The driver was old and young, twenty-five and fifty, dressed in a business suit and white shirt with a bow tie, and in hunting clothes, and in a leather jacket and hat. He was also husky and slender, balding with a full head of bushy, black hair. One account: "He was a two-hundred-pound Mexican or Portagee with dark hair and sunglasses."

Only certain conclusion: Stephanie Bryan was missing, and a thin man in a General Motors car was overwhelming a smaller female passenger proximate to the time and place she had disappeared.

II

Berkeley, 1955: A somnolent, tree-lined university town of 110,000, third-largest city in Alameda County, one-third the population of contiguous Oakland, one-seventh of San Francisco, but with a police department at least as sophisticated as either. Return to to 1905. Citizen reformers tired of open prostitution, gambling, and narcotics elected a twenty-nine-year-old mail carrier/fireman named August Vollmer as town marshal. Vollmer served four years before being appointed Berkeley's first police chief.

Vollmer ran BPD from 1909 to 1931, bringing the department out of the caves. He imposed ethics while rooting out graft and corruption. He prohibited rubber-hose interrogations. He recruited high-intellect officers from the university. He hired on merit without regard for race or gender. Later in life Vollmer became a law-enforcement educator. He served on the faculties of the University of Chicago and his hometown UC Berkeley. He studied international police programs on location—Scotland Yard and the Surete, among dozens of other European and Asian departments. He published books that still serve as texts for police administration.

Vollmer established a training academy; he mobilized the department by putting all patrolmen first into bicycles (1910), then motorcycles (1911), then into squad cars (1913); he formed the first juvenile division in the country; he innovated with two-way radios and established the West Coast's first fingerprint bureau; he established the first school of criminology at UC Berkeley. Under his supervision, UCB developed the world's first polygraph testing system. BPD under Vollmer was among the first in the world to use fingerprints to identify suspects.

Berkeley PD in 1955 was the cat's ass in law enforcement, an August Vollmer legacy, maybe the best-situated on the West Coast for handling a case such as the disappearance of Stephanie Bryan. BPD rolled on Charles Bryan's telephone call the night of April 28, 1955...but seemed to stall with every initiative.

BPD had worked with Pacific Telephone to trap the Bryan's residential line on a reel-to-reel recorder. Thirty-two hours after Stephanie disappeared, right around midnight Friday, the phone rang. Charles Bryan fingered the switch and picked up the receiver. A male voice—Dr. Bryan said it sounded like an ill-educated Southern black dialect—offered to return Stephanie for $5,000 in small bills delivered to the corner of Eighth and Brush Street (the caller spelled it "B-r-e-s-h" and pronounced it *Bersh*) in West Oakland. The caller warned against contacting the police.

Dr. Bryan dialed BPD immediately. Within 90 minutes, he was on the move, policewoman Marian Clark in the passenger seat posing as Mary Bryan, a dummy package of cash between them. On the backseat and rear floorboard, in radio contact with Oakland and BPD stakeouts: detectives Willard Hutchins and Art Lyman.

Dr. Bryan parked at the southwest corner of Eighth and Brush. A black man approached: "You the doctor who's supposed to deliver the package here?" Dr. Bryan signaled. Police converged. The black man, ID'd as L. C. Elliot, eighteen, turned out to be a discharged mental patient from Sonoma State Hospital. Under severe questioning by detectives, L. C. Elliot admitted to a scam masterminded by an accomplice, an unemployed twenty-five-year-old fry cook. Neither had anything to do with Stephanie Bryan. L. C. Elliot eventually was tried for attempted extortion, convicted and returned to the bughouse in Sonoma. The accomplice was nabbed in Alabama, extradited to Alameda County, convicted, and sentenced five to life in San Quentin.

BPD had placed a mail cover on anything addressed to 131 Alvarado Road. May 3: An anonymous letter postmarked Oakland the day before issued a demand for $10,000 in fives, tens, and twenties, delivered to a "contact" in the back row of the television lounge inside the T&D Theater on Twelfth and Broadway, downtown Oakland, at nine forty-five the next night. Dr. Bryan arrived as directed with another package of bills.

The letter writer no-showed, but his MO activated the FBI. Under provisions of the Little Lindbergh law, the use of mails for extortion is a federal crime. The feds weighed in under the direction of San Francisco division SAC (special agent in charge) William Whelan, working through the Oakland RA (resident agency) located at the main Post Office building. Charles Bryan received a follow-up letter postmarked May 4 castigating him for "tipping the law," but nothing after. William Whelan sent both letters to Washington, but the FBI lab could raise no prints.

Early leads went as wispy as the extortion letters. By Tuesday, May 3, officials had produced and mailed five thousand fliers featuring Stephanie's picture and dental charts to law-enforcement agencies and radio/television outlets in eleven Western states. BPD canvassed the neighborhood and interviewed Willard Junior High students and staff. They pulled in known sex offenders and checked them one by tedious one.

Cops dispatched search teams into hills and ravines east of the university and the Claremont. Charles Bryan and Stephanie's siblings roamed outlying roadways as far away as the Sacramento-San Joaquin Delta. They posted fliers on telephone poles offering a $2,500 reward. Mary Bryan's brother, colonel Alfred Marks, commanded the Michigan Air National Guard. Colonel Marks came west with two pilots. They borrowed observation planes and flew over the wilderness between the Berkeley Hills and the 3,849-foot peak of Mount Diablo 16.8 miles to the east.

Charles Bryan had a little juice. One of his patients was Stanley Norton, assistant managing editor of the *Oakland Tribune*. Bryan called Norton. The *Trib* pressured law enforcement to organize squads of volunteers for extensive exploration of the wild ground along Tunnel Road and Monte Diablo Boulevard.

May 8, Sunday: Twelve hundred showed for the larger of two full-scale searches over a two-week span. The Boy Scouts, Explorer Scouts, Dads' Clubs, and the Council of Scouts' Fathers met with the sheriff's mounted patrol and six National Guard jeeps. They combed thirty-two square miles for eight hours along a fifteen-mile front.

They went bush to bush through Oakland Canyon east from the Claremont grounds to the edge of Orinda, north eleven miles as far as Pinole, south ten miles to Castro Valley. The yield: one decomposed body of a toothless fifty-five-year-old woman in a culvert not far from the hotel and a bloody blanket off Mount Diablo Boulevard a mile east of the tunnel. Useless. Doctor's kid Stephanie had never been blood-typed.

Monday, May 2, 7:30 a.m.: Sixty-seven-year-old electrician David Tyree was motoring with his wife Effie and son Ernest. The Tyrees had recently moved to San Pablo. The boy was finishing the academic year at Loma Vista Junior High in Concord, staying with a friend's family in Clayton. David and Effie were taking him to start the week. They cut off San Pablo Avenue (US 40) at the Route 4 *Y* in Hercules. They drove through the Crockett Hills on Franklin Canyon Road.

David Tyree was taking prescribed diuretics. He pulled over on Franklin Canyon Road to pee near a copse of trees on the other side of a fence. Returning to the car, he noticed a book lying on the shoulder ten feet off the pavement—a textbook. He handed it to Ernest: beginning French. Ernest kept the book but tossed the tattered cover.

Monday, May 9: Effie Tyree lounged at home with the *Oakland Tribune*. She read about the hunt for Stephanie Bryan. She saw that Stephanie Bryan was carrying schoolbooks when she vanished. She remembered Franklin Canyon Road a week prior. She told her husband. Lightbulbs flicked on.

David Tyree called the number published in the *Trib*. He was patched through to Willard Hutchins in Berkeley. David Tyree told his story. Willard Hutchins picked up David Tyree in San Pablo and drove to Clayton. They found Ernest, drove to Concord, and retrieved the textbook from his locker: *Modern French, Course I*. Willard Hutchins flipped it open. Last name scrawled on a borrower slip pasted to the inside cover: Stephanie Bryan. The book was weathered from dew but not warped. BPD lab analysis: no rain after April 30; book degraded by no more than a day. The book had been flung from a car on Sunday, May 1, seventy-two hours after its owner went missing.

BPD and FBI searchers poured into surrounding Briones Regional Park, spent all day and past nightfall until 1:00 a.m. but came up dry. Detectives plotted the book's location against the Claremont Hotel and Broadway Tunnel. They factored travel times between the disappearance, the probable disposal of the book, and since. They protracted route lines from Franklin Canyon Road. The lines boxed the compass. Manifold roads leading everywhere. They were looking for a single needle in a panoramic horizon of haystacks.

Chronic confessors called in. Beaten wives snitched off abusive husbands. Red herrings propagated. Sightings were reported and followed.

May 4, Keyes, a tiny farm town on SR 99 in the Central Valley between Modesto and Turlock: A man stopping for gas at a frontage road filling station in a '49 or '50 Pontiac. The night-shift attendant spotted what looked like purplish, discolored human finger ends sticking from the seal of a slammed-down trunk. He called out to the driver. The driver, dark-haired, medium-medium, thirty-five through forty, peeled rubber. The attendant looked down. No rear plate. He ran down the road to a bar and called the Stanislaus County sheriff's department in Modesto.

Undersheriff Harry Oliver took the call. He issued an all-regions APB, dispatched five patrol cars for an overnight BOLO (be on the lookout), and alerted the highway patrol. Berkeley PD caught the dispatch and noted the similarity in automobiles to the Tunnel Road incident. Sergeant Ralph Bischop accompanied Willard Hutchins for a midnight ride across Altamont Pass on two-lane Highway 50 (now 580), past Tracy and into the Central Valley. They tracked the story and believed it, but car and driver vanished. Nothing left to connect the fingers to Stephanie Bryan.

The FBI threw itself into the case. At one point the bureau assembled every witness to the Tunnel Road episode for brainstorming. The feds obtained a DMV list of '49/'50 Chevys/Pontiacs in the Bay Area with a *Y* in the license plate. None warranted a recheck. Agent interrogations dug up bogus leads. Representative: A man with a 1949 Oldsmobile was washing his car in anticipation of selling it. A passerby reported what looked like blood colors sluicing onto the driveway. The car owner freely admitted it. He said his brother had borrowed the car recently and had banged a married woman on the front bench seat the first day of her period. The feds investigated. The story checked.

May into June: BPD and FBI no closer to a solution. Buzzards circled a ravine near a golf course in Orinda. Agents found a deer carcass. Stephanie was spotted simultaneously at bus depots in San Francisco and San Rafael. She was ID'd as a new tenant of a rooming house in Oakland, recently married to a serviceman. She was seen wearing a scarf riding in a car with two Mexicans, stopping at a San Pablo fruit stand.

June into July, thirteen weeks into the case: Stephanie Bryan's sensational disappearance dropped below the fold of Bay Area dailies. The best efforts of a pioneering police department, combined with the authority of the Federal Bureau of Investigation, stuck at an aggravating standstill. The Bryans bore on, heartbroken, maintaining as normal a family presence as possible, including a camping trip with the children—all but Stephanie. After the Fourth of July, the Bryans, Berkeley PD, and the FBI faced the prospect that the case wouldn't clear without a gift from the gods.

III

July 15, 1955, 1408 San Jose Avenue, Alameda: East Bay bungalow, white-stucco siding, gray Pabco roof, located on a tree-lined street across from Franklin Park, Franklin Elementary on the other side of the park. Anywhere, USA, middle-class residence: single-car driveway with a mow strip between concrete wheel paths. Garage at the end of the driveway. Clothesline connected to a pole strung on a back-porch pulley for pinning wash to dry in the sun over a small backyard. Three bedrooms, single bath. A one-story place built over a basement with L-pattern cement steps offset to the right of a front facade, rising to a covered porch.

A retired railroad man from Hayward, Clyde Wood, owned the property. A married couple, Burton W. "Bud" Abbott and his wife, Georgia, rented it. Their four-year-old son, Chris, and Burton's mother, Elsie, lived with them. Elsie worked as a civilian seamstress at Alameda Naval Air Station (ANAS). Red-haired Georgia, thirty-three, a hairdresser, was employed by Morton's Beauty Salon, 1414 Encinal Avenue in Alameda, five minutes' drive away, owned by family friend Leona Dezman. Burton, nicknamed "Bud" after the comedian: twenty-seven years old, scrawny, five foot eleven, 135 pounds, narrow shoulders, long fingers, dust-blond hair, and no ass. Bud Abbott wore horned-rim glasses and sported a pencil-thin mustache. He attended UC Berkeley as an accounting major under the GI bill's Veterans Disability Act.

6:30 p.m.: Burton Abbott in the kitchen, broiling steaks. Chris was staying with a babysitter on the other side of town. Just home from work, Georgia bustled down to the basement and was digging through a clutter of cardboard boxes looking for a 1920s-era cloche for a skit at an upcoming hairstyling contest staged by the Oakland Cosmetologists Association. Georgia was the association president. She had performed the same skit wearing the same hat the year before.

Doorbell. Burton answered. Otto Dezman, Leona Dezman's husband, family friend, retired Navy chief warrant officer. Burton: "Come on in. If I'd known you were coming, I'd have put on another steak." Dezman said he couldn't stay long. Burton mixed him a highball. Georgia bounced up the stairs calling, "Abbott, Abbott," holding a red rectangular object. She'd been combing through a cardboard carton—ALL laundry soap label on its side—sorting through packed-away aprons, socks, shorts, and T-shirts.

Underneath familiar items she had uncovered a plastic dime-store red purse with a broken clasp, not hers. She dumped the contents on the dining room table and itemized the spread. Three pennies, a white plastic comb, two bobby pins, green-and-gold Paper Mate pen, blue wooden pencil, pink rubber eraser, letter to "Teddy," and a man's red-leather wallet. In the wallet, a Junior Red Cross card in the name of Stephanie Bryan and a special-privilege card from Willard JH, also in the name of Stephanie Bryan.

"Isn't this the girl who disappeared in Berkeley?" Georgia asked the house, pointing to the cards from the purse. Elsie looked at the purse and contents. Burton looked. Dezman looked. They all handled the merchandise. Dezman connected too late. "Don't ruin the fingerprints," he said. Later, Otto Dezman claimed he suggested phoning Berkeley PD. Abbott would make the same claim, adding that he had looked up the number. Elsie feared adverse publicity. Georgia made the call. She reached desk sergeant Victor

Viera. She said, "I found a purse...it has a junior high school ID in it with the name of Stephanie Bryan." Sergeant Viera: "Don't touch anything. We'll be right over."

"Let's eat," Burton said. "Steaks are getting cold." Georgia set the purse and contents on a side table. Elsie, distracted, had left for a dinner date with a friend, Devere King. Georgia, puzzled, chatty through dinner. Otto Dezman, anxious that a bad day was turning worse, wishing he were elsewhere, poured another drink. Abbott, thinking out loud: "How could that purse have gotten down there? Why our house of all the houses in Alameda...the only thing I can think of, someone's trying to put us on the spot."

Inspector Charles O'Meara, in command of J-22219, showed up at 7:30 p.m. with Willard Hutchins and three other plainclothesmen. Five more BPD detectives followed within the hour, along with three FBI agents from the Oakland resident agency. Dezman suggested the living room. Abbotts on the sofa; Dezman in an upholstered wing chair; O'Meara and Hutchins semicircled with Dezman in dining room chairs. O'Meara and Hutchins interviewed Burton Abbott, Georgia Abbott, and Otto Dezman for three hours. The others catalogued the purse and contents for crime-lab examination. They checked the basement and backyard. They asked for the keys to the cars in the driveway: Georgia's 1955 Pontiac Chieftain hardtop and Burton's 1949 slope-back, four-door, gray-green Chevrolet Fleet Line.

Routine inquiry, nobody targeted...yet. O'Meara and Hutchins mostly focusing on access to the basement. Occupants, of course. Friends, possibly. Babysitters, certainly. Burton's older (by a year) brother Mark and his new wife since December, Mary. Landlord Clyde Wood had a key. Clyde Wood stored tools in the basement. He maintained the property. Tradesmen, mail carriers, milk men, garbage haulers. The garage doubled as a polling place; 150 registered voters shuffled through on election days, most recently in late May.

O'Meara and Hutchins asked about the householders' whereabouts on the afternoon of April 28. Georgia and Burton jogged their memories for ninety-day-old calendar clues. Georgia said the last week of April was the same as every week that month. She said she must have worked all day at Morton's—she could verify this with her appointment book. Georgia and Burton said Elsie carpooled to and from her sewing table at ANAS every weekday. April 28 would have been no different. Abbott remembered he had been fishing. He said he had left Alameda in his '49 Chevy to a cabin owned by his wife's family located 275 miles away near Wildwood, in Trinity County. He said trout season in California opened Saturday, April 30. He explained that UC was recessed for spring break until Monday, May 2.

The way he told it, he had a tire repaired and had gassed up the night before at a Standard station on Webster Street in Alameda. He had parked the car at the station while he and Georgia took dancing lessons on the same block. They were home by nine thirty or ten. Burton parked in the driveway and packed the trunk with a Coleman stove, an oil lantern, a canvas cot, pots, pans, utensils, and three sleeping bags. In the morning, he left Chris with the babysitter, Hilda Frakes. He stopped at the Lewis Grocery Store next to the Morton Salon on Encinal Avenue, where he bought a box of food he placed in the backseat. He dropped into Morton's to say goodbye to Georgia. He said he was on the road no later than 11:00 a.m.

He said he exited Alameda Island through the Posey Tube, the tunnel underneath the harbor's shipping channel. He drove along Harrison Street in Oakland to Eighth and turned left onto Cypress in Berkeley. He merged onto the East Shore Highway toward El Cerrito. He picked up Highway 40, a.k.a. San Pablo Avenue (now the route of I-80), the main line to the Sacramento Valley. He followed San Pablo Avenue along the Bay front around the Crockett Hills and crossed the Carquinez Bridge. He said he drove past Benicia, Vallejo, Vacaville, and Fairfield. At Davis, he turned north to 99 W (now the route of Interstate 5). He stopped for lunch in Dunnigan. He had trouble remembering the restaurant's name, only that "it had two names, a woman's and man's…" (Actually, it was Bill and Kathy's.)

He said he stopped again in Corning at a Shell station, "I would say at 4:30 or a quarter of five." He said he patronized Shell instead of Standard because his wife had been nagging him about credit-card bills. Elsie had given him fifteen dollars for the trip; he stopped at the most convenient place and bought gas from his fresh fifteen.

He said he drove to Red Bluff. He said he stopped for dinner on the west side of 99 W at the south end of town. He said it was still daylight: probably about six o'clock by then. He couldn't remember the name of the restaurant. He said it "had something to do with chicken, something like 'Chicken Fry Spot,' maybe." (It was the Chuck Wagon Café.) He said he took SR 36 off 99 W out of Red Bluff. Abbott said the weather worsened—rain turning to snow as he gained elevation. He said his car had bad tires, and it took him almost two hours to travel sixty miles from 99 W. He said he turned off SR 36 for the mile drop to Wildwood around eight. He said he had dropped in for one drink at the Wildwood Inn, where he said hello to innkeeper Delbert Cox, busy with customers, before driving two miles to the cabin on unpaved Hayfork Road.

He said he puttered around the cabin Friday morning. He said he drank and ate at the Wildwood Inn all afternoon and into the night, talking mostly to a local miller, Tom Daly. He said he drank too much. His brother and his sister-in-law, Mark and Mary, had arrived by the time he woke. Abbott said he was nursing a "brilliant hangover." He said the drizzly weather ruined fishing. Said he and his brother drove back tandem on Sunday.

O'Meara noted throughout the interview that Georgia answered questions eagerly, looking at Otto Dezman for corroboration. Dezman contributed to the dialogue. Burton Abbott said little beyond providing details of his fishing trip. Willard Hutchins's cop instinct perked up: Georgia Abbott and Otto Dezman about normal for the circumstance; Burton Abbott trying too hard to appear calm, stifling nervous gestures, forcing laughter at remarks not especially funny. When not directly questioned, Burton

Abbott worked a crossword from a newspaper on his lap. Most of the police left by 10:30 p.m. Willard Hutchins stood guard until relieved by a two-man BPD detail at eleven thirty. Otto Dezman drove Hutchins to the Berkeley police station at 2171 McKinley Street. He stopped at a liquor store and returned to the Abbotts' with a pint of bourbon. He and Burton drained the pint while they played chess until dawn.

9:00 a.m., Saturday, July 16: FBI agent Marvin Buchanan at the door with a consent-to-search form. Burton Abbott signed it. Georgia signed it. Rights waived by signature. Three BPD detectives with shovels trailed through the door behind agent Buchanan. A half hour later, they were joined downstairs by three FBI agents. Cop sedans, marked and unmarked, lined the street. Suits and fedoras buzzed in and out of the Abbott's white stucco house. Uniforms, ditto. Morning papers hit the stoops. Radio news reports broke in over coffee and corn flakes. Party lines crackled. Onlookers gathered across the street, speading under fir trees into the grass at Franklin Park. Reporters arrived with photographers. Radio and newsreel crews arrived, clogging sidewalks. 1408 San Jose avenue on a pleasant Sabbath in July—a cynosure for rubbernecks.

Alameda County district attorney Frank Coakley showed with his chief assistant, Folger Emerson. BPD brought in UC criminology professor and criminalist Dr. Paul Kirk to examine the Abbotts' cars. Number 1408 had a full basement running the length and width of the house with concrete footings supporting the floor joists. The front half of the basement was paved; the rear all sandy soil.

4:00 p.m.: FBI/BPD double team. Burton accompanying Charles O'Meara and special agent Donald Hallahan to the RA at the Post Office building. Georgia, home from work by then, went with BPD inspector William Robinson and federal agent Marvin Buchanan to Alameda police headquarters. Still eleven years before *Miranda v. Arizona*: a free shot for law enforcement. The Abbotts did not ask for counsel. They didn't waive their rights to remain silent. Police described them to the press as "most cooperative."

Elsie was interviewed at 1408 San Jose by BPD detective Wilbur Plantz and federal agent William Poole. She said Burton returned from his fishing trip tired. She said his car was dirty from snow and mud. Said he dumped all his soiled clothes for her to wash. She rambled on about being downstairs a day or so later looking for chenille bedspreads. Said she saw the purse in the ALL box. She had mentioned it to agents who were digging in the basement. She confirmed it in her interview with Plantz and Poole. She said she opened the purse, thought Stephanie Bryan might be a friend of Georgia's. Said that was the first week in May. Elsie inadvertently destroying a voter/kidnap-killer alternative, someone else who could have planted the goods.

Thirty minutes after the Abbotts had left, FBI agent Richard Nichols was probing subbasement dirt opposite the third stud from the northeast corner. He hit something solid six to eight inches from the footing. He called out to another agent. They dug with their fingertips and unearthed a book: *Sue Barton, Staff Nurse*. They dug deeper. Two more books: *Two's Company* and *Everything about Parakeets*. They sifted the immediate context and unearthed a spiral notebook with Stephanie Bryan's name on it, an exercise book for French lessons, Stephanie's blue-tipped eyeglasses, and a white DuPont nylon brassiere with an I. Magnin label.

Georgia, hearing the news at Alameda police headquarters, blurted: "He could have done it! He must have done it if they found that stuff in the basement." Elsie, upstairs, broke the only time from insistence on her son's innocence: "If Burton did this, I wish he were dead. He would be better off."

Burton, confronted with the new discoveries three hours deep into his interrogation by O'Meara and Hallahan: "This makes the thing even more impossible. Why would these things be buried, and the other things put into a box?" Hallahan, boring in: "Burton, think of the ordeal these parents are going through. If you have any compassion at all, tell us where she is. You owe that much to the Bryan family." Burton, on edge: "I don't give a damn about the Bryan family. I care about my family. When do we get to eat?"

IV

Georgia Schorch Abbott was from Kansas. Her parents moved to Trinity County as resort managers when Georgia was young. In the 1930s, her father staked a mining claim near Hayfork Creek and built a rough shelter near the claim. The family relocated to San Anselmo, where Georgia attended high school. Her father died when she was nineteen, in 1940. Two-thirds interest to the claim and cabin fell to Georgia's mother, one third to his mining partner, Lloyd Snyder, former husband of one of Georgia's cousins.

Lloyd Snyder, a semi-affable lush, spent the bleak winter of 1947/48 snowbound in Wildwood, bunking in the Hayfork Creek cabin with another alcoholic miner, a cantankerous slob named Ray Latham. Didn't take long for a bad mix to sour. Lloyd Snyder and Ray Latham picked at each other, boozing through long frigid nights and short gray days. In one bibulous dispute, Ray Latham threatened to slice Lloyd Snyder. Snyder glanced in a mirror and glimpsed Latham raising a butcher's knife. Snyder grabbed a shotgun and blew Latham apart.

Wilderness hovel, knee-deep slush outside—no way to summon the law or dispose of the body. Lloyd Snyder wasn't eager to ride out the winter in a one-room shack with a decomposing corpse ripening in the heat from a half-barrel stove. Solution: he dismembered Ray Latham with a wood ax, packed a half-dozen gunnysacks with body parts, and buried the sacks outside the cabin just below the snow. Lloyd Snyder never bothered to mention the loss of his roommate. Nobody liked Ray Latham anyway. With the spring thaw after a hard winter, the locals forgot him.

A local rancher, Harold "Bud" Jackson, foiled the play. Bud Jackson was versatile, a local legend. He moonlighted as a miner, a deputy sheriff, a county-road boss, bear hunter, and cat tracker—he bounty hunted mountain lions that threatened farm and ranch livestock. Bud Jackson owned highly evolved tracking dogs, bloodhound/blue-tick crosses, Shorty and Spot. Bud Jackson was traveling the Hayfork road with Shorty and Spot in the bed of his pickup after the snowmelt. Shorty and Spot picked up the scent of the recently departed and defrosting Ray Latham.

Bud Jackson ignored his baying dogs—until Lloyd Snyder showed up days later at the local post office in Platina, nine miles west on SR 36, asking about Ray Latham's mail. Backwoods sociology: everything is everybody's business with the postmistress at the center of information. The postmistress thought Lloyd Snyder was acting funny. She mentioned it to the sheriff's deputy in charge of the Hayfork substation. The deputy sent Bud Jackson to check. Bud Jackson brought Shorty and Spot. Shorty and Spot howled. Bud Jackson followed their noses. He shoveled up six sacks of Ray Latham's remains. Lloyd Snyder might have skated with self-defense except for the ax work and his subsequent silence. The jury had no choice. Lloyd Snyder was convicted of second-degree murder and sentenced to five to life.

Before departure for San Quentin, Snyder signed his one-third ownership of the cabin and claim to Georgia's older brother, Robert. Robert and Georgia had inherited their mother's original two-thirds share. Owners now: two-thirds/one-third, Robert and Georgia. Georgia's husband, Burton Abbott frequently roughed it in Wildwood, Sometimes alone, Sometimes with Georgia, often with his brother Mark. He was well known by face and name in the area.

The Schorch cabin fronted the gravel road to Hayfork, two miles past Wildwood. It was situated on a wide spot in the road that sloped gradually downhill thirty yards to the creek. The cabin was stilted in back to accommodate the slope, making it level with the road. It was built out of untreated 2 x 4s and 1 x 12 barn wood, culled from the local mill, single-wall construction, roofed with corrugated tin. Inside, a main room and small kitchen, rough plank floor, and exposed rafters. No indoor plumbing or electricity. Water was pumped from the creek or gathered from snowmelt. Winter heat came from the vented half-barrel, summer air from opening doors and windows. The front door was saw-cut through the 1 x 12s, Z-framed with 2 x 4s, and strap-hinged. It was secured from intrusion with a galvanized hasp and a padlock.

Charles O'Meara and Donald Hallahan stepped it up after hearing about the new discoveries in the basement of 1408 San Jose Avenue. They grilled Burton Abbott for specifics of his April 28 alibi. The FBI had accumulated signed receipts from Burton Abbott's Standard Oil gas card. Not everything computed. Burton's twitchy explanations were studded with "I don't know...I don't think...I'm not sure...I'm sorry, I don't recall..." One gas ticket showed a purchase at Fulton and Durant in Berkeley the afternoon of April 27. UCB on recess—no reason for him to be in town.

Another receipt recorded a fill-up at Twentieth and Harrison in Oakland midmorning on the twenty-eighth. Didn't track. Abbott said he had gassed up for his trip on Webster Street in Alameda the night before. Twentieth and Harrison is at least twelve blocks out of the way for accessing the East Shore Highway at Eighth and Cypress in Berkeley, but it is a straight shot through downtown Oakland and Berkeley to the interior of the UC campus. O'Meara asked him about his customary route to the campus. Burton: "I'm sorry, I'm not sure of the street names..."

O'Meara flashed another gas tag for May 2 in Pinole on the day UCB was back in session. Burton said his tires were bad; he said between classes he had trolled San Pablo Avenue junkyards for used replacements. BPD and FBI had interviewed Mark Abbott earlier that day. Mark had said Burton had told him he detoured through Sacramento en route to Wildwood. Burton had said nothing about Sacramento. O'Meara braced him on the discrepancy. Burton backtracked: he said Mark wanted him to file another mining claim near Hayfork Creek. Burton: "I remember now...I did go to Sacramento. We are thinking about additional property near the cabin. I went to the Bureau of Land Management office in San

Francisco, and the man there said we should go to their office in Sacramento. He told me where it was, and I went there."

O'Meara and Hallahan pressed him for details. Burton scratched out a map to the BLM office and a drawing of same. O'Meara and Hallahan looked skeptically at his page. Kid-crude lines with arrow tips. From Burton Abbott's rudimentary renditions, they didn't think he'd been to either place. Mark Abbott had said they'd driven back on May 1. Mark said Burton followed him home to Castro Valley before returning to Alameda. Past the Carquinez Bridge, he said they'd teed off on Highway 4 through Franklin Canyon, eventually cutting onto SR 75 (now 680). He said Burton was three to four car lengths behind most of the way.

O'Meara and Hallahan hammered the alibi until 10:55 p.m. Burton had been interrogated since four thirty: the better part of six hours. Burton Abbott was a "lunger," diagnosed with pulmonary tuberculosis during an Army boot-camp physical in 1947. He was given a medical discharge but retained veteran's benefits, including prolonged treatment at an Army sanitarium in Livermore. Surgeons excised a lobe of his left lung in 1951, leaving a concave scar across the back of his left shoulder trailing under his armpit. He was routinely described in the media as "frail." He claimed he tired easily and needed to eat often. He appealed to O'Meara and Hallahan. They said, one more stop.

Alameda County district attorney Frank J. Coakley tended to work late in his office at the Alameda County courthouse across the street from Lake Merritt. He wasn't taking time off now. O'Meara and Hallahan drove Abbott to see Frank Coakley at eleven thirty. Coakley asked him his name and address and went random from there, spiking inquiries into the alibi with disjointed questions designed to trip him: whether he ever drove through the Broadway Tunnel; if he had ever been to Keyes; if he was in the neighborhood of the Claremont Hotel on April 28; if he had ever stayed at the Claremont Hotel. Coakley meandered. Finally, at almost one in the morning, he said, "All right, that's all."

1408 San Jose, a half hour later: Area bright from floodlights, law-enforcement crews still sifting basement dirt and taking apart a backyard patio paved with 3 x 6 wooden bricks. They were excavating to a depth of two feet. The reason was obvious: they were looking for Stephanie Bryan's corpse. Leona Dezman had returned from a beauticians' convention in Louisville, Kentucky. Georgia was home, nerves shot, Leona and Otto Dezman in attendance, when Burton returned. The Abbotts accepted the Dezmans' offer to spend the rest of the night at their house.

Sunday morning, July 17: Banner, headline, and bold lead paragraph in the *SF Chronicle*:

NEW STEPHANIE CLUES DISCOVERED
POLICE QUESTIONING UC STUDENT

> The anguishing and mysterious Stephanie
> Bryan Case seemed closer to solution than it has
> at any time since the 14-year-old Berkeley
> girl disappeared on her way home from school
> one afternoon nearly three months ago...

Burton Abbott all over the front pages of Bay Area dailies. Burton still said he didn't need an attorney. Georgia overruled. She consulted a prominent neighbor, mortician Chesley Anderson, an Alameda city councilman, through his wife, a client at Morton's Beauty Salon. Chesley Anderson contacted high-end civil attorney Stanley Whitney at the Encinal Yacht Club. Stan Whitney agreed to represent the Abbotts virtually pro bono—low legal fees in return for high-profile exposure.

Sunday afternoon, May 17: Frank Coakley called Burton back for interrogation. Stan Whitney arrived at the courthouse during the session and demanded to see his new client. Coakley acceded. By then, Burton had overcome his reluctance to have legal counsel. In a private room, Burton broached an immediate concern to

Stan Whitney: he said he had misled police regarding his detour through Sacramento. He laid it out. Whitney didn't see it as a huge problem. Client and counsel reconvened with Frank Coakley.

Burton told Coakley he had been afraid of disappointing his brother. He said he told Mark he had stopped at the BLM office but left without information after a bureaucratic runaround. In fact, he said now, "I went to Sacramento and drove around, but I couldn't find the place. It was getting later and later, it got darker, so I said the heck with it and went on to the cabin." Burton said when Mark Abbott confirmed the account during his own interrogation, he felt trapped into repeating the same story to O'Meara and Hallahan. Different sides of the adversarial bar. Stan Whitney for the defense saw incorrect testimony amended after an honest mistake. Frank Coakley for the people sensed intimations of guilt. On an inconsequential issue, Abbott had lied to his brother and had lied to the police.

Frank Coakley had come across as a bumbler the night before. He wasn't. He had served in the Navy in World War I before attending UC Berkeley and Stanford. He passed the bar and went to work in the Alameda County DA's office, training under future California governor and US Supreme Court justice Earl Warren, running the same fast track as state attorney general (and future governor) Pat Brown.

Coakley asked Abbott if he had stopped between Alameda and Sacramento on April 28. Abbott said no. Coakley asked what time he arrived. Abbott: "Probably about one or one thirty." Frank Coakley asked what time he had headed west out of Sacramento. Abbott: "About three o'clock or so." Frank Coakley flashed to an Abbott phrase he had bookmarked earlier: "...it was getting later and later, it got darker..."

April 28, daylight savings time: Sundown on record at 8:01 p.m., dusk extending at least half an hour. Abbott in an unconscious slip? Frank Coakley thought so. He interpreted Abbott's "it got darker" remark as subconscious admission that he had traveled on 99 W five hours later than previously claimed.

Three BPD detectives and three FBI agents had driven to Wildwood almost immediately after the items were uncovered in Burton Abbott's basement. They interviewed the few locals, including Delbert Cox and Tom Daly. Del Cox remembered pouring for Abbott's nine-hour bender with Tom Daly on April 29. Del Cox insisted he didn't see him the night before. Broadside hit on Abbott's alibi.

Agents and detectives conducted a forensic examination of the cabin and outbuildings. They dusted tools and utensils for fingerprints and bloodstains. They scoured a thirty-yard area between the cabin and the creek, extending two hundred yards through the woods upstream and down. Forty-eight hours later, they drove home with sweat stains on their dress shirts and red dirt on their city brogues, but no clues.

Tuesday, July 19: *San Francisco Examiner* managing editor Bill Wren convinced the answer was to be found in the Trinity Alps. He thought the BPD/FBI crews had given up too easily. That afternoon, he secured use of a small plane and a pilot, Bill Kelly. He dispatched reporter Ed Montgomery and photographer Bob Bryant with Kelly to the Hayfork Air Field with the assignment to scoop out a story.

Montgomery was high profile. He had won a Pulitzer for local reporting in 1951 by uncovering kickbacks at the San Francisco branch of the IRS. On his own time, he was scrambling to exonerate convicted LA murderess Barbara Graham, "Bloody Babs," executed with two male accomplices in San Quentin six weeks earlier.

Montgomery, Bob Bryant, and Bill Kelly borrowed a car in Hayfork and wound around the gravel road to Wildwood. They mixed with locals at the inn before driving to the cabin. They stood on the road. Sweltering summer heat. Shift in the scalding evening breeze. Ed Montgomery scanned the mountain on the other side of the road. He saw a two-foot bank at the bottom of a forty-five-degree slope holding stands of tall pines. Ed Montgomery caught a sour whiff. Breeze reshift. Whiff dissipated into hot air.

Montgomery, Bryant, and Kelly drove twenty-one miles back to Hayfork, renting rooms in the only hotel. They asked about hunting dogs. The hotel keeper recommended the best bear and lion hunter in the county, Bud Jackson. They found Bud Jackson the next day, operating heavy equipment on a county road. Bud Jackson was eager to help.

He arranged to meet at the Snyder/Schorch cabin at six thirty. Ed Montgomery called deputy Frank Wyckoff at the sheriff's substation in Hayfork. Wyckoff said Montgomery and his crew were wasting their time; the FBI had already searched. Wyckoff notified the *Redding Searchlight*. Reporter Bill Mayer joined the *Examiner* party with a Redding car dealer. Bud Jackson brought Shorty and Spot and a rancher friend.

BPD and the FBI had searched behind the hovel, from the cabin to the creek. Ed Montgomery's group retraced that pattern for an hour. Ed Montgomery recalled the scent from the night before—up the slope. He asked Bud Jackson to send the dogs across the road. Shorty and Spot bounded ahead. Bud Jackson held their leads while hoisting himself up the mulch-slick bank by grabbing a manzanita limb. The others followed.

8:20 p.m.: Ed Montgomery forged ahead of the two men from Redding and Bob Bryant who was lugging photo gear. He trailed Bud Jackson, the rancher, and the pilot, Bill Kelly. Montgomery pushed through bushes into a small clearing a hundred yards above the road and saw Bud Jackson with Shorty and Spot standing over a slight indentation of loose dirt.

The indentation ended at the base of an old-growth ponderosa pine. Navy-blue fabric showed through the loose dirt, the color of Stephanie Bryan's cardigan. Bud Jackson called for shovels and a pinch bar. Ed Montgomery scampered downhill to the cabin's garage and brought back the tools. Bud Jackson dug around, exposing a protrusion. He dropped to his knees, brushing away dirt. Ed Montgomery recoiled at the emerging sight:

a mud-caked saddle oxford twisted perpendicular, skeletal foot inside a frayed sock.

Things went frantic. Ed Montgomery, feeling the terror but thinking scoop. Bud Jackson: "Call the coroner and the Sheriff in Weaverville. I'll stay here." Ed Montgomery slip-slid down the hill and saw that the *Searchlight* reporter had beat him to the road. One public phone in Wildwood, a retro rig on a wall at the inn. Ed Montgomery's car was closer and pointed in the right direction. Bill Mayer U-turned on the narrow road, losing his edge. Ed Montgomery spun gravel toward the inn. He bolted from his car at the parking lot, ran inside, and cranked up the operator: Long distance, San Francisco, Sutter 1-2424. He held. Dial tone. Connection. City editor Walter Tremaine answered. He heard Ed Montgomery's breathless few words. He turned him over to deskman Gale Cook for dictation.

Walter Tremaine snapped orders. He rushed one reporter, Frank Purcell, to 1408 San Jose. He assigned another, Francis O'Gara, to call the Bryans. He posted a third, Dick Pollard, for standby to BPD. Ed Montgomery tied up the hick phone line for twenty minutes, securing it from leaks. Walter Tremaine obstructing justice—wanting raw reaction from Burton Abbott and the Bryans before authorities were brought in. Ed Montgomery finished dictation with Gale Cook. Walter Tremaine back on the line: "Wait 10 minutes before calling Sheriff Wilson in Weaverville."

Frank Purcell wormed his way into Burton Abbott's house and broke the news. Burton, gone pale: "Near the cabin?" Elsie, bursting into tears: "Oh Burton!" Georgia, stunned, speechless, her arms cradling her husband. Burton, again: "How far from the cabin? How far from the cabin was it found?" Burton shook his head. "It can't be. I don't know how it got there. I don't know anything about it."

Active flurry. Francis O'Gara's phone call to Charles Bryan prompted Bryan to phone BPD, sergeant Victor Viera answering. Sergeant Viera notified acting chief Addison Fording. Fording directed Viera to contact the Trinity County sheriff. Events still inside Walter Tremaine's ten-minute window. Sheriff Wilson hadn't heard a thing. Viera hung up as Dick Pollard walked in. Dick Pollard: "Ed Montgomery has found Stephanie Bryan's body near the Abbott cabin in Trinity County." Telephone ringing. Outside line. Victor Viera picking up. Sheriff Wilson calling to confirm Dick Pollard's story. Victor Viera buzzed Acting Chief Fording.

Addison Fording: "Notify everyone on our call list. Teletype Alameda to pick up Burton Abbott on suspicion of 187 PC and hold for this department."

V

The *Examiner*'s Friday, July 22, banner headline, subhead, and lead paragraph:

GIRL'S BODY FOUND
NEAR ABBOTT CABIN
STUDENT ARRESTED
PLEADS INNOCENT

By Gale Cook

The body of a young girl believed to be Stephanie Bryan was found by the Examiner last night near the Trinity County family cabin of Burton W. Abbott. Authorities were first informed of the grisly find by reporter Ed Montgomery, who discovered the body in a small grave—together with Examiner photographer Bob Bryant, two Trinity County ranchers and a pair of bloodhounds...

BPD and FBI teams sped back to Wildwood, along with Frank Coakley, Alameda County chief pathologist Dr. George Loquvam, and Bryan family dentist Dr. Reginald Hanson. At first light, cops, agents, and local deputies scoured the place for evidence within the context of the foot-deep grave. Dr. Loquvam said he needed an autopsy table and water. Sheriff's deputies placed the remains in a coroner's basket and tucked them in with a sheet of canvas. They bore the basket down to the road and transported it by coroner's wagon seventy miles to a mortuary in Redding.

Dr. Hanson compared his charts with the uncovered skull. Positive ID: Stephanie Bryan. Dr. Loquvam's preliminary analysis—Stephanie's body too badly decomposed to yield forensic clues. Her panties were wrapped around her neck, but he couldn't find evidence of strangulation or molestation. From skull depressions, he could say she had been struck on the back of the head, but he couldn't pinpoint a fatal blow. Postmortem would not determine time or place of death, or cause of death. Two things certain: from the hard clay clinging to her garments, Stephanie was buried when the ground was wet—during or closely after a period of rain, and she was in rigor at the time of burial. The rigor item was never made public.

Burton Abbott, still claiming innocence, was taken to Berkeley city jail at the police station, 2171 McKinley. Judging by the headlines, he was as good as gassed. Case geometry incriminated him beyond coincidence. The crime triangulated between Alameda, Berkeley, and Wildwood: dead girl's belongings found in Abbott's Alameda basement; dead girl frequented the area Abbott traveled to and from the UC Berkeley campus; dead girl buried when the ground was wet 339 feet from the cabin Abbott visited on the rainy day she disappeared.

Charles O'Meara, irate over the *Examiner*'s headline grab, felt robbed from confronting Burton Abbott, maybe extracting a confession. In Washington, J. Edgar Hoover found no humor in his elite Federal Bureau of Investigation being upstaged by a news crew abetted by a hillbilly with hunting dogs. The three agents investigating Wildwood were transferred forthwith by Hoover edict to Butte, Montana.

Frank Coakley, pushing for the prize: a gas chamber conviction in the hottest case he would ever try. Once Stephanie's body was ID'd, he could have charged Burton Abbott with murder and kidnapping on the strength of a complaint signed by Charles Bryan. Charges would have held through a preliminary hearing before a superior court judge. Instead, he convened the grand jury, a one-edged legal-system weapon, the DA alone swinging the blade. Grand juries number between sixteen and twenty-three. They aren't challenged for bias. They operate in secrecy, without a presiding judge. Defense counsel cannot cross-examine because defense counsel is barred from the proceedings. Witnesses appear under subpoena; they testify under oath, subjecting them to perjury if their testimony changes during open court—especially critical if, like Mark Abbott, they were defense witnesses. Grand jury transcripts are sealed. GJs' charge is to weigh the evidence and hand down or deny "true bill" indictments.

Alameda County courthouse, Twelfth and Oak, Wednesday, July 27: One significant absentee, Elsie Abbott. Frank Coakley wanted the record to reflect Elsie's sworn testimony that she had seen the purse in the basement days after Burton Abbott's late-April fishing trip (well before the next election, in late May), but subpoena servers couldn't find her. Stan Whitney was riding point on the Burton Abbott case. His junior partner, John Hanson, conducted research and filings. Stan Whitney hired private-practice criminal attorney Harold Hove, ex-FBI field agent, for legwork, primarily for breaking down the prosecutor's case. Days after Abbott's arrest, Harold Hove ordered Elsie Abbott into hiding. She wasn't served because process servers couldn't find her.

Testimony ran for three and a half days through Saturday, July 30. Frank Coakley paraded witnesses through the criminal sequence. He started with three who spoke of the Tunnel Road scuffle. One, Sam Marshall, said: "A man in the front seat swung around to the right…I saw a small person…. fall back, and her feet come up so the tips of her toes were above the window sill of the car. The man was reaching back as if to choke her..." Coakley called classmate Mary Ann Stewart and librarian Lydia Barton. He walked them through the teenager's carefree after-school stroll to the Claremont branch of the Berkeley public library.

He propped up an easel with a site map. He had Mary Bryan take a pointer and show Stephanie's route behind the Claremont. He called Georgia Abbott, who invoked spousal privilege, refusing to testify. He called Mark Abbott, who couldn't. Coakley asked Mark about his mother's whereabouts. Mark didn't know. Coakley asked about the fishing trip. Coakley wanted the grand jury to connect the shallow grave and exhumation with Abbott—he wanted to put a shovel in Burton's hands. He homed in: "Did your brother use a shovel at any time during the trip?" Mark only said they both dug hellgrammites from the creek for bait. Coakley brought Mark back twice more. He asked about any tools Burton might have brought to the cabin. He asked about the May 1 trip home—the detour through Franklin Canyon. He asked about Burton's May 2 drive along San Pablo Avenue, allegedly to buy used tires.

Coakley called Ed Montgomery, Dr. George Loquvam, and the dentist, Dr. Reginald Hanson. In the absence of Elsie and Georgia, he called Otto Dezman to talk about the night Georgia had found Stephanie's purse in the ALL box. He called FBI agent Richard Nichols regarding the discoveries of Stephanie's books, bra, and eyeglasses. He called Charles O'Meara to sequence the investigation and catalogue the inconsistencies in Abbott's alibi.

Most intriguing witnesses: Delores Pring, owner, and Laverne Malloy, waitress, at Pring's Donuts, located at 2811 Telegraph, half a block south of Willard JH. Willard students routinely milled at Pring's before and after school and during lunch. The full name, Pring's Dutch Girl Donuts, was blazoned on a sign at the top of the building, along with the logo of a fresh-faced girl in blond braids, pinafore, and wooden clogs. BPD officers had canvassed the Willard neighborhood early in the investigation of Burton Abbott. They hit Pring's with pictures. The pictures rang the gong.

Delores Pring and Laverne Malloy both said that Stephanie Bryan was an after-school regular. They testified that Burton Abbott routinely stopped for coffee and donuts after his UC classes. Laverne Malloy said he lingered afternoons while catching up with the morning *Chronicle* and often would discuss the news. They couldn't say that Stephanie Bryan and Burton Abbott knew each other. They said he always left a tip.

Burton Abbott had stumbled over street names when Charles O'Meara had asked him about his route to UC. O'Meara brought out a city map. Abbott finger-traced a route from Alameda to Broadway in downtown Oakland, merging with College Avenue into campus. Odd. College Avenue is a bottleneck, two lanes always thick with traffic, cars and delivery trucks. Telegraph or San Pablo Avenues—both straight-shot four-lane thoroughfares from Oakland—would make more sense. Burton Abbott, subconsciously steering inquisitors from the spot where he conceived the crime?

Incriminating possibilities on two grounds:

First, in initial interrogation of Burton Abbott, July 16, Frank Coakley had asked Abbott if he knew much about the case. Abbott: "I don't remember reading about it...I think my wife, my mother, and I might have said Something about it...my wife said Something about a reward being offered...We are not prone to reading newspapers." Abbott elaborated on this. He said he had never subscribed to a newspaper until the previous February. He was enrolled in a labor-economics class and thought he should stay current. He said he might buy the Sunday *Tribune* for the comics and the crossword puzzles. On the same day that the Pring's lead was developed, Frank Coakley's captain of inspectors, Clarence Severin, talked to a court bailiff who had been a pulmonary patient with Burton Abbott in Livermore. The bailiff said that he and Abbott both subscribed to the *Oakland Tribune* and both read it every day. Detectives catalogued every item in Burton Abbott's cellar. Listed with everything else: stacks of old newspapers.

Second, on July 26, the day before the grand jury convened, *San Francisco Call-Bulletin* reporter Bill Hall had located a potential witness, William Russell. BPD was tipped in time to conscript Russell as a prosecution witness. Russell worked for the Berkeley Unified School District repairing typewriters. He said that on April 28, he was delivering a renovated Woodstock to the typing teacher at Willard School in anticipation of the open house that night. He said afterward that he walked the half block to Pring's. He knew Abbott as a Pring's regular. Russell said he saw Abbott at Pring's between three and three twenty on April 28; he said Bud Abbott always read the *Chronicle*—usually Russell's. He said Abbott customarily dressed in slacks and a collared shirt. This time he was geared for the outdoors, wearing jeans, a heavy plaid shirt, and a fur-collared leather jacket. He said Abbott left the same time he did, around three thirty.

Coakley had the BPD report on Russell, but not in time for the grand jury the next day. He could save him. He thought it was a done deal anyway, and he was right. No surprise: on Saturday, July 30, the grand jury true-billed Burton Abbott for kidnap and murder. He was arrested in the Berkeley city jail and transported to county, the tenth floor of the courthouse building on Twelfth and Oak, and bound over for trial.

The jury trial would be different—a judge presiding, and a defense allowed to cross examine. Coakley grasped the soft spots. No confession; no murder weapon; no incriminating fingerprints; no eyewitnesses to the abduction, the murder, and/or the burial. Under the law, direct and circumstantial weigh the same. Coakley could convict with circumstantial, but it's tricky. Circumstantial evidence requires jury inference, as in: Can we reasonably infer factual guilt from the chain of circumstances presented? Coakley said they could "beyond reasonable doubt, beyond *peradventure* of guilt."

On the other side of the bar, Stan Whitney saw a pile of coincidence without a shred of direct evidence. Abbott was arraigned on August 3. Trial would begin November 7, 1955, in the court of judge Charles Wade Snook. Snook's reputation: expert on law and evidence, noticeable bias toward the prosecution. Defense attorneys derogated him as "Judge Schnook."

Frank Coakley had ninety days to forge an incriminating chain of circumstance. Stan Whitney, the same ninety to chisel through weak links. Both were governed by 1955 rules enabling underhanded maneuvers. Discovery didn't exist in California law and wouldn't until 1986. Neither did exclusion. Discovery obligates contending parties to make available all information they planned to use in trial. Exclusion throws out all evidence illegally obtained, or obtained in violation of suspect rights.

Criminalist (investigative technician with a background in science) Dr. Paul Kirk found hairs in Burton Abbott's car that "were similar" to strands lifted from Stephanie Bryan's remains. He found fibers "resembling" those in Stephanie Bryan's garments. Georgia Abbott was a hairdresser. The strands in the trunk were "similar" to those of countless beauty salon clients. Fabric fibers were generic, "resembling" off-the-rack duds worn by almost everyone. Modern DNA would have settled the case on the hair evidence alone. It would have had to. The items that were dug from Abbott's basement were excavated without benefit of warrant. By modern rules of exclusion, they would have been tossed.

Case procedure was routine for its time. Witnesses were stashed, vital documents withheld, surprise witnesses sprung. At issue in both camps: Abbott's alibi. Harold Hove traveled to Trinity County. He browbeat Del Cox into admitting that Burton Abbott could have appeared in his saloon without him knowing or remembering. Harold Hove found a waitress from the Chuck Wagon, Rosa Arnone, who remembered Abbott and confirmed the timelines of his alibi.

Rosa Arnone had since moved to a trailer park in San Leandro. Stan Whitney and Harold Hove instructed her not to talk with anyone from the DA's office. He did the same with a young man who remembered Abbott crossing a one-lane bridge over Cottonwood

Creek between Red Bluff and Wildwood about 7:30 p.m. the night of April 28—consistent with Abbott's contention that he ate at a Red Bluff diner and left at about six. They tried and failed to build a case against known Wildwood killer Lloyd Snyder. Snyder was paroled April 7, 1955, three weeks before the murder. He settled in Markleeville, Alpine County, between Lake Tahoe and Yosemite National Park. Up-country witnesses placed him in town the day Stephanie Bryan disappeared.

Prosecution and defense whipsawed William Russell. Russell was certain he had serviced Willard JH on a Thursday, the last week in April. Could he have been off by a day in spotting Abbott? BPD checked. His time cards showed him signed out to Willard on Wednesday but to Berkeley High, across town, on Thursday. Russell said he was chronically careless about filling out the "place" line on his time cards. He said his supervisors cared only about total hours tallied.

Harold Hove threatened to "tear him apart on the stand" over the time cards. Hove intimated they would be fingering Russell as a suspect for the crime. Hove and Whitney pressed the typing teacher, Eleanor Rice, for a statement saying William Russell never appeared at Willard that Thursday. She refused. Through five interviews with Berkeley PD detectives, Russell finally remembered that it was overcast the afternoon he saw Abbott at Pring's. Investigators dug up weather reports for that week: clear on Wednesday, cloudy on Thursday, April 28.

Another Pring's regular, a goateed interior decorator named Alexander Marten, showed at BPD. His story: about 3:30 p.m. on April 28, he was traveling south on College Avenue in his GMC pickup toward a go signal at the intersection of Ashby. A 1949 gray/green Chevy barreling east up Ashby blew the stop and almost collided with Marten's pickup.

Alexander Marten claimed he saw the driver clearly. He picked Burton Abbott out of a lineup. Marten said he jotted the license number on the inside of a packet of Dill pipe cleaners. He gave police his appointment book with a notation of April 28 at 4:00 p.m. and a customer address near College and Ashby. He gave them the Dill pack with the license number of IL53486: Abbott's Chevy. Shaky. The number had been in the papers. Marten's bohemian appearance might not play to the jury. FBI agents sent the Dill package to the FBI lab in Washington, hoping technicians could time/date Marten's pencil marks. They couldn't.

VI

November 7, 1955, 10:00 a.m.: *The People of the State of California v. Burton W. Abbott* underway. Frank Coakley and Folger Emerson for the people; Charles Whitney and Harold Hove for the defense. Jury selection on hold through the Armistice Day weekend. Epidemic challenges and dismissals. Adversaries couldn't agree on any twelve out of the first fifty-six. Sixty-five more brought in. The jury finally was paneled on Tuesday, November 13. Spectators were permitted the next day. *People v. Abbott:* a circus. Onlookers showed early. Seating for 150, but overflow spilled seventy-five more into the alcove. Room for thirty-two reporters and four newspaper artists. Retro policies in play: photographers prohibited. Radio microphones barred. Double-glass doors were frosted to prevent pictures snapped from the lobby. Court TV coverage as yet unheard of.

Frank Coakley set the tone in the opener, stringing "We will prove" for forty-five bombastic minutes: everything from the Tunnel Road incident to the French book on Franklin Canyon Road to discoveries of items in Burton Abbott's basement and burial uphill from his cabin. DA Coakley promised he would place Abbott at Pring's between three and three twenty and at the intersection of College and Ashby at three thirty. Harold Hove smirked. He anticipated Frank Coakley calling Alexander Marten. In the Red Scare '50s, Harold Hove was confident he could discount Marten as a subversive swish.

Frank Coakley struck at the heart of Abbott's alibi. He called Marian Morgan: the epitome of a dignified, middle-aged matron. Gray hair coiffed, well groomed in a business suit, eyeglasses, smartly dressed. Marian Morgan carried an 8 x 10 manila envelope. She was an insurance underwriter. Inside the envelope: an appointment book that placed her in the Claremont/Elmwood district the afternoon of April 28. Defense counsel had never heard of her.

Her testimony:

3:30 p.m., April 28: She was stopped at a red signal on College Avenue at the Ashby intersection headed north. (Across the street from Alexander Marten's GMC pickup?) Stop flipped to go. She inched off the line. From her left, she saw a 1949 or 1950 Chevrolet speeding east toward the intersection. She slammed her brakes. The driver, a young man, ran the stop, almost colliding with a pickup (Marten's?).

> Frank Coakley: Have you seen the young man since?
> Marian Morgan: Yes, I saw a man that looked like him in a lineup at the jail.
> Coakley: I call your attention to Mr. Abbott. Does he look like the man?
> Morgan: That's right.

Frank Coakley called William Russell. William Russell put Burton Abbott inside Pring's at 3:00 p.m. on April 28. He placed him outside at the curb in his '49 Chevy at 3:20 p.m., minutes before the incident at the intersection described by Marian Morgan (and Alexander Marten, who was never called to the stand). Harold Hove crossed with a vengeance. He intimated that Russell was a suspect because he left early from work that day. He twisted a remark Russell had offered during interrogation at Russell's house a few weeks earlier, Russell saying that his mother had made a joke about him as a suspect because of his proximity to the case. Hove: "Do you recall telling us your own mother accused you of the crime?"

Folger Emerson on redirect: "What else did defense attorneys say when they interviewed you?"

William Russell: "They offered me a job. They said if I would water down the testimony they might employ me as an expert witness in future cases."

Coakley called Del Cox, who iterated that he didn't remember seeing Burton Abbott inside the Wildwood Inn on Thursday, April 28. He remembered starting him off with a shot of Old Hermitage the next afternoon. On cross, Del Cox repeated his statement. Harold Hove showed him a signed statement obtained from Cox, in which he said, "He may have come in [that Thursday] but I didn't see him." Harold Hove read the statement. Del Cox registered uncertainty with body language. Frank Coakley lost momentum. He regained it with his next witness, another surprise: Reva Leidicker.

Reva Leidicker was a Tunnel Road witness with a repressed memory. She had been traveling with her family from Concord on April 28, and had seen it all at a speed of fifteen to twenty miles per hour. She had seen Stephanie Bryan's picture in the paper but wasn't sure she was the girl in the car. She read Frank Coakley's "We will prove" string on the car struggle. She said that at four the next morning she woke, perfect recall popping into her skull. She forced her husband to call BPD. Her version differed from the others in one respect: she could positively ID Burton Abbott as the driver. "The man in the blue suit," she said, pointing at the defendant.

Coakley rode the momentum, reprising his grand jury case. Stan Whitney and Harold Hove poked holes here and there. Physical evidence, laughable by today's standards, carried weight. Maybe bloodstains in Abbott's trunk. Maybe fish blood or tomato juice. Maybe garment fibers matched; maybe they were generic. Maybe hair strands.

UCB criminalist Dr. Paul Kirk was a leader in his field but sloppy with chain-of-custody protocols. He vacuumed Abbott's car. Detectives gathered samples from Stephanie Bryan's hairbrush and garments. Cross-contamination probable. Comparisons established hair and fiber matches only to the point of being "similar." Except: Dr. Paul Kirk determined the mud that was caked inside the heels of Burton Abbott's field boots compared precisely to the soil nine inches deep at the grave site. No way for the defense to mitigate the impact of the burial dirt under Abbott's heel.

December 13: Five weeks in. Prosecution had rested. Circumstances piled up. Prosecution ahead on points. Defense punching away. Defense desperate for an edge, needing a knockout blow. Whitney and Hove swung wild. They called Burton Abbott. Through four days on the stand, Abbott came across as a supercilious shithead. Whitney and Hove had prepped him on tone and body language. They pounded him on humility and truth. Hove opened with twenty-seven questions, each eliciting one word: no.

"Did you bury the eyeglasses in your basement?"
"Was Stephanie Bryan ever in your car?"
"Has that brassiere ever been in your possession?"
"Did you at any time ever take Stephanie Bryan to your cabin?"

As the finale, Harold Hove displayed a graveside blowup, asking, "Did you do this horrible crime to Stephanie Bryan?"

Frank Coakley baited him on cross, and Abbott bit. Coakley had combed the reports from BPD, the FBI, and his own staff. He drilled Abbott on every inconsistency. He brought up the lies about the Sacramento detour; the fact that Abbott called himself a graduate student, when he wasn't; that he joined the Army two days before the GI bill was set to expire; that he had lied on his Army enrollment—said he took university courses in 1946 (he didn't begin at UC until 1949). Coakley went back to high school when Abbott falsely claimed to have been a lieutenant in the Junior ROTC.

Abbott responded like a truculent teen facing expulsion, trying to impress his punk friends by smart-mouthing the dean of boys. Representative exchanges:

Regarding his BLM sketches:

Coakley: Is this the picture you drew?
Abbott: I don't know—*sir!*
Coakley: What do you mean you don't know?
Abbott: It doesn't have my signature on it—*sir!* It looks like my picture, but I wouldn't trust law officers as far as I could throw them right now!

Regarding his May 2 tire shopping when he said he was tapped from his fishing trip:

Coakley: What you were going to use for money?
Abbott: Legal currency, *sir!*

Regarding his habitual stops at Pring's:

Coakley: Why did you go to Pring's?
Abbott: To get donuts, *sir!*
Coakley: Isn't Pring's on the same side of the street as Willard, just a half block down?
Abbott: It could be, *sir!*

Went like that for four days. Abbott couldn't contain his attitude, oblivious to its impact. Coakley sealed it in during sur-rebuttal. Bessie Wells, a Morton's Beauty Salon client, testified that she saw Abbott in the shop at 2:00 p.m. on April 28. Alma Segal worked at the state land office in Oakland. She claimed that Burton Abbott approached her at 1:30 p.m. on April 28 for information on mining claims in Trinity County. She said she directed him to the BLM office in Sacramento.

All along, BPD had received reports of Abbott attempting to lure children into his car. Trolling for little girls: Explanation for the excess number of gas charges for which Georgia had berated him? Witnesses had been brought to 2171 McKinley to ID him through a glass window. No legal way to wedge that information into testimony—until Harold Hove reacted during sur-rebuttal while cross-questioning Willard Hutchins.

Hutchins admitted to bullying a potential witness: Robert Hall, the owner of the Chuck Wagon restaurant in Red Bluff.

Hutchins: "I believe I told him, in part, 'Of course the son-of-a-bitch is guilty.'"

Hove: "Well, what was the other part?"

Hutchins: "I told him we had reports of Abbott molesting other children."

Pattern unexplored at the time: Abbott lived across from a park and a school. Of the myriad donut shops between Alameda and the UC campus, he picks one half a block away from a junior high that features a logo of a happy little Dutch girl in braids, clogs, and a pinafore.

Judge Snook handed the case to the jury on January 19, 1956. Jurors needed fifty-one hours and fifty-six minutes to deliberate through four thousand pages of testimony transcribed from forty-two days of trial. They worked through deadlocks, ten to two and eleven to one against Abbott. They sequestered at the Hotel Leamington downtown for the better part of a week. They filed back on Wednesday, January 25, none looking at Abbott. From averted glances, he *knew*: guilty of kidnapping and murder, no mercy.

Stan Whitney and Harold Hove checked out after the verdict. Leo Sullivan and George T. Davis ran the perfunctory appeals. Appellate courts heard no new evidence, discovered no errors in the law. The last attempt at a stay was fumbled while George T. Davis tried to contact governor Goodwin Knight, who was being hosted by the US Navy on the USS *Hancock* outside the Golden Gate. Wires crossed between the state house and the carrier. George Davis was told that the governor was airborne, when actually he was aboard ship. By the time Goodwin Knight dialed the death house in San Quentin, the executioner had already plunged cyanide eggs into the reservoir of sulfuric acid. Fatal fumes were rising when the call finally came.

Burton Abbott drew his last breath at 11:25 a.m. on Friday, March 15, 1957.

VII

He had been tried, convicted, executed, and buried, but doubt over Abbott's guilt still lingered. All along, he said he was framed. By whom? At different points, Elsie offered Georgia, Georgia abetted by Otto Dezman, and her brother, Wilbur Moore. None of it washes—frame too elaborate. They all had access to the basement. But why stash the purse in a box and bury the books, bra, and eyeglasses? Who would kidnap and kill an innocent girl and frame a nobody like Burton Abbott? Who would risk exposure to witnesses at the abduction or murder site during the eight-hour trip to the Trinity Alps and at the burial in Wildwood?

Much was made of Burton Abbott's frailty, the impossibility of his 135-pound frame dragging a dead (or live) body (plus digging tools) up the snowy banks of a forty-five-degree mountainside 339 feet to the burial site. Much was made of his personality—passive, quiet, inward, intellectual, a chess player, not the killer type—and of his lack of apparent motive.

Two days after Georgia had found the purse, Abbott volunteered for the black box. Lie detection was invented at UC Berkeley under August Vollmer. Detective Albert Riedel was a descendant, as good as anyone in America at administering a polygraph. Abbott was strapped for sessions that extended over Monday and Tuesday, July 18 and 19. They took frequent breaks, sickly Abbott citing fatigue. Riedel pressed him ruthlessly (probably in violation of his rights) on guilt/innocence questions. Burton Abbott told the *Chronicle*: "...he spent two hours asking two questions...one question...32 times...the other 42..." Public version: results inconclusive—inadmissible in court anyway.

For the polygraph, Albert Riedel had mapped out gridlines of two areas: The East Bay hills along San Pablo Dam Road and the area around Wildwood. He pointed to spots at the first and asked, "Did you kill Stephanie here? Did you kill her here?" He replicated the technique for Wildwood, only changing the verb from "kill" to "bury." Abbott fluttered the needles too often to write off. Results: legally moot, but from July 19 forward, BPD and Frank Coakley were absolutely certain that Burton Abbott killed Stephanie Bryan on a back road between Orinda and Pinole and buried her in the Trinity Alps uphill and across the road from his cabin.

January 28, 1957: Six weeks before the execution, a five-part copyright story ran in the *San Francisco Chronicle*, byline John Douglas Cober (as told to Bernice Freeman and Charles Rudabaugh). Banner headline, headline, and lead paragraph:

Exclusive
'BUD ABBOTT TOLD ME
HE'S GUILTY'
ABBOTT'S CELLMATE TALKS: 'HE
MADE IT PLAIN HE KILLED HER'

Burton W. Abbott is as guilty as hell of the kidnapping and murder of Stephanie Bryan.

I was his cellmate day after day during his long trial, and he gave me everything but a written confession...

Cober was a check kiter whom Frank Coakley planted in Abbott's cell. Coakley never used Cober as a witness. The case was already in the rebuttal phase when Cober delivered. Frank Coakley thought he had the case won without him; he wouldn't risk breaking momentum by allowing Stan Whitney and Harold Hove to cross-question a potentially impeachable jailhouse snitch. Excerpts from the *Chronicle* series:

Cober: You'll get a ticket to the gas chamber if they find any dirt from the grave on your boots.
Abbott: I'm not worried about that. We brushed the boots before we turned them over to the police.

Regarding the bra in the basement:

Abbott: Do they think I undressed that girl and took off her brassiere? Her last class that day was gym, and she didn't put it back on.

Cober explaining about Abbott hiding incriminating evidence in his own basement:

...I came to realize that Abbott killed the girl merely to make himself the center of attention...the mystery of the purse was simply another of the contradictions that he deliberately built into the murder. He thought these contradictions would absolve him...that they would be so clever and confusing no one could ever explain them... [and] he would be acquitted.

About Abbott being too frail to drag Stephanie's body and the shovels to the grave site:

Cober: You made two trips, the first to carry the shovel and dig the grave.
Abbott [surprised]: How do you know?
Cober: ...Couldn't carry both body and shovel at once...it would be only reasonable to reconnoiter first and dig the grave; then take the body up.

Cober's explication of motive:

Bud Abbott planned murder for years. He plotted the specific abduction of Stephanie Bryan for months. It was to be a spectacular murder...a famous case. Abbott will never confess publicly, not even when the moment comes for him to step into the gas chamber...that moment will be his highest pinnacle in his own sick mind...

Cober to Abbott:
No matter what happens, you can't lose. If you are acquitted, you are forever the famous Bud Abbott...And if you are sent to the gas chamber you will leave behind a world of doubt about your guilt...There will be thousands of people who will always say you were innocent.
Abbott: You're shrewd.

Cober asked no compensation for his story. He said he had a daughter Stephanie's age. Said Abbott's crime disgusted him. Cober's version makes sense, as much as any that is connected to the case. Frank Coakley had believed him. BPD psychiatrist Dr. Douglas Kelley, had interviewed war criminals at Nuremberg. He said the two most self-centered people he had ever met were fat Hermann Goering, Reichsmarschall of the Luftwaffe, and Burton W. Abbott. Cober's take fits: An interior motive classic through time, from Iago to Leopold/Loeb. Pure Freud: underdeveloped superego spurring self-absorption, riding it into a homicidal rampage.

Abbott was a mama's boy married to an oversexed wife six years his senior. When Mark married in December before Stephanie Bryan disappeared, Elsie Abbott gave her Castro Valley house to the newlyweds and moved in with Burton and Georgia. Two women competed to run him. Pressures building. (John Cober said Burton had been planning the Bryan murder for months.) Elsie did his laundry. Elsie made the suits Burton wore to court. Georgia nagged him about gas-card bills. Elsie palmed him fifteen bucks for his trip—he used it for gas.

Georgia was a bed-hopper. Burton admitted he couldn't keep up. Georgia and Elsie separately concurred. Eavesdropping Elsie said Georgia demanded it nightly but Burton was good for only a couple of times a month. Stands to psychotic reason: passive-aggressive Burton diagnosed as inadequate by TB, overmatched by dominant mother figures, acting out.

Weak-ass Burton could control only a female child. Cober said Abbott spoke in implications: implied the murder weapon was a ketchup bottle. Implied Abbott whacked Stephanie twice more when she was already dead to spread false clues. Implied she was in rigor, making burial difficult (rigor never made public—only the killer would know). Implied he was planning to scatter clues over Contra Costa County (the same as the French book) but never managed to do it.

Burton Abbott boasting his brilliance in late-night jailhouse patter, reconstructing to John Douglas Cober the abduction as a hypothetical. The kidnap killer was...

> ...shifting the grocery box to the front seat. Killer removing handles from the rear doors and windows, lying in wait on Stephanie's route behind the Claremont, stopping her, saying he has to deliver groceries to 131 Alvarado, asking directions. Stephanie, tired, arms full of books, saying, "That's my house..." Killer saying, "Jump in, and you can show me." Killer stepping out and opening the rear door...

Burton Abbott: One twisted son-of-a-bitch.

John Douglas Cober's jailbird analysis: verdict affirming and credible beyond Frank J. Coakley's "peradventure of any doubt." Cober said Abbott was incensed over Frank Coakley characterizing the Bryan abduction as a sex crime. Burton Abbott, disinclined to think of himself as a pervert. In his mind, it wasn't a sex crime because it didn't involve physical penetration. He sliced her panties off with a knife and wrapped them around her neck postmortem. He buried the bra as a trophy. He violated her by fact of murder. He didn't have sex with her because he couldn't. Burton Abbott, only dimly acquainted with the pathology of psychosexual symbolism.

Add one more element: mama's boy Abbott's eve-of-execution exchange with Dr. David Schmidt, San Quentin chief psychiatrist, revealed by Schmidt in 1961, as reported in the *San Francisco Chronicle*:

> Schmidt: Burton, why don't you admit your guilt and throw yourself on the mercy of the Governor and ask for Executive Clemency?
>
> Abbott: Doc, I can't admit it. Think of what it would do to my mother...she couldn't take it.

People v. Abbott: American justice pre-Miranda, pre-Discovery, pre-Exclusion, pre-OJ. Judge, jury, and system all arriving still at the correct resolution.

Postscript

Late at night on April Fools' Day, 1956: A trio of drunken Trinity County hicks set fire to the Abbott/Schorch cabin in Wildwood, reducing it to a rubble of smoldering coals. Their explanation? "We figured two murders was enough."

CHAPTER 3
WILLOW SPRINGS: SPADE COOLEY

The Antelope Valley stretches between the San Gabriel and Techapi mountain ranges—twenty-two hundred arid square miles of sand, wind, and sage split by the LA/Kern County border, located at the western tip of the Mojave Desert. The pronged elk of the valley's name has been extinct since the nineteenth century. Fur hunters took out a portion; harsh winters in the 1880s drove the surviving herds from the hills. Confused pronghorns couldn't discern between train tracks and barbed-wire fences. They wouldn't cross the rails to forage, and they starved.

Most of the valley looks as it always does: desolate high-desert scrub dotted by jackrabbits and Joshua trees. Part doesn't. Scenery is soundtracked by Edwards AFB sonic booms. Housing tracts splay across the windswept terrain around Lancaster and Palmdale along State Routes 14 and 138—monotonous split-level stuccos painted pale green/tan/peach/ocher and marketed to commuters from LA and Kern.

Progress has encroached. Pristine Mojave Desert topography has been breached by wind turbines on hillsides, spinning propellers chasing off vultures, kicking the natural food chain off its sprocket. Fields of low-profile collection panels beam solar energy to long rows of forty-story derricks humming with juice, disturbing native species—desert tortoises, kit foxes, and Pacific rattlesnakes. Alfalfa farms, fruit orchards, and vineyards have sprung up, draining the fragile aquifer. Closer look: medical marijuana collectives skirt drug laws; rusted trailer homes and beat-down shotgun hovels pop up behind forbidding chain-link fences. Figure crystal meth among AV enterprises.

Willow Springs sits off the Tehachapi Road, seven miles west of Rosamond, population seventeen hundred. "Howdy, neighbor" biscuits-and-gravy down-home hospitality gone with the howling desert winds. Gates and fences posted No Trespassing, enforced by packs of mangy dogs snapping with menace. Junkyard security around remote dwellings: Something mean simmering subsurface.

Three-quarters of a mile down a dusty path off dirt 105th Street: a twelve-foot sand embankment surrounds a desiccated sixteen-hundred-acre-foot basin once a shitkicker's pipe dream called Water Wonderland. Envisioned: three lakes—one for speedboats and water skiing; one each for bass fishing and swimming; a twenty-thousand-square-foot dance-band pavilion wired for radio and television broadcasting; an Indian village plus hotels, motels, restaurants, golf course, and bowling alley. A water park in the Mojave?

Go figure. The project never made it past blueprints, bullshit, and bad debts.

I

April 4, 1961: Page-one headline, subhead, and first paragraph of the *Bakersfield Californian*:

> SPADE COOLEY HELD
> IN SLAYING OF WIFE
> MATE DIES
> AFTER DESERT
> RANCH FIGHT

Spade Cooley, nationally-known western-style band-leader and developer of a $15 million Water Wonderland Park under construction near Willow Springs has been booked at the Kern County jail on suspicion of murdering his wife, Ella Mae...

The day before: Spade Cooley, a has-been at fifty, the "King of Western Swing," had been stewing over Water Wonderland financing issues at his 1,320-acre SC Ranch. Spade, twitchy and distracted, snapped at staff. He chain-smoked unfiltered Camels. He was zonked on booze and pills prescribed by Hollywood doctors, his life a mess. Spade was an epic womanizer. He boned every female he could but was crazy jealous that his thirty-seven-year-old wife had been stepping out on him.

Spade's aqua-paradise was hemorrhaging money. The ranch house was a disaster of unmade beds, dirty dishes, discarded laundry and food cartons, overflowing ash trays, and Jim Beam empties. Scrip bottles everywhere. Spade had nitro pills for his heart; capsules for urinary tract disorders, hypertension, and nausea; uppers, downers, and antipsychotics. His kids, fourteen-year-old Melody and Donnell Jr., twelve, were farmed to friends in Rosamond, seven miles northeast, the McWhorters. Ella Mae was confined to the bedroom badly damaged. Spade routinely knocked the shit out of her.

Spade's agent, Barbara "Bobbie" Bennett, lived in North Hollywood but maintained office space in a Quonset hut at the SC Ranch. His project manager, Beal Whitlock, lived in a trailer 150 feet behind the twenty-six-hundred-square-foot ranch house.

6:00 p.m.: Beal Whitlock heard gunshots. He called Spade, fearing the worst—he knew what Spade had been doing to Ella Mae. Spade reassured him: he hadn't shot his wife; he had fired .410 and .22 shots into the air. He asked Whitlock not to call the cops. He didn't bother to mention the beatings.

Spade had filed for divorce on March 21 in Sherman Oaks. Ella Mae had filed in February but pulled it back. Spade had retained celebrity private investigator Billy Lewis to dredge up evidence of two-timing. Lewis turned up nothing. Spade slugged a confession out of Ella Mae—had her talk to Lewis on the phone, admitting to an affair with Roy Rogers and involvement with a "free love cult"—Spade's words—in a Route 66 motel in Rosamond with two homosexuals. Clifton "Bud" Davenport, thirty-six, and Luther Jackson, twenty-eight were UCLA med center male nurses living in a trailer in Northridge. Spade had braced them a few days earlier at their trailer park. He brought Beal Whitlock and another Water Wonderland exec, Jerry Enfield, with him. He pounded Davenport and threatened to kill both him and Jackson.

Under Spade's prodding, Ella Mae had called Melody at the McWhorters and begged her to come home. Spade grabbed the phone and said her mother had "Something to tell her." Melody was scared to death of her father. She told Mrs. Lilya McWhorter to drop her off at the SC Ranch but please return in twenty minutes. Melody walked in; Spade frenzied. Spade on the phone with Beal Whitlock after the gunshot spree. Melody heard: "Beal, don't call the police." Spade surrounded himself with toadies. Against all noble instincts, Beal Whitlock obeyed.

Spade motioned Melody into the master bedroom. He was slurring words. He said, "Come in here. I want you to see your mother. She's going to tell you something." Melody heard shower water in the bathroom. Spade yelled through the open door, "Get up. Melody's here. Talk to her." Spade burst into the stall, grabbed Ella Mae by the hair, and dragged her naked into the bedroom, banging her head twice on the floor. Spade dumped her on the rug by the bed. He demanded that she confess her sins.

Ella Mae inert, comatose; couldn't confess anything. Spade burned Ella Mae's breasts with the smoke end of his cigarette. Melody screamed. Spade wore range gear, including black cowboy boots. He stomped her stomach with boot tips and heels. He made Melody help her mother onto the bed. Melody swabbed Ella Mae's forehead with a wet towel. She tried to give her a glass of water. Ella Mae unresponsive. She labored for air; her chest heaved; her breath rattled morbid injury.

Spade ushered the tearful Melody into the den. He sat her on his lap in the sofa. He kissed and pawed her, said he was transferring his love from her mother. Her account, creepy: "He told me to kiss him sweet."

6:20 p.m.: Phone rang. Spade rose to answer. Melody saw headlights from Mrs. McWhorter driving in. She ran frantically to the McWhorter car and jumped in.

Spade's thirty-year-old son John (by his first marriage) lived in a Lancaster house trailer with his wife, Dorothy. Back in Rosamond, Lilya McWhorter dialed Lancaster. Dorothy answered; John was in LA on business. Mrs. McWhorter spilled Melody's story. Dorothy drove toward Willow Springs.

7:00 p.m.: An unidentified female called the LA County sheriff's substation in Lancaster to report a wife-beating in Willow Springs—Kern County jurisdiction. She would deny it later in court, but figure 80/20 Lilya McWhorter the caller.

Back at SC Ranch, Spade wasn't done. He penetrated Ella Mae vaginally and anally with a broomstick. He called Bobbie Bennett in North Hollywood—said something was wrong with Ella Mae. Bobbie Bennett was night-blind—couldn't drive after dark. She enlisted Spade's music engineer, Ed Borgelin, as a chauffer. They arrived at SC Ranch around eight. Dorothy already inside. They caught blood spots on Spade's pants and shirt; blood streaks on his cut and swollen knuckles.

Bobbie said she wanted to talk to Ella Mae. Spade told her to send Ed Borgelin home. She did—reluctantly. Ed Borgelin, agitated, knew enough to call the sheriff but couldn't work up the nerve. Another toady. In the bedroom, Bobbie Bennett saw Ella

Mae's legs stiffening. Bobbie tried to convince Spade to call a doctor. Spade: "No, we're going to leave her sleep." Spade oblivious. He tucked his wife in a blanket, said she was in a "little coma and needs rest, that's all."

They repaired to the kitchen. Telephone ringing: Spade took it. Billy Lewis on the phone saying he couldn't find motel records for Spade's "free love cult." Spade losing interest in what he didn't want to hear. He handed the phone to Bobbie Bennett. Billy Lewis: "What's going on?" Bobbie Bennett: "Nothing good." Spade swilled Jim Beam and gulped Thorazine. His attention swayed. Bobbie Bennett dialed Dorothy "Dottie" Davis, a nurse friend of hers and the Cooleys, on hospital duty in North Hollywood.

Bobbie Bennett coded her conversation with Spade's word, *coma*. Dottie Davis: "Or worse?" Bobbie Bennett: "Yes, I believe so, yes." Dottie Davis arrived in two hours and took charge. She told Spade to change out of his bloody clothes. She said she had to call an ambulance: "Ella Mae is a very sick little girl." Spade reeled toward his closet.

10:05 p.m.: Dorothy Cooley faded back to Lancaster. Dottie Davis dialed Mojave, twenty miles away. She made two calls—one for an ambulance, another to the Kern County sheriff's substation.

Richard Stickel, manager of Turner Ambulance, took an hour to navigate the dark dirt roads to the ranch. Spade told Stickel the same thing he had told the deputies: his wife was ill. Ella Mae nude, wrapped in a blanket on the bed. Richard Stickel feared she was a corpse. Stickel saw bruises and burns but kept his thoughts to himself. "I didn't know what was going on," he said, "only that something violent had occurred." Spade helped Stickel lug Ella Mae on a stretcher into the ambulance. Spade climbed in with her. Richard Stickel heard Spade moaning: "Don't be dead…she can't be dead."

12:20 a.m., April 4, 1961: Ella Mae Cooley declared DOA by attending Tehachapi Valley Hospital physician Dr. Vincent Troy.

Violent fatality—Kern County sheriff's department (KCSD) Mojave substation alerted. Preliminary report to sergeant Tom Scheull and deputy Marion Dickey: injuries not consistent with Spade's contention that she had fallen in the shower. Report showed burn marks on her breasts, neck and abdominal bruising, plus anal and vaginal trauma. Preliminary cause of death: ruptured aorta or hyoid bone. Preliminary assumption: felonious assault. Tom Scheull reported to headquarters in Bakersfield. Kern County's chief homicide investigator, Harmon Cooper, motored to Tehachapi. Cooper grilled Spade in a side room at the TV hospital before ordering him removed to the substation in Mojave.

1:00 a.m., April 4, 1961: Pre-Miranda. Spade Cooley had no rights by law and none by Western desert tradition. Cooper, Scheull, and Dickey interrogated him for two hours Solid. Spade, eager to talk, lied out his ass. He ascribed damage to an incident three days earlier—Ella Mae falling from his speeding car, Spade pulling her back in by her hair. He repeated what he'd told the doctors at TVH: Ella Mae fell in the shower. They asked him about domestic abuse. He admitted they had quarreled. He admitted he had slapped her but denied hitting her with his fists, let alone boot-stomping her. They asked about the burn marks. Spade said Ella Mae grabbed his smoke and branded her own boobs to show how much she loved him. Spade couldn't explain how a fall in the shower could cause internal bleeding and bruises on her neck.

Harmon Cooper called in a photographer. He wanted color stills of Spade's bruised, cut, and bloody knuckles. Spade recoiled. He tried to hide his hands on his thighs under the table. Spade babbled innocence. He clung to his story. He was crashing hard, unraveling from fear, booze, and pills, sweat dripping from his pores.

4:00 a.m.: KCSD made it official: Donnell Clyde Cooley arrested on suspicion of murder. John and Dorothy showed. Spade manacled, awaiting transfer to county jail in Bakersfield, sixty-three miles away. Spade could only stare. John: "Oh, Dad."

5:30 a.m.: Kern County coroner Stanley Newman arrived in Tehachapi. He ordered Ella Mae's body moved to Kern General in Bakersfield for autopsy. Stanley Newman said it appeared Mrs. Cooley had been dead before she was transported from SC Ranch, four to five hours before the ambulance reached hospital.

Stanley Newman drove with a medical-examination team to join deputies at SC Ranch. They found a broom handle with blood, mucous, Vaseline, and hair six inches up the shaft. They found Spade's pills and guns. They found bloody clothes in the laundry room dropped where Spade had changed into fresh garments. A set of deputies drove to Rosamond and took statements from Melody and Lilya McWhorters. They talked to Bobbie Bennett, Beal Whitlock, and Dottie Davis. The subject of infidelity was broached. Bobbie Bennett said it was preposterous. She said Ella Mae confessed just to stop the abuse. Dottie Davis: "Ella Mae was incapable of having an affair."

Dr. Robert Huntington cut Ella Mae postmortem. His findings confirmed the preliminary report. Cause of death: shattered hyoid bone from strangulation and/or ruptured aorta from blunt-force trauma. Either could have been fatal. Dr. Huntington cited anal and vaginal mutilation.

11:00 a.m.: Spade Cooley processed into Kern County jail on an open charge of murder (degree TBD)—in time to make the page-one banner story in that afternoon's *Bakersfield Californian*. He was arraigned in municipal court a day later, April 5, at 1:30 p.m. The spectator section accommodated seventy. It overflowed. Hayseed fiddler stomping his old lady: big news in Okie Bakersfield. Kern County district attorney Kit Nelson called for a grand jury coroner's inquest for Friday, April 7. Nelson: "Injuries suggest torture and if proved we have and open and shut case of first-degree murder."

Thursday, April 6: Spade collapsed in his cell. He had chronic heart issues: another in a string of mild cardiac infarctions. Coroner's inquest delayed one week.

April 14: The coroner's jury ruled Ella Mae's death as "homicide at the hands of Donnell Clyde Cooley." Forensic evidence verified the charges. Testimony from Melody Faith Cooley sealed it. Among her statements: "When I entered he was talking on the phone to his business partner Beal Whitlock. I heard him say, 'Beal, don't call the police.' He was real sweaty, and he had blood spots on his pants." Odds running long against the King of Western Swing. An ambitious DA looking at incontrovertible evidence in the biggest case he would ever prosecute; a jury pool drawn from oil fields and cotton farms steeped in Old Testament attitudes and cowboy justice.

The rise and fall of Donnell C. Cooley: a Country and Western Song twanging toward a long bad end.

II

Oklahoma Territory became the state of Oklahoma in 1907, the forty-sixth in the union. Statehood reconfigured boundaries. Day County near the South Canadian River became Ellis County, with the tiny town of Grand established as its first county seat. Grand was backcountry agrarian, impoverished with a demography dominated by poor whites and Indians. The Cooleys were both. John Cooley was one-half Cherokee; his wife, Emma, pale-skinned British Isles Euro. John and Emma Cooley had six children. Donnell Clyde in the middle, born December 17 or February 22, 1910, depending on the source consulted. C&W historian Rich Kienzle, in *Southwest Shuffle* (Routledge 2003), subtitled *Pioneers of Honky Tonk, Western Swing, and Country Jazz*, writes that Spade was "born on a ranch near Grand, Oklahoma." He sets the date as February 22, 1910.

The *Comprehensive Country Music Encyclopedia* (Times Books 1994) lists Rich Kienzle in its masthead as "Research Editor." *CCME* also says Spade was born February 22, 1910, in Grand, Oklahoma. A C&W reference tome, *Country Musicians* (Thomson Gall 2005), says it was December 17, 1910, in Pack Saddle Creek, Oklahoma. Kurt Wolff, in *Country Music: The Rough Guide* (Rough Guides 2000), has him born December 17, 1910, in Grand. Bruce Henstell, in a 1979 article for *Los Angeles* Magazine titled "How the King of Western Swing Reached the End of His Rope," wrote: "He was born Donnell Clyde Cooley on December 17, 1910, in the storm cellar of his family's small house in Pack Saddle Creek, Oklahoma. His father, John Cooley, was half Cherokee Indian, and his mother, Emma, Scotch-Irish."

A self-published author named Robert J. Joling, JD, a retired jurist since deceased, wrote *Shame! Shame!* (2009), subtitled *A Saga of Spade Cooley, King of Western Swing!;* sub-subtitled a split infinitive, *The Most Brutal Murder to Ever Occur in Hollywood!* Joling, JD, laces his narrative with judgmental guesswork rife with error: "Clyde Donnell Cooley [reversing the order of his names] was born among the pitiful trappings of a sure loser. Birthed on top of a dirt floor in a one-room shack outside Pack Saddle Creek, Oklahoma, in 1910, he was a sickly runt of hopelessly alcoholic parents..." Storm cellar or dirt floor in a one-room shack: Someone has it wrong.

Understood: Okie/Indian sharecroppers worked sorghum, corn, and wheat with shovels and hoes under hot prairie sun. They wouldn't spend much time scratching out volumes of personal history. The Cooleys would be typical of their times and stations. Literacy improbable; instinct to record their genealogies unlikely. Not much in the way of reliable fact has survived to chronicle Donnell Cooley's early years.

Typical confusion: Pack Saddle Creek. The Cooleys lived in Ellis County, near enough to an area called the Pack Saddle Preserve—six hundred thousand acres of prairie and shrubland along the South Canadian River. The Cooleys would later push their way to apple country east of Salem, Oregon, in Merion County, near Pack Saddle Creek in the Willamette Valley.

Two Pack Saddles in two different states starting with *O*: Merely a coincidence fated to confuse sloppy biographers. In *Shame! Shame!* (title of Spade Cooley's first big hit), Joling, JD, writes: "The Great Depression forced this dirt-poor family to migrate westward in the late 1920s when tiny Clyde was not yet four." One paragraph earlier, Joling, JD, has "tiny Clyde"—still not his correct first name— "birthed…in 1910." By Joling's sense of history, a fifteen-year-old was actually four when the migration occurred. Safe to say: from scarce records, biographers have traced the trail of one another's mistakes. Small sample: *Los Angeles Times*, in an unsigned article, April 5, 1961: "…but he left school during the Depression…"

Donnell, born in 1910, was nineteen when the stock market crashed; twenty-one—well past high school age—when the Depression hit. The chances of him enrolling in college, good times or bad, hovered zero. He married his first wife, Anna, in 1930. They were parents within a year, hard-scrabbling bare sustenance off crop work.

Joling, JD, elaborates with presumption of fact that invites skepticism:

> His father was an inveterate losing-gambler and "dime-a-day" fiddle player. He had long since driven his half-Apache wife, Emma, into a ranting nut case. The Cooley's bloodline was variously described as "Injun," German, Italian, Arab, Jewish, Welsh, Polish, Turk, or even Pomeranian, although more often than not, "plain ole trash" In short, the Cooley's epitomized a real life embodiment of *Tobacco Road*, albeit they never managed to climb far enough up, let alone out of their sociological swill bin to even qualify as "White Trash" …

Alcoholic parents; mad half-Apache mother; degenerate gambler father; "sociological swill bin"—none of that shows up anywhere else. Joling confuses Erskine Caldwell's work with John Steinbeck's. Joling, JD, suspect. His ill-documented invective benefits from legal proscriptions against libeling the dead. His loose grip on facts and his amateur prose suggest he's embellishing from his own interior motive—perhaps projecting Calvinist disapprobation of Spade Cooley's dissolute adult behavior.

Joling claims he connected to the Cooley story through a writer named Jonn Christian. Christian investigated and wrote about Robert F. Kennedy's assassination. Christian's two-part premise: Sirhan Sirhan, a "Manchurian candidate"; a massive cover-up ensued involving law-enforcement agencies from LAPD to the FBI. Joling says Christian met Bobbie Bennett when she was in her seventies, dying of cancer.

He says Bennett admired Christian's book, *The Assassination of Robert F. Kennedy*, subtitled *The Conspiracy and the Cover-Up*. Christian wrote the book with former FBI agent William Turner. Random House published the book in 1978 but pulled it from the shelves and burned all copies under threat of lawsuits. It remained unavailable until it was reissued in 2006. Bobbie Bennett had read one of the early copies. She arranged a meeting with Christian through her nephew, James Barton. Bobbie Bennett said she held the rights to Spade Cooley's complicated life story.

Bennett spent hours in the early 1980s talking to Christian. Christian brought Joling into the project. Joling had worked background on the Kennedy theories. Besides his legal credential, he had experience in crime-scene forensics.

Joling says he and Christian disagreed in style, which delayed the Cooley project; says Christian wanted raw content in a literary context. Born-again Joling says in *Shame* that he wanted it properly sanitized. Christian died before the book materialized. Joling published through a vanity press in 2009. The cover alone indicts accuracy. Above the title: a graphic of the green room in San Quentin. Spade never received a death sentence. Below the title: caricature of Spade gripping cell bars, staring ahead, his finger, fist, and face tinted bronze. Spade in life was pale from his mother's Euro stock. The graphic is red Injun racial stereotype. The book's sole value: Bobbie Bennett's interviews transcribed verbatim, though her accounts begin only when she met Cooley in Los Angeles in the 1940s. Until then, reasonable inference has to suffice.

Accordingly:

John and Emma Cooley sharecropped in Oklahoma until 1914, when they drifted toward Oregon, working their way cross-country. Donnell was four at the time. Figure iconic fruit-tramp images, foreshadowing Dorothea Lange's WPA photos: gaunt men with bad teeth dripping plug juice into beard stubble. They wore tattered bib overalls, scuffed high-top shoes, and shapeless sweat-stained hats, cloth or straw. They looked at life through defeated eyes, old men at forty. Poor souls at the ass end of the social caste system without prospects for gain or protections from the law—American peons who knew depression long before the Great Depression had a name.

No unions for migrants. Congress passed the Wagner Act in 1935, permitting labor to organize under the First Amendment's "right to peaceable assembly" clause. The farm lobby was powerful. The Wagner Act passed the Senate and the House only because agricultural labor was exempt. Same with child labor.

1938: FDR signed the Fair Labor Standards Act into law, preventing children under twelve from entering the job market. Underage farm labor was excluded. Migrant kids worked up calluses with their adult parents, cousins, aunts, and uncles, reaping fruit and row crops for subpoverty pay in subacceptable conditions.

Migrants organized hoedowns for escape. They tippled moonshine from jugs. They played card games on upturned barrels.

They sparked romance under trees and behind barns. Their music scored hard times—down-home syncopations twanging from banjos, washboards, Jew's harps, and fiddles. John Cooley performed for pennies plunked into his fiddle case. His father had fiddled. Donnell emulated his forebears, a prodigy at age six, aping his ancestry with kindling sticks as instrument and bow.

John was half Cherokee, Donnell a quarter. Fortuitous. Donnell's first big break: John Cooley earned a local reputation. He became friends with P. F. Thomas, a Salem music teacher. During sessions, P. F. Thomas grew intrigued by Donnell's little-kid kindling-sticks act. He promised to train Donnell in strings when he was old enough. Second break: proximity to the Chemewa Indian School, located five miles north of Salem. Open since 1883, Chemewa was part of the Bureau of Indian Affairs' plan to integrate Indians into mainstream American culture through education.

Donnell qualified for a scholarship at age thirteen. P. F. Thomas passed Donnell to the Chemewa music teacher. She had more than enough violin students (fiddle and violin, the same thing, differentiated by genre). She handed Donnell a cello. Upshot: he was formally trained in both strings by the time he left Chemewa in his teens. Donnell was unique among hillbilly entertainers. He had a grasp of European classical composition, and he could sight-read sheet music.

1929: Donnell, nineteen, picking apples with his family in Oregon. The American dream for most people within his status an energy drain for exhausted imaginations. "I was born poor, and I was raised poor," he said. Donnell was different. He had aspirations. Like anyone who has transcending assets, he felt primed for elevation. He had the talent and the drive. Like most Okies stuck in a low-end social caste, he had no idea how to escalate. Like everyone else at the end of the Jazz Age in the United States, he was about to be blasted by the Great Depression.

September 3, 1929: Stock peaked at a record 381.

October 24, Thursday before the crash: Market dropped 9 percent, a harbinger.

October 28, Monday: Thirty-eight-point/13 percent plunge.

The next day, October 29, Black Tuesday: 12.5 percent more, another forty-one points. Financial panic. The ticker bottomed out at 41.32 by July 1930, a drop of 89 percent in the past ten months.

Grim numbers. The week of the crash, the stock market lost $14 billion. Between 1929 and 1932, the average American family's income dropped by 40 percent, $2,300 a year to $1,500. In that same span, half of all residential-mortgage loans in America fell delinquent. In 1932, 273,000 families were evicted. New-home construction fell by 80 percent. Shorthand formula for economic catastrophe: huge supply of goods stuck in warehouses; stagnating demand for same because no one had liquid capital.

Economy stalled. Theory in vogue since the nineteenth century: a capitalistic economy worked by itself. The eighteenth-century philospher Adam Smith called it the "invisible hand": competition for resources, coupled with human self-interest, regulated the pendulum forces of supply and demand. Demand drove supply until prices rose high enough for demand to decrease. Oversupply resulted, lowering prices until demand returned. Back and forth. Tick tock: metronomic fiscal forces swinging down into equilibrium, restarting the cycles.

Twentieth century: The invisible hand palsied as agrarian dominance in America yielded to industrial. Social shifts from country to city grew complexities that Adam Smith could not have anticipated. The British economist John Maynard Keynes studied business cycles through the microscope of depression reality. He offered a new theory: a modern economy can reach equilibrium at a depressed level and cease cycling. Evidence of Keynesian insight all around.

Forty percent of all US banks failed from 1929 through 1932. By the end of 1930, three million children had quit school. The

GNP shriveled by 50 percent. Government records estimated that 50 percent of children in the country didn't have adequate food, shelter, and medical care. Seventy-five thousand farms were lost to bankruptcy. The Dust Bowl of 1934 and 1935 heaped misery upon misfortune. Between 1935 and 1938, eight hundred thousand people left Arkansas, Missouri, Texas, Kansas, and Oklahoma, abandoning the only homes they ever knew because of depression and drought.

Unemployment soared from 3.2 percent in precrash 1929 to 8.9 in 1930, rising to a peak of 24.9 in 1933, sinking no lower than 17.2 through the decade of the 1930s—until the United States began mobilizing for World War II. FDR's New Deal wouldn't kick in until the second half of the decade. Despair over poverty was breaking hearts and spirits all across the country. Suicides spiked from 12.1 per year per one hundred thousand population from 1920 to 1928 to 18.1 in 1929 before leveling to 15.4 from 1930 to 1934. Herbert Hoover needed a staff of one to handle his mail. During the Depression, Franklin D. Roosevelt hired fifty. Most of the mail was homespun—hand-scrawled from plain folks out of work, deprived of hope, asking relief for hunger.

Bad everywhere, worse in the sticks. Supply for unskilled farm labor glutted. Keynesian forces in motion: labor supply exceeded demand for workers, wages dropping like stones. More workers than jobs by a bunch. Growers offered pennies; hungry crop hands fought to have them, and their children ate flour-and-water dough fried in lard. The Cooleys had migrated south in 1931, to Modesto, California, and they were caught in the Depression vise. Donnell had married Anna in 1930; they had John in '31. Donnell eked dismal crop wages fiddling in roadhouses along Highway 99. He had a nickname by then. Different versions of its origin. Joling, JD, probably not accurately, claims he was tagged at Chemewa School: "...he studied violin and cello, and demonstrated a formidable poker-playing talent earning respect, spare bucks, and a lifelong nickname, 'Spade' after he dealt himself six straight spade-suit flushes, thereby fleecing unsuspecting classmates." Other accounts have it three straight spade flushes and place it in Oregon in the early '30s while touring the northwest with a group called the Southern Stars or while playing poker between sets at C&W dives on the outskirts of Modesto.

Firmly established by all: he was Spade Cooley when he finally shot into the world of entertainment.

III

Hollywood had escaped direct-hit damage from the Depression. Warner Brothers had introduced talkies in 1927 with Al Jolson in *The Jazz Singer.* Smash success. Fifty-seven million Americans attended movies that year. In 1930, the year after the crash, ninety million. During the trough year of 1932, sixty million found solace in dark auditoriums, mesmerized by flickering images. Every downtown in America had a least one theater. Ten cents a ticket for a double feature with newsreels, shorts, serials, and cartoons. A dime for Saturday Western matinees. Cheap escape from utter despair.

Assumed: Spade watched weekend movies like the rest of America. The pre-1927 silents featured action in pantomime, dialogue captured in interlude frames across the screen. Melodramatic organ music enhanced cornball damsel-in-distress, good-guy/bad-guy plots. Western heroes galloped across the silver screen with soundless effects—hoof beats billowing dust from posse chases; gun smoke flaring from Colt .45 barrels wielded by western heroes Harry Carey, William S. Hart, Ken Maynard, Hoot Gibson, Tim McCoy, and Tom Mix. White-hat good guys prevailed through tribulation over bad guys wearing black—amusing diversions for the Roaring Twenties.

Spade's people fled the prairie winds in search of farm labor in Oregon and California. They saw no horizon beyond squeaking by. Spade wanted more: he turned his back on Hicksville poverty.

1934: Spade took his fiddle, a few coins, and hopped a southbound freight. He jumped off at the yard limit north of Glendale and thumbed his way into the confusion of LA entertainment. He slept in city parks and wandered the streets of Los Angeles, ignorant of locale and protocol for achieving stardom.

He talked to a street guy who directed him to a club in the San Fernando Valley called the Black Cat Cafe. The Valley in Depression 1934: rural, small towns sprouting up along Ventura Boulevard between truck farms, olive orchards, orange groves, and meadows of grazing sheep. The Black Cat—lost to history, long-since paved over. Figure the Black Cat a country dive stuck between LAPD/LASD jurisdictions. Figure a vice-crime clientele sloshing beer and straight shots, sucking down first and secondhand smoke. Spade sat in with the house band until two in the morning. He didn't know how to ask for pay, and no one offered. He left predawn, as penniless as when he'd entered. He rode the rods back to Modesto.

Spade was poorly educated and impoverished like most migrants, but he wasn't just an Okie stereotype. He was a high-IQ schemer scrapping for prominence. He receded into day work around Modesto. At a picnic one Sunday, he riffed an impromptu jam with a blind fiddler. Someone in the audience liked what he heard and contracted both for a local honky-tonk at fifteen bucks a week. Spade's life as a field hand was over.

From roadhouse bars, he found sideman gigs in Western bands. He expanded beyond the Central Valley. He toured with Chuck Woods's Southern Stars out of Klamath Falls, before the Stars went broke. He caught on with Missouri-born Walt and Cal Schrum's Colorado Hillbillies out of Denver, before the Schrum brothers broke up the Hillbillies in 1934. Cal would re-form in 1940 as the Rhythm Rangers and play background to B-Westerns featuring Tex Ritter, Charles Starrett, and Johnny Mack Brown. Spade was broke from the Hillbillies venture, but he was starting to figure out a few things.

1937: He hoboed south. He jumped off again near Glendale with pennies in his pocket and a head full of hopes. He had watched movies like the rest of America, from the silent Gilbert "Broncho Billy" Anderson two-reel oaters of his boyhood to the feature-length wagon-train talkie and box-office bomb *The Big Trail*, directed by Raoul Walsh and starring a young John Wayne. *The Big Trail* broke new ground. Vitaphone had figured out how to soundtrack motion pictures. With more innovation, the company advanced to outdoor locations and was able to filter unwanted ambient noise. No record of how, but Spade apparently snapped Western movies into his dreamscape.

Westerns had been big since movies began. Among the primitive cinema milestones: *The Great Train Robbery* (1903), a one-reel (ten-minute) flick shot in New Jersey, fourteen scenes dramatizing Butch Cassidy's Hole-in-the-Wall Gang blowing a safe inside a train car they had uncoupled. Westerns, especially B Westerns, were a Depression era lifeline. Impoverished citizens flocked to films; the industry couldn't afford to price such a vast audience out of the market. Hollywood innovated to manufacture dirt-cheap flicks.

Five big studios dominated the 1920s and '30s: Paramount, United Artists Columbia, Twentieth Century Fox, and Metro-Goldwyn-Mayer. Then as now, the star system ruled. Bankable talent drew big bucks. Full-length A-list features with a cast of stars cost time and money. Low-budget production was in demand. "Poverty Row" independents rushed to fill it: Monogram, Liberty, Mascot, Majestic, Century, and Chesterfield. They held offices in faux-baroque two-story stuccos on Sunset east of Gower Street.

They built code-violating barn-and-corral sets and soundstage Western towns. They cranked out a flick a week, ten days at the most. They traded/shared the stock scenes—posse chases, overturned stagecoaches, cattle stampedes—from footage filmed wholesale among the desert boulders in the Alabama Hills in the eastern Sierra near Lone Pine on Highway 395, in the Santa

Susana Mountains near Chatsworth, or around Vasquez Rocks in the high desert above Santa Clarita.

Cattle ranches had consolidated into corporations after the turn of the twentieth century and downsized the labor pool. The American cowboy was fading into history. The Depression dispersed them off the plains. Cowboys found Hollywood. They might not have money for meals, but they wore sixty-dollar Stetsons and hand-tooled boots. They hung around the Columbia Drug Store at the corner of Sunset and Gower, ushering in the phrases "Drugstore Cowboy" and "Gower Gulch." They all were desperate—if not for star status, at least for the $7.50/day the studios paid the extras.

An opportunist named Herbert J. Yates figures into the background. Yates was a Brooklyn Jew just past fifty when the Depression hit. He had made a fortune as a mogul in the tobacco industry before he was thirty and gravitated toward Tinseltown. He acquired film laboratories and record companies and backed motion pictures. In the 1920s he had financed Fatty Arbuckle and Mack Sennett silents. He called his own company Consolidated Film Laboratories.

Consolidated provided film processing and financing for most of the Poverty Row studios, which one by one sank into Yates's debt. In 1935, he called in notes and merged Mascot and Monogram, among others (including the offshoot Lone Star, which produced fifty or more John Wayne movies in the 1930s), into a conglomerate he would call Republic Pictures.

Desperate Depression audiences loved Republic's output. Straight-shooting heroes atop majestic horses—early John Wayne and Gene Autry and later Roy Rogers on palominos Champion and Trigger. A recurring plot line: the broad-shouldered good guy with a colorful sidekick—Cannonball, Froggy, Soapy, or Fuzzy—rescuing plucky single women whose grandpas, fathers, or uncles were dry-gulched by desperados covertly employed by prominent but corrupt townsmen—bankers, lawyers, judges—or by slick-talking strangers fronting for pernicious land grabbers from the East trying to monopolize grazing land or water rights.

The Jazz Singer had changed everything. Al Jolson introduced soundtrack dialogue synced with music. Herbert J. Yates loved Broadway musicals and clicked on the entertainment implications for Western movies. Ken Maynard had singing-cowboy roles in the silents. John Wayne starred as "Singing Sandy Saunders" in a 1933 Lone Star flick, *Riders of Destiny*. John Wayne couldn't carry a tune, but...miracle of talking pictures, an actual crooner dubbed in. Bad fidelity was typical for the times. Singing Sandy paces into the climactic shootout against the town villain, distorting a dark dirge.

Singing cowboys with backup groups stuck as B-Western staples. Plots formed around barn dances or barroom bandstands featuring the Riders of the Sky or the Sons of the Pioneers. Individual white hats with guns and guitars belted out numbers from the saddle. Eddie Dean sang horseback tunes ("Wild Prairie Rose"); so did Gene Autry ("Back in the Saddle Again"), Roy Rogers ("Tumbling Tumbleweed"), Tex Ritter ("Git Along, Little Dogies"); and Monte Hale ("Home on the Range").

John Wayne was A-list ascendant and a Republic graduate, as was director John Ford. Gene Autry came with the Mascot merger. He was the biggest of the B performers. He starred in fifty-six Republic features between 1935 and 1947. Gene Autry was business shrewd. He would exploit his fame well beyond the ninety-three Westerns he starred in from 1934 to 1953. He diversified into radio and television. He bought into Golden West Radio and had significant holdings in Signal Oil. He became synonymous with Christmas music: "Rudolph the Red-Nosed Reindeer," "Here Comes Santa Claus," and "Frosty the Snowman."

Gene Autry was Hollywood's foremost singing cowboy under Republic's control. In 1937, he made salary demands, betting that his status would open Herbert J. Yates's wallet. Yates wouldn't cave.

Autry walked. Yates brought in a white hat from the Sons of the Pioneers: a twenty-six-year-old crooner from Cincinnati, Ohio, named Leonard Slye. Leonard Slye would adopt the stage name Roy Rogers and within a year would make the first of his eighty Republic flicks: *Under Western Stars.*

Herbert Yates had bought the twenty-acre Mack Sennett lot on Radford Avenue in Studio City (originally the neighborhood of Laurelwood; renamed because of Mack Sennett) just off Ventura Boulevard. Yates moved Republic into the lot. He modernized production technologies and enlarged the complex from six stage sets to nineteen. Spade Cooley zeroed in on Republic for his 1937 trip to Los Angeles. He invested his last dollars into custom boots, a Stetson, and a checkered shirt with arrow-point pocket flaps and pearlescent snap buttons.

He sported his new look on a spec trip to Studio City one morning, joining the cowboy mendicants at the Republic gates. He waited. Spade, like all the hillbilly extras, knew about Len Slye. In the summer of 1931, Slye had auditioned for a talent contest on a radio station in Inglewood, playing the guitar, singing, and yodeling. A country group called the Rocky Mountaineers heard the voice and asked him to join them.

The group eventually split. Len Slye and two others became the Pioneer Trio, and eventually the Sons of the Pioneers. They played country bars and radio gigs. They signed with Decca; their first commercial recording was "Tumbling Tumbleweeds." From that beginning, Len Slye branched out.

1935/1936: He was featured in three Westerns for Columbia.

1938: Gene Autry entered the Army Air Force. Republic plugged in Len Slye (as Roy Rogers) to replace Gene Autry. No formula changes necessary. Roy for Gene, Trigger for Champion, Gabby Hayes for Smiley Burnette as the colorful sidekick.

Spade bumped into Lenny Slye—no clear record of how or when. Len Slye had the juice of a comer. He responded to Spade

Cooley's pitch. Spade was shorter than Slye by four to five inches. Both men had squint eyes. Maybe Len Slye responded to the fact of their common Depression deprivation. Len Slye had picked peaches in Tulare in 1931, same time Donnell Cooley was working stone-fruit near Modesto.

Spade exuded fervent purpose. Len Slye bit; he told Spade to report back the next day. Spade was still a rube. While on trial for murder in 1961, he told Long Beach *Press-Telegram* reporter George C. Flowers, "All of a sudden I realized I didn't even have a place to stay or nothing to eat." Spade scanned Ventura Boulevard. He saw a billboard. He lifted empty boxes from the back of a store. He camped under the billboard with cardboard blankets. That was Tuesday. Spade worked Wednesday. He had no idea that he could have asked for an advance until payday. He stayed two more nights beneath the billboard. Spade was an Okie surviving on desperate optimism.

IV

Spade worked as an extra and stunt double and sideman with the Sons in Roy Rogers's movies. He toured with Roy and the Sons. His Oregon training kicked in. He could sight-read sheet music. He understood symphonic intricacies that applied to C&W music. He grasped how disparate instruments fused into a single orchestration. His backcountry peers tended to improvise by ear. Spade sunk boot heels in both camps—in classical strings by formal education; in improv fiddling by upbringing and DNA. Big-band sounds swung to rural rhythms in his head.

1939–1942: Spade jammed on Western music movie sets. He reunited with Walt Schrum as a sideman with the Rhythm Rangers. He branched out to clubs, benefits, ballrooms, and county fairs. Spade was a perfectionist and a tireless worker. He was flush for the first time in his life. With money, Spade brought Anna and John up from Modesto and bought a small house in North Hollywood.

Celebrity nightlife drew him to the flame. Spade drank hard and caved to priapic impulses.

He never bothered to card his dates. Under California law in 40s, statutory rape rotated around the age of twenty-one: any man over that age flinging with any girl under qualified for arrest. Spade sported with San Quentin quail without regard for consequence. He was a serial statch rapist and spousal cheat. He fought with Anna over his wild habits. Spade flew into rages. He was a mean drunk; he knocked Anna around more than a little.

1942/1943: War heating up in Europe and the South Pacific. Spade 4-F—something about a distended liver. He was discovered by a WWI Navy vet named Bert A. Phillips, who went by the name Foreman. Foreman Phillips had recognized an entertainment trend and moved on it. He hustled radio programming out of the C&W dance halls growing throughout the San Fernando Valley and the LA Basin. Spade Cooley had worked with bands around LA and Orange Counties; Foreman Phillips couldn't help but notice. Phillips saw more than fiddle talent. He saw a showman. He signed him in 1943 and told him to organize a group and headline the Venice Pier Ballroom. Spade's run in Venice would last seventy-four weeks.

Phillips recruited legitimate talent. Teenager Joaquin Murphey played steel guitar; so did Noel Boggs later on. Tex Williams sang. Smoky Rogers sang and wrote music. A vocalist named Helen Hagstram changed her name to Carolina Cotton and became the featured yodeler. Deuce Spriggens played bass viol; Eddie Bennett, piano. The Spade Cooley Orchestra dazzled overflow Okie audiences, three thousand or more, in Venice. Spade was fueled. "I got it into my head...," he said, "the idea of making money because being born poor and staying poor and being satisfied with it wasn't how I saw living out the rest of my natural life."

Spade pushed. He crashed a Glenn Miller band rehearsal at a country club in Northridge one Saturday. He was looking for

Eleanor "Bobbie" Bennett, an attorney and entertainment agent. Spade knew about Bobbie from his piano player, Edgar Bennett, Bobbie's husband—like Spade, a slave to late-night booze and round-heeled babes. Spade found her backstage in Northridge and offered her his last (he said) $2,000 to represent him. Bobbie Bennett and her assistant, Bernice Allen, laughed at him. Bobbie Bennett pointed to elegant dinner-jacketed Glenn Miller. She snickered at Spade's Okie patter and lowbrow act. Spade dared her to see for herself. He induced her with coupons for free beer. Bobbie Bennett deferred to Eddie. Eddie vouched. Bobbie suffered as Eddie Bennett's wife—what was one more indignity?

Pre-freeway LA: long-ass drive from Northridge to Venice over Sepulveda Pass to the beach via surface streets. Bobbie left in a limo after Glenn Miller's final set with a supply of cold champagne. She hated beer, even free beer. She was surprised to discover that she liked the act. Spade had integrated pop music forms. Spade himself fiddled. His thirty-piece band fused barn-dance twang and yodeling with jazz improv overlaid with a Benny Goodman/Artie Shaw type of big-band resonance. Spade was diminutive, only five foot four and slight, built like a gymnast, with footwork like Sugar Ray Robinson—a little white Okie with rhythm.

Foreman Phillips had instructed his acts to stick to the melody. Spade knew better. Depression, migration, and war broke down inhibitions. Spade fused rowdy rhythm and beat with melody and jumped into it. Between solo riffs, he conducted. He hip-swiveled pre-Elvis. He sashayed the stage, arcing his bow at country women in hoopskirts and cowboy boots. He held fiddle and bow with one hand and rocked his elbow with the other, snapping fingers and beaming a big-tooth smile that exaggerated his natural squint. Bobbie Bennett felt a thrill she probably could not articulate: cornball Spade Cooley with the stuff to outdraw her society bookings. She gripped it: a whooping subculture of cash-flush hay shakers. She could make them both rich.

The audience was built in. Midwestern and Southern state populations had headed West since the Depression. Prewar servicemen poured into military bases from Camp Pendleton to Fort Irwin. Okies, Arkies, hillbillies, peckerwoods, rednecks, and crackers cascaded into Southern California. William Mulholland had built an aqueduct in 1913, pirating water for the city of Los Angeles from the Owens Valley in the eastern Sierra. San Fernando Valley settlements could access city water only by incorporating into the city of Los Angeles.

LA boomed. Valley towns sprang up along Ventura Boulevard. Valley Ag began to flourish. Rural enclaves blew up. The Depression had masked what had been burgeoning but never stopped it. Late-thirties hostilities brought it out. Hitler stormed the Sudetenland. Hirohito overtook Nanking and railed against a US oil embargo. World war clouds gathered. The aviation industry was drawn to LA anyway. War mobilization and munitions manufacturing followed.

Cheap open land, 340 rain-free days a year: perfect for jerry-building bomb factories, slamming up Quonset huts, and grading runways. LA was going nuts. Emigrants were finding work in Anaheim citrus groves and San Fernando Valley truck farms. Shade-tree mechanics able to fix tractors or keep a '31 Ford from leaking oil all over Route 66 transformed into assembly-line labor for aeronautics and weapons production. The postwar boom wouldn't begin to pave over LA for a decade. LA still had its sticks. Future ghettos—East LA and Watts—still were fully integrated.

C&W music wasn't mainstream Hollywood or national pop chart hot, but twenty-four-hour cowboy dance joints sprang up where rural LA still showed through. The best known: Riverside Rancho in Glendale on the border of Las Feliz. The others: 97th Street Corral in South Central; the Jubilee Ballroom in Baldwin Park; Venice Pier Ballroom on the beach; McDonald's Ballroom in Compton; the Lighthouse Dance Hall, also in Compton; Pop's Willow Lake in Sunland; Tex Williams's Village in Newhall; the Sunset Rancho on the Strip.

They catered to cowboys, soldiers, sailors, and farmworkers, to swing and graveyard-shift workers from aircraft and war-mobilization factories. Honky-tonk juke joints filled in: The Band Box, the Cowtown, and the Saddle Club on Vermont Avenue; Hoot Gibson's Painted Post on Ventura Boulevard; the Hitching Post in Gardena; Henri's Lariat in Torrance; Maybo's in Culver City; the B&R Club in East LA; the Palomino on Lankersheim in North Hollywood. C&W in LA wasn't as concentrated as it was in Nashville, but it was bigger. Bobbie Bennett pressed for profit.

Spade had a name for his music: Western Swing. He didn't originate the term or the genre, but he would be most notably associated with it. Two Texans pioneered the sound. Bob Wills broadcast it from a radio station in Tulsa, Oklahoma, with his group, the Texas Playboys. Milton Brown and his Musical Brownies performed it out of Fort Worth. Both made enduring music history. Bob Wills is listed among the most influential country musicians of all time. Spade Cooley is mentioned as a media-driven '40s/'50s meteor flash better known for beating his wife to death in the desert than for innovating the Country and Western genre.

Spade had Hollywood press agency as an ally. Entertainment media tends to dub stars with royal stature. Gene Autry was the "King of the Cowboys," Clark Gable was the "King of Hollywood," big-band leader Benny Goodwin was the "King of Swing." A decade in the future, Elvis Presley would be crowned the "King of Rock and Roll." No reason Spade Cooley should hide his light under a bushel. He would overtake Milton Brown and Bob Wills in popular awareness with the simple expedients of headquartering in Los Angeles and nicknaming himself the "King of Western Swing."

1943–1946: Inevitable—Spade's private life slopped over the side. Spade philandered out of control; his marriage to Anna was on the shoals and heading toward a crash. Spade held a talent contest in 1943. One entry: Ella Mae Evans, a blond, twenty-year-old clarinetist and singer from Baldwin Park by way of a hick town in Missouri. Ella Mae was earnest but couldn't play or sing. Spade fell hard, and not for her music. Spade had an exceptional ear; he knew she was terrible. He hid his true intentions. He rigged the vote; Ella Mae won the competition. Spade beamed teeth and spritzed hillbilly charm over her renditions. She flashed shy smiles and fluttered her eyelashes.

Spade stashed Ella Mae in a Hollywood Hills house he had bought at 8623 Franklin, uphill from his office on the Sunset Strip. He scampered between home, work, and his shack pad. Spade was rolling in money. He could afford peccadilloes but couldn't contain them. Band bookings, rehearsals, radio broadcasts, travel between, and flings with other babes already strained him. Anna and Ella Mae saw each other's lipstick on his shirt collar. Hollywood gossip spread the rumors.

Bobbie Bennett advised Anna to split the sheets.

1945: Spade arrested for statch rape in Glendale. A squad car spotted his car late at night on the side of the road. Cops caught him in the backseat of his 1940 Buick with an eighteen-year-old. Spade called in the juice. Gene Autry intervened. Charges were heard in judicial chambers and squashed. Hollywood: Cash changed hands via high-priced lawyers and *poof*—crime wasn't crime.

Arguments at home; duplicity, recriminations, lies, and evasions led to inevitable outcome. Anna filed; the divorce was finalized in September 1945. Anna kept the house. Spade lived out of his office and the shack pad. Ella Mae turned up pregnant. She and Spade eloped to Vegas on December 9, 1945. They had Melody Faith in June 1946. Spade retired his new wife to motherhood. Donnell Clyde Jr. was born two years later.

Bobbie Bennett kept him hopping. Foreman Phillips broadcast *County Barn Dances* from the Venice pier on his radio program, *Western Hit Parade Show*. Spade had his own show in '46, on KFVD: *Spade Cooley Time*. He played Venice for eighteen months and moved on. Spade appeared in more movies, all bad. He was featured in *Rockin' in the Rockies,* a 1945 contemporary Western with Moe Howard and Larry and Curly Fine, not as the Three Stooges. He made three flicks in the late 1940s, all released in 1950: *The Kid from Gower Gulch, Silver Bandit,* and *Border Outlaws. Border Outlaws* wrapped around a rustling plot but never included a single frame that included cattle. Spade cloned new bands, all as the Spade Cooley Orchestra, so that they could meet every booking demand. Bobbie Bennett's idea. Spade appeared in multiple locations on the same night.

1943: Spade leased the top spot, Riverside Rancho in Glendale. He outgrew the Riverside by 1946 and signed a seven-year agreement with the more spacious Santa Monica Ballroom. Spade cut records for Columbia, RCA, and Decca. He hit it big with his second single in '44, "Shame, Shame on You!"

"Shame" bounced through the top-ten charts for nine weeks in 1945, hitting number one nine times. "Shame" became his theme. Spade piled on the hits: "Crazy 'Cause I Love You," "Forgive Me One More Time," and "Oklahoma Stomp." Spade had a gift for song-title irony. Six of Spade's Songs made the Billboard charts from 1945 to 1947.

Spade launched from Santa Monica. Bobbie B. booked him through his own lease. Thousands paid to see him live. *Spade Cooley Time* on KFVD radio broadcast to tens of thousands more. Something new on the horizon: television. The German wunderkind, electrical engineer Klaus Landsberg, had fled der fatherland after the 1936 Berlin Olympics when the Nazis wanted to classify one of his inventions as a state secret. Landsberg hit LA at age twenty-three, way ahead of his time. He was a technical whiz with an instinct for pop entertainment programming. Paramount Pictures hired him in 1941 to experiment with television.

January, 1947: Landsberg pioneered innovations for Paramount. He obtained the first commercial license for broadcast television in Los Angeles, the first west of the Mississippi, W6-XYZ. W6-XYZ morphed into KTLA, Channel 5. Bobbie Bennett broached Klaus Landsberg. Landsberg caught Spade Cooley's act in Santa Monica and foresaw a live TV hit.

V

1948: Maybe nine hundred television sets in LA living rooms. NBC, CBS, ABC: nominal networks only. Syndication and transcription not yet technically possible. Only way to package programming is kinescope: film a TV picture tube on 16 or 35 mm and ship copies via airmail. Programming by default: live and local.

Hoffman Radio established itself postwar, 1946, downtown, at 3430 Hill Street, manufacturing tabletop radio consoles. Convergences: Hoffman ready to retool into a progressive new medium; Klaus Landsberg reaching for local programming, eager to secure sponsor money. Simple dovetail market push: Hoffman advertises TV hit program; hit program sells Hoffman TV sets.

Landsberg offered Hoffman Spade Cooley performing from the Santa Monica Ballroom. Hoffman reluctant but yielding. Landsberg hired character actor Dick Lane as emcee. The *Hoffman Hayride* with Spade Cooley a smash from its debut. Variety format predating Ed Sullivan a decade later. Spade's orchestra performed between cornball comedy skits and guest appearances. Lowbrow Spade fit with early television. KTLA broadcast wrestling from the Olympic Auditorium—Gorgeous George vs. Lord Blears; Bomber Kulkowski vs. Sheik Lawrence. Wrestlers took nicknames for show; Gorgeous George (George Wagner) dyed his curly hair platinum; he atomized perfume on his torso before entering the ring. He called himself the "Human Orchid." LA audiences ate it up.

Novelty time, before the inevitable and exponential explosions in TV technology and sophistication. Early viewers watched everything Klaus Landsberg could conjure up. A game show playing charades (*Pantomime Quiz Show*). A game show based bingo (*Play Marco*). A dog show. An Indian tribe show featuring Iron

Eyes Cody. A Bob Clampett puppet show (*Time for Beany*). News, sports, cartoons, cooking shows, live wrestling, and gimmick features. Landsberg hired an organist named John Roland Redd, a light-skinned black from Missouri. Redd had renamed himself Korla Pandit; he wore sequined robes and a jeweled turban. Landsberg had him stare into the camera with a dream-trance expression and play exotic music on a Steinway grand piano and a Hammond organ. Incense misted from a smudge pot behind the instruments. Eerie. Landsberg gave Korla Pandit a fifteen-minute daily slot called *Adventures in Music*. Audiences marveled.

1948-1952: Spade Cooley time at KTLA. The *Hoffman Hayride*—featuring "Spade Cooley, your fiddling friend"—debuted August 5, 1948, and aired live on Saturday nights at eight from the Santa Monica Ballroom. Bags of fan letters confirmed the call. Estimated 75 percent of all receivers in Los Angeles were tuned to the *Hayride* at its peak. Spade bounced bad jokes and worse puns off straight-man Dick Lane. He brought in country singer Hank Penny as a rube comic.

He hosted Hollywood buddies eager to marquee their names: Frank Sinatra (before *From Here to Eternity*); Jerry Lewis; his old rival Bob Wills; Ronald Reagan; Sara Vaughn. Spade wasn't a slave to refined culure. He staged his orchestra on risers behind him. He brought in animal acts: a talking dog from Iowa, "Pal O'Malley" (and his human ventriloquist); the dog said he was hungry. He brought in a trained ape named Joe. Joe was leashed to his two-hundred-pound trainer. Monkey Joe went ape shit over the hanging mike. He reached up and yanked it from its mooring. He ran amok, dragging the trainer, mike, and mike cord backstage. Spade brought in a baby elephant. The elephant crapped on the stage. Hee Haw.

Early LA TV: Spade was the biggest name of all. Spade rode the comet, burning it from both ends.

1951: He and Ella Mae left the Hollywood Hills. They moved to a four-thousand-square-foot rambler on three leafy acres at 4509

Noeline Avenue in Encino, painted-wood siding and a weathered shake roof, half a mile south of Ventura Boulevard. Roy Rogers and Dale Evans their nearest neighbors. Roy and Spade were best friends until...

Fierce storm in the winter of 1952. Mudslides and floods threatening both properties. Spade in Santa Monica rehearsing for the show. Ella Mae terrified. Ella Mae called Roy and Dale. Roy owned an earth-moving Cat.

Roy fired it up. In hard wind and pounding rain, he graded dikes around his property and Spade's. Ella Mae grateful and relieved. She called Spade at the Ballroom, extolling Roy's heroics. Something in her tone fired up Spade's dark demons. Two-timing had left him paranoid. He projected his own subcutaneous guilt. He festered the worst interpretation of events. Roy was a hound too, which didn't help. Spade imagined Roy and Ella Mae playing bury the brisket behind his back. He stayed away two days and returned drunk. He pounded Ella Mae, accusing her of bopping his sneaking used-to-be best friend. He forbade the mention of Roy Rogers's name in his presence.

Spade had abundant guilt to project. Offstage and backstage, Spade caroused. Bobbie Bennett paid quacks for penicillin shots every time Spade contracted the clap. Her lawyers bought off bimbos whose affections Spade had alienated. She sent Spade's sad conquests to scrape clinics in Ventura and San Berdoo Counties and paid bills out of band proceeds.

He ran with dysfunctional Hollywood buddies. He bopped wannabes from his auditions; he wenched with pickups in Sunset Strip saloons. He pimped leftovers to Gene Autry and—before they split—Roy Rogers. Alan Ladd was bipolar before the condition was medically ID'ed. He drank to mask depression. Audie Murphy, World War II's most decorated GI, suffered from post-traumatic stress syndrome well before PTS was an acknowledged pathology. He drank to modulate downer moods. Spade drank with both.

He drank and chased young chicks with Errol Flynn. He drank and chain-smoked with Humphrey Bogart. He bounced along the Sunset Strip with notorious Tinsel Town red asses Richard Boone, John Carradine, and Aldo Ray.

He drove a souped-up 1940 Buick, often drunk. Spade rode his palomino, Golden Nugget, in sheriff Eugene Biscailuz's honor posse; he fiddled for police/sheriff-sponsored widow-and-orphan benefits; he was a reserve police captain in Santa Monica. He had an honorary LAPD badge.

1954 to 1956: Encino a community, not an incorporated town—ceremonial government only. Spade installed as honorary mayor of Encino by the Encino Chamber of Commerce; he termed out in favor of John Wayne. Spade was a protected LA celebrity. Hot talent in Hollywood always had a pass.

Spade won Emmys as LA's top local program in 1952 and 1953. He dressed the part. A Ukrainian tailor named Nudie Cohn (Nuta Kotylarenko) opened a shop, Nudie's of Hollywood, on the corner of Victory and Vineland in North Hollywood in the late '40s, staked (among others) by Spade Cooley and Tex Williams. Nudie spun outrageous threads. He chain-stitched celebrity designs into suits adorned with rhinestones. Think Robert Redford's title duds in 1979's *The Electric Horseman*—a Nudie creation. Nudie's fop duds caught on huge with C&W performers from the late '40s. Nudie embroidered aces of spades and fiddles and bows on Spade Cooley's gear. Spade had a hundred Nudie suits hanging in his Encino closet in the 1950s, along with three-dozen pair of hand-cobbled boots and shelves stacked with fifty 4x beaver Stetsons.

1954: Spade's family appeared with him on his annual Christmas show from the Santa Monica Ballroom. Ella Mae, Melody Faith, and little Donnie. Ella Mae wore mink. Ella Mae's coat sleeves pushed up during a sequence. Gauze wrapping showed on an exposed wrist—dark truth underneath happy holiday image. After the show, Spade replenished himself with beer, cigars, whiskey, and

Chinese takeout. Something gave: Spade gripped his chest—his second heart attack. Intensive-care at Mount Sinai. Cardiac docs recommended excising tobacco, spicy foods, and alcohol from his intake. They prescribed nitro tablets. Except for the nitro, Spade ignored their advice.

Errol Flynn and Humphrey Bogart kept yachts anchored in Santa Monica. Spade bought a 40-footer and named it *The Idler*. Spade was an Okie. He knew zero about boating, but that didn't faze him. One day in 1955 he sailed in Santa Monica Bay in thirty-five-knot winds. Down the coast near El Segundo, Spade, drunk, rammed *The Idler* into a barely submerged cistern engineered to carry coastal city sepsis into the sea. Big damage—45k in boat repairs; millions to fix the sewer system. Twenty miles of beaches were posted for weeks as unsafe for swimmers. Spade had chutzpah. He retained engineers to testify that the septic pipes had been constructed far too shallow to avoid catastrophe. He skated on liability.

1954: Spade had at least one innocent hobby—lapidary. He liked working with rocks. Pure Okie pastime: Collect desert stones, cut and polish them, set them in silver for adornment on belts, rings, money clips, and bolo-tie slides. In his free time, he and Ella Mae rock-hounded open spaces in the Mojave, hunting for trilobite shale, black dendrites, petrified wood, and fossilized arrowheads. On one outing, he came across acreage for sale in Willow Springs. He bought the property—started with eighty acres—and broke ground on a twenty-six-hundred-square-foot house. He named it the SC Ranch.

1956: Spade's orbit cresting the apogee and plunging toward splashdown. Spade's core audience came from a niche of the Depression population—shitkickers who married young and aged fast. Their children tended to transition into more contemporary interests; their grandchildren were baby boomers rocking and rolling to Bill Haley and the Comets. They themselves would mellow into more sedate entertainment.

KTLA had been airing Lawrence Welk and his Champagne Music Makers from the Aragon Ballroom in Venice since 1951. Spade and Larry: unfriendly rivals. Larry had arranged a tepid rendition of "Shame." Larry fingered an accordion and conducted granny music. He affected a *Plattdeutsch* accent from his North Dakota roots— "Wunnerfull, Wunnerfull"; "a-one, a-two." His bubbly acts featured innocuous house talents such as Myron Floren on the accordion and the five Lennon Sisters in tepid acappella. He ascended his own house-trailer arc. Too many of Spade's followers defected Larry's way.

Television programming techno-progressing into TV's golden age. Network feeds overtook local schmaltz. Networks now could transcribe, syndicate, and cover America. Think Bishop Fulton J. Sheen from New York on Sunday mornings. Think Ed Sullivan on CBS introducing Elvis Presley or the Smothers Brothers on national television. Think Spade Cooley on KLTA Channel 5, Los Angeles, bringing in a baby pachyderm to shit on the stage. Think golden-age sitcoms, kid's shows, Westerns, and crime shows: *I Love Lucy, Howdy Doody, Gunsmoke,* and *Dragnet*. Spade found difficulty securing guests. Lucy and Desi, James Garner, James Arness, Richard Boone—all interdicted by network contracts. Spade was down to second-rate lounge acts like Tennessee Ernie Ford and Morey Amsterdam. His ratings slipped precipitously.

Spade became increasingly hard to work with—half the time soused and always grinding. He fired musicians when he was smashed and tried hiring them back when he was sober. Some left and spun off with their own groups—Tex Williams, Deuce Spriggens, and Carolina Cotton long gone. Spade's talent bag was near empty. Spade retooled—he formed an all-girl orchestra. Dual purposes: fresh acts plus a replenished supply of pliable women. The idea bombed. KTLA fired him in 1957; he retired from television in 1958. He worked Vegas until 1960.

February 28, 1960: His last blast. The Hollywood Chamber of Commerce embedded a Spade Cooley brass star in the Walk of

Fame across Hollywood Boulevard from Grauman's Chinese, on the 6800 block just west of Highland Avenue.

By then, Spade had moved to SC Ranch, where he was cooking up a whole new enterprise. He looked across the desert and saw Mafia-made Las Vegas: Cactus and tumbleweed transformed into sinful neon delight. Looked down the coast and saw Walt Disney paving over Anaheim orange groves and pepper trees and creating tourist bonanza Disneyland—Mr. Toad's Wild Ride, the Matterhorn, and Main Street, USA. He looked around his own Mojave backyard and envisioned theme-park attractions.

Spade still played dance halls around the state. He had a new fiddler he was bopping on the side, a leftover from his all-girl band named Anita Aros. He was obsessing on Water Wonderland. In theory it could have worked. Allowing for its projected size, the project would require sixteen-hundred-acre-feet of water inside a dammed basin roughly half a mile long by a quarter mile wide, with depths varying up to twelve feet. It would have to be lined with compacted layers of hard retention clay. Pumps would draw water from the aquifer to fill the lakes and replenish evaporation losses. Seems preposterous for the arid Mojave—but once filled, Water Wonderland would require no more hydration than an irrigated alfalfa field of the same dimensions.

Spade sunk his own capital into Water Wonderland, Inc., but he needed more. His television income had plummeted from millions to zero. Bobbie Bennett signed on as business manager to flak the scheme—she put all her personal holdings into the project. A few Hollywood buddies bought in—Jack Benny, Lucy and Desi, James Garner, Jim Davis. Two who didn't provide a clue: William Boyd and Gene Autry, the two most scheme-savvy B-Western stars wouldn't touch it. Spade found alternate (and high-vig) financing from Las Vegas and from Texas oil money.

His overhead was huge. Spade kept project managers, engineers, and architects on salary. He leased high-end earth movers and retained crews of operators. He bought options on peripheral property for subdivision into residential lots and accumulated mortgages for 1,320 acres. The lots never caught on. Prospective buyers scoped a horizon of dust. In sizzling heat, wind drifts flapped their pant legs and blew grit into their eyes. They saw WW as a mirage and shied away.

Spade held it off for a while—he stayed in Encino with his late-night floozies. He kept Ella Mae in Willow Springs, far away from any temptations he could imagine. Progress slow on Water Wonderland. He piped in a publicity stunt. Engineers designed and installed a groundwater generator. Big show for potential investors and press—the clay liner that would keep water from sinking back into the desert soil yet to be applied—still a sand bottom. Spade spun the big wheel. A gusher flowed from the spigot. A puddle formed. Flashbulbs popped. Investors and press applauded. Spade and Bobbie Bennett slapped backs and glad-handed. They escorted the customers and flaks to a big room at SC Ranch. They unveiled a scale model of Water Wonderland. Spade and Bobbie plied them with free food and booze. Back at the basin, engineers wheeled back the spigot. The puddle bubbled and sank back into the sand.

Spade Cooley's Water Wonderland never held another drop.

VI

Fact is, Spade was running a Ponzi scheme. He serviced loans with proceeds from new backers. He couldn't contain the inevitable. Two years since ground breaking, the basin was excavated and the sides dammed, but that was it. Bobbie Bennett could see it: she was losing her life savings. Spade lapsed deep into lifelong bad habits. He chased women; he chased whiskey with pills. He kept Ella Mae as a virtual prisoner in Willow Springs. He knocked her around. Pressures built. Signs for bloody denouement flashed red. March 1961: Ella Mae was hospitalized at UCLA med center with a nervous breakdown. She met male nurses Bud Davenport and Luther Jackson. She confided; they commiserated. She sent them money to invest for her in Water Wonderland in the event she got free from Spade. They never did, fearing a Spade backlash. Ella Mae filed for divorce and backed off when Spade threatened to kill her and the children. Spade filed.

March 23: Spade brought in a notary from Lancaster, Catherine Polino, and had Ella Mae sign eleven quitclaim deeds to SC Ranch and Water Wonderland. Four were valued at 80k each, the other seven left blank. In return Spade was obligated to place 10k in escrow per deed. Big laugh: Spade, SC, and WW were mortgaged past redemption. Ella Mae was signing over future bankruptcy. Spade never funded the escrow. Mrs. Polino noticed that Ella Mae wore dark glasses indoors.

Things escalating. Spade knew about Davenport and Jackson. He had hired PI Billy Lewis to dig dirt. He beat confessions out of Ella Mae. He pounded her until she conceded that his paranoia was the truth. Spade fixated on two points: Ella Mae bopping Roy Rogers and Ella Mae joining the free love cult with Davenport and Jackson. Ella Mae would say anything to stop the abuse. Spade forced her to call acquaintances and confess her adulteries and perversions.

March 24: Spade called Anita Aros and proposed—said they could marry in seven weeks, after he obtained a decree in Nevada.

March 30: Spade dropped Ella Mae in North Hollywood at Bobbie Bennett's while he was in LA on business. Ella Mae telephoned her sister in Duarte, Elizabeth Kidwell. She told Kidwell she was in "bad shape" and needed a place to hide if she could escape from Willow Springs.

March 31: Spade and Ella Mae driving back, arguing. Ella Mae jumped/was pushed from their moving car—maybe more than once. She sustained a black eye, brush burns on her arms and legs, and bruised back and coccyx.

April 2: Ella Mae told Melody that Spade had pushed her from the car. Dottie Davis visited SC Ranch. Spade showed her telephone bills he claimed were from calls she'd made in which she confessed her infidelities. Billy Lewis called in. Spade made her confess about Jackson and Davenport. Spade ordered Lewis to find motel records for the days and times in question.

April 3, late morning: Spade told WW exec Jerry Enfield he had proof in Ella Mae's own handwriting—her confession of a three-way with Davenport and Jackson. Jerry Enfield: "Yes, that's Ella Mae's handwriting, but I know how you got it." Spade: "What's the difference as long as it's true?"

April 3, 6:00 p.m.: Spade made Ella Mae telephone the McWhorters and summon Melody to "explain what this is all about"—meaning confess her adulteries to her daughter. By the time Melody arrived, Spade had beaten Ella Mae to death, claiming she had fallen in the shower and hit her head. Seventeen hours later he was sitting in Kern County jail cell awaiting trial on a murder charge.

Spade hired a slick Beverly Hills attorney, thirty-seven-year-old P. Basil Lambros, as his defense counsel. P. Basil Lambros was conspicuously well dressed at trial. He sported tailored dark suits, a different one each day, black alligator shoes, and matching cuff links and stick pins. His 2010 *LA Times* obit highlighted two cases from his long career, neither a win—the Spade Cooley trial and one in 1962, where an Arcadia man charged with arson was granted a new trial because superior court judge William F. Fox believed that "...the jury was biased and prejudicial against [the] defense counsel." Two female jurors, citing his dandy appearance, signed affidavits claiming that they had voted to convict because the defendant had hired Lambros as his lawyer.

July 6, 1961: Spade in Kern County slammer since early April. Next day's headline in the *Bakersfield Californian*: Spade Weeps at Death Scene. P. Basil arranged a day-trip furlough under armed KCSD guard—Spade brought back to Willows Springs. P. Basil played to press—a dozen reporters and photographers on site from Bakersfield, Mojave, Lancaster, and Los Angeles. P. Basil: "There are a lot of blank spots in Spade's memory," he said. "We thought it would refresh his recall to come home." Spade walked the grounds, surveyed the house, cried, and checked on his heifers and horses. He was back in his Kern County cell the same afternoon.

Spade scratched out two songs inside. One called "Faith," a hymn dedicated to an Oregon church; another dedicated to Ella Mae, called "Cold Gray Bars."

> Cold gray bars for windows
> Cold gray bars in view
> Makes no difference, Darling
> All I see is you.

Bobbie Bennett snatched both and had them recorded in LA. "Faith" and "Cold Gray Bars" were marketed on the same platter. Spade: "Any other song on the record would be sacrilegious." Spade broke: anything for a buck.

July 10 through 13: Jury selected and paneled—ten men, two women. *Voir dire* revealing. Kit Nelson aiming for the gas chamber. He charged Spade Cooley with first-degree "murder by torture." On Spade's behalf, P. Basil Lambros entered dual pleas: not guilty, and not guilty by reason of insanity.

Differences at bar showed. Kit Nelson grilled prospects on points of law, whether jurors could decide a capital case, whether they could stay trained to facts without distractions of sympathy or passion on the defendant's behalf. P. Basil Lambros prepping for insanity. He asked candidates whether they would give psychiatric testimony equal credence as law enforcement would. He probed for cracks.

He inquired about biases against Okies, Indians, wife-beaters, and country entertainers. He asked if the victim's/defendant's daughter's testimony would be accorded more weight than that of other witnesses. He diverted the focus to himself. He asked about attitudes toward out-of-town attorneys. End of day: P. Basil made Spade available for the press. Spade: "I've had much time to think…I am deeply sorry…I am crushed…Without her [Ella Mae] life has no meaning for me." P. Basil: "Spade is a wonderful person to work with, and he is heartbroken, very, very sad over the whole tragedy."

July 14, Friday: Opening arguments in a thirty-one-day proceeding, the longest murder trial in Kern County history. Standard three-phase capital case under California law: Same judge and jury determining (1) guilt/innocence, (2) sanity, and (3) sentence. Kit Nelson had filed first-degree "murder by torture." Good strategy with an asterisk. By law, if torture is proved, no need to establish premeditation for a gas chamber verdict. No mystery to his approach. He could prove Ella Mae was stomped to death—with Spade the stomper—and he could demonstrate a pattern of wife-beating.

Kit Nelson gambling on only one point: premeditation implies sufficient reasoning faculties to offset an insanity plea. Without it, P. Basil Lambros could claim diminished capacity, and Spade could walk. For his part, P. Basil was operating in shackles. He had no "other guy" defense: no way to reconstruct the crime sequence. P. Basil was left to chip at the edges of the state's case and hint that his client was nuts.

July 15 headline, *Bakersfield California*: Lawyers Clash on Cooley Trial Photos; subhead: Judge Rules Jury Can See Pictures. Kit Nelson moving to introduce into evidence pictures of Ella Mae taken postmortem at Kern General the night she was killed. P. Basil objecting vehemently, saying the pictures would "inflame the jury at this time" and that their admission "would be grossly unfair." First pivotal moment: Judge Bradshaw overruled P. Basil's objection. The jury saw a ten-picture spread: a Kodachromatic horror show revealing multiple bruises and abrasions; blackened left eye; bruised nose and lips; split lips; cracked chin; contusions on her neck, shoulder, chest, hips, arms, wrists, and legs; abraded right breast—blackened and discolored nipple, partially separated from the breast.

The impact on the jury was indelible. P. Basil tried to counter. He said, "The colors in the pictures do not fairly portray what the people are trying to portray." He quibbled over halftones and color values with prosecution witness John Harmon, production manager of the Glendale film company that processed the death snaps. He belabored a contention—that the photo spread did not accurately distinguish between bruising from assault and postmortem lividity. John Harmon agreed: 100 percent fidelity was unlikely. He added, "But the difference is too slight to matter." No rebuttal.

July 16: P. Basil Lambros reaching. He rigged a presession visit in the anteroom—Spade with his grandchildren by John and Dorothy, five-and-a-half-year-old Debra Lee and thirteen-month-old Melody. Debra Lee chirped little-kid stuff—she told Spade she could hold her head under water. Spade smiled and cried. A bailiff escorted Spade into court. Little Debra Lee asked, "Where is grandpa going?" P. Basil working the loving-family angle. Reporters witnessed and wrote about it.

Defense wobbly from the photos forward. Kit Nelson called Bud Davenport and Luther Jackson. They denied having an affair with Ella Mae. They said Spade bullied them. Jackson: "Spade called and threatened to kick my teeth in and kill me." Bud Davenport recalled the night Spade, Beal Whitlock, and Jerry Enfield stormed his and Jackson's trailer in Northridge: "They came into our patio area like a cyclone."

Davenport and Jackson both said Ella Mae routinely called and told them of Spade's abuse. They said Ella Mae called one time from Palm Springs after Spade had choked her. P. Basil asked on cross if Ella Mae was ever unfaithful to Spade. Jackson: "To my knowledge, never." P. Basil's strategy subtle. He wasn't trying to impugn the truth of fact—he was implying the fact of insanity.

July 27: Melody took the stand for the prosecution. She told of chronic beatings in Encino and Willow Springs. She referred to her father as "Spade." She said the beatings occurred mostly on Saturdays when Spade returned from band bookings. Melody testified about events on April 3. She said Spade kicked Ella Mae in the stomach and back and said, "Look, Melody she only cries when you hit her." She said it had been ongoing punishment. The week before, Spade was out with John. She and Ella Mae tried to think of ways to escape. John's car was in the driveway, but "she was too weak to drive." Melody said she overheard Spade on the phone with Anita Aros on April 3, talking about marriage. She recalled Spade dragging Ella Mae from the shower. She recalled him holding a rifle and a broomstick. She recalled the kicking and slugging.

She recalled Spade holding his Camel ash to her mother's breasts. She recalled Spade fondling her on the living room couch. She recalled fleeing the house when she saw Lilya McWhorter's headlights reflecting off the gravel driveway into SC Ranch.

P. Basil on cross: "When did you stop referring to Mr. Cooley as 'Daddy'?"

Melody: "When this happened."

P. Basil, flailing to mitigate. He intimated Melody was a problem child, sexually precocious. He mentioned her running away from home to meet older boys. Kit Nelson objected. Judge Bradshaw sustained, with an admonition: "You do not have the right to besmirch her character." P. Basil jabbing at Spade's paranoia. He asked if her parents fought about Roy Rogers. Melody said multiple arguments centered on that name—Roy Rogers. She didn't know why.

2:45 p.m.: Judge Bradshaw gaveled recess.

2:50 p.m.: Spade in the anteroom puffing a cigarette. He was talking about Melody's testimony to P. Basil and his PI, Leonard Winter: "Wasn't she beautiful up there? Wasn't she beautiful?" His hands trembled.

Leonard Winter: "The cigarette dropped to his lap, and he began to sink downward." Spade was transported to Kern General Hospital, treated for another seizure.

VII

July 28: Spade back in court. Melody still on the stand. P. Basil backfiring with every shot. P. Basil: "Did your father ever deny you anything?"

Melody: "He denied me my mother."

P. Basil grilled Melody on her precocities: "Did your father object to you going out with older boys?"

Judge Bradshaw: "You have the right to attempt to establish bias, but you need to stop this line of questioning right here." P. Basil asked if Ella Mae ever asked her for forgiveness.

Melody: "I know very well why—she was forced." P. Basil tried everything to shake her. Fourteen-year-old Melody aced him with three terse replies. P. Basil insinuating Melody's account was excited, hence inaccurate: "Sir, I am not exaggerating. I saw what I saw." P. Basil implying inconsistent recall of the bedroom sequence on the evening of April 3: "I saw what I saw. I'm sorry. I can't change my story to please you." P. Basil suggesting contradiction in her testimony over the phone calls she overheard: "They just told me my mother had died. Am I supposed to get everything straight?"

Melody left the stand in tears. The jury noticed. Trial proceeded pro forma from there. Kit Nelson, meticulous, calling experts; P. Basil badgering same, filibustering technicalities, moving the trial at a glacial pace.

July 18: Kit Nelson called Kern County pathologist Dr. Robert Huntington. He prepped the moment with the introduction of twenty-nine exhibits, including photographs of bloodstains on furniture, doors, and windows, and on the headboard of the bed. He included pix of bloodstained sheets and pillowcases. Dr. Huntington testified about the te burn scars on Ella Mae's breasts. He said he experimented on his own arms. He held a burning cigarette against his own skin for a minute twenty seconds to replicate the lesions he noticed on Ella Mae.

July 20: The aforementioned Dr. Paul Kirk, renowned criminalist from the University of California, Berkeley, took the stand. He said, "Blood leaves a good record of how it was placed there." He talked about "impact areas." Dr. Kirk affirmed that the bloodstains on the bedspread were consistent with mutilation by a broomstick. Dr. Vincent Troy of Tehachapi Valley Hospital followed Dr. Kirk and recalled that Spade had told him that Ella Mae had fallen in the shower. Dr. Troy said he told Spade that Ella Mae was too badly damaged for a shower spill. He said Spade added that she had jumped out of a moving car days prior. In cross, P. Basil asked Dr. Troy if Ella Mae's injuries might be consistent with jumping from a speeding car. Dr. Troy: "It was obvious Mrs. Cooley's injuries did not result from falling in a shower or jumping from a car."

July 31: Nobody had read Spade his rights in the early morning of April 4. Deputy Harmon Cooper of the KCSD criminal division had recorded the interview. Spade blabbed without the presence of counsel. Two years before Miranda, three before Escobedo, and pre-OJ by three and a half decades—P. Basil Lambros had no grounds for exclusion. Kit Nelson played the rambling transcription to the jury with legal impunity. Highlights: Spade said "Rockets went off in my head" when he heard about the "free love cult." He said, "I hit things when I am hopelessly lost. I never hit people."

August 3: P. Basil called a parade of twelve witnesses—family retainers, neighbors in Willow Springs, a security guard from the Santa Monica Ballroom, a writer from the *Hoffman Hayride*, a PR guy from Burbank who flakked Some of Spade's radio and TV programs, and a gas jockey from Rosamond. They all testified to a negative: they had never witnessed Spade beating his wife.

August 6: Spade on the stand. He talked for forty-three minutes, never mentioning the events of April 3. P. Basil led him into sentimental reminiscences about a happy home and how much he loved his daughter.

"We got along wonderfully and didn't have any trouble until nine years ago," Spade said.

P. Basil: "What happened nine years ago?"

Spade: "A friend of mine, like my dearest brother…" Kit Nelson objected before Spade could impugn Roy Rogers by name. Judge Bradshaw sustained—he cautioned Spade to confine his remarks to troubles between himself and his wife, "not to details."

Spade: "There was another man involved—a famous figure. We certainly had some scraps over that cowboy star, but there were no beatings." Spade mentioned swatting Melody earlier in the year because she ran away from home. "I paddled my little daughter for the first and only time." In her testimony of July 27/28, Melody had stated that he had strapped her with hard leather and that she still bore the marks.

August 16, Wednesday: P. Basil Lambros wrapped up nine hours of closing arguments over two trial days. "Now it is up to the jury and up to God," he said, "and I think you can work together."

August 17, Thursday, 2:10 p.m.: Kit Nelson concluded remarks for the state. He took a shot at P. Basil's overly long summation. He said the defense attempted to "get the jury's eye off the case by ignoring evidence. It was a defense of nothingness…"

3:00 p.m.: Judge Bradshaw delivered instructions and handed the case to the jury. The jurors deliberated until near midnight before sequestering in the Hotel Tejon downtown.

August 18, Friday, twenty-ninth day of the trial: Most of the morning spent in court listening to the steno reread 314 pages of transcript and dealing with pathologists' and crime-scene technicians' testimonies plus Spade's taped statement to deputies in the Mojave substation.

The panel resumed deliberations after lunch and worked late into a second sequestered night.

August 19, Saturday, 2:20 p.m., verdict in: The jury had taken nineteen hours, fourteen minutes, to agree. The first ballot taken that morning, eleven to one; the next, after lunch, unanimous: Donnell Clyde Cooley guilty of murder by torture. Spade slumped in his seat when foreman Leonard Allison read the verdict, his face devoid of expression, the color of cold ashes from yesterday's fire.

August 22, Tuesday: Sanity phase in Judge Bradshaw's court. Likely to be a battle between bearded shrinks. P. Basil had retained five distinguished psychiatrists from Beverly Hills, Los Angeles, and San Francisco. Two had examined Spade in April. Kit Nelson had summoned four of his own. P. Basil counting on a five-on-four blitz, though one of his experts was in Massachusetts and another en route to Europe. P. Basil intended to ask Judge Bradshaw for a two-week continuance to guarantee testimony from all five.

The next day's *Bakersfield Californian* headline and subhead, Wednesday, August 23, 1961, a shocker:

COOLEY WHISKED TO PRISON TO BEGIN SENTENCE OF LIFE
DROPS INSANITY PLEA, WAIVES RULING BY JURY

P. Basil had met with Spade, Bobbie Bennett, and PI Leonard Winter in Kern County jail after the verdict on Saturday evening of August 19l. P. Basil directing full-on prep for the sanity phase—the core of his defense strategy all along. Spade read the shrinks' evaluations; boiled down, they viewed the subject as "paranoid, schizophrenic, and psychotic, with latent homosexual tendencies." Spade flipped. Doubtful that he could clinically define *paranoid*, *schizophrenic*, *psychotic*, or even *latent*, but he sure as hell could grip *homosexual*. Doubtful that Spade ever examined his interpersonal flaws for deeper motives. He was incensed that anyone would deduce latent fairy from homophobia, wife-beating, and habitual priapism. Anathematic slurs crashed through his skull: *queer, fruit, limp-wrist, butt-fucker*. He couldn't be reduced to those labels. Over counsel's vociferous objections, he redirected strategy.

Bobbie Bennett and P. Basil begged him to endure the sanity hearing. Spade envisioned the shrinks pulling him apart—the whole sordid mess on parade before his once-adoring public, complete with clinical judgments impugning his masculinity. Bobbie Bennett and P. Basil conceded the possibility but argued 75/25 the jury would rule diminished capacity and that no one would remember shrink jargon. They said he'd be confined to Atascadero but would skate free after ninety days. Spade held tight to his brittle ego. Nothing harder than the head of an American Okie. P. Basil, Bobbie Bennett, and Leonard Winters all tried. Nothing they said would loosen him even a notch. Spade was willing to roll the bones against green-room gas.

August 22: P. Basil in chambers moving for a continuance, but with a different reason now. He was buying time to change Spade's mind. Judge Bradshaw denied the motion but recessed until after lunch.

1:30 p.m.: P. Basil tried again. Judge Bradshaw allowed him to confer in the anteroom. P. Basil lobbied Spade until 3:12 p.m. No dice. He returned to court with his announcement: Spade would withdraw his guilty-by-reason-of-insanity plea. He would introduce no evidence during deliberations over penalty.

Judge Bradshaw to Spade: "and this is [in] accordance with your wishes?"

Spade: "It's been a long and horrible trial…It's been a very, very wretched thing. Ashamed ain't [the] word for how I feel…."

Judge Bradshaw excused the jury but permitted the jurors to remain in the box as spectators. Judge Bradshaw weighed arguments. No surprises. Kit Nelson asked for cyanide, and P. Basil pled for leniency.

3:30 p.m.: Judge Bradshaw rolled into his preamble on the tradition of an eye for an eye, dropping a hint about his inclination: "…but that has no place as we now view it…" He droned into a double negative, "…Mr. Cooley has been…a source of pleasure and entertainment for quite a segment of our people…and there is nothing in his life that indicates he would not be amenable to rehabilitation…" He ordered Spade to rise: "…It is the judgment of this court that you be committed to the state prison for life."

Spade went to Chino for processing. Sixties murderers routinely were confined in hard-time joints—Folsom or San Quentin. Spade started in San Quentin, but the California Adult Authority deemed the Big Q medically inadequate for heart patients. AA shipped him to Vacaville. Under California law, he would qualify for parole no earlier than summer '68.

In stir, Spade exceeded Judge Bradshaw's projections. Bobbie Bennett donated his rock-processing equipment and sent him a few instruments. Spade passed his time teaching lapidary to his fellow inmates. He gave music lessons. He fiddled with a prison band. He was a broken man plagued with remorse, but a model prisoner.

Eight years into his sentence, Bobbie Bennett and country singer Hank Snow lobbied for his freedom. Ronald Reagan was California's governor now. Spade had bolstered Ronnie's film career with regular appearances on the *Hoffman Hayride*. Right-wing, pro–death penalty Ronnie couldn't afford to align himself publically with a wife-beating murderer, but he remembered.

Bobbie Bennett knew Reagan from both entertainment and politics. Bobbie Bennett once swung show-business political weight. Hank Snow petitioned for parole in a letter countersigned by two hillbilly state governors. Ronald Reagan had long-range presidential-candidate aspirations. Hillbilly governors tended to sway votes in nominally Democratic states. Right-wing Ronnie pulled strings with the Adult Authority. The AA approved Spade for release on his sixtieth birthday, February 22, 1970.

November 24, 1969: Spade was furloughed for seventy-two hours to Oakland for a benefit concert at the Oakland Civic Auditorium sponsored by the Alameda County Sheriff's Deputies Association. Huge wingding with twenty-eight-hundred raucous country fans ready to romp. Chill Wills, raspy sidekick actor and comic singer, emceed. Chill Wills played Uncle Bawly in the 1956 movie *Giant*. Uncle Bawly pounded annoying "Clare de Lune" on the drawing-room organ at *Reata* ranch, asking Rock Hudson if the sun was over the yardarm so he could drink. Chill Wills was Beekeeper in

John Wayne's 1960 movie *The Alamo*. Chill Wills was best known as the voice of Francis the Talking Mule in the Donald O'Connor movie series of the 1950s.

Bobbie Bennett had supplied a dark-brown Nudie suit brocaded with fiddles, bows, and spade aces. She brought boots and a white Stetson. John Wayne, Jimmy Stewart, Jack Benny, LAPD chief Ed Davis, LA County sheriff Eugene Biscailuz, and mayor Sam Yorty all sent sprays of flowers. Spade glided into the spotlight. He thanked the deputies for allowing him to breathe free. The country fans applauded.

Spade Cooley glimpsed a future he thought he'd lost. He arced his bow at the twenty-four-piece band—including a few members from his former group—and riffed a twenty-five-minute set of his standards: "Fidoolin'," "Hayseed Heifetz," "Devil's Dream," "Hollywood Hoedown," and, finally, "Shame, Shame on You!" He was sweat-drenched. He bowed. He savored the moment before fading backstage into his dressing room. He never came out. Chill Wills and Bobbie Bennett found him sprawled on the floor, stricken with his final coronary.

Chill Wills, weak-kneed, faced the audience with a cracking voice: "Ladies and gentlemen, it, it's my sad job…to come out here…to say there ain't going to be a second half of any show. Our fiddling friend, Spade Cooley is, well, podnahs…he is dead."

The band twanged into the cowboy taps, "Goin' Home." Spectators sat disbelieving and hushed. Backstage, shock broke from wild tears. Spade Cooley, the only convicted murderer with a Walk of Fame star on Hollywood Boulevard, was gone at fifty-nine.

A bad long end for the King of Western Swing.

CHAPTER 4
BEL AIR: THE MANSON FAMILY

September 26, 1970: Southern California temperatures stifling in the high nineties. A drought year: 1.72 inches of rain since March 4, less than half of normal. So-Cal foliage as combustible as old kindling. The daily marine layer of fog and wind off the Pacific reversed by the dreaded Santa Anas—desert blasts whistling west, inverting intense heat into LA at speeds up to seventy miles per hour. Prime conditions for a big-ass inferno.

Something sparked it. Specific cause moot: anything could have. Flames rode the rampaging gales, crackling destruction east to west; 256 homes burned to the ground overnight. Fire raged through hills and canyons across forty thousand acres from the eastern San Fernando Valley to Malibu, brimstone smoke rising into the ozone. *LA Times*, the next day:

> ...The Sheriff's department said the fire also destroyed the Spahn ranch, one-time home of the [Charles] Manson family, several members of which are accused murderers of actress Sharon Tate and six others last summer...

For most of the charred remains, heartbreaking disaster and destruction: massive property damage and personal loss. For the tumbledown 511-acre Spahn Movie Ranch nestled into the base of the Santa Susana Mountains near the Simi Hills north of Chatsworth, purgative: hellfire catharsis from the Tate-LaBianca slaughters thirteen months earlier, fomented by freaky Charles Manson, staged at Spahn and carried out by depraved killers, his infamous "family."

Clock back to July 20, 1969: Literal high point of the final year of a tumultuous decade. NASA launched astronauts Neil Armstrong, Buzz Aldrin, and Michael Collins. *Apollo 11* landed on the surface of the moon, winning the interstellar sweepstakes with the Soviet Union. Neil Armstrong boot-printed the lunar plain, uttering, "One small step for man, one giant leap for mankind." Total triumph for the USA.

August 9, 1969, twenty days later: A waning crescent shed penumbra light on a nightmare slashing. Next day's page-one *LA Times*, Dial Torgeson byline:

'RITUALISTIC SLAYINGS'
SHARON TATE,
FOUR OTHERS MURDERED

Film star Sharon Tate, another woman and three men were found slain Saturday, their bodies scattered around a Benedict Canyon estate...

I

Spahn Ranch: A Western movie set gone to seed, a late-sixties rat's nest. Hippies squatted on Spahn like green flies buzzing horse apples. They pitched a hobo camp among weathered wooden sidewalks along a ramshackle stage set—a ghost-town saloon and general store. Communal living at its worst: epic filth, indiscriminate sex, rampant drug intake, bad hygiene, zero productivity, zero humor, chronic outbreaks of herpes and clap. Abandoned vehicles rusted in the sun across back acres of sand and scrub brush, inoperable from thrown rods and flat tires. Only one sled working: a yellow '58 Ford Fairlane belonging to ranch hand Johnny Swartz.

Just past midnight, August 9, 1969, Charles Manson glommed the Ford without asking Swartz. He gave orders to Charles "Tex" Watson, twenty-three. He told baby-boomer hippie chicks Patricia Krenwinkel, age twenty-one, and Susan Atkins and Linda Kasabian, both twenty, to dress dark and bring a change of clothes. He said, "Go with Tex and do what he says." Tex grabbed Krenwinkel. They dipped into a secret stash of crystal meth. Charlie's rule: only he could dispense drugs and control dosages. Tex and Pat violating the rule: zorched for the mission, edgy and aggressive. Tex drove. Tex had a gun, a High Standard nine-shot .22 long-barrel Buntline Special. He and the girls carried Buck knives. Tex brought wire cutters and a four-foot coil of triple-strand nylon rope.

He headed out Devonshire and ramped onto the 405 south. He rolled through the Valley past the 101 interchange, climbing Sepulveda Pass crossing into the LA Basin. Near the summit, he exited onto Mulholland Drive but lost his way around the winding roads fronting the 405. He eventually found Sunset and headed east. He turned into Bel Air on Benedict Canyon Drive and climbed between secluded mansions on hillsides dotted with palm trees and rioting with red bougainvillea.

He parked near an eight-foot wrought-iron security gate at 10050 W. Cielo Drive. Charlie had directed the play. He told the girls: "Do what Tex says." What Tex said, per Charlie: "Get all the money inside and kill everybody there."

Tex shinnied up a high-tension pole with his cutters. He snipped the phone lines. He backed the Ford down the hill and parked off to the side. He and the girls walked back up to 10050. They feared electricity or alarms on the driveway gate. They scaled the chain-link fence at a low spot on the embankment to the right. They saw headlights moving toward them. The girls hid in the bushes. Luckless Steve Parent, eighteen, driving a white Rambler, headed downhill toward the gate. Tex hailed him. Steve Parent was a junior college student from El Monte, a hi-fi/stereo wizard visiting the caretaker in the guesthouse. Tex shot Steve Parent four times and stabbed him repeatedly after he was dead.

Tex signaled the girls. They soft-stepped to the house. Tex climbed through an unsecured dining room window. He opened the front door. Susan Atkins and Patricia Krenwinkel padded in; Linda Kasabian stayed outside. Tex had slung the rope over his shoulder. They found Voytek Frykowski asleep on the couch. Tex woke him at gunpoint. Susan Atkins walked the hall, opening doors. Coffee heiress Abigail Folger reclined in one bedroom; jet-set hairdresser Jay Sebring and eight-and-a-half-month-pregnant actress Sharon Tate sat in another. Strangers wandering the property: common in a Hollywood party house. Menace never registered.

Susan Atkins reported back to Tex. Tex handed her a length of rope and told her to tie up Voytek Frykowski. Tex headed down the hall. He brought Abigail Folger back at knifepoint. Patricia Krenwinkel did the same with Jay Sebring and Sharon Tate. Tex ordered them to lie on their stomachs. Jay Sebring resisted. Tex shot him with the .22. Sharon Tate and Abigail Folger screamed.

Tex demanded money. Big-deal heist: seventy-two dollars plus credit cards. Tex told Susan Atkins to retie Frykowski with a bath towel. He noosed one end of the rope around the necks of Jay Sebring, Sharon Tate, and Abigail Folger. He tossed the other over an exposed ceiling beam and tugged it to the edge of asphyxiation. One of the victims: "What are going to do to us?"

Tex: "I'm the Devil, here to do the Devil's work. You're all going to die."

Tex told Susan Atkins to kill Voytek Frykowski. Frykowski broke loose. He struggled with Atkins. She stabbed him multiple times in the leg. He tumbled outside. Tex gun-whipped Frykowski's head, breaking pieces off the grip, and stabbed him to death. Inside, Abigail Folger wriggled free and bolted out the front door.

Patricia Krenwinkel caught her and struggled to subdue her. Tex finished off Jay Sebring. He moved off the porch toward

Abigail Folger, who was clawing at Krenwinkel. Atkins was holding on to pregnant Sharon Tate. Sharon Tate shrieked, begging for her unborn baby's life. Tex stabbed Abigail Folger in the belly. Tex told Krenwinkel to kill Sharon Tate. Sharon Tate keened death-throe decibels. Pat Krenwinkel slashed her until the screaming stopped. Tex ripped his blade into her upper torso.

Tex, Atkins, and Krenwinkel turned to Abigail Folger, out on the lawn dying. Ghoulish Tex stabbed her again multiple times. Voytek Frykowski was nearby, also dead. He had been shot twice, hit on the head thirteen times, and stabbed fifty-one times. Tex kicked him in the skull. Tex sent Patricia Krenwinkel back inside to write something "that will shock the world." Krenwinkel dipped the Frykowski towel in Sharon Tate's blood and in large letters on the inside of the front door wrote: *PIG*.

They exited Cielo just past one in the morning and changed in the car. They dumped the gun and bloody kill clothes at intervals off the road into Benedict Canyon on the Valley side. Two miles down, they veered off to a house in a cul-de-sac to rinse the blood with a garden hose. The homeowner, Rudolph Weber, flashed a beam and chased them off. They were back at Spahn by two in the morning.

Charlie wasn't happy with their recap. He was angry that Linda Kasabian had failed to participate. He judged the Cielo massacre as sloppy. He thought Tex had caused useless panic by telling the victims that they would be killed. Charlie preached gibberish about murder killing only the diseased ego and releasing the soul into its purity—a beautiful thing that had to be done right. Charlie based his beliefs on someone else committing murder and himself avoiding death. The killers went to bed. Charlie drove back to Cielo. He rearranged the crime scene. He dropped a random pair of prescription eyeglasses on the living room floor—false clue for pigs.

Next night, same drill, but with a slightly different crew, also in Johnny Swartz's Fairlane. Still Tex, Susan Atkins, Linda Kasabian, and Patricia Krenwinkel. This time, Charlie in charge, followed by stupid Steve Grogan, seventeen, and Leslie Van Houten, twenty-one. Charlie alternated driving with Linda Kasabian. They wound around Griffith Park to Waverly Street in Los Feliz. They stopped at a Spanish stucco on a grassy slope.

3301 Waverly belonged to Leno and Rosemary LaBianca, prominent citizens. Leno had followed his father into the grocery business. He was CEO of a four-franchise chain of stores in the Pasadena area called Gateway Markets. Rosemary had bootstrapped herself from an orphan's beginnings in Arizona. She co-owned a dress/gift boutique on N. Figueroa off the Arroyo Seco Parkway. She had done well trading stocks.

The LaBiancas had just returned from Lake Isabella east of Bakersfield, their fifteen-foot inboard still hitched to Leno LaBianca's '68 Thunderbird. Susan Atkins had fallen asleep in the Fairlane's backseat. She woke to see Charlie slipping up the driveway. He carried a gun, a Buck knife, and leather thongs. Some minutes later he returned. He sent Tex, Krenwinkel, and Van Houten to the house. He said he had bound the occupants with deer-hide thongs and left them feeling calm.

Charlie told them to "paint a picture more gruesome than anyone [has] ever seen." He told them to hitchhike back to Spahn when they finished. He left with Steve Grogan, Kasabian, and Atkins. Charlie had lifted a wallet thick with credit cards from Rosemary LaBianca. He told Linda Kasabian that they'd dump it on a ghetto street. He said blackie would try to use the cards. He said cops would nab him and profile Black Panthers for the murders. Charlie's logic often took huge leaps. They stopped at a Standard station next door to a Denny's in Sylmar. Charlie dipped into Denny's for milkshakes and forgot about the Panthers. Kasabian dropped the wallet in a toilet tank in the gas station's ladies' room.

Charlie wanted more. Kasabian driving. Charlie riding shotgun. Atkins and Grogan in back. They wound around the beach near Venice. Charlie recalled a few weeks back: Linda Kasabian and Sandra Good hitchhiking, picked up by an actor named Saladin Nader who lived in Venice. Charlie told her to drive by

Nader's apartment building, 1101 Ocean Front Walk, and park the Ford. He handed her a Buck knife and Steve Grogan a gun. He outlined: Linda Kasabian knocking at the door, slitting Saladin Nader's throat as he opened it, while Steve Grogan shot him. Linda Kasabian balked: "I'm not you, Charlie, I can't just kill someone."

Charlie amended. He handed the blade to Atkins. He ushered them upstairs four floors. He left, saying they could thumb a ride home when they finished. Kasabian led them to 403. Deliberately. Saladin Nader lived one floor above, in 501. She knocked. Susan Atkins and Steve Grogan could see: The citizen who answered was not Saladin Nader. Linda Kasabian said she must have forgotten where he lived. Steve Grogan had the IQ of a broccoli. He didn't care. Susan Atkins was off her rocker: she took a dump on the hallway floor. Charlie had left them with no plan B. They buried the gun in the beach sand and hitched back to Chatsworth.

Inside 3301 Waverly, Leslie Van Houten and Patricia Krenwinkel dragged Rosemary LaBianca, bound with thongs, a pillowcase over her head, into a bedroom. Tex stayed back to slash Leno. Rosemary heard Leno yelling and struggled in panic futilely against the thongs.

Van Houten and Krenwinkel held her down. Muffled screams escaped her hood. Patricia Krenwinkel stabbed at her. Rosemary fought and lost. Leslie Van Houten slashed her repeatedly. In blood on the north living room wall, they wrote "Death to all Pigs." On the South wall: "Rise." Misspelled on the refrigerator door: "Healter Skelter." Patricia Krenwinkel found a carving fork in the kitchen. She plunged it into Leno LaBianca's belly. It wobbled like a metronome. She watched with fascination. With a steak knife, she etched "War" in stomach skin below the fork.

The killers showered. They scrounged the LaBianca refrigerator. They sat in the dining room, eating watermelon slices washed down with chocolate milk. Clean and fed, they hitched to Spahn. Seven murders in twenty-four hours: most of the known kills the Manson family racked up in the bloody summer of 1969.

II

10050 Cielo Drive: Owned by Hollywood A-lister Rudi Altobelli, agent to actors and musicians, including Henry Fonda and Katherine Hepburn. In 1968, Altobelli leased the place to twenty-seven-year-old music producer Terry Melcher—only son of Doris Day—and his girlfriend, actress Candice Bergen. Melcher and Bergen moved out in February 1969. The Polish film director Roman Polanski moved in with his pregnant wife, Sharon Tate. Rudi Altobelli stayed in the guesthouse. Leading up to August 8, Altobelli was in Rome. He employed nineteen-year-old William Garretson as a live-in caretaker.

8:30 a.m., August 9: Bodies found by housekeeper Winifred Chapman when she reported for work. She freaked over the blood and bodies. She fumbled her fingers trying to dial 911 from a dead phone line. She ran screaming toward neighbors at 10070, who didn't answer, and 10090, who did. The neighbor kid at 10090, a Boy Scout police cadet, called it in, noting the time: 8:33 a.m.

9:14 a.m.: Two West LA patrol units blew in, lights and sirens. A third WLA sector car arrived. Beverly Hills PD swooped in. Officers secured the crime scene and noticed the guesthouse on the left, past the pool, a hundred away. They saw William Garretson in profile through a sheer window curtain.

They kicked their way in, guns drawn. Probable cause: Garretson only one alive on the property. They yanked him handcuffed past the carnage. Garretson: disoriented, stumbled over answers to aggressive questions. He misidentified the dead bodies. The murders occurred within eye and earshot of the guesthouse. He said he saw nothing. He said he'd amped his music the night before. He claimed he blasted rock tunes until sunrise. The West LA cops saw the volume button on his stereo tuned midway, only to 4 or 5. They doubted his story. They thought they had their killer. Officer Robert Burbridge radioed in: five dead, suspect in custody.

The crime scene gave up forensic evidence but no clues: lengths of three-strand nylon rope; eyeglasses belonging to none of the victims, Roman Polanski, Rudi Altobelli, or William Garretson; a piece of a handgun gun grip; bullet fragments from a .22; twenty-five sets of fingerprints; a blood-spattered Buck knife near Sharon Tate's body. Evidence implicated no one, including the suspect. They carded Garretson's prints: no match. Scientific investigation division (SID) techs found no blood on him or his garments, and no wounds, scratches, bruises, foreign fibers, or skin on his person.

Detectives transported Garretson to Parker Center and strapped him to the black box. Steel needles flatlined all key questions. They fluttered inconclusively about whether he had seen or heard the slaughter. Lie detector results: inadmissible as evidence, but credible to the cops. They booked him a night in the West LA jail pro forma but released him in the morning. He might have been stoned, deafened by his tunes, or skulking from fear, but he hadn't murdered anyone.

First-step homicide question: *Cui bono?* Who benefits? Flash answer from the Tate crime scene: *nemo*—nobody. Cops stalled over easy assumptions. Murders committed by friends, relatives, and acquaintances: zip. Murders motivated by sex, greed, or revenge: zilch. They had rich victims with no known enemies. No evidence of sexual assault. Stock solutions leading nowhere. Cops grasping. SID found traces of drug use at Cielo. No shit. Drugs in the Hollywood fast lane in the 1960s? In that era, simpler to find celebs who refrained. Cops worked up a bogus hypothesis: big-money drug deal gone bad.

The cops denied a link between Cielo Drive and Waverly Place, except to concede a copycat possibility. They cited proximity of place and time. Leno LaBianca was Italian. He played the ponies at Hollywood Park and Santa Anita. He lost big. First guess, mindless stereotype: Mafia loan sharks snuffing a deadbeat. The Tate and LaBianca detectives split into separate investigations, perspectives crippled by their preposterous presuppositions and by law-enforcement realities unique to Southern California.

LAPD: Third-largest law-enforcement entity in the nation, behind New York City and Chicago. Number four? The Los Angeles County sheriff's department. Statistic holding over time: LA County accounts for 40 percent of all crime committed in the state of California. LA County, population near ten million, runs from Kern County to Orange County, from Santa Monica to San Bernardino: four thousand square miles, taking in eighty-eight municipalities, thirty-nine unincorporated communities, fifty-three "census designated places," and sixty-five ghost towns, plus parts of the 700,746-acre Angeles National Forest.

City and county cops blurred boundaries. The city of Los Angeles itself, with 469 square miles of districts and neighborhoods and a population of nearly four million, weaves city limits in, out, and around the other eighty-seven towns. To protect and serve, LAPD employs plus or minus ten thousand officers organized into twenty-one divisional station houses under four bureau commands.

Forty-six towns in LA County have independent departments, among them—Burbank, Beverly Hills, Santa Monica, Whittier... The sheriff's department (LASD) commands the rest: forty-two municipalities, ranging in size from one to one hundred square miles and in population to 177,000. A few incorporated independents such as Compton and West Hollywood contract with the LASD. The LASD runs the county jail and provides bailiffs for the superior court. The LASD is staffed by roughly eighteen thousand people: nine thousand sworn deputies, eight thousand civilian personnel, and nine hundred reserve officers. The sheriff's department oversees more than forty-two hundred civilian volunteers.

Competing bureaucracies too large and politically complex to contain. Too many cracks; too much falling through. Too many hidey-holes. The whole sprawling multimunicipal mess: acutely susceptible to mismanagement, corruption, and backbiting. The departments share a corrosive range-war history. They maintain a distance that was prominent during the Tate/LaBianca investigations. No one from the LAPD bothered to ask the sheriff's homicide department whether similar MOs had shown on their docket, and they should have.

July 31, 1969: LASD investigated a murder in Topanga Canyon. A man named Gary Hinman had been stabbed and suffocated, his left ear sliced off and sewn back on with dental floss. The words "Political Piggy" were scripted in blood on an interior wall. Hinman's '65 VW Bus and Fiat station wagon were missing. The sheriffs BOLO'd the plates. Two days before Tate-LaBianca, August 6, a California Highway Patrol (CHP) cruiser spotted the Fiat on the shoulder of Highway 101 near San Luis Obispo. The driver was inside, asleep; patrolmen ID'd him Robert Beausoleil, twenty-four, from Santa Barbara.

They called in his license and the vehicle registration. It came back hot, belonging to the murdered Gary Hinman. They cuffed Beausoleil and searched the car. They found a bloody knife in the Fiat's wheel well. They saw spatter on Beausoleil's shirt. The blood types on the knife and shirt would match Gary Hinman's blood. Hinman's house had been wiped, but not very well. Print techs black-lighted the walls. They raised finger and palm impressions: Bobby Beausoleil's.

August 10, 1969: Twenty-four hours after the Tate atrocities. Bobby Beausoleil jugged in the LA County jail in the Hall of Justice building on Broadway and Temple—four blocks north of Parker Center, at 150 N. Los Angeles Street. LASD homicide detectives noted that Beausoleil lived at Spahn Ranch with a band of hippies who followed a charismatic strange-o named Charles Manson. Sheriff's sergeant Paul Whitely walked the four blocks. He talked to LAPD Tate detective Jess Buckles about crime-scene similarities between Hinman and Tate-LaBianca. Buckles dismissed it, said the murders were dope related. He asked no questions.

October 13, 1969: Sixty-plus days without a sniff. The Hinman-LaBianca connection recurred. LASD detectives combing for Hinman witnesses learned that Bobby Beausoleil had a pregnant girlfriend named Kitty Lutesinger, age seventeen. They called in an APB. Inyo County SD buzzed a quick return.

Three days earlier, in the Mojave Desert, a strike force composed of Inyo County sheriff's deputies, the CHP, and national park rangers had rousted hippies at a property called Barker Ranch—a cluster of crude prospector dwellings situated five miles up the slopes of the Panamint Range, at the western rim of Death Valley. Barker was as remote as the other side of the moon, accessible by a rock-strewn goat path across the Panamint called Goler Wash. Nearest civilization: Ballarat, a ghost town, twenty-two miles southeast along a gravel road, population two—the husband-and-wife proprietors of a general store selling beer and jerky to desert rats in ATVs.

The strike force was acting on information pertinent to arson committed one month earlier in Death Valley Monument National Park. On September 9, someone had set fire to a big-rig front-scoop, called a Michigan Loader. Ranger Dick Powell followed tire tracks through Goler Wash to Barker. He spotted a disabled dune buggy and a red Toyota Land Cruiser with California plates. Powell relayed the plate numbers to James Pursell, at the CHP's one-man Death Valley resident post in Furnace Creek.

The license plates had been issued to a Dodge, whose owner had reported them stolen. The Land Cruiser matched the description of a missing Hertz vehiclel from Encino, rented with a credit card stolen during a residential burglary. Subsequent inquiry uncovered reports from prospectors of unfriendly longhairs residing at Barker.

October 10 and 12, 1969: In two separate incursions, the three agencies rounded up twenty-four hippies, including a freaky dude, thirty-four, five foot two, 130 pounds, scraggly, with black weasel eyes, dressed in buckskins, who identified himself alternately as "Jesus Christ," "God," and "the Devil."

Jim Pursell found him in the bathroom of the stone and mortar house, corkscrewed into the vanity under a wash basin. His long hair gave him up. He had shut the cabinet door on loose ends that showed. The hippies were handcuffed and transported in truck beds over back roads three hours to the Inyo County jail in Independence. They were detained for grand theft auto and arson on a government reservation.

At Barker on October 12, 1969, two young women emerged from the bushes a few miles west of the road and flagged down deputies. Stephanie Schram and pregnant Kitty Lutesinger identified the Jesus/God/Devil guy as Charles Manson. They said they were runaways from the Manson family, afraid for their lives. Deputies clicked on Lutesinger. They transported both women to Independence and placed them on an LASD hold.

The LASD knew about Manson already. Acting on a tip (by wrangler Shorty Shea), deputies had raided Spahn one week after Tate and LaBianca, August 16. They arrested twenty-six hippies: eleven men and fifteen women, including Charles Manson. They confiscated seven rifles, a .43 caliber automatic pistol, and a 9mm machine gun. They towed off an aggregation of disassembled VWs and Jeeps. Everybody who was hauled in eventually was cut loose— no direct ties to the stolen cars or weapons.

Sheriff's sergeants Whitely and Guenther drove 225 miles up State Route 395 along the desolate eastern Sierra. They talked to Kitty Lutesinger at the Inyo County courthouse. Lutesinger told them what she had heard at Spahn (she couldn't remember from whom): that Charles Manson had sent Bobby Beausoleil and a girl, Susan Atkins, to Gary Hinman's house to appropriate money. She said a fight had broken out, and Hinman was dead. She said Atkins was one of the Manson women who were jailed in Independence, booked as "Sadie May Glutz."

Susan Atkins, desperate for attention and detached from reality, confirmed all details, apparently unconcerned that she was confessing to first-degree murder. Atkins's account: Charlie had heard that Gary Hinman had inherited $21,000. Charlie believed he was entitled to a sizable share. Hinman balked—the 21k probably never existed. Bobby Beausoleil tore into him. Gary Hinman fought back. Beausoleil slashed him. Beausoleil and Atkins tied him up. They tortured him for two days. He suffocated when they pressed a pillow over his face. Bobby Beausoleil hot-wired the VW and Fiat. The killers drove themselves back to Chatsworth.

Whitely and Guenther arrested Susan Atkins on suspicion of penal code 187, unlawful killing of a human being. They released Kitty Lutesinger to her parents, who had driven in from their Simi Valley horse ranch. They booked Atkins at the San Dimas substation and shuttled her to Sybil Brand Institute, LA County's women's lockup in City Terraces, East Los Angeles.

October 20, 1969: LASD dicks stuck on a detail. Kitty Lutesinger said that Susan Atkins rambled about stabbing a man three or four times in the leg. Gary Hinman wasn't stabbed, but on Cielo Drive, Voytek Frykowski was. Whitely contacted Jess Buckles. Buckles still not enthused. Tate detectives didn't interview Lutesinger for another eleven days.

The Tate and LaBianca detectives were myopic. They burned phone lines and wore out shoe soles and tire tread for three months. They filed reports. They followed leads into dead ends. By the estimate of LAPD chief Edward M. Davis, between August 9 and December 1, they interviewed more than six hundred relevant parties and ran up 8,750 man-hours of police work with nothing to show. Pushed by reporters, Parker Center brass dissembled with stats.

They stressed hard work, citing "tremendous progress." They elided the obvious: no smoking scoops or imminent arrests. The murders stoked rumors of madmen with celebrity hit lists targeting rank Sinatra and Steve McQueen, among others. LA big shots nervous: killer cult on the loose. Boom time for gun shops, dog breeders, and security specialists. Sales skyrocketed for sidearms and Rottweilers. Home-alarm installation orders backed up to Christmas.

In their defense, the cops in LA and everywhere had fallen behind the curve of fast-acting counterculture convolution. They couldn't conceive of a creature such as Charles Manson and the evil that metastasized through his skull.

III

Toxins bubbled in Charlie's makeup from birth. His mother, Kathleen Maddox, by many accounts a hooker, was at least was young and loose. They had Charlie when she was sixteen. Charlie: unplanned and unwanted, paternity pinned on a grifter named Scott from her hometown of Ashland, Kentucky. Scott was never in the military, but his first name was Colonel. Zany hillbillies tagging children from God knows what impulse.

Kathleen married William Manson before she gave birth. She charged Colonel Darwin Scott with "bastardy" (the crime of begetting an illegitimate child). The judge fined C. D. Scott twenty-five dollars and gaveled down five dollars a month in child support. Colonel Scott forked over the twenty-five but stiffed Kathleen on monthly support. He took an early powder. Charlie never knew a father.

Charlie was born in Cincinnati General Hospital in 1934, labeled for weeks as "no name Maddox," eventually Charles Milles Maddox, changed to Charles Milles Manson. Kathleen divorced William Manson in 1937 and went on the prowl. One night in 1939, in Charleston, West Virginia, she picked up a drunk and lured him into a hotel room. The drunk flashed a wad. Kathleen excused herself, went into the hall, and phoned her older brother, Luther. Luther tiptoed in and pistol-whipped the guy. Brother and sister grabbed his roll. They were caught and charged—Luther with armed robbery and assault, Kathleen as an accessory. Luther: ten years of hard time in the state pen at Moundsville; Kathleen, five in the women's wing of the same Gothic joint.

Charlie was shuttled off to relatives. He lived a year in Ashland with his grandmother, Nancy Maddox, Kathleen's mother, a Bible-thumping Nazarene. Nancy sent him on to Kathleen's sister Glenna and her husband, Bob Thomas, in McMechen, West Virginia, near the Ohio River. Charlie lived with the Thomases from the first through fourth grades. Uncle Bob was a hard-ass, a blue-collar redneck. He thought Charlie was whiny. Charlie's first-grade teacher was a heartless old bat named Mrs. Varner, a cliché spinster schoolmarm.

Mrs. Varner wasn't partial to simpering little Charlie. She humiliated him by broadcasting details of Kathleen's stay in Moundsville. Charlie, in tears, complained of his treatment to Uncle Bob and Aunt Glenna. Uncle Bob scorned him. Object lesson: Uncle Bob picked a dress—too big—from Charlie's cousin JoAnn's closet and made Charlie wear it to school the next day.

Charlie's formative years were beyond fucked up. Go figure: he turned into a crappy kid. He lied, stole, and cheated. He could beam a smile when he wanted something, but mostly he was defiant. He flashed a creepy temper. He was fascinated with knives and guns. His only positive interest, music. His only outlet for same: belting out hosannas with scowling Nazarenes.

1942: Kathleen on parole, reprieved Charlie from West Virginia kin. Mother and son lived in flophouses in Charleston while Kathleen worked menial jobs and resumed fast living with numerous men. They drifted to Indianapolis, Indiana. Kathleen was conflicted. She no doubt loved her Charlie at some level, but she liked to carouse, and she was beginning to realize that her eight-year-old boy was an incorrigible liar, thief, and truant, a burden who was pulling her apart.

1943: Kathleen met an ex-GI named Lewis at an Alcoholics Anonymous meeting. Kathleen had a knack for picking winners. Lewis stumbled over AA's twelve steps to sobriety as if his shoelaces were tied together. He couldn't stay off the hooch. He couldn't hold a job. He had no ambitions for stepfatherhood. The next few years, the three of them were a dysfunctional mess. They had moved back to McMechen. Lewis wanted Kathleen but resented Charlie. Kathleen wanted a productive husband and an obedient child. Charlie wanted family stability and acceptance. They all were destined for serious disappointment.

Kathleen rationalized a plan. She would park Charlie and reform Lewis. She and the new Lewis would reclaim Charlie and raise him right. She tried pawning Charlie off on relatives. No dice. She tried foster care. Same. Finally, she placed him in the Gibault School for Boys in Terre Haute, a cross between a parochial school and a reformatory, founded by the Knights of Columbus. He lasted ten months before wandering off to find Kathleen. Still stuck with Lewis, she had no place for Charlie.

Charlie drifted back to Indiana. He robbed stores for spending money. He wasn't much of a criminal at age thirteen—or later. He was caught and processed through the juvenile center in Indianapolis. He escaped the next day. He was caught again. The court sent him to Boys Town in Omaha, Nebraska. Boys Town followed the beliefs of its founder, Father Edward Flanagan (d. 1948). Boys Town: an orphanage, not a jail. Boys Town had no walls, no fences. Father Flanagan believed that "There are no bad boys."

Charlie was a bad boy who saw fenceless fields as an exit sign. He left after four days with another kid, Blackie Nielson. The two committed armed robberies on the way to Blackie's uncle's hometown of Peoria, Illinois. The uncle, a Fagin, used the boys' small stature to gain second-story access to grocery stores. They were nabbed after the second of two break-ins. The court sent Charlie to reform school, this one with walls: the Indiana Boys School. Charlie rode out puberty as the catamite of bigger kids.

1951: Charlie, age seventeen, escaped with two other boys. The trio was caught in a stolen car in Utah, apparently en route to California, paying their way by sticking up gas stations. They had crossed state lines in stolen cars, a violation of the federal Dyer Act, an offense that sent him to the National Training School for Boys in Washington, DC. Rehab: a futile concept in the 1950s, and probably always, the term itself ironic. Rehabilitation defined: to "restore to a former condition."

Charlie's former condition was constant rejection, ongoing abuse, and incipient rage. By then, Charlie had the civil instincts of a wolverine. He was labeled by reformatory shrinks as "aggressively anti-social." In 1951, in minimum security at Natural Bridges Honor Camp in Petersburg, Virginia, less than a month before a parole hearing, Charlie held a razor blade to the throat of a meeker inmate and sodomized him. Instead of parole, he landed in a harsh federal reformatory located in Chillicothe, Ohio.

In Chillicothe, he detoured for a time toward personal rehab. He took classes and approached literacy. He achieved what amounted to a seventh-grade education. He scored a 121 on the IQ test (previously tested at 109). He learned a few skills while working on automobile engines. He paroled out at age nineteen to West Virginia. He bounced between Wheeling, where his mother and Lewis had moved, and McMechen, where Bill and Glenna Thomas lived and where Granny Maddox had relocated from Kentucky. He worked odd jobs. He met and married a local girl named Rosalie Willis. He acquired an acoustic guitar and taught himself the basics.

1955: Rosalie pregnant; money tight. Charlie reverting. He stole cars across the river in Ohio and unloaded them wherever he found a market, one time as far away as Florida. Kathleen had separated from Lewis by this time and had moved to Southern California.

In July, Charlie heisted a '53 Mercury in Bridgeport, Ohio. He and Rosalie drove it to Los Angeles to see his mother. Kathleen lived in one of LA's homogenous two-story stucco apartment buildings. Charlie and Rosalie moved in. Charlie worked shitty jobs and tooled around town in his hot Merc, oblivious to the LAPD's obsession with rousting out-of-state crooks. In September, a sector unit spotted his Ohio plates. Arrested again. During arraignment, Charlie spilled out a sob story of his tormented upbringing.

The judge ordered a psychiatric work-up. The shrink, Dr. Edwin McNiel, thought Charlie a bad bet for leniency but allowed that a pregnant wife might make a difference. On November 7, the judge granted probation subject to a court appearance in February 1956 to face Dyer Act charges for the sled he stole in Ohio and drove to Florida. Charlie figured the system would plunk him back inside. He and Rosalie split to Indianapolis, where Charlie Jr. was born.

Charlie had a gift for arrest. The Indiana cops nabbed him in March and returned him to California. He was twenty-one. The judge sentenced him to three years in the Terminal Island federal penitentiary in San Pedro Harbor. Rosalie hung in for a while. She and Charlie Jr. stayed with Kathleen, visiting Charlie on Sundays. Kathleen showed up alone one visiting day after a few months. She informed Charlie that Rosalie had moved in with another man, filed for divorce, and moved back to West Virginia.

Penned up with Mann Act (crossing state lines for lewd purposes) violators, among other federal prisoners, Charlie gravitated toward the pimps. The calling answered to a voice inside him. Pimps possess women as property and turn them out for profit. Women under a pimp's control do not abandon or desert them. The pimps schooled Charlie on methods for reshaping girls who had hardcore daddy issues. They advised alternating beatings with episodes of reassuring affection. They suggested methods for severing the girls from all contact with family and friends and for hooking them on drugs, eventually making them totally dependent on the pimp.

Terminal Island offered self-improvement classes. One of them: Dale Carnegie's 1936 correspondence course called *How to Win Friends and Influence People.* Dale Carnegie was a salesman, a prairie-state huckster, the kind Sinclair Lewis imagined when he wrote *Elmer Gantry.* Carnegie: "Begin in a friendly way." He suggested: "Let the other person feel the idea is his." Dale Carnegie resonated with Charlie. Dale Carnegie was smooth. Dale Carnegie packaged false sincerity as a first step along the road to success. Charlie never finished the course, but he picked off what he could use.

1958: Charlie made parole. He lived with his mother and worked menial jobs. Fact is, Charlie worked only to shuck his parole officer with proof of employment while moonlighting felonies. In the next year, Charlie committed crimes against people and property. He pimped. He shoplifted. He stole cars. He became a serial Dyer Act and Mann Act offender. He forged signatures on government checks he stole from residential mailboxes. He was caught for forgery of a treasury check in May 1959.

One of his whores, nineteen-year-old Leona Rae Musser, informed Charlie's probation officer that she was pregnant by Charlie. She begged for his release, promising they would marry and Charlie would reform while they were raising their child. Same drill as before: a court-ordered psych work-up (in fact, with the same shrink who had examined him four years earlier). Dr. Edwin McNiel iterated that Charlie belonged behind bars. Leona Rae turned on the tears. She was convincing. The judge sentenced Charlie to ten years suspended sentence plus probation. No one in authority thought to have Leona tested. No hurry to wed—she wasn't pregnant.

December 1959: Charlie expanded. He escorted Leona and another whore to Lordsburg, New Mexico. Charlie never learned. The three were arrested and charged under the Mann Act. Charlie countered. He married Leona; wives couldn't turn state's evidence.

Charlie made bail but with his record couldn't foresee leniency. He skipped. Alone. Leona, now pregnant, faced federal prostitution charges on her own.

Charlie miscalculated. By law, Leona couldn't be forced to testify, but she could on her own volition. She cut a deal, verifying that Charlie had crossed state lines to pander her and others in New Mexico. Charlie's record corroborated. The judge revoked probation and issued a bench warrant. Charlie lasted less than a month on the run. In Laredo, Texas, cops arrested a sixteen-year-old hooker. The hooker, one in Charlie's string, shopped him for a lighter sentence.

June 1, 1960: Charlie extradited back to LA. Three weeks later, a federal judge sentenced him to finish his ten-year term in prison.

He strung out appeals for a year and even managed to have the Mann Act charges dropped, but by the summer of 1961, he was transported to McNeil Island in the dank climate of Puget Sound. At McNeil, Charlie found fresh inspiration in L. Ron Hubbard's *Dianetics: The Modern Science of Mental Health*, a new-age pseudoreligious formula for elevating self-esteem. Hubbard called it Scientology. Perfect. Dale Carnegie had furnished tools for manipulating hookers— "be friendly; let it be their idea." L. Ron Hubbard now provided more. Boiled down, Dianetics coins jargon and brainwashes converts into believing their issues are illusory, thereby wiping out the square-john burdens of guilt and remorse.

At McNeil, Charlie also met Alvin "Creepy" Karpis. Karpis was a Depression-era killer and bank robber, part of the murderous Barker Gang. Karpis was a lifer in Alcatraz, serving twenty-six years until 1962 when the government closed down the Rock and shipped him to McNeil. Creepy Karpis had what Charlie wanted: advanced guitar aptitude. Charlie had caught fire from 1960s music he'd seen/heard on radio and television at McNeil, especially the Beatles. Charlie obsessed over the Beatles phenomenon. Alvin

Karpis tutored Charlie. Charlie wrote tunes. Charlie fantasized about Beatles-type fame. Creepy Karpis neglected to tell Charlie that his music stunk.

March, 1967: federal prisons overcrowded. Charlie kicked loose, a bad candidate for freedom. Charlie knew it. He pleaded to stay. Prison records acknowledged that he had "deep-seated personality problems," but the system released him anyway. He walked off the island a truly dangerous man: a maladjusted pimp with a head full of half-ass beliefs and zero conscience. At thirty-three, he held all authority in contempt. He could scam teenyboppers, parole officers, and liberal judges. Underneath, he ranked among the most megalomaniacal creatures in literature and history—Iago, Rasputin, Adolph Hitler—in that he answered only to the bell of his own rapacious ego.

IV

Charlie entered Terminal Island during the Wonder Bread era of *American Graffiti*. He exited McNeil in the Summer of Love during the excitement from the Age of Aquarius. All his years inside, he sharpened feral, not civil, traits. Charlie was oblivious to current events and the sweep of time. He couldn't tell the difference between the baby boom and a sonic boom, but he was about to find out. The Manson family all would be baby boomers. The worst person they possibly could meet was Charles Manson.

He lived day to day upon release, with no plans. He pondered landing spots. He had phone numbers from inmate acquaintances. He made calls. One contact suggested Berkeley. Sounded good. He had paroled out in Los Angeles. He received permission instead for transfer to the San Francisco Bay Area. He headed north lacking current awareness of the world outside the gates.

Mid-1960s: total global goat fuck. Big problems. No solutions. The social order in the USA under fire. Political assassinations. Race riots. Riots on campuses. Civil dissidence. Wars abroad.

Force of law, traditional values, political platitudes, and religious bromides powerless to push back the onrushing chaos.

Politics reconfigured for the jet age. One world now. Trouble somewhere: trouble everywhere. Berlin, Korea, Indochina, the Congo, Cuba—hot spots choosing sides, communist or capitalist, dictatorship or democracy, both military camps desperate to exercise influence enforced by nuclear threat. Supreme ETO commander from World War II general Dwight David Eisenhower hit the White House in a landslide. Hot war transitioned to cold. Cold Somehow scarier under the prospect of mutual annihilation. Ike's secretary of state, John Foster Dulles, invented "brinkmanship," the strategy of stalemating Moscow with threats of H-bomb aggression. Citizens in both countries scared shitless: Dr. Strangelove felt more like truth than movie fiction.

Boomers exacerbated everything. Sixties kids: the most populous, pampered, and publicized generation of all time. Exploited by Madison Avenue, monitored by Dr. Spock, influenced by Harvard dope professor Dr. Timothy Leary, and studied by sociologists, psychologists, anthropologists, sexologists, and pharmacologists, they sang, smoked, snorted, spiked, protested, marched, sat in, tuned in, and dropped out. They were outraged by the material complacency of their 1950s upbringings. They levered anger against the Vietnam War. They opposed military conscription and were empathetic to the oppressed. They revolted against norms. They barged into politics, music, and culture. They felt entitled. They made a difference. They were a mess.

Charlie dropped into their midst. He thumbed his way from McNeil with thirty-five dollars in release money, a cardboard suitcase, and his guitar. He trolled Telegraph Avenue, his pimp's antenna fine-tuned to signals from needy women. He met a drab UC Berkeley assistant librarian from Eau Claire, Wisconsin, twenty-six-year-old Mary Brunner. He pitched pseudohip drivel, amalgamated by Dale Carnegie, L. Ron Hubbard, and the Beatles. Mary

Brunner was spellbound. Charlie felt the intake, the first rush of messianic delusion. He pushed it. He was crashing in a parole board–certified flophouse. He panhandled for pocket change. Mary Brunner had an apartment and a salary. Charlie leeched a large share of both. Charlie was a predatory recidivist, not a hippie. He was apolitical via indifference, a racist and sexist by temperament, not doctrine, and he was sensing opportunity arranged by counterculture dupes.

He found Haight-Ashbury, a psychedelic street fair gone berserk. Placards/slogans. Message tees. Anti-war. Anti-establishment. Pro-feminism. Black militants. White revolt. Braless women with underarm hair in peasant blouses and broomstick skirts. Bearded men in fatigue jackets and bell bottoms and John Lennon wire-rim glasses. Love all around. VW Bugs and Birkenstocks. Head-shop fixings. Total strangers sharing spliffs on the streets. Legitimate San Francisco artists playing background: Joan Baez, Janis Joplin, Grace Slick, the Doors, and the Jefferson Airplane. Folk and rock stars scoring theme music for 24/7/365 counterculture be-ins.

Adult oversight threw up its hands and ran. The absence of establishment rules and order greased epic self-absorption. Youthful energy exploded with social causes; pretense hitched along for the ride. Charlie extended his thumb and hitched with the pretenders: the ragged radicals with drug-glazed glares; the mountebanks spouting hippie homilies; the tin ears with pan pipes or banjos posturing as musicians; the longhairs in sandals and serapes setting up sidewalk displays of beaded belts and incense candles.

The Haight was overrun with drugs: Both the standard street stuff—marijuana, hashish, cocaine, and heroin—and the new-age LSD, PCP, and psilocybin. Illusion, delusion, and confusion followed. A certain strain of hippies transposed into lost-soul druggies in search of certitude. Charlie in his element: full of shit but dead-ass certain. Charlie rapped his pitch and drew in the weak.

Charlie didn't label himself with Dale Carnegie or Dianetics. He dipped from both and preyed. Mary Brunner was first; Charlie added Lynette Fromme after a trip to LA. Charlie had no car, but he bummed a '48 Chevy from time to time and hit the road. In Venice, he saw Lynette Fromme at a bus-stop bench, looking forlorn: redheaded, high-voiced, unattractive, at odds with her strict parents, a drug abuser, sexually active, a student at El Camino Community College.

Lynette Fromme had twice attempted suicide. Charlie sat with her. He guessed she'd been kicked out of her house, which was obvious to anyone with a scintilla of street smarts. Lynette Fromme thought Charlie had tapped her essence. They talked. Charlie spieled. He rose to leave. Lynette was hooked—JC student cum dropout. She jumped into the Chevy. Charlie worked Lynette and Mary into threesomes. Charlie told them they were beautiful—they were dogs. He said uninhibited sex was liberating. They bought in. They moved to the Haight. Mary Brunner was now a cross-bay commuter.

A lapsed Congregational minister named Dean Moorehouse picked up Charlie while he was hitchhiking with the girls. Charlie insinuated himself into the Moorehouse house. Charlie admired an old piano in the corner of the living room. Charlie also admired Dean Moorehouse's sixteen-year-old daughter, Ruth Ann. Moorehouse gave Charlie the piano. Charlie traded the piano to one of Moorehouse's neighbors for a beater VW Microbus. He drove his new bus with runaway Ruth Ann a willing passenger. They headed up north on Highway101 toward the Mendocino coast.

Dean Moorehouse and his wife called the cops. As usual, the cops caught Charlie. The cops couldn't prove statutory rape or kidnapping—not without corroboration from the smitten and rebellious Ruth Ann. They charged him with interfering in the questioning of a runaway and hauled him off. Over his shoulder, he told Ruth Ann to find a husband—didn't matter whom. Marriage would emancipate her legally. He said he would call for her later. Ruth Ann hooked a lonely bus driver and waited. Charlie received thirty days suspended and ten years tacked onto his probation.

Mary and Lynette gutted the Microbus of everything but the driver's seat. They spread rugs and pillows on the floorboards. Mary Brunner flushed her job at UCB. She was all the way in and pregnant with Charlie's love child. They took Lynette Fromme and hit the road. They drove to Manhattan Beach so Charlie could visit a prison buddy; said buddy introduced him to nineteen-year-old Patricia Krenwinkel.

Krenwinkel had a crappy home life. Her parents were divorced. Her mother had moved to Mobile, Alabama. Her father sold life insurance in Inglewood. Pat lacked direction. She went to Mobile for a time. She taught catechism in a Catholic school and thought of becoming a nun. She returned to California and took a clerk's job. She shared an apartment in Manhattan Beach with a strung-out half-sister and an obnoxious nine-year-old nephew. She was making payments on a VW Bug. She bought gas with her father's Standard Oil credit card. Pat's endocrine flowed out of whack. She was overweight and cursed by unwanted body hair. Schoolkids had picked on her for both. Charlie told her she was beautiful. First she'd heard of it.

Patricia Krenwinkel apparently didn't mind sharing Charlie with Mary Brunner and Lynette Fromme. Group love still was love. She hopped aboard. Charlie took her gas card. Pat wrote her father that she had finally found inner peace. Parents are only as happy as their saddest child. Charlie's monthly charge-card bill: a small price for the short-term illusion of Pat's serenity.

Charlie found topless dancer Susan Atkins in the Haight. Susan Atkins was from San Jose and Los Banos. Susan Atkins was desperate for attention. Her mother had died of cancer when Atkins was fifteen. Her father dove into a bottle, lost jobs, and argued with his headstrong daughter. She found '60s anodynes—sex, alcohol, and drugs. She attempted suicide. She turned eighteen in 1966 and fled to the Haight. She shacked at a second-story Victorian flat on Lyons Street, an overcrowded '60s commune: dope and bedmates freely exchanged, rent paid sporadically if at all.

Charlie showed up one night with his guitar. He sat cross-legged on a shoe-worn hardwood floor. He picked his strings and sang cornball lounge songs. His music still stunk. Susan Atkins not a music critic. She felt a pull. Charlie let her touch his instrument. He rapped his usual horseshit. They had sex. Some days later, an SFPD narco squad raided the flat. Evictions followed. Charlie invited her to join a real family. Charlie took his real family to Sacramento. He knew a pimp named Pete who operated three whorehouses. The girls worked Pete's houses for money.

The VW was too small for the growing group. In Sacramento, Charlie traded the van for a discarded school bus. As with the Microbus, the girls removed the seats and replaced them with psychedelic pattern rugs and pillows. They painted the bus black. Charlie was through with the Haight. His ambition was worldwide stardom like the Beatles. The big action was LA. Charlie transferred his parole back to Southern California. He schlepped the family down I-5 into infamy.

V

September 1967: Charlie's rootless group road-tripped remote routes from Mendocino to the Mojave but always returned to LA. They slept on the bus at the beach or in crash pads discovered by rumor. They shoplifted staples and begged on the streets. They scrounged for food, Dumpster-diving behind high-end restaurants and grocery stores. Charlie found a place in Topanga Canyon known as the Spiral Staircase, a wide-open, multistory mystery house that welcomed hippies. Charlie met Bobby Beausoleil at the Staircase. Beausoleil was an itinerant musician, a ladies' man from Santa Barbara traveling with his girlfriend, Gail, and another disaffected woman, Catherine Share, a.k.a. "Gypsy."

Charlie was twitchy for contacts inside the music industry. Prison buddy and drug runner Phil Kaufman, still in stir at Terminal Island, referred him to Gary Stromberg, a talent hunter at Universal Studios. Kaufman's name actually counted. Stromberg scheduled a three-hour session. Charlie arrived at Universal in his bus with Mary, Lynette, Susan, and Pat. He walked into the studio barefoot.

Charlie figured he'd sit on a stool, finger a few frets, strum his strings, and the rest would happen. He'd riff himself into universal fame. Charlie was clueless about modern music production: headsets, sound booths, amp boosters, co-ax wires snaking around mike stands plugged into Moog synthesizers, with studio engineers directing. He flopped with anxiety from the congestion. Gary Stromberg amused himself with girls. He wrote off Charlie as a wannabe with no game.

Bobby Beausoleil introduced him to Gary Hinman, an aspiring Buddhist, music teacher (piano, bagpipes, drums), and low-level drug dealer. Gary Hinman lived near the Spiral Staircase in Topanga Canyon. He opened his house to anyone in need. Charlie was grateful for the introduction: someone new to use.

June 1968: Charlie stressed over his musical destiny. He sent the girls to scout for patrons. Patricia Krenwinkel and Ella Jo Bailey, thumbing rides along Sunset Strip, came through big. Big blond guy in a Rolls stopped: Dennis Wilson, the black sheep of the Beach Boys, asking if they'd like to visit his house for refreshments.

Dennis Wilson, separated from his wife, had leased Will Rogers's log-sided hunting lodge at the western edge of Sunset Boulevard, off the Pacific Palisades. The lodge was enormous, set on three acres: a party pad stocked with food, drugs, and booze, doors open and revolving with raucous company. Krenwinkel and Bailey didn't know Dennis Wilson from from a Wilson A2000 baseball glove. They talked up their spiritual master, Charlie. Dennis Wilson dropped them at Topanga on his way to a recording jam.

Krenwinkel and Bailey told Charlie about their day. By nightfall, Charlie had moved the family into the lodge. Sometime after midnight: Dennis Wilson pulled up. He thought he was walking into an empty house. He found the Manson entourage draped over his furniture, helping themselves to food and drink. Charlie greeted Dennis Wilson as if he were the prodigal returning to Charlie's own domain. Charlie dropped down and kissed Dennis Wilson's feet. Total weirdness.

The family crashed at the hunting lodge for the better part of two months. Charlie pimped the girls to Wilson and his friends. Charlie hounded Dennis Wilson for an audition with Brother Records, the Beach Boys' company. Brother execs humored Dennis Wilson. They had no faith in his judgment but agreed to a session. Charlie flopped again. He hadn't bothered to bathe. Brother big shots thought he was a strange dude with BO. Worse: his music didn't register. They shitcanned his session tapes.

September 1968: Dennis Wilson didn't mind humping the girls, but he was tired of permanent parasites who had no regard for his stuff. Steve Grogan had crashed Wilson's uninsured Ferrari: $21,000 repair. The girls had run up dental and medical (mostly VD treatment) bills, all reverting to bean counters at Brother. The hunting lodge lease expired. Dennis Wilson ditched the Manson clan, moving to his family's Malibu beach house without telling Charlie. Out on the street again, Charlie looked toward Simi Valley, a location the family had discovered a year earlier.

The Spahn movie ranch was perfect: acres of rundown shelters, large boulders, dry dirt, and scrub brush, with mountains in the horizon. Charlie feared his flock had softened from creature comforts at the hunting lodge. Only the main house at Spahn featured indoor plumbing. The rest of the property: wells, outhouses, and bushes. Spahn was owned originally by silent Western star William S. Hart. David O. Selznick filmed his overblown 1946 Gregory Peck/Jennifer Jones epic *A Duel in the Sun* at Spahn. TV Westerns in the 1960s did likewise. Charlie and the family often camped nearby.

George Spahn had bought the place in 1948. By 1968, the glory days were long gone. The Western genre—movies and TV—had faded. George Spahn was an aging widower—eighty years old and half-blind. His ten children had scattered, none interested in the aroma of horseshit and straw. Spahn eked it out. He employed stuntmen—Juan Flynn, Shorty Shea, and Johnny Swartz—as wranglers. He kept the place in business by renting horses to television producers and offering weekend riding lessons. Charlie saw a chance. He volunteered crew labor in trade for free rent.

George Spahn thought it would be a few people for a short time. He had no idea. Charlie sweetened the pot: Lynette Fromme as personal cook, housekeeper, and concubine. Spahn agreed, especially to the Lynette Fromme clause. She had a high voice and willing body parts. George Spahn liked her. He nicknamed her "Squeaky," for the sound she made when he grabbed her ass. George Spahn was unaware the dimensions of Charlie's intentions: three-dozen parasites as indeterminate tenants; Squeaky pillow-talking George Spahn, leaking information to Charlie; Squeaky ingratiating Spahn until he changed his will, leaving her—meaning Charlie—the property. Inferred: Old man George Spahn soon dead by natural or other causes.

1968/69: The family expanded. Ruth Ann Moorehouse dumped her bus-driver husband. She turned up at Spahn. Others dropped in: Bruce Davis, Ella Jo Bailey, Diane Lake, Paul Watkins, Sandra

Good. Sandra Good came with a $200-per-month remittance and a $6,000 trust fund, control of which she turned over to Charlie. Charlie's baby by Mary Brunner arrived in April 1968. Dean Moorehouse visited; he raged over Charlie's hold on Ruth Ann. Charlie dosed him with LSD. Dean Moorehouse transcended from irate father to '60s druggie. Phil Kaufman, paroled, turned up. Phil Kaufman squired Charlie around LA, among other places, to peyote and crash parties at the house of a man named Harold True. Harold True lived in the Los Feliz district, on Waverly Drive. One house east, at 3301: the home of Leno and Rosemary LaBianca.

Earlier in the summer, Dennis Wilson had thumbed a ride in a rattletrap pickup along the Pacific Coast Highway near Malibu. The driver: Charles Watson, from a one-stop Texas town north of Dallas called Copeville. In high school, "Tex" Watson had been a crew-cut A-student athlete at Farmersville (Copeville was too small to have its own high school). He discovered drugs in college at North Texas State in Denton. He grew his hair and fled to Southern California. He worked at a wig shop in Laurel Canyon, chased hippie girls, and smoked weed. He drove Dennis Wilson to the lodge and stayed.

Tex Watson was magnetized by the Manson family. Tex lived without purpose beyond pussy and weed. Charlie could provide girls and drugs, plus he had what Tex lacked—certitude. Tex was spiritually unglued. He had been raised with cow-town core values that he was crapping on. Charlie espoused philosophies that dismissed his guilt. Tex could fix cars and didn't mind taking orders. Charlie stole cars that were in need of work. Charlie obsessed over domination of others, and he needed another male flunky. Adolph Hitler meets Heinrich Himmler.

Bobby Beausoleil drove in from San Francisco with his harem in the summer of 1968. He had been jamming in the Haight with the Satanist Anton LaVey and picked up a female stray, Leslie Van

Houten, a classic boomer dropout. She grew up in Monrovia, in the San Gabriel foothills above the Santa Anita racetrack. Her parents had divorced when she was fourteen. She was twice a high school homecoming queen with no mind of her own. She drank, smoked weed, dropped acid, and put out for boys unprotected. She was pregnant at fifteen; her mother made her abort. At eighteen, she jumped for the Haight. Bobby Beausoleil and Gail were inclined to roam. Leslie Van Houten and Catherine Share stayed back as part of Charlie's inner circle at Spahn.

Charlie ran things. Tex carried out orders. Charlie believed in open sex and personal domination. He dictated pairings. The family was one large group home. Charlie wouldn't let children near their biological parents—experience taught him that mothers and fathers only screwed up kids. Charlie believed women were put on earth to serve men. He worked them like coolies around the ranch. He sent them into the city to scrounge Dumpsters. He sent them on "creepy crawlies"—late-night break-ins of upscale houses, inhabitants snoring through nocturnal home invasions.

Most evenings, Charlie gathered them around to listen to music (his own and the Beatles'). He deconstructed British Invasion lyrics, distorting anything the Beatles intended. He dosed the family with acid and preached the apocalypse. The family sang chorus to his mania.

Charlie hadn't abandoned his dream of musical immortality. He clung to his connection with Dennis Wilson. Wilson ran in a pack with recording session arranger/ talent procurer Gregg Jakobson and music producer Terry Melcher, the only Son of wholesome movie star Doris Day. Charlie was in the backseat of Dennis Wilson's car one night when Wilson dropped Terry Melcher at his home, high on a hill in Benedict Canyon: 10050 Cielo Drive.

March 1969: Dennis Wilson, Gregg Jakobson, and Terry Melcher occasionally visited Spahn. Charlie flattered himself. He thought they were intrigued by him and his music. Gregg Jakobson prattled on about filming a documentary of life at Spahn within a commune of counterculture hippies. Charlie didn't catch on: they viewed him as a pet freak who bestowed benefits. His big attractions: drugs and women. Terry Melcher liked Ruth Ann Moorehouse. Charlie dogged Dennis Wilson for an audition with Terry Melcher on location at Spahn. Dennis Wilson scheduled it for March 18.

Charlie preened. The girls sewed him a deerskin outfit laced with thongs—long-sleeve V-neck shirt and bell-bottom pants. Charlie pulled a stiff comb through the rats in his hair. He bathed. He scissor-groomed his beard scrag. He waited for the Saturday moment, but Terry Melcher was a no-show. Charlie was enraged. He stormed into Benedict Canyon—he didn't know that Terry Melcher and Candice Bergen had moved a month earlier. At 10050 Cielo, he ran into Rudi Altobelli, snarling. Rudi Altobelli scoped him as a dangerous mutt. He didn't reveal Terry Melcher's new address.

Charlie didn't stop. He hassled Dennis Wilson, who in turn hounded Terry Melcher until Melcher consented to a redo on May 23, another Saturday. Charlie was ready. Dennis Wilson and Terry Melcher made it this time. Charlie anticipated raves and a rich contract. Terry Melcher was bored. He looked past Charlie toward Ruth Ann Moorehouse. He dismissed the performance. "Maybe later…"

Charlie uncorked. The previous November, Dennis Wilson had reworked one of Charlie's songs, "Cease to Exist." He titled it "Never Learn Not to Love" and credited it as his own on the Beach Boys album *20/20*, released in January 1969. Dennis Wilson felt justified by the bills the family members had run up at the hunting lodge. Charlie still seethed at the plagiarism. He copped to the truth after the May 23 fiasco. He had been punked by Hollywood slicks.

Payback to the world now on full go. He spiked the dosages of LSD. He himself held back but tripped the family beyond sanity.

The previous November, Charlie had found alternate digs in the Mojave Desert. The grandmother of one of the marginal family members, Catherine Gillies, owned property near Death Valley called Myers Ranch. Barker Ranch sat a quarter mile up Goler Wash from Myers and was more remote. The family spilled over to Barker and squatted.

Charlie's message darkened. He preached end-of-days lunacy. He envisioned himself avatar of almighty God. He called himself Jesus Christ and the Devil. He dipped into his Nazarene Bible, particularly Revelation 9. He thought he was the fifth angel handed the keys to the "pit of the abyss." He prophesized that when each of the twelve lost tribes amassed one thousand followers, he would guide the 12,000 and outwait the apocalypse.

Charlie translated. He logic-leaped from the locusts of Revelation to "beetles" and from there to the "Beatles," the modern prophets. He called his vision "Helter Skelter" from *The White Album* Song of the same name. The Beatles believed they were using the name of a carnival ride in Liverpool to symbolize the Tilt-A-Whirl of life. John Lennon's eventual take on Charlie's view: "He's barmy."

Charlie saw Helter Skelter as a final battle, the blacks overwhelming white oppression. Charlie was confused about blacks. He was brought up a peckerwood racist, but he had been intimidated by blacks in prison. He was impressed with the organized ferocity of the 1960s black militants, but he thought blacks were inferior. He put it together: blacks will revolt against whites during Armageddon and overcome. But…blacks? They were incapable of organizing a revolution. Incapable even of knowing how to ignite the war. No problem. Charlie would handle all that.

VI

Tuesday, December 2, 1969, *LA Times* page-three headline and story excerpts, Dial Torgeson byline:

TENACIOUS PROBE
CHIEF TELLS HOW
MURDER CASE
WAS UNRAVELED

Police Chief Edward M. Davis ended the Tate mystery at 2 p.m. Monday.

Under bright lights, behind 15 microphones, the chief announced an official end to 8,750 man hours of police work—the "tenacious investigation by detectives" which, he said, solved Hollywood's most savage murder case...

...Today, warrants have been issued for the arrest of three individuals in connection with the murders...The same people, he explained, also were involved in the murders of Rosemary and Leno LaBianca...

Ed Davis, desperate to deflect heat, scheduled the December 1 press conference without consulting the DA's office. The DA's central operations manager, J. Miller Leavy, had assigned Tate and LaBianca to thirty-five-year-old deputy DA Vincent Bugliosi on November 17. Since then, Bugliosi had scrambled to develop leads but was nowhere close to securing sufficient evidence for conviction. Ed Davis referred to three warrants. It had taken two weeks just to figure out real names. Manson was in custody for stolen vehicles and arson. At booking he called himself "Jesus Christ" and "God." Susan Atkins had checked in as "Sadie May Glutz.,"

Ed Davis suggested the imminent arrest of the Tate and LaBianca killers. He was bullshitting big-time. Manson was in custody in Independence for arson; Susan Atkins in the Sybil Brand Institute on the Hinman murder. The DA's case was tenuous and had nothing to do with relentless police work. It had turned on the drop of an informant's dime two weeks earlier.

At Sybil Brand, Susan Atkins bunked in dormitory 8000 with hookers Ronnie Howard and Virginia Graham, both serving county time—Howard for prescription-pill forgery and Graham for violation of probation. Idle hours led to girl talk. Topics ranged from men, clothes, and sex to drugs and murder. Howard and Graham hadn't killed anyone, but, to their amazement, Susan Atkins copped to Hinman and…Sharon Tate. She provided details on what happened August 9 at Cielo Drive, from Tex cutting the phone lines, to the slashings, to them flinging their bloody kill clothes and Tex's .22 High Standard into Benedict Canyon.

Howard and Graham shared an aversion to snitching. They agreed to tell no one…until the thing grew so big between them that they could no longer hold it in. Virginia Graham eventually was transferred to the women's prison at Corona. She unloaded Atkins's confessions to a Corona shrink, but not until December. By then, the story already had blown hot through the HOJ and Parker Center.

November 13: LaBianca detective units hadn't communicated any better across their own homicide table than the LAPD had with the LASD. Both teams were rigid, denying a link and working at cross purposes. One name popped the assumption: Charles Manson. The LaBianca detectives had received tips from bikers linking the hippies at Spahn Ranch to the killings. They put it out that they were looking for a member of the Straight Satans biker gang from Venice named Danny DeCarlo who was tied into Spahn. Venice PD detectives called in. They couldn't locate DeCarlo, but they were holding a Straight Satan named Al Springer on an unrelated charge. LAPD jumped on it. Venice PD delivered him to Parker Center.

Al Springer told a story. He said a Manson guy named Tex had burned a street dealer named Bernard "Lotsapoppa" Crowe on a drug deal. Crowe paid Tex $2,500 out front for twenty-five kilos of weed. Tex was lying: he had no weed. He took the money and gave it to Charlie. Lotsapoppa phoned Charlies at Spahn. Lotsapoppa said he was a Black Panther. Produce the dope, or his boys would spill blood. Charlie arranged a July 1, 1969, meeting at Crowe's North Hollywood apartment.

He brought a family member named T. J. Walleman. They drove Johnny Swartz's Ford. He handed Walleman a gun, a .22 High Standard Buntline. He told Walleman at his signal to fire on Bernard Crowe. Crowe had two blacks with him. Charlie signaled. Walleman lost his guts. Charlie grabbed the .22 and shot Crowe in the chest. He and Walleman backed out of the apartment. Charlie feared a Black Panther reprisal. Al Springer said Charlie wanted a biker gang at Spahn as security and offered sex privileges and drugs to the Straight Satans.

Al Springer said Spahn was too unsanitary for him, but another Straight Satan, club treasurer Danny DeCarlo, loved the place. He said DeCarlo shammed repairs on motorcycles, sat in the sun, chugged beer, and boned the family girls. Al Springer said that sometime around August 11 or 12, Charles Manson had bragged to DeCarlo about killing: "We knocked off five just the other night."

November 17: Ronnie Howard scheduled to appear in Santa Monica on the prescription-forgery charge. She was bussed from Sybil Brand to the Men's Central Jail at 441 Bauchet Street downtown, the hub for shuttling inmates to various county courthouses. She was between buses and had access to a pay phone. She dialed Beverly Hills PD and said she had information on Tate-LaBianca. BHPD referred her to Hollywood homicide. She dialed Hollywood station on Wilcox Street.

5:00 p.m.: Back at Sybil Brand. Two LAPD homicide detectives, sergeants Mossman and Brown, visited. They interviewed Ronnie Howard, who coughed up the whole story. Her info spiked adrenaline. Every cop in LA was padding overtime chasing his own tail, and these two pegged it. They judged Susan Atkins to be an extreme danger to any witness. They stashed Ronnie Howard in isolation and hustled back to Parker Center.

November 17: same day. LAPD detectives had found Danny DeCarlo. They grilled him for seven hours. Danny DeCarlo spilled big, all of it hearsay, but most of it incriminating or illuminating. High points: Mary Brunner was with Atkins and Beausoleil for the Hinman kill; Charlie sliced Hinman's ear the second day with a souvenir sword obtained from a Straight Satan; Charlie ordered the Hinman kill; Charlie ordered the killing of Spahn ranch hand Shorty Shea; the night after LaBianca, Steve Grogan, a.k.a. Clem Tufts, said: "We got us five piggies."

November 24: LAPD moved five Manson girls—Dianne Lake, Ruth Ann Moorehouse, Catherine Share, and Leslie Van Houten—from Independence to Sybil Brand, placing them on "keep away" (from one another) status. All five still used aliases. None had police records; print cards were useless. Detectives bore in. Four of the five gave up nothing. Leslie Van Houten, a.k.a. Leslie Sankston, dropped hints.

She said four people were involved in Tate. She said Charlie wasn't one of them, and three were female. She said one woman named Linda didn't participate. She didn't know Linda's last name, only that she showed up at Spahn around the Fourth of July. She said "Katie" was one of the women. Katie was one more name for Marnie Kay Reeves, arrested at Barker, released a few days later. At one point, Leslie Van Houten clammed up. Interrogators asked why. Answer, paraphrased: If Zero suddenly was found playing Russian roulette, I could be found playing Russian roulette. Big-time click. Zero, a.k.a. John Phillip Haught, a.k.a. Christopher Jesus, a weak-minded Manson acolyte.

November, 1969: Venice PD investigating a gunshot death on Clubhouse Avenue near the beach. John Phillip Haught, twenty-two, dead on a mattress, a hole in his temple, an eight-shot Ivers & Johnson .22 revolver on the floor next to him. Four witnesses said Haught was playing Russian roulette and spun the chamber on a live round.

Venice wrote it off initially as hippie madness, probably drug-induced: death by suicide. The witnesses—Bruce Davis, Sue Bartell, Linda Baldwin, and Catharine Gillies—were ID'd later as Manson associates released from custody after Barker. Triple implications: Charlie eliminating witnesses susceptible to police pressure; Charlie kiting messages for his flock to shut up; Leslie Sankston, a.k.a. Van Houten, eager to obey Charlie, and not eager to join Zero. Venice PD had never penetrated the case. The gun had been wiped and was fully loaded—seven live after the kill shot. Suicide.

Traction. Detectives cross-checked field reports, this time with the LASD. They brought in Marnie Kay Reeves, hauled in during the August 16 raid on Spahn. Her booking card showed that she had been bailed out by Joseph P. Krenwinkel from Inglewood. Techs compared her print card with lifts from Cielo Drive. Bingo. A match from Sharon Tate's bedroom: M. K. Reeves at the scene. Phone call to Pop Krenwinkel confirmed. M. K. was his daughter Patricia, living now in Mobile with her mother. Vincent Bugliosi wired an arrest warrant. Mobile PD scooped her up within the day.

November 30, 1969: Blanks filling in. LaBianca detective sergeant Robert Patchett interviewed Gregg Jakobson. Key question: Did he know a Charles "Tex" Montgomery? Answer: "Yes, but his last name is Watson." Patchett ran Watson's name through the system. Click: Charles D. Watson had been arrested in Van Nuys seven months earlier for narcotics possession. Techs compared Watson's card with extractions from the Cielo Drive slaughters. Another match. Tex tied to the Sharon Tate crime scene. Detectives located Watson in his *Last Picture Show* high-school hometown of Farmersville, Texas, and wired a warrant.

LAPD grilled ranch hands at Spahn and caught a last name for Linda: Kasabian. They heard she was hiding out in a New Mexico convent. In fact, she had returned to her native New Hampshire, overcome by guilt. She confessed all to her mother.

December 2, 1969: Mom urged her to surrender to the police in Concord, New Hampshire. Mom said Linda admitted she was present at the Tate slayings. She denied any participation in the killings. Kasabian waived extradition. Two days later, December 4, 1969, she was in custody at Sybil Brand.

By order of deputy DA Vincent Bugliosi, the LAPD backtracked its investigation. Evidence surfaced. The case teetered on the twisted psyche of multiple-murderess Susan Atkins, who was staring at a gas chamber conviction. Atkins was represented by Richard Caballero, who was agitating for a plea bargain. He offered full disclosure, grand jury, and trial testimony in exchange for wiping the death penalty. Vince Bugliosi opposed the idea. He wasn't inclined to deal, not with seven innocents slaughtered. He was overruled by big-brass interests. LAPD chief Ed Davis's regime had been in the glare of the spotlight for too long; DA Evelle Younger was campaigning for state attorney general. Both wanted case closure. Their call.

December 4, 1969: Head deputy DA for trials Aaron Stovitz memoed Evelle Younger regarding the agreement with Caballero on December 4. Susan Atkins opened the bag the next day. She testified for three days. The grand jury began deliberations on December 8 at 4:17 p.m. Twenty minutes later, at 4:37 p.m., the verdict was in. A true bill on Van Houten (two counts murder and one count conspiracy to commit murder) and on Manson, Watson, Krenwinkel, and Kasabian (seven counts murder and one count conspiracy). Testimony supposedly sealed.

December 14, 1969: LA's official record an open book. Susan Atkins's statements capsuled into a three-page story in the *LA Times*—publishing rights fenced to European tabloids—doubtless leaked by attorney Caballero. Destitute hippies weren't compensating his billable hours; he needed money from outside the box.

Local news outlets followed with frenzy. That day, a Channel 7 camera crew backtracked the murder sequence and found the kill clothes dumped in Benedict Canyon. Two days later, a man named Bernard Weiss called the homicide desk at Parker Center, a referral from the LAPD Valley Services Division (VSO) in Van Nuys. Bernard Weiss said on September 1 that his ten-year-old son Steven had found a .22 High Standard Buntline Special in the weeds near Cielo Drive. He said the gun had a broken trigger guard, with part of its grip missing.

Weiss said that it sounded like the gun described in the paper; said he'd given the gun to the police in Van Nuys in September. Weiss had talked to three cops at Parker Center, none of whom seemed to care. Weiss called his neighbor, Clete Roberts, a Channel 2 newscaster. Roberts shook Parker Center phone lines until two detectives drove to Van Nuys and retrieved the weapon from the VSO evidence locker. Shell casings matched. A missing grip confirmed the .22 Buntline as a Tate murder weapon.

December 26: Rudolf Weber called. Vince Bugliosi interviewed him at his home, 9870 Portola Drive, 1.8 miles from 10050 Cielo. Weber's description captured similarities to all four defendants. He remembered Johnny Swartz's Ford, down to the

faded yellow paint around the license plate. He remembered the license number, GYY 435. Bugliosi wondered how. Rudolf Weber said he was a restaurant steward at the Brentwood Country Club; he recalled numbers as an occupational necessity. At Spahn, Johnny Swartz confirmed the August 9 and 10 use of his car.

March 1970, three months later: Bernard "Lotsapoppa" Crowe surfaced through his attorney, Ed Tolmas. Crowe hadn't died, though his friends put out a story that he had. He was critical for eighteen days with a .22 bullet near his spine, but he recovered. Classic Charlie. He had bragged about capping a Panther. Bernard Crowe wasn't dead, and he wasn't a Panther, just a low-level drug dealer with a line. Bugliosi wanted the bullet tied to the Tate murder guns. Risky to extract. Lotsapoppa faced paralysis with the procedure. He declined. Charlie's bullet stayed in his back.

VII

Vince Bugliosi navigated tricky waters pertinent to Susan Atkins. Precedents, *People v. Aranda* (1965) and *Bruton v. The United States* (1968), established that codefendants may not implicate one another with confessions. Bugliosi could indict with Susan Atkins's GJ testimony, but implication of others from her grand-jury record could not be entered as evidence. The alternative: trying all four separately, quadrupling court costs and tangling witness logistics. Severance ruled out.

Developments:

February 18, 1970: Patricia Krenwinkel waived extradition and was transported from Mobile to Sybil Brand. All warranted defendants in custody in Los Angeles except Tex Watson, who stayed bunkered in Collins County, Texas. He reverted to his short-hair, A-student athlete persona. He was jailed in Texas on the LA County murder warrant, but provincial Texans resisted extradition.

May 11, 1970: Susan Atkins fired attorney Richard Caballero, replacing him with Daye Shinn. Shinn filed a declaration repudiating her grand-jury testimony. Atkins renounced her GJ statement for the same reason Leslie Van Houten had stopping blabbing: Charlie was sending instructions between the HOJJ and Sybil Brand, often using Sandra Good and Squeaky Fromme as runners. Charlie controlled the women from his jail cell. They obeyed without questions. They believed him omniscient. They thought he could see through walls and bars. Charlie's message: deny everything. If codefendants refuse to testify, the state has no case. Implied: anyone ratting will die.

Examples: Zero and Joel Pugh, weak-willed husband of Sandra Good. On December 2, 1969, Pugh was found in a guest room in the Tagarth Hotel in London with slash marks on his wrists, a bruise on his forward, and his throat slit. A coroner's inquest ruled it a suicide. Charlie had sent Bruce Davis and Sandra Good to London on October 27 with Pugh for reasons never explained. The others returned. Joel Pugh did not.

Ranch hand Shorty Shea had become a problem. Shorty married a black woman; Charlie detested blacks. Shorty was loyal to George Spahn. Shorty Shea despised Manson. He lobbied Spahn to evict the family or sell the ranch to developers. Shorty snitched for the August 16, 1969, raid.

Midnight, August 26: Shorty Shea stepped into a car with Charlie, Tex, Bruce Davis, and Steve Grogan. He was never seen again. Seventeen-year-old Manson girl, Barbara Hoyt, remembers hearing horrific screams that night. She tried to run way the next day.

Danny DeCarlo said on November 17 that he'd heard they'd chopped up Shorty Shea and buried his body parts in lime on random plots around the property. He also said that Mary Brunner was present at the Hinman slaying. Mary Brunner had fled to Eau Claire upon release from jail for a credit card fraud charge. Bugliosi granted her immunity on Hinman. Among her statements: Tex told her that Bruce Davis and Steve Grogan had dismembered Shorty Shea and dumped his car in Canoga Park.

During the trial in September 1970, Squeaky Fromme and Sandra Goode pressured Barbara Hoyt, offering her a Hawaiian vacation in exchange for her refusal to testify. Ruth Ann Moorehouse flew with her to the islands, where they basked for a few days in tropical paradise. Ruth Ann said she had to return to LA. At the airport, she bought Barbara Hoyt a hamburger. Barbara Hoyt tucked into it. Ruth Ann waited. She told Barbara she had plugged ten tabs of acid into the burger. She strolled for the gate. Barbara Hoyt went bad-trip berserk. She ran shrieking through traffic before collapsing into a coma. Backfire: Barbara Hoyt survived and was talking.

Atkins's repudiation handed Bugliosi the case on a platter. In private, he agreed with Charlie: without an eyewitness, the state's case was weak. Atkins's plea bargain precluded her GJ testimony from appearing in open court. *Aranda-Bruton* held that incriminating statements against codefendants were inadmissible. Gary

Fleischman and his client snapped at the opportunity she left behind.

Linda Kasabian had come late to Spahn, recruited by Catherine Share. She was from Concord, New Hampshire. Her mother admitted that she had too many other children and had no time for Linda. Linda cited mistreatment by her stepfather. She left home in 1965 at age sixteen. She returned three years later after separating from husband Robert in New Mexico—her second husband. Robert drifted west. He called from Los Angeles in the summer of 1969. Robert was sharing a trailer in Topanga Canyon with a hippie adventurer named Charlie Melton. Melton had money. He and Robert were rigging a sailboat for a South American voyage. Robert invited Linda to join them.

Catherine Share, a.k.a. Gypsy, stopped one day to visit Melton. She talked about the peace-love-beauty aura at Spahn. She talked in mystical tones about the abyss in the desert at Barker. Linda's reconciliation with Robert was floundering. She weighed her bad options: stuck on a small boat with Bob, or back in Concord with her mom and stepdad. She believed a hole in the ground in Panamint was an improvement over both. She left with Gypsy for Spahn. She met Tex. They talked into the night and screwed. She was hooked. Common knowledge in Topanga: Charlie Melton had money. Tex knew about it. He told Linda to grab her daughter and money from Melton.

July 4, 1969: Linda Kasabian anted into Spahn with 5k stolen from Charlie Melton. She met Charlie that night and was mesmerized.

Five weeks later: Helter Skelter. Kasabian was present at Tate, but she stood guard and hadn't actually killed anyone. She drove for Charlie the night of the LaBianca slaughters, but she prevented the murder of Saladin Nader. She had a working conscience. "I'm not like you, Charlie. I can't just kill someone." She was articulate and desperate to atone. She could impress the jury. Despite countless acid trips, her recall was sharp, her mind clear. Bugliosi had enough physical evidence to indict Charlie and the others but not to convict. Star-witness affirmation tipped the scales his way. He took Kasabian off the table as a codefendant. *Aranda-Bruton* no longer in play.

Motive stumped him initially. He bore no legal burden to prove motive, but he knew it was essential in this case. He sensed that the girls would swing on physical evidence and corroboration from Linda Kasabian. He feared that Charlie could skate. Charlie never shot nor stabbed a Tate-LaBianca victim. He wasn't present during any of the murders. He was charged with conspiracy, not homicide. Bugliosi knew that Charlie directed the bloodshed; he was obligated to demonstrate why. Articulate motive carries direct and circumstantial evidence into assumption of guilt. Without it, juries can wobble over reasonable doubt.

He couldn't see it at first; no rational intellect could—until too many witnesses confirmed. It hit him as a gestalt that tied up every loose end, the literal handwriting on the wall: Helter Skelter. Breathtaking in its lunacy: megalomaniacal Charlie directing slasher kills he could blame on blackie in the racial tinderbox of '60s militancy. Murders would ignite black/white Armageddon. Blackie would overcome, but inherent deficiencies would botch any attempt to organize a new world order. Charlie as Jesus, God, and the Devil with his Army of 12,000 Aryans would levitate from the pit of the abyss in Panamint and assume control. Sheer madness.

Charlie's vision was common knowledge around Spahn and Barker. Bugliosi could produce any number of witnesses to verify. He could smell conviction.

June 15, 1970, Monday. Department 104, eighth floor of the LA County HOJ. The honorable judge Charles H. Older dropped the gavel on what would be the longest, most expensive trial in American history to that point: nine and a half months from preliminary motions to the penalties. The proceedings would pile up 31,762 pages of trial transcript and 225 sequestered jury days. It would score twenty on a ten-point bizarro scale.

Items, now etched in lore as legends of evil:

Death threats to court officers. Attempt bribes to bailiffs. Xs cut into foreheads—Charlie's and the girls'. The girls shaving their heads. Unincarcerated family girls sitting on the sidewalk outside the HOJ, occupying the corner of Temple and Broadway like Hari Krishnas at airport loading and unloading zones. Charlie and the girls turning their backs to the bench until bailiffs carried them out. The girls giggling at graphic exhibits of seven corpses and 169 stab wounds. Krenwinkel doodling Satanic symbols during testimony. Attorneys hired and fired. And killed: Ronald Hughes murdered on a camping trip in Sespe Hot Springs in Las Padres National Forest. Hughes represented Leslie Van Houten. He made the fatal mistake of working in his client's best interest.

Guilt was foregone. Vince Bugliosi laid out the physical evidence tying all four defendants to the crimes of conspiracy and murder. Linda Kasabian corroborated. The others jeered at her and threatened her. One of them said, "You're killing us." Kasabian, unfazed: "You killed you." Manson's attorney, Irving Kanarak, tried to break her on drug use and sex habits. She wouldn't buckle. She testified for eighteen days. She gave the jury the whole package. When she stood down, Judge Older granted the prosecution's motion for full immunity. She walked on all charges.

November 16, 1970: The prosecution rested. The defense spent three days filing futile motions for dismissal. Judge Older denied them all pro forma. Shocker: all four defense attorneys rested their cases without calling a single witness. Atkins, Krenwinkel, and Van Houten howled. They asked to testify. Their attorneys refused. Charlie had programmed them to sacrifice—themselves for him. Charlie's play: the girls would affirm their own guilt under oath while maintaining his innocence. Ronald Hughes's counter: keep them off the stand. Hughes: "I will not push a client out the window."

November 20, 1970: Charlie asked if he could testify. Irving Kanarek ratified the move. Because of *Aranda-Bruton*, Judge Older removed the jury. In lieu of questions from Kanarek, Charlie ran a monologue. He rambled, repeated, droned, and digressed for one strange hour. Excerpt:

> You eat meat and you kill things that are better than you are, and then you say how bad, and even killers, your children are. You made your children what they are...These children that come at you with knives, they are your children. You taught them. I didn't teach them. I just tried to help them stand up...

Charlie left the stand. He passed the killer girls at the counsel table. He told them: "You don't have to testify now."

November 30, 1970: Court back in session. Ronald Hughes missing—last seen on November 27, camping above Ojai with two hippies. Court recessed until December 21.

December 18, 1970: Grand jury indicted five family members for conspiracy to prevent and dissuade a witness, Barbara Hoyt, from attending a trial.

December 21, 1970: Closing arguments underway. Judge Older, sick of obstreperous antics, removed all four defendants from the court. Bugliosi bookended a Christmas recess to state his case for the obvious. He finished on Monday, December 28. Paul Fitzgerald for Patricia Krenwinkel, and Daye Shinn for Susan Atkins, made half-ass attempts at impeaching witness credibility, especially Linda Kasabian's. They were mercifully brief. Not Manson's counsel. Irving Kanarek took seven court days and nearly twelve-hundred transcript pages, annoying even his own client. At one point, Charlie yelled out, "Why don't you sit down. You're making things worse." Judge Older: "This isn't a summation; it's a filibuster." Wouldn't matter. Clarence Darrow couldn't have sprung the Tate-LaBianca killers.

Vince Bugliosi nailed it. Bugliosi wrote the bible on the case, *Helter Skelter* (W. W. Norton 1974). An episode from his text: Charlie asking to see him one noon recess during Irving Kanarek's endless closing oration. Charlie to Bugliosi: "I don't want you to think they're [the] best I could do. I've screwed girls that would make these three look like boys…I'm a very selfish guy. I don't give a fuck for these girls. I'm only out for myself." Charlie said it to a listener, not an audience. Pure candor: he admitted to the definition of evil—conscience carried off by a runaway ego.

January 15, 1971: Seven months after the first gavel, Judge Older delivered instructions, and the jury began deliberations.

January 25, 10:15 a.m., judgment day: Verdict reached—court reconvening. LASD intelligence picking up chatter of "disruption to proceedings." Extra security measures put in place. Bugliosi and Older both flanked by three armed bodyguards. Pat-downs and metal detectors at all HOJ entrances. Verdict forms to the bailiff, who passed them to Judge Older. Judge Older back to the bailiff, and back to the jury foreman. Judge Older stone-faced: "The clerk will read the verdicts."

The court clerk, Gene Darrow, rattled off twenty-seven counts. Twenty-seven repetitions: "We the jury in the above-entitled action" find…

On all counts, guilty as charged.

Postscripts

March 29, 1971, penalty-phase verdict: death for all.

March 29, 1971: Two fishermen discovered Ronald Hughes's decomposed body stuck at an angle between two boulders in high elevation above Ventura.

April 19, 1971: Sentencing date. Judge Older: "If this is not a case for the death penalty, what would be?"

April 21, 1971: Bobby Beausoleil and Steve Grogan convicted for the murder of Gary Hinman. Sentences: death for Beausoleil; life imprisonment for Grogan.

August to October, 1971: Charles "Tex" Watson tried, convicted, and sentenced to death for Tate-LaBianca murders.

November 8, 1971 to June 4, 1972: Charles Manson tried and convicted for the murder of Gary Hinman. (Susan Atkins would plead guilty for the same crime seven months later.)

December 23, 1971: Charles Manson, Steve Grogan (a.k.a. Clem Tufts), and Bruce MacGregor Davis convicted of the murder of Donald "Shorty" Shea. Barbara Hoyt testified about the screams she heard the night he disappeared.

February 18, 1972: The California supreme court ruled the death penalty unconstitutional. All capital sentences automatically commuted.

The Tate-LaBianca killers living on, parole applications routinely denied, more than four decades in cages and counting. Murderous legends, the quintessence of evil.

CHAPTER 5

SANTA CRUZ: FRAZIER, MULLIN, AND KEMPER

Surf City, USA, pre-1967: idyllic. Monterey Bay's best weather. Roaring Pacific rollers lapping onto sheltered white beaches. Locals mixing with tourists in getaway coastal villages. Postcard images in pastel: wharf, boardwalk, yacht harbor with slips of sailboats moored in tight formation. A real-life watercolor running from West Cliff to Capitola, the waterfront backdropped to the north by a high wilderness dense with evergreens of the Santa Cruz Mountains. Literal PR slogan: "Where the Redwoods meet the Sea."

Santa Cruz then—surfers and Republicans basking in Mediterranean microclimates. Doris Day social simplicity—nothing heavier than a Gidget movie plot. Oceanside innocence. School kids rolling skateboards to the beach and back. Surf rats shooting curls from point break to ebb tide. Silicon Valley dropouts in aloha shirts and sandals launching start-ups from workbenches in one-car garages. Old duffers in golf hats and Madras shorts gazing into brilliant sunsets.

Santa Cruz, later, post-1967: a culture in convulsion. Age of Aquarius zeroing in. UCSC liberals overwhelming conservative civics. A center that cannot hold.

1970–1973 in specific: thirty months of horror riding in on the wakes of hippie incursions. Trepidation bearing in. Square johns squinting at longhairs. Longhairs stepping lightly around square-john scrutiny. Dove hunters sleeping with loaded 16 gauge shotguns at arms length. Schoolteachers, volunteer firemen, and Pacific Street merchants buying sidearms. Citizens dead-bolting doors. Santa Cruz County DA Peter Chang captioned it. "This must be Murderville, USA," he blurted to *Watsonville Pajaronian* crime reporter Marj von Beroldingen at a multiple-victim crime scene in the forest of Henry Cowell Park off Highway 9. It hit the newswires as, "This must be the murder capital of the world."

The misquote stuck.

I

999 Rodeo Gulch Road: up the Soquel Hills on a two-lane path through eucalyptus, scrub oaks, and redwoods. Modern house designed by Aaron Green, a Frank Lloyd Wright protégé: 4,166 square feet, five bedrooms, three baths, blending with the terrain, reflecting an Asian reverence for nature in which no trees are hewed to accommodate construction. Long, low, and flowing—native rock and wood; no right angles. Backyard pool: free form, sunk into the earth, a lagoon with a flagstone deck. Floor to ceiling windows on all sides, no curtains or drapes. Unobstructed views into the hills and the Bay. Oriental shrubs obscuring a hydrant installed in case of fire.

The place belonged to Victor Ohta, forty-six, and his family—wife, Virginia, forty-three, and four children—Taura, eighteen; Lark, fifteen; Derrick, twelve; Taggert, eleven. The Ohta family lived large on the summit. Victor earned big money as an eye surgeon. He co-owned an expansive medical complex, 550 Water Street, with an ENT specialist named Dr. Daniel Seftel. The complex featured a koi pond and also was designed by Aaron Green. Victor Ohta's house on Rodeo Gulch cost between 250 and 300k to build, an extravagant price for the times.

Victor drove a maroon Rolls Royce—classic cars his hobby. He wore showy silk scarves in lieu of neckties—he had a drawer full in a spectrum of bright patterns and colors. He paid private-school tuition for four children. The older daughter, Taura, attended a design college in New York. Lark went to Santa Catalina, a Catholic boarding school in Monterey; she was a classmate of future kidnap victim Patty Hearst.

October 19, 1970, 1:30 p.m.: Both girls away at school. Virginia driving home after visiting Lucienne Seftel, the wife of Victor Ohta's partner. Front door unlocked. Santa Cruz until the '70s—nobody took precautions against intruders. Virginia entered and gasped in terror. A man wielding a .38 standing in her entry hall. The man was short, five foot six, with long hair and a beard. He gibbered, agitated, castigating her for destroying the earth. He held her at gun point. He tied her wrists with Victor Ohta's silk scarves. He sliced the phone lines with a survivalist knife.

4:00 p.m.: Taggert's school, Good Shepherd Catholic, called the medical office. Virginia Ohta, usually prompt, had not picked up Tag at two forty-five. Dr. Ohta's secretary, Dorothy Cadwallader, dialed Thorp Manor, a small school in a large downtown house: Derrick still waiting as well. Victor called home: busy signal. No worry. Virginia on the line, must have lost track of time.

Dorothy Cadwallader, thirty-eight, offered to pick up Tag at Good Shepherd. She left the office at four fifteen, driving her black and gold Lincoln Continental. Dr. Ohta said he'd gather Derrick at Thorp and swing by his mother's house. He left work in his Rolls at four thirty, about the time Dorothy and Tag stepped through the front door and stared into the bearded man's gun. The bearded man bound them with scarves. Victor and Derrick rolled in at 6:10 p.m. Another surprise: more scarves.

The longhair berated Victor Ohta. He gestured for him to go outside toward the patio. He ranted about the evils of materialism. He screeched at Ohta that he was desecrating the planet. He urged him to help burn down the house. Ohta offered desperate bribes—money, goods, anything. The offer amped the longhair's rage. He invaded Ohta's home to punish profligate pigs, not profit from them.

He pushed Victor Ohta, who reeled backward into the pool. Ohta worked his hands free and surfaced for air. He spit water iterating bribes. The man reached down to pull him to the deck. Victor Ohta tried to yank him into the pool. The man straightened and fired into Ohta's chest. Ohta floated over. The man shot him twice in the back. He took out a .22 revolver and went back inside. He brought Virginia Ohta to the pool deck.

He asked if she believed in God. She said yes. He said, "You'll be fine." He shot her behind the ear and shoved her into the pool. He repeated the ritual with Dorothy Cadwallader. He hesitated at the boys. Innocent children? He consulted God. Them too? God insisted. The man obeyed. *Pop. Pop.* Two more shots. Two more dead bodies splashed into the pool.

He found car keys and pulled Ohta's Rolls across the road, blocking access to the rear of the house. He moved Dorothy Cadwallader's Continental across the driveway to the front. He drank a can of beer. He composed a note on the Ohtas' typewriter. He stuck the note under the wiper blade of the Rolls. He flashed tinder at different spots inside the house. He drove off in Virginia Ohta's '68 Oldsmobile station wagon.

8:10 p.m.: Santa Cruz sheriff's deputies on patrol saw smoke rising through the treetops. Soquel Fire answered the call. Trucks sirened into Rodeo Gulch and up a macadam driveway that switched back sharply uphill to the Ohtas' summit. They braked at the cars blocking access. They saw the roof on fire. No inhabitants outside with buckets and hoses. Figured no one home, but cars jamming the roads? One fireman axed the Connie's driver's-side window, reached through the shattered glass, and popped the door. He shifted into neutral and wedged the Lincoln into the landscaping.

Firemen swarmed. Chief Ted Pound grabbed his flashlight and shined it through the shrubbery looking for the hydrant. He flashed toward the pool: a floater, a young boy. Closer look: four bodies visible, blood streaks in the water. He beamed the deck—bloodstains. He radioed the sheriff, Doug James. Told him he had a major crime scene.

Deputies sealed the premises. Firefighters sluiced the flames. The house on its way to total loss. Sheriff James doubled as coroner. He was on site examining bodies. Santa Cruz County DA Peter Chang rushed in. Pre-CSI. Santa Cruz a slow coastal town of twenty-five thousand. Deputies worked with Mayberry technology. They shined black Mags into dark corners. They probed with index fingers and picked odd ojects off the ground. First take: multiple assailants—five victims too many for a single killer.

They found clues: a discarded beer can; a note under the wiper blade on the driver's side of Ohta's Roller. The message disjointed, illiterate:

Halloween...1970. world war 3 will begin as brought to you by the pepople of the free universe.

From this day forward anyone and ?/or everyone or company of persons who missuses the natural environment or destroys same will suffer the penalty of death by the people of the free universe.

I and my comrads from this day forth will fight until death or freedom, against anything or anyone who dose not support natural life on this planet, materialiusm must die or man-kind will.

Knight Of Wands
Knight Of Cups;
Night Of Penticles
Night Of Swords

Oddball occult allusions. Snap profile: a band of hippie whack jobs orbiting Jupiter. Surf City USA growing weird. Wasn't hard to find a soothsayer to translate the Tarot references: peaking energy (swords) mixing with spiritual change (cups), new realms (cups again), and new vision (wands). Killer cult paranoia creeped in. Charles Manson and his heinous family standing trial 352 miles south: headline news for fifteen months. Nerve ends popping Helter Skelter anxieties in Santa Cruz.

October 20, the next day, 4:45 p.m.: A South-bound SP switch engine ploughed into Virginia Ohta's Olds. It was abandoned on the tracks, halfway through the 282-foot Rincon Tunnel in Henry Cowell Redwoods State Park. Someone had set fire to the front and backseats. Engine still warm. Engineer said the Olds had not been on the tracks when he'd chugged north two hours earlier.

Two-hundred-man callout with sheriff's deputies, Santa Cruz PD, CHP, firemen, and a flyover of choppers co-opted from the Bay Area. They fanned a perimeter through the wilderness around the San Lorenzo River gorge. Rumor: three longhairs, two men and a woman driving the Olds. Hot clue: three sets of footprints from the tunnel toward the gorge. Paranoia edging both ways. Longhairs feeling heat. Straights thumping vigilante tubs. "The Catalyst," a counterculture music lounge on the upper end of Front Street downtown, fielded the first of multiple unsigned bomb threats. Retro Wild West message: "only good hippie is a dead hippie."

The search ended at nightfall. Henry Cowell Park: four-thousand-plus acres of redwoods, high ridges, and steep canyons. Futile. Madman slayer(s) still at large. Community spooked. Jack Cadwallader, Dorothy's husband, wouldn't allow the *Santa Cruz Sentinel* to publish his address. He talked of "crazed killers." He slept with a loaded gun. Reactionaries demanded martial law. Handgun sales spiked fivefold. County pound slammed by panic rush for guard dogs.

Mayor Ernest Wickslund called for calm. The *Sentinel*'s next-day lead didn't help: "The grisly murder of five people has set a fuse burning on long smoldering tensions in this oceanside city." Neither did the politicians. The chairman of the board of supervisors: "We have to start looking at the transient element and those people who come here with no visible way of making a living." Another supervisor called for "laws against itinerants." The board voted for a $25,000 reward for information leading to capture and conviction.

October 22: Sheriff Doug James called a press conference at which he released the full text of the note. The *Sentinel* published it verbatim. Three longhairs read it in the paper. They asked through an intermediary to meet with DA Chang at 3:00 a.m. They were reluctant to snitch off a hippie, but five murders—too heavy to hold.

One of them, Roger Krone, said the wording of the note echoed the ranting of a weirdo who lived off Cornwell Road, in the woods west of Old San Jose Road, half a mile downhill and east of 999 Rodeo Gulch. Roger Krone lived in a commune among old farm buildings they rented on outback property called Bunny Haven, owned by a rabbit breeder named Pat Pascal. The ecofreak was her Son, John Linley Frazier, a.k.a. John Linley Pascal. Frazier himself stayed in a converted milking shed across a ravine bridged precariously with mismatched slats suspended by thin cables. Roger Krone said Frazier had talked as recently as three days before about snuffing materialists who were destroying the planet.

Quick check by sheriff's deputies. John Linley Frazier: twenty-four, local, married with a child, a mechanic who had quit his job at Putney and Perry Auto Repair, 325 Front Street, six months before. Gave old man Putney some drivel about "refusing to contribute to the death cycle of the planet." Frazier's wife, Delores, said she last saw her husband on October 17, two days before the murders.

They were separated, but he had spent the night—Saturday—at their house in San Lorenzo. He left his driver's license and a book on tarot cards—said he wouldn't need them. She said he stuffed a pack with food and stuck a .45 automatic in his waistband. She said he carried a spring-blade survivalist knife and had been dosing heavily on LSD and mescaline since spring. She said he harbored radical views on ecology.

October 22, Thursday: Warrant filed on hot suspect who was nowhere to be found. Sheriff's deputies Rod Sanford and Brad Arbsland walked across the creaking bridge. They reconned the shack and the perimeter woods. No sign of John Linley Frazier. They set an ankle-high twig on the first plank of the bridge and another against the doorway of the dwelling. They recrossed the bridge and bivouacked in a brushy hill across the ravine.

October 23, daybreak: Deputies checked the foot span. Someone had slipped past in the night and tripped the twigs. Rod Sanford went over first, swaying on the unstable span, both hands gripping the cables, a sitting duck if the suspect burst from the door and opened fire. Sanford inhaled and stepped across. Arbsland hung back to cover his partner. Nothing stirred from inside the shanty.

Arbsland followed across the bridge. Both deputies framed the door, Sanford with a 12 gauge Remington pump. Arbsland kicked in the door from the right. Rod Sanford ducked in low from the left, Arbsland behind. Six-by-six one-room shack. They took it in with an eyeball sweep: a pile of sleeping bags on the floor near the far wall. Rod Sanford pointed his shotgun. Brad Arbsland pulled back the top bag. Bearded man in a leather headband underneath, eyes open.

Sanford: "Make a move, and I'll shoot."

John Linley Frazier, grinning off-kilter: "Why don't you just give me what I deserve?"

Rod Sanford tempted...holding his discipline.

II

Rod Sanford and Brad Arbsland humped Frazier to the county jail on upper Front Street. They booked him, mugged him, and rolled his prints. The prints returned a positive match with crime-scene impressions lifted off the beer can that had been discarded at the Ohta place and off the maroon Rolls. Things moving now.

Burglary ruled out—expensive jewelry and electronics left behind. Single killer now a plausible explanation. Interviews with the school and the medical-complex staff charted time frames. Virginia Ohta was home alone three hours before Dorothy Cadwallader and Taggert arrived—an hour and a half in front of Victor and Derrick. One maniac with a weapon could have done it.

October 23, 1:00 p.m.: John Linley Frazier hustled into a lineup. Six separate witnesses ID'ed him as the driver of Virginia Ohta's dark-green Olds in Felton the day after the murders.

October 26, Monday, 10:00 a.m.: John Frazier arraigned on five counts of murder before municipal court judge Donald O. May. Judge May had appointed local attorney James Jackson, former Alameda County deputy DA, as his public defender. Jim Jackson moved to dismiss. Judge May denied the motion. On Frazier's behalf, Jackson entered a plea of not guilty and asked for bail. Judge May considered the slaughter of a prominent citizen and most of his family. No bail.

October 26, same arraignment hearing: deputy DA Art Danner submitted an affidavit announcing Peter Chang's intent to seek a grand-jury indictment. Judge May granted a forty-eight-hour delay. Pete Chang eager to bypass a preliminary hearing in the municipal court. The DA controls the action with a grand jury, serving evidence to a GJ panel under a seal of secrecy. No judges; no defense counsel. The DA can lock grand-jury witnesses under oath that will constitute perjury if changed at trial.

October 27: Jim Jackson filed a motion of discovery. Pre-OJ: discovery a one-way street. The DA's office obligated to share evidence without expectation of reciprocity. Initial read: case against his client porous—no direct evidence, no confession, no eyewitnesses. No evidence proving Frazier was present at the times of the murders. Jim Jackson's investigator, Harold Cartwright, searched the property around Frazier's shack. In a chicken coop, he found the orange backpack, the .45, a Swiss watch, and a pair of expensive binoculars stolen from Victor Ohta.

Jackson ceded the items to the police and the prosecution. Why not? None of them placed him at the scene during the murders. Multiple Sources claimed John Linley Frazier creeped houses in Soquel Hills. The binoculars had been missing for months—Taura Ohta verified. The .45 wasn't a murder weapon. The Swiss watch was trickier: Taura Ohta said it belonged to her brother Derrick.

Judge Charles Franich denied bail. Jackson reentered a not guilty plea. Pretrial publicity a huge concern. Judge Franich imposed a gag order and set a post–New Year trial date, January 25, 1971.

Events pushed it back six months:

January 9, 1971: Frazier slashed his wrists with a razor. He survived; medical attention required—four to six stitches. Frazier trying suicide but not very hard.

January 19, 1971: Jim Jackson drafted Dr. Donald T. Lunde, assistant professor of psychiatry at Stanford. Frazier's backstory revealed little. He went to San Lorenzo Valley elementary. His parents divorced, like half the parents in his generation. Dad fell out of sight. John Frazier dropped out of high school and was popped for petty crimes before stabilizing with marriage and steady work as an automobile mechanic.

No markers for murder, but something tripped him. From one interview, Don Lunde knew Frazier was red-lining paranoid schizophrenia. He said Frazier believed the book of Revelation (the revelation of Saint John the Divine) was speaking directly to him because his first name was John. From New Testament misreads, street drug delusion, and tarot-card mumbo jumbo, Frazier heard lordly voices directing him to kill on behalf of the planet. Jim Jackson amended the plea: not guilty and not guilty by reason of insanity. Judge Franich ordered psychiatric evals.

Dr. John Peschau from Agnews State Mental Hospital in Santa Clara and a practicing Salinas shrink, Dr. Robert Noce, assessed him. Judge Franich asked for reports by February 9 and scheduled a hearing one week later.

February 16: Dr. Peschau reported that Frazier was sociopathic, not psychotic. Dr. Noce said Frazier was mentally defective. Judge Franich ruled him legally competent—meaning sufficiently lucid to participate in his own defense.

Jim Jackson moved for change in venue. Judge Franich noted the gag order on pretrial publicity and denied the motion. Jim Jackson filed a writ with the First Circuit Court of Appeals in San Francisco. He cited adverse public opinion and the size of Santa Cruz County. His pitch: Judge Franich's order controlled only court officers and law enforcement. It couldn't stifle compulsive chatter at gas pumps or break rooms, in checkout lines, or over back fences.

By area, Santa Cruz is the smallest county in California. Word travels. Word of disaster travels faster. The Ohta funeral made headlines, with full-page art showing the distraught faces of grieving survivors, notably Victor Ohta's mother and his two daughters sniffling under black mantillas. Services at Holy Cross Catholic, the church at Mission Santa Cruz, drew more than a thousand mourners. Dorothy Cadwallader's funeral attracted three hundred. It would be impossible to find potential jurors without attitudes about the Ohta massacre.

The First Circuit Court of Appeals issued a summary dismissal on the writ. Jim Jackson filed an automatic appeal, kicking it to the state supreme court.

July 7, 1971: In a six-to-one ruling, the higher court reversed the lower. Chief justice Stanley Mosk cited three precedents involving murder, kidnap, and rape in Lassen, Mendocino, and Stanislaus Counties. All involved thrill-killers preying on teenagers. None was innocent, but their verdicts and/or penalties paralleled the Frazier case. They'd committed crimes in rural parts of the state where word-of-mouth spun viral hate and fear, rendering defendants "friendless in the community."

The state's Judicial Council moved the trial to Redwood City, San Mateo County. Judges in short supply in San Mateo. Charles Franich traveled. From October to December, he stayed with the prosecution and defense teams in separate wings under the same orange roof, a Howard Johnson's in Redwood City. The proceedings trifurcated: determination of guilt, determination of sanity, and penalty.

Peter Chang took it personally. He identified with Victor Ohta. Pete was a Korean American, twelve years younger than Ohta. He went to Stanford law. He was elected SC County DA in 1966 at age twenty-nine, the youngest DA in the nation at the time, and the only Asian. He had fought stereotypes—criminal-law firms couldn't feature an oriental Perry Mason. He took speech and acting lessons to enhance his courtroom presence. Pete empathized beyond the Asian thing. He had three children of his own, of similar ages. A wacko had slaughtered two-thirds of his friend's family.

Chang argued for the prosecution; Jim Jackson for the defense. Jackson fought hard in a lost cause. The prosecution called sixty-eight witnesses; the defense, twelve. Deputy DA Chris Cottle was assigned to organize the string of exhibits for Peter Chang to argue. Cottle started with a jigsaw challenge—more than a hundred separate pieces of evidence. Chang: "The case was a circumstantial monster." Chris Cottle equal to the job; he fit the facts into an irrefutable pattern of guilt.

Circumstantial often is more reliable than direct. Witnesses can be impeached or cancelled out, or they can perform badly on the stand. Circumstances don't change. Arranged effectively, they permit the jury to infer guilt. Peter Chang entered Frazier's hunting knife as an exhibit. Chris Cottle ran state's evidence through the attorney general's office in Sacramento. State crime-lab technicians noted metallic elements on Frazier's knife blade that matched the insulated phone wires that had been sliced in the Ohtas' house at the time of the murders.

Jim Jackson introduced an expert to demonstrate that the wire could have been cut by anything sharp. Pete Chang handed the expert a length of the same wire and a pocket knife. The expert struggled and strained through the task. He couldn't sever the insulation. Jim Jackson moved to strike the testimony of his own expert. Defense credibility took a large hit.

The biggest hole in the prosecution's case was the absence of murder weapons. Chris Cottle covered. A family named Muni lived in the vicinity of the Ohtas' hillside estate. Their house had been burglarized some time before the murder. Among the missing items: .38 and .22 caliber revolvers, and ammo for both. DA's investigators had retrieved a briefcase from Delores Frazier's house. Inside: fifty-six .22 caliber cartridges and four for .38s. The state crime lab ran ballistics. The bullets recovered from the five Ohta corpses matched the Munis' ammo and the cartridges found in the Frazier briefcase.

November 29, 1971: An eight-woman, four-man jury deliberated twenty-one hours and found John Linley Frazier guilty on five counts of murder.

November 31, 1971: sanity phase. California is one of twenty-one states that employ the nineteenth-century M'Naghten standard. Under M'Naghten, sanity is a rebuttable presumption weighed by a jury upon presented evidence. Backstory, England, 1843: a Scottish woodturner named Daniel M'Naghten fixated on Prime Minister

Sir Robert Peel, originator of the modern British police force who worked out of Scotland Yard. Peel was a Tory big shot; M'Naghten an insignificant Whig. One day on Downing Street, M'Naghten fired a pistol into what he thought was the back of Sir Robert Peel. In fact, he killed Peel's secretary, Edward Drummond.

M'Naghten's barrister, Sir Alexander Cockburn, stipulated his client's guilt. His defense rested solely on M'Naghten's mental condition, easily established as disturbed. Jurors found Daniel M'Naghten "Not guilty on reason of insanity" and set him free. Outraged, Queen Victoria demanded a retrial in the House of Lords, but double jeopardy under English law prevented it. The House of Lords instead commissioned chief justice of common pleas, Sir Nicholas Conyngham Tindal, to convene a panel of black robes and powdered wigs to close the loophole.

The result was the M'Naghten test, the judicial standard ever since. The defendant is not responsible if he is "…labouring under such a defect of reason, from disease of the mind, as to not know the nature and quality of the act he was doing, or if he did know, he did not know what he was doing was wrong." Simplified: Was the defendant aware the crime was wrong at the moment of commission?

In jailhouse sessions, Frazier detailed the murders to Don Lunde and UCSC doctor of psychology David Marlowe. Both were free to testify; the insanity plea waives doctor-patient privilege. As witnesses, the doctors had to re-create the crime to demo the workings of a disordered brain. Hard for a jury to assimilate complex jargon; easier to fall back on M'Naghten, in which premeditation and cover-up imply legal sanity. John Frazier stalked the Ohtas. He planned his crimes. He ditched murder weapons and dumped a stolen escape car. He was nuts, but he knew what he was doing.

December 3, 1971: J. L. Frazier in court with his head shaved vertically in half: full beard, mustache, and shoulder-length hair to the left side of his nose; bare skin on the right. One foolscap with bells away from a full harlequin. Dr. Marlowe said Frazier was feigning insanity so the jury would see through his act—Frazier on record preferring death row to a "fascist head factory." Dr. Marlowe noted the fresh hairstyle. Said it was the product of a distorted mind. Dr. Peschau testified that the same ploy proved Frazier was able to think clearly and strategize. Frazier favored death row over a padded cell: Proof of functional ability. Dr. Peshau called him "crafty."

Dr. Don Lunde's opinion was pivotal. In direct examination, Lunde maintained that Frazier's delusions morally impelled him to kill. On cross, Pete Chang hooked him with M'Naghten. Chang: "Was he capable of knowing the acts violated the standard of conduct that had been formulated by Society?"

Lunde, reluctantly: "I'd have to say he was."

December 9, 1971: The jury took five and a half hours to find the defendant legally sane; one week later, four hours to establish the penalty. One of the jurors suffered from a significant stuttering problem. He locked up during the final tally and couldn't spit out his vote. The other eleven, eager to end an eight-week sequester, drummed impatiently, making it worse. Frustrated, the stutterer mimed his vote—he slashed an index finger across his throat. Twelve-to-zero verdict: John Linley Frazier headed to the green room.

III

1971/1972: Americans shell-shocked from the '60s, when nightly news anchors Walter Cronkite, Frank Reynolds, and Howard K. Smith brought sensory overload into their living rooms around dinnertime.

Graphic images of a nightmare era reverberating: Lee Harvey Oswald sniping JFK in Dallas. Shady Jack Ruby gunning down Oswald the dupe in a police station corridor. Warren Commission whitewashing the truth. Zapgruder film zealots chattering conspiracy frame by frame. Mississippi rednecks lynching and shooting Freedom Riders. Alabama peace officers fire-hosing civil rights demonstrators. C-130s lifting off from Da Nang cargoed with body bags of American Soldiers. FBI wiretapping Martin Luther King Jr. and storm-trooping Black Panthers in Chicago. MLK gunned down in Memphis by a Tennessee cracker (or parties unknown).

Black Power shootouts with police. Bobby Kennedy assassinated by Sirhan Sirhan (the Manchurian candidate?) in the ballroom of the Ambassador Hotel in Los Angeles. Richard Nixon's Watergate White House—a band of political thugs and hard-core perjurers. Images: Kent State; Woodstock; Altamont. Campus shutdowns at San Francisco State; race riots in LA and Detroit.

Fallout:

Longhairs flooded back to nature, pouring into Mendocino County, Yosemite, eastern Sierra deserts, and the Santa Cruz Mountains. An estimated seventeen thousand scattered into Santa Cruz, carving out new-age experiments behind tall trees. They formed communes in sheltered glens. They squatted in vacation shacks and rustic lean-tos. They pitched nylon tents and built hovels from scrap wood. They lived off the land and on it. They drank run-off creek water from the San Lorenzo River. They cultivated arable patches between redwood groves. They harvested vegetables for food and weed for profit and use. They tucked into macrobiotic rice and sipped herbal tea. They scavenged food and clothing; they panhandled for spending money. They shit in the woods and breast-fed in public. They dropped acid. They scammed welfare. They passed fatties around Kumbaya campfires.

Meanwhile:

The University of California, Santa Cruz, had opened for business in 1965 as the progressive ninth campus in the university system. New ideas turned loose in Surf City. The campus spread over two thousand upland acres between Wilder Ranch and Henry

Cowell Redwoods State Park. UCSC was chartered with forward vision. It was built on a foothill slope—285 feet at the entrance gate to 1,195 feet at the northern boundary, where an RV park spilling east into Henry Cowell functions as student housing. It was designed to blend into oak and redwood groves overlooking Monterey Bay to the south, the wild Pacific coast to the west, and the heart of the Santa Cruz Mountains to the north and east.

UCSC opened with 650 students. Planners projected a cap of nineteen thousand by 1980. UCSC broke with stuffy traditions; the school attracted surfers, ecofreaks, and liberals. The school mascot: a banana slug.

1971: The state of California lowered the voting age to eighteen. UCSC student body plus faculty and staff vested themselves into the community as voters in an electorate now trending left. Motorcycle mechanic Mike Rotkin was a symbol. Mike Rotkin attended UCSC. He laddered degrees through a "history of consciousness" PhD. UCSC appointed him adjunct (non-tenured) lecturer in human studies. He taught Marxist theory. He transfused left-wing scholarship into local politics. He was elected six times to the city council; was six times town mayor. Santa Cruz spent 80k per annum on social services in 1979, the year Rotkin first was elected. Two decades later, the figure was $2 million. UCSC influenced beneficence to the dispossessed. Societal rejects noticed. They swarmed toward the generous new Santa Cruz.

Meanwhile:

1967: Governor Ronald Reagan signed the Lanterman-Petris-Short Act into law, crippling the state's capacity to provide mental-health care. Bleeding hearts blasted Reagan for his insensitivity, but the governor was not acting alone. In fact, he was massaging a bizarre coalition of right-wing fiscal conservatives, an uber-liberal patients' rights lobby, and the American Civil Liberties Union. Fully operational by 1972, LPS amplified section 5000 of the California Welfare & Institutions Code, introducing into the lexicon the term

"5150." Section 5150 of the amended code prohibits law enforcement, judges, and doctors from detaining patients longer than seventy-two hours—and only then for evaluation in the face of imminent danger.

Right-wingers loved the new law. It constricted the supply of mental patients, rendering state institutions cost-ineffective, greasing closures, permitting the state to pork-barrel budget money elsewhere. Patients' rights lobbyists loved it. The state could no longer warehouse the insane. ACLU leftists loved it. They viewed forcible commitment as trampling nutcase civil rights. One by one, the state hospitals in Northern California shut down. Mendocino. Dewitt in Auburn. Stockton. Sonoma. Napa. Agnews in Santa Clara. The burden shifted. The feds promised subsidies to offset but reneged. The private sector and the counties stood the cost for halfway houses, homeless shelters, group homes, and sanitariums.

Proponents rationalized that modern psychotropic drugs would compensate. The nuts could pop magic meds as outpatients. The proponents didn't account for patients dosing themselves erratically or mixing antipsychotics with street drugs. They didn't account for side effects pushing patients off their meds or reeling them into counterpsychoses. They didn't differentiate between manic-depressive mood swingers, sad-sack schizos skipping on reality, and compulsive killers. They didn't account for lost souls surviving like stray cats, swatting at imaginary insects and conversing with the wind, sleeping in downtown doorways, and scarfing food from Dumpsters. They didn't account for the fact that they had set the madmen loose.

1972: women roaring about Helen Reddy liberation usurped men-only privileges—underarm hair, tattoos, F-word fluency, and hitchhiking. Hippie chicks with outstretched thumbs on roadsides and on-ramps: as common in the era as pierced navels and bell bottoms. Hitchhiking offered advantages. It brought a sense of adventure. It was less creepy, cramped, and smelly than Greyhound buses and cheaper than trains and planes. Hitchhiking involved no security checkers pawing backpacks. It was faster than muni buses. One drawback—and a big one—hitchhiking was as dangerous for women as Russian roulette.

Two Fresno State coeds, Mary Anne Pesce, nineteen, and Anita Luchese, eighteen, from Camarillo and Modesto, respectively, hit the road in early May. They thumbed up 99, over 580 to Berkeley.

May 7: They headed for Stanford. They scratched out a cardboard destination sign— Palo Alto. They stood on a corner on the north side of Ashby Avenue, toward the Bay. A yellow two-door Ford Galaxie stopped. Big man driving said he had business at Stanford. All the way in one shot—a hitchhiker's dream.

The big man picked up I-80 at the foot of Ashby and cloverleafed south down the Nimitz freeway (SR 17 then; now I-880), the road along the east shore of the Bay from San Rafael to Santa Cruz. He exited near Hayward. The girls lived in Clovis—they had no idea Palo Alto was across the water. The big man turned onto a dirt road leading to a remote area in the hills above the Hayward. He had tricked the passenger's door lock with an empty ChapStick tube. The man pulled to a stop in an underbrush cutout. The girls were locked in.

He forced Anita Luchese into the trunk and slammed the lid. He handcuffed Mary Ann Pesce and placed her facedown in the backseat. He hooded her with a plastic bag. He strangled her with toweling. She bit through the plastic; the terrycloth ripped. He pulled a knife and stabbed her to death. He popped the rear lid and stabbed Anita Luchese. He slammed Mary Ann Pesce in the trunk and spun wheels to SR 17 toward the Santa Cruz Mountains. He beheaded and dismembered both girls, disposing of their body parts in the wilds around Loma Prieta Mountain.

September 14, 1972: Fifteen-year-old Aiko Koo just missing a bus on University Avenue in Berkeley. Aiko Koo was a precocious Korean dance student running late for a ballet lesson in San

Francisco. Her mother worked in the library at UC Berkeley. The Koos had no car. Skaidrite Koo usually accompanied her daughter by muni, but she was overbooked that evening. Aiko insisted on traveling alone.

Skaidrite relented against her instincts, but only if Aiko took the bus—Aiko had started hitchhiking, which worried her mother. Aiko agreed, but…diesel smells, sardine-tin seating, airbrakes hissing to a halt at every lamppost. Teenage impulse vs. abstract parental alarm: an easy call. She jumped to the curb and stuck out her thumb. A yellow Ford stopped—big man asking about her destination. She said San Francisco. He said hop in. Aiko Koo was smart with directions. She knew something was wrong when they crossed the bridge and ramped down Highway 101.

She started to scream. He pulled a .22 revolver. Said he was planning to use it on himself. Said if she didn't cry out or signal for help, he wouldn't hurt her. He lied. They drove south on 17 past Campbell and Los Gatos, gaining in elevation across Patchen Summit, exiting onto narrow S-turn mountain roads. The big man braked at a spot off Two-Bar Road near Bonny Doon.

Aiko Koo was fifteen and ballet petite. The man was huge—six foot nine, 280 pounds. He easily overwhelmed her. He duct-taped her mouth. He stuck his thumb and index finger into her nostrils and snuffed her breath. He strangled her with a scarf. He lifted her from the car and raped her postmortem. He hacked off her head with an ornamental sword. He threw her body into a ravine, stashed her head in the trunk.

Santa Cruz County, 1970--73: Tripling the FBI's annual US statistical average of homocides per 100,000 population (8.4). City cops and sheriff's deputies overwhelmed. City and county murder victims were stacked in body bags, and law enforcement had nothing. The operating theories—hippie killer cult; single maniac; one or both of the above plus copycat(s)—produced no leads, let alone suspects.

Peter Chang: "We'd get together, all the chiefs, meeting at the Holiday Inn [on Ocean Street next to the county administration building], but invariably we'd end up getting drunk and accomplish nothing...couldn't even form a task force without stepping on each other's jurisdiction."

October 13, 1972: Lawrence White, fifty-five, fruit tramp, had spent the night in Henry Cowell Park with a jug of muscatel under redwood needles dripping rain. He was stumbling along Highway 9, three miles south of Felton, above a stretch of canyon overlooking the San Lorenzo River. He saw a Chevy station wagon parked in a dirt cutout, hood up. A young man gestured. Lawrence White had experience with engines. Through his alky fuzz he formed a plan: help the kid, maybe bum a ride downtown and panhandle bus fare to Watsonville for harvest season peaking in the Pajaro Valley. Friends from the streets said he worked winter crops in the Coachella Valley. Two weeks on an orchard ladder picking cider apples could net a travel stake.

The young man asked White if he knew anything about cars—his wouldn't start. Lawrence White ducked under the hood. He checked the battery posts and tugged the distributor wires. He straightened and turned. The young man had a baseball bat. He swung both hands in an overhand arc that crushed Lawrence White's skull. He dragged White's corpse into roadside underbrush. He fired up the Chevy and spun off.

No one stressed about a dead wino discovered by a hiker later that day, Friday the thirteenth. SCSD detective Terry Medina ID'ed Lawrence White from prints matching a D&D arrest in September. Medina mingled with street bums downtown and obtained a scatter of bio facts. The booking card listed the name and address of a sister in Chicago. Routine teletype returned no such street. Next-of-kin notice: we tried. White was buried at county expense, gravediggers only in attendance.

October 24, 1972, Tuesday, 3:30 p.m.: Mary Guilfoyle, twenty-four, had a 4:30 p.m. job interview downtown at the unemployment office. Guilfoyle lived with her boyfriend in a small apartment on E. Cliff Drive. Mary Guilfoyle was from Buffalo, New York. She was majoring in English at Cabrillo College in Aptos, a part-time TA looking to augment her meager wages. She feared missing the appointment. Santa Cruz County's crappy bus system a consideration. Anxiety overtook caution. She stepped into the pavement. A blue/white Chevy station wagon stopped. Young man driving.

She told him where she was headed. He said, "Get in." He exited off 1 and drove past the social-services complex on Emeline until Emeline turned into El Rancho Avenue. Mary Guilfoyle looked at him. El Rancho turned rural. He stopped on the shoulder. No houses around; area profuse with trees. Mary Guilfoyle confused.

The man raised a Finn Double-X hunting knife and stabbed her in the chest. She slumped forward. He stabbed her twice more in the back. The force of the blows dropped her onto the floor. The man geared up the Chevy. He wound through the mountains—west at Sims Road, north on Graham Hill, past Henry Cowell Park. Graham Hill to Felton-Empire Road to Empire Grade Road. Left on Empire Grade three miles. Right on Smith Grade, a twisting two-lane road dipping into a vast gully thick with redwood groves. He drove five miles and stopped. He dragged Guilfoyle's body 125 yards into an opening between the trees. He eviscerated her with his Finn Double-X. He wiped his knife with a spatter-free tail of his shirt and sped off.

November 2, 1972: Saint Mary's Catholic Church in Los Gatos, twenty miles from Santa Cruz over SR 17. All Souls' Day—big deal for Catholics: Solemn time of prayer for the dead still confined to purgatory. Catholics tend to complicate transmission to the hereafter. They celebrate anxiety with ritual. Afternoon: too early in the day for Catholics to process their devotion. Saint Mary's empty. A man walked into the sanctuary. He dipped his fingers into the stoup. He genuflected. He looked around. He noticed the confessional. The light above the door was on.

He stumbled on a kneeler on his way to the booth. He grabbed violently at the knob: booth locked. He rattled the knob. Inside,

Father Henry Tomei heard. He opened the door. The man knifed him in the chest. They grappled, and both fell back into the confessional. The priest kicked the man in the ear. The man stabbed Father Henry Tomei twice more, killing him.

A Santa Cruz derelict, three female hitchhikers in the Bay Area, another in Aptos, and a Los Gatos priest. Six dead or missing. Both genders. Age range from fifteen to sixty-four. Three counties, multiple MOs. City cops and sheriff's deputies hitting walls chasing false leads.

January 24, 1973: SCPD captain Richard Overton: "This thing has a pattern to it. It's not [a] case of some crazy man running around shooting people." He had no idea. Nobody did. The Carpenters caught the grisly paradigm in sappy pop lyrics airing the previous August: "We've only just begun."

IV

Murders piling up:

January 8, 1973: A nineteen-year-old Cabrillo College student thumbing to class from her rented room on Cleveland Avenue off Business 1, on the west side of Santa Cruz. An eight-mile hop; twelve minutes by car; forever by bus. Cynthia Schall elated when a yellow Ford rolled up and waved her in. Big man driving. "Where you headed?" She said Cabrillo; he said he'd take her to campus. She had noticed the car had a "UCSC Staff Lot A" parking sticker on the front bumper. He picked up SR 1 at Soquel Avenue. She thought he'd exit at Park Avenue.

He passed the ramp and stayed on SR 1 toward Watsonville. Cynthia Schall alarmed. He exited onto Freedom Road toward Corralitos and cut into the woods up a ridge route and parked. He took out a .22 pistol and ordered Schall into the trunk of his car. She complied. He shot her…and more. A CHP cruiser found two severed arms and legs the next day on Highway 1 South of Big Sur.

A week later, a mutilated human torso bobbed to the surface in a lagoon off the San Lorenzo River near Santa Cruz. Two days after that, a surfer in Capitola found a left hand. Three days after that, a citizen walking the beach stumbled across a female pelvis along the Santa Cruz shoreline. The medical examiner gathered body parts. He pieced together everything but a head and a right hand. Fingerprints from the left hand matched prints lifted from Cynthia Schall's room. She had had a chest X-ray three months earlier. Her lungs matched the torso from the lagoon.

January 24, 1973, 9:00 a.m.: The man in the '58 Chevy wheeled through pounding rain up Branciforte Drive toward the world-famous Mystery Spot, an old-house tourist trap constructed in such a way that round objects on the floor roll uphill. He stopped at a dirt driveway turned to mud. He walked to a clearing between underbrush and wild berry vines toward four crude dwellings—a tree-limb log cabin, a brick hovel, and two turtleback trailers—that shared a bootlegged mailing address, 1965 Branciforte.

None of the dwellings had utility hookups; only one of the trailers had phone service. The man knocked at the cabin. Kathy Prentiss, a.k.a. Kathy Francis, age twenty-nine, opened. The man asked for Jim Gianera. Kathy Francis said the Gianeras had moved three months earlier to a small two-story Jim had built on Western Avenue off the coast road. The man slogged back toward his car.

Jim Gianera, age twenty-five, from San Lorenzo High and Cabrillo College. An out-of-work carpenter who dealt dope with a partner, Bob Francis, Kathy Prentiss's common-law husband, the father of her youngest, four-year-old Daemon. Daemon's half-brother, nine-year-old David, was the product of Kathy's union with an Albany musician named Robert Hughes. Jim Gianera and Bob Francis had picked up seven pounds of weed the day before. Bob Francis was hauling it to Berkeley.

Jim needed the money from his share. His new house had electricity. PG&E charged for same. Jim fell behind; PG&E had turned off his utilities nine days earlier. Gianera dealt dope. He owned a panel truck that didn't run and that he couldn't afford to fix. He borrowed a beater pickup from Bob Francis for round-town transportation. Jim Gianera was hanging around the house when he heard a knock on the door. His wife, Joan, twenty-one, was upstairs.

Jim Gianera opened the door and recognized the man who drove the '58 Chevy wagon. No invitation to enter. The man fumbled through a conversation. Gianera asked him what he wanted. The man pulled a .22 revolver from his pocket. The man shrieked, "You're claptrapping me." Gianera bolted for the kitchen. The man shot him in the right arm. Gianera groped frantically for a weapon. All he reached was a plastic half-gallon milk bottle, but his ruined right arm couldn't form a grip. Gianera stumbled toward the stairs. Another shot shattered his right elbow. A third penetrated his lung. A fourth went wide and splintered a doorjamb.

Joan heard noises like firecracker pops. She rushed to the stairwell. The man's fifth shot hit Jim Gianera in the head. The sixth slammed Joan in the chest. The man pulled a knife and stabbed her in the back. He popped empty shells from the cylinder. He reloaded from a cartridge box in his pocket. He shot Joan Gianera three times in the neck.

January 24, 1973: Half an hour later. The man fretted about witnesses. He drove south on Mission and crossed Pacific onto Water Street. He drove to Market Street and turned left. Market snake-curves through downtown residences into Branciforte Drive. Anxiety pulled at him. He passed Delaveaga Park on Branciforte and stopped near the Mystery Spot. He trudged through mud to the cabin. Inside, Kathy Francis faced a rainy day with two small children. The boys played Chinese checkers on their bunk. She fed the wood stove with loose logs from a pile on the floor. She had worries like the Gianeras'. Bob built kayaks and dealt dope. She drew welfare. They never had enough. Six weeks past Christmas, her tree still stood in the living room, brown needles and sparse ornaments. Her life was depressing. She often was stoned.

She heard a noise at the front door. Same dude as before pushed his way into the house. He had a gun. He blasted Kathy Francis twice: once in the chest, the other in her head. He turned to the boys. He shot four-year-old Daemon through the left eye and nine-year-childhood David in the forehead. He drew his knife and stabbed Kathy in the chest and the boys in the back. They were already dead.

Panic spreading throughout Santa Cruz County. UCSC posted warnings:

> When possible, girls especially, stay in dorms after midnight with the doors locked. If you must be out at night, walk in pairs. If you see a campus police car and wave, they will give you a ride. Use the bus even if somewhat inconvenient. Your safety is important. If you are leaving campus, advise someone where you are going, where you can be reached, and the approximate time of your return.
>
> DON'T HITCH A RIDE, PLEASE!!!

UCSC was designed to blend with nature. The master plans excluded space-eating parking lots but carved walking paths through foliage; no part of campus was more than a leafy, twenty-minute stroll from another. UCSC advertised itself as a residential college. Naive assumption: students would live all four years in residence halls. The 1970s reality was that the school was four miles uphill from town.

Students tended to peel off after a semester in the dorms and join subcultural pilgrims in downtown rooms and apartments or communes in the woods. Policy discouraged UCSC students from driving cars. Students were surcharged $3.50 a semester so that the university could contract with the city of Santa Cruz for inadequate transit services. Buses into town filled fast during peak hours, stranding passengers on every run. The busses were scheduled every half hour.

February 5, 1973: Rosalind Thorpe, twenty-three, a senior from Carmel, rushed through the front doors of the science library at 9:00 p.m. She lived downtown, on Mott Street. She'd read the flyers but couldn't see a cruiser. She had missed the latest bus; thirty minutes until the next one. She stood at the curb schlepping a handful of heavy books. A yellow '69 Ford Galaxie two-door dragged by. She noticed a "UCSC Staff Lot A" decal on the front bumper. The Ford stopped. The driver, a big man, asked if she needed a ride. She was reassured by the campus parking sticker. She was tired. She wanted to go home. She hopped in.

They drove two blocks. Alice Liu, twenty-one, from Torrance, stood in front of the main library in the same predicament. She saw the Ford. A couple in front, a man and a woman. A university decal on the bumper. No red flags. She stuck out her thumb. The big man wended his way around campus roads to a secluded spot.

He stopped the car and shot both women with a .22 revolver. He dropped them to the floorboards and covered them in blankets. The guard-shack guy saw the bumper decal and waved the Ford through the gate. Classmates reported the girls missing the next day. Campus fire marshal Mike Hughes organized eight search teams from students, staff, faculty, and volunteers. They combed two-thousand acres of forest without success.

Two days later, an Alameda County road crew was surveying storm damage in Eden Canyon. Down a ravine, they spotted what they thought were discarded mannequins. Hard to tell—the mannequins had no heads. Closer look: human. One nude, missing her hands. From her skin tone, they speculated that she was Asian. The other was Caucasian, in a bra and panties. The ME used X-rays and dental charts. IDs established within a week: Alice Liu and Rosalind Thorpe.

February 9, 1973: Brian Scott Card, nineteen, had graduated from Van Nuys High the previous June. He and his older brother

Jeff set off to backpack through Northern California. In August, they found a spot off Oxtail Trail uphill a quarter of a mile from Highway 9 in a seldom-traveled section of Henry Cowell State Park called the Garden of Eden overlook. They fashioned a five-sided ten-by-ten shelter out of tree limbs and rolls of opaque plastic. They built a teepee roof and a plastic entry hall. They camped without hassle for six months.

They had met a fifteen-year-old who helped them construct the tent. He told them his name was Mark Johnson. In fact, he was a runaway from Pennsylvania named Mark John Dreibelis who had skipped the jurisdiction after a marijuana bust. Jeff Card had moved out in late January; he was staying with friends in an actual house in Boulder Creek. Two buddies from So-Cal had showed ten days earlier: Rob Spector and David Oliker, both eighteen. They had hitchhiked from Van Nuys, en route to Humboldt County. Rob Spector intended to enroll for the spring semester at the College of the Redwoods in Arcata. Oliker, a student at Valley CC in Van Nuys, was along for the adventure.

Early morning, drizzling: Scott Card trying to start a fire with wet twigs. He sensed a shadow in the entry. He looked up. A young man standing in silence, rain dripping off his hair. Eight sets of eyes fixed on the intruder. He told the boys they were camping on federal land without a permit. He wore no uniform and showed no badge. They F-bombed his pretense of authority. The man pulled a .22 revolver.

He fired six shots into four bodies, hitting each one at least once. He dipped into a coat pocket for a box of cartridges. He snicked out the spent shells and thumbed in fresh bullets. He emptied the gun into the four boys. No survivors.

The young man picked their pockets for twenty-one dollars. He saw a .22 rifle propped against one plastic wall. He grabbed it and split down Oxtail Trail to a cut-out on the side of Highway 9, where he had parked his blue/white '58 Chevrolet Nomad.

February 12, 1973: Schools closed for Lincoln's birthday. Teenage target shooters chipping bark off trees near Majors Creek on Smith Grade Road stumbled across a skeleton. They ran for their car and jammed eight miles to the Fall Creek fire station on Empire Grade Road. The firemen called the sheriffs. Sirens screamed through Felton. Pathologists confirmed the identity of the remains via charts from a local dentist: Mary Guilfoyle, twenty-four, Cabrillo College student.

V

The Gianeras were city; Francises, county. Ballistics matched slugs from both jurisdictions. The same .22 revolver killed the Gianeras, Kathy Francis, David Hughes, and Daemon Francis. SCSD and SCPD collaborating. Investigators knee-jerking stock theories—bloody love triangle or drug burn. They braced neighbors from the trailers and the brick hut. Nothing. They checked out Robert Hughes. He was distraught over losing his son. Nothing suspicious. He was cordial with his ex. He played the bassoon and lived in Albany. He was alibied out his ass.

They waited for Bob Francis. He showed up two days after the murders, at 9:00 p.m. on January 26, 1973, a Friday. They brought him downtown in handcuffs. Bob Francis could prove his whereabouts elsewhere. He had crashed at a hostel in Berkeley and had driven to Marysville to visit friends. Investigators searched his '67 El Camino. They found empty smuggling compartments cut into wheel wells and in the bed behind the cab. Bob Francis volunteered for a polygraph. They brought in a technician from the state attorney general's office. The technician thought Francis was lying about something—'70s dope dealers tended to double-talk their livelihoods—but not the murders.

Investigators grasping. Santa Cruz in the '70s: hippies passed around partners like glowing joints. The Francises lived in a shit-hole commune. The Gianeras couldn't pay their bills. Hippies wouldn't kill over shared sex. Bob Francis and Jim Gianera: small-time dealers. If they scored big enough to warrant killing, Bob Francis would have moved someplace with thermostatic heat and running water. Jim Gianera would have gas and lights. He could have fixed his piece-of-shit truck.

February 13, 1973: Fred Perez, seventy-two, lived in a small house on Lighthouse Avenue, one block north of oceanfront West Cliff Boulevard. He was descended from one of the original Santa Cruz settlers—his grandfather founded a fish company on the wharf in 1863. His ancestors were wholesalers to the Stagnaro family's seafood retail and restaurant businesses. Fred Perez served with the Marine Corps in China in World War I. He boxed in the corps, a middleweight. He fought professionally in the 1920s along the Central Coast as Fighting Freddie Bell. He went into the family fish business, worked forty years, and retired in 1969. He owned two houses: the cottage at 511 Lighthouse and a rental next door. He was shoveling dirt into a chuckhole off the curb near the driveway of the rental early on a foggy Tuesday morning.

A young man in a blue/white Chevrolet Nomad creeped east on Lighthouse. He pulled to the left-hand curb at the corner of Gharkey Street, seventy-five yards from where Fred Perez was hauling dirt. Through his open rear window, he sighted in with a .22 rifle he had taken four days earlier from the tent near Oxtail Trail. Fred Perez was straining over a wheelbarrow. The man squeezed off a shot. The bullet ripped through Fred Perez's chest, exploding a lung and blowing out his aorta. He hit the ground gushing blood. An off-duty sheriff's deputy, Chuck Weaver, was coming off graveyard. He saw Fred Perez stagger near the wheelbarrow.

Across the street, a neighbor Joan Stagnaro, lived on Gharkey at the corner of Lighthouse in a large Victorian with a wrap-around front porch that faced both streets. She had heard the rifle crack on the Lighthouse side.

She walked to the porch. She saw a blue-and-white station wagon parked on the wrong side of the street in front of her house, engine running, car pointed northeast. She couldn't see a plate but noticed a red oval STP sticker near the right-front door. She glanced at the driver, a young man, looking over his shoulder as he pulled out toward Bay Street.

Joan Stagnaro registered fast. She sent her two sons running to Fred Perez's house while she called the police. Sirens in two minutes. Rick Weaver attended to Perez. Blood bubbled through Perez's jacket. More sirens. Sergeant Dan Fite approached. Dan Fite kneeled down, probing Fred Perez's neck for a pulse. None.

Joan Stagnaro told the cops what she'd witnessed. Details dispatched within minutes of the shooting. Patrolman Sean Upton was cruising the west side when he heard the BOLO. He figured the killer would head north on Bay. He saw the blue/white station wagon pulling right onto Mission. He followed, calling for backup as the station wagon split left toward Highway 1 North and jogged across an overpass to River Street, the junction with Highway 9.

The station wagon turned onto River Street. Upton held back until he reached a clear section of River near Coral Street. He hit his flasher. The wagon steered to the curb. Upton IDed himself as SCPD. He told the driver he was under arrest for suspicion of murder. He ordered him to flatten his palms against the windshield.

Sergeant Burt Witte moved another cruiser into position. Upton and Witte approached the Nomad, guns drawn. A third unit veed in. Sean Upton jerked the door and yanked out the driver. He forced him facedown on the sidewalk and cuffed him behind his back. He frisked him for weapons. Clean. He dragged him into the backseat of his squad car. He went back to the station wagon. Inside he saw a .22 rifle in the front seat, a paper bag covering the muzzle.

Cops checked the suspect's license: Herbert William Mullin; DOB April 18, 1947; 1541 McClellan Road, Felton; brown/green;

five foot seven, 135 pounds. Cops hauled him to headquarters. Herbert Mullin said nothing during the ride. They mugged, printed, and booked him for suspicion of murder, 187 PC. Upton escorted him to the county hospital for drug and alcohol testing. Mullin's only words: "I don't have to say anything. I choose to remain silent."

The duty doctor examined him without his spoken consent. Normal pulse, blood pressure, and temperature. Mullin showed no signs of alcohol impairment or drug addiction. Hearing, vision, or neurological tests were moot: Herbert Mullin wouldn't speak. He resisted a blood sample. Officers pinned his arms and legs on the table. The doctor spiked a syringe into a wriggling vein. The doctor wouldn't hazard an official guess on the mental state of a subject who was standing mute.

Others could. Mullin opened his shirt for the stethoscope. Cops noted four tattoos: "LEGALIZE ACID" in block letters across his midbelly, "Eagle Eyes Marijuana" directly below; two crosses and the words "birth" and "Mahashadmadhi" on his left forearm; the words "Kriya Yoga" on the inside of his left ankle. Mullin dropped his drawers for the rubber glove digit probe. The doctor noted scars on his crank that he speculated were inflicted by burning cigarettes. Snap first take: Herbie Mullin, one fucked-up dude.

Momentum on the murders, finally:

Rossi's tow yard on the Capitola Avenue extension off Soquel Avenue impounded the Chevy. Sheriffs' investigators drove to 1541 McClellan Road in Felton and spoke with Jean Mullin. She confirmed that the Nomad belonged to her son, Herbert. Said he was a woodcutter; used the wagon to haul logs. He was supposed to deliver a cord to her that morning. She said he cut wood around Empire Grade. Cops perked: Mary Guilfoyle's body dumped on Smith Grade Road off Empire Grade. She said Herbie kept a place downtown at the Pacific View Apartments, 81 Front Street, a 1940s era flop near the Boardwalk, vacancies filled with transients and surf bums. Cops obtained search warrants on Mullin's parent's house, his apartment, and the Chevy wagon.

Technicians dusted prints. Rifle ballistics tied him to Fred Perez. Prints slammed it. Investigators found loose receipts in the Chevy's glove box—one from Western Auto for a .22 revolver bought for $22.99 plus tax on December 16, 1972. Western Auto in Santa Cruz had no record, but the Felton store did: for a German-made Rohm RG-14 six-shot purchased by Herbert Mullin of 1541 McClellan, Felton, on December 16, 1972. Mullin picked it up on December 22 after the mandated five-day waiting period. In the wagon, they also found a brown canvas overnight bag on the passenger seat. A technician with gloves unzipped the bag and pulled out a cloth sack with a drawstring pull. In it: a Rohm RG-14 six-shot .22, three-inch barrel.

Hasty summit of city and county cops: big buzz from everyone connected with investigations on Perez, Gianera, and Francis. SCPD, without technical facilities of its own, worked through the San Mateo County crime lab. Cops couriered the evidence to Redwood City. Ballistics confirmed that the Rohm six-shot killed Jim and Joan Gianera as well as Kathy Francis and her two boys.

Traction:

February 15: Pete Chang charged Mullin with six counts of murder.

February 16: Santa Clara County stepped in. Los Gatos PD had distributed print exemplars lifted from Father Henry Tomei's confessional booth. SCPD patrolman Dave Larson had worked with the DOJ on print classification. He compared the Los Gatos exemplar with Mullin's booking card. Positive match.

February 17, 2:00 p.m.: Jeff Card, twenty-two, burst into SCPD. He'd been to Oxtail Trail. He found Scott and three other boys dead in their plastic tent, blood everywhere. He said the boys camped near the Garden of Eden overlook at Inspiration Point above Highway 9. He said he had hitched down from Boulder

Creek to visit his brother. Henry Cowell Park was county. SCPD brought in the sheriffs. Scanners squawking. Jeff Card led SD detective Terry Medina and a team of deputies. Newshounds followed, along with forestry crews, the sheriff coroner, and the district attorney.

February sun sinking behind treetops. Law enforcement, CDF, and media milling in the woods. The ME couldn't process the scene until morning light. DA, reporters, still photographers, news camera crews dispersing. Pete Chang dropped his "Murderville, USA" line on Marj von B. within earshot of the AP stringer. SCSD sealed the area. Terry Medina had investigated Lawrence White and the Mystery Spot killings. He drew the short straw. He and a three-man deputy team posted guard over the four dead campers until daybreak.

February 18: The ME determined that all four were killed by a .22. Jeff Card said a .22 rifle was missing. Cops snapped on Fred Perez: Herbie Mullin for the Garden of Eden tent slaughter? They tracked the rifle through the ATF registry. Original owner: a woman from Ukiah who had married and had moved to Santa Cruz under her new name.

She sold the rifle in October 1972 to the owner of Trusty's Furniture in Felton. Tom Trusty (his actual name) displayed it for sale in his showroom. He said three young men had come in just before closing in mid-November and tried to sell him a banjo. They inquired about the gun, but the fifty-five-dollar price tag was too steep. The next morning, he found a window jimmied, the rifle missing. SCSD had the theft report. Assumption: the campers stole Tom Trusty's .22, and Mullin snatched it before or after he shot them.

February 20: DA Chang amended the charge from six murders to ten. Ten crimes wrapped up in one haul: epic coup for small-town cops with a bad residual: coed killings still unsolved. Mary Guilfoyle maybe pinned to Mullins—she was dumped off Empire Grade. Herbert Mullin gathered logs around Empire Grade. Thin.

Cynthia Schall. Rosalind Thorpe. Alice Liu. All dismembered and beheaded and/or raped. Nothing to connect that MO with Mullin. His weren't ultra twisted sex crimes: necrophilia with missing heads and hands. Santa Cruz still sweating.

April 24, 1973, post-midnight, Tuesday after Easter: Collect call from a pay phone in Pueblo, Colorado, person-to-person to SCPD for detective lieutenant Chuck Scherer from a man calling himself Ed Kemper. The caller claimed he wanted to turn himself in for doing some bad things. Chuck Scherer was off shift. The Ed Kemper voice said to find him—he'd call back later. The duty officer shrugged it off as a crank call.

2:00 a.m. shift change: Another collect call. New desk officer refused charges. He told the caller that Lieutenant Scherer would be in at 9:00 a.m. The Kemper voice tried again after five that same morning. Day watch drifting in. A third desk cop answered. The Kemper voice said he'd been trying to call lieutenant Scherer. He repeated that he'd done bad things. He said he had murdered his mother and her friend in Aptos on Friday. Said he was messed up in the head and feared that he'd launch a killing spree. He said he was in his car near a pay phone. He added that he was the "Coed Killer." The desk cop waved to detective sergeant Jim Connor, signaling him to pick up an extension.

Jim Conner knew Ed Kemper. Kemper was a six-foot-nine-inch, 280-pound police groupie who hung out at the Jury Room, a dive bar across Ocean Avenue from the city and county buildings that catered to off-duty cops. Jim Connor had trouble processing. On one hand, Big Ed: likeable, a wannabe cop who surpassed the height maximum. On the other: Cynthia Schall had babysat his kids. Jim Connor asked the Kemper voice for a precise location. Ed Kemper dangled the phone while he walked to the corner, scoped street signs, and reported the coordinates to Jim Connor.

Adrenaline surge. Connor punched into an open line. He dialed Pueblo PD for a pickup order and warned: subject armed, dangerous, and King Kong big. Kemper relayed his mother's Aptos address, 609A Ord. Said it was hard to find but they needed to investigate the premises. Said Mickey Aluffi (sheriff's detective) had been to the house a few days before. Unincorporated Aptos was SCSD jurisdiction. The desk guy kept Big Ed on the line. Jim Conner reached Aluffi at home in Capitola. Aluffi phoned sheriff's dispatch. Patrol sergeant Stony Brook moving with the squawk. Lights and sirens: two sheriff's squad cars screaming toward Aptos.

609A, bottom unit of a split-level duplex behind 609: no answer. Aluffi and Brook braced upstairs neighbors. 609C reported an odor from 609A. Stony Brook popped a rear window. Flesh rot whiffed out. Aluffi and Brook pushed in. Woman's head on the mantle; decapped body in a bedroom closet, nude. A second closet: naked woman hooded with a plastic bag.

Meanwhile, Pueblo had dispatched a two-man patrol car. A cruiser with a solo cop already in the neighborhood caught the call. He saw Big Ed's back filling the booth. He switched on his red light, drew down, and tapped on the glass. Big Ed opened the accordion door, one hand on the phone. The patrolman ordered him out. Big Ed didn't know what to do with the receiver. "Hang it up," the cop said. "Raise your hands and flatten your palms against the side."

Big Ed's hands reached over the top of the booth. Lone cop freezing Gargantua at gunpoint. The tableau held. Four minutes crawled like four hours. The two-man unit screeched in. Big Ed submitted. Coed Killer captured. Pueblo PD read him his rights. He waived everything. Rapid action at the brass level in Surf City: Lieutenant Scherer, DA Peter Chang, and DA's investigator Dick Verbrugge booked the next flight to Colorado from San Jose International.

Pueblo PD had confiscated two loaded rifles, a shotgun, a .22 revolver, and a hundred rounds of ammunition from the trunk of the car Ed Kemper was driving, a Chevy with Nevada plates. Big Ed had a near-genius 136 IQ, but his getaway scheme left some holes. He had fled Ord Avenue in his mother's friend's car on Easter Sunday. The friend's name was Sarah (Sally) Hallet. He dumped Sally Hallet's sled and rented an Impala from Hertz in Sparks. He tore east on I-80. He expected radio bulletin break-ins of a desperate nationwide manhunt. He spun the knob. He heard mostly Wolfman Jack—no bulletins Ed drove thirty-six hours through Nevada, Utah, Wyoming, and into Colorado fueled by cheeseburgers and NoDoz. He cut south on I-25 at Cheyenne. In Pueblo, he realized he had no destination and no purpose. He gave it up. He ramped off the expressway to contact Santa Cruz PD.

April 25, Wednesday: Peter Chang had figured on flying back to California, but no airline would take an oversized serial slayer, even with his three police escorts. Dick Verbrugge called Hertz about Big Ed's rental. He worked a deal to return the rental to Sparks and drive Sally Hallet's car back to Santa Cruz. They held an extradition hearing in Pueblo. Big Ed signed away his Miranda rights. Chang flew back to San Jose right after, leaving Chuck Scherer and Dick Verbrugge to escort Big Ed in the Impala. They planned to jug Big Ed in jail in Laramie that night and find lodging for themselves.

They drove north on I-25 to Cheyenne and west on I-80. In the dark, everything about a prairie looks like prairie, including towns. They blew past Laramie without realising it. Pre-cellphone; pre-Garmin. They said, what the hell. They didn't stop until they had crossed Wyoming and Utah and reached Elko, Nevada. They planted Big Ed in a jail cell and found a motel. They clicked on the news. They'd made headlines. They hadn't turned up in Laramie. Laramie alerted Pueblo. Pueblo alerted Santa Cruz. TV picked it up. Talking heads speculated that Verbrugge and Scherer had been overwhelmed by their gigantic prisoner.

Big Ed rode in shackles and handcuffs. He took his waivers seriously, especially the "presence of counsel" and the "right to silence" parts. He copped in detail to killing his mother and Sally Hallet; to kidnapping and dismembering Cynthia Schall; to kidnapping the Fresno State coeds Anita Luchese and Mary Ann Pesce; to kidnapping Aiko Koo in Berkeley and Rosalind Thorpe and Alice Liu off the UCSC campus. Big Ed screwed himself for trial. Jim Jackson: "He confessed from Colorado to California by way of Montana." Big Ed didn't care. He had nothing left to defend. Dick Verbugge rolled tape across five Western states.

Big Ed blabbed guilt all the way home.

VI

April 30, 1973: Edmund Kemper arraigned in Santa Cruz; Santa Cruz County jail inadequate for epic monsters. Herb Mullin was riding out pretrial procedures under high security in Redwood City at the San Mateo County jail. After arraignment, Kemper followed. Turnkey humor: jailors slammed Big Ed into a cell next to Mullin. The two grew to hate each other. Big Ed: Herbie was a "no-class killer." Herbie: Big Ed a sex maniac. Big Ed was alpha. Herbie like to chant yoga. Ed heard it as atonal shrieking. He tended to throw toilet water on him. Later, he said, he'd reward him with peanuts if he was good. He called it "behavioral modification."

Herbie was cooked legally. The stolen .22 rifle with his prints killed Fred Perez. Neighbor Joan Stagnaro ID'ed his car at the scene of the shooting. He was arrested in the same car minutes later. Cops found his RG-14 in a bag in his car. Ballistics and prints tied it to nine killings—the two Gianeras, Kathy Francis and her two sons, and the four campers. Herbie's father, Martin W. (Bill) Mullin, retained Richard Pease, the DA before Peter Chang. Pease met with Herbie before arraignment. Herbie had no property or assets. His father worked for the post office. Billable hours would bankrupt him.

The Mullins fired Pease and asked for a public defender. Judge May designated Jim Jackson. Jackson had long hair. Mullin said he wanted a lawyer who looked more like Richard Nixon. Jim Jackson ignored him. He filed for discovery and ran through evidence. He interviewed Mullin who had no defense except insanity. Jim Jackson: "I thought Mullin was the craziest son of a bitch I had ever met."

March 1, 1973: Herbert Mullin arraigned in municipal court. Herbie scribbled sentences on a legal pad that was sitting at the defendant's table. He ripped off the page and handed it to the clerk, who handed it to Judge May. May read it aloud: "The defendant pleads *nolo contendre*." Judge May looked to Jim Jackson. Jackson said Mullin wanted to represent himself, contrary to counsel's advice. Judge May refused the request. Mullin wrote out another page. It said: "The defendant pleads that he is guilty to the offenses charged." Jim Jackson shook his head. Judge May refused again. He scheduled a new prelim to determine whether Mullin was competent to participate in his own defense. Chang intervened. He said he was taking the case to the grand jury. Judge May relieved to gavel down his part in Mullin's clown act.

Jackson retained Harold Cartwright to dig up Mullin's history and Don Lunde to dig through Mullin's skull. Nobody wanted another change of venue; the nightmare costs and logistics from the Frazier trial were still fresh. Jackson bartered. He said he wouldn't file, in exchange for unlimited juror challenges. Judge Franich bought it; Chang seconded. A change of venue would be a foolish distraction anyway. Everyone in California knew about Santa Cruz. Walter Cronkite headlined Mullin's February 13 arrest on CBS national news. Judge Franich would hear the case.

Harold Cartwright backgrounded Herbie for the defense. He found no predictors from his early life. Mullin hadn't decapped or tortured house pets or set fire to neighborhood houses. Cartwright thought Mullin's parents, Bill and Jean, were "wonderful people." Bill, a WWII vet from Oregon, mustered out of Fort Ord. He sold furniture in Salinas after the war. Herbie was born on April 18, 1947. He had an older sister, Patricia. Bill moved the family to

Walnut Creek and San Francisco. Herbie attended Catholic schools in the City—Saint Stephens elementary and Riordan High. Bill took a job with the Santa Cruz post office.

Herbie entered San Lorenzo Valley High as a junior. He played football with Jim Gianera. He made friends. He earned good grades. His senior yearbook tagged him "Most likely to succeed." He had a girlfriend, Loretta Ricketts. Home life: normal, within bounds. Bill Mullin was a Lutheran, not overly expressive; Jean a devout Catholic. Both parents were strict. Bill said the household might have been "oppressively religious." He meant Jean's Catholic obsessions, not his own Lutheran indifference. Bill may have been excessive recalling his war stories. He was a tough guy, a boxer in the service. He may have sparred with his son without checking whether Herbie thought it was fun. Multimillions have survived worse without turning into homicidal madmen.

Herb had a close friend in high school named Dean Richardson who was killed in a car wreck the summer after graduation, in 1965. Herbie went morose with grief. He propped a picture of Dean Richardson on his dresser flanked with burning candles. The shrinks cited Richardson's death as the beginning. Herbie attended Cabrillo College in the fall, studying engineering in the school's highway-technology department. He worked summers for county public works. He graduated from Cabrillo in the spring of 1967 with an AA degree.

He ran into Jim Gianera on Capitola Beach a month before graduation. Gianera turned him on to drugs, mostly weed, but also LSD. Herbie grew interested in Eastern religions and joined protests against the Vietnam War. He enrolled at San Jose State. He changed his major from engineering to philosophy. He filed with the draft board as a conscientious objector. He dropped out of school and drifted. He broke up with Loretta.

He was hired as an executive trainee with Goodwill Industries. Selective Service granted his CO status. He moved to San Luis Obispo to manage a thrift store. He quit Goodwill and told his parents he was going to study yoga in India. His sister Patricia's husband, Albert Bocca, owned a Christmas tree farm in Sebastapol. His parents convinced him to live in an empty trailer on the Bocca property.

Bill and Jean drove to Sebastopol to celebrate their twenty-ninth anniversary with their children. At dinner, Herbie mimed Albert's every gesture, what the shrinks call echopraxia. The family freaked. Bill called a family priest, who brokered a voluntary stay at the Mendocino State Hospital. Herbie resisted treatment. He checked himself out after six weeks. He drifted to Lake Tahoe, where he worked as a dishwasher before returning to Santa Cruz. He signed up for rehab. Bill and Jean were relieved: they thought his problem was drugs.

November 1969: Herbie orbited out of town; 5150 not yet fully enacted. Herbie was forcibly detained at the psychiatric ward of San Luis Obispo General Hospital. He wrote his parents. They drove down to visit. He told them he was homosexual—he had been committed by a local doctor after he'd made aggressive passes at the doctor's nephew. Herbie had shaved his head and scarred his own dick with tobacco fire. Bill and Jean brought him home on the condition that he enroll as an outpatient at a mental-health clinic.

December 1969: He flew to Hawaii with a fortyish female addict he had met in a commune. She dumped him. He checked into a Maui mental hospital. A month later he wrote home for plane fare. He returned to outpatient rehab status.

March 1970: he drifted to San Francisco. He stayed in Haight-Ashbury crash pads and Tenderloin flops reeking of mold and Lysol. He ran with hippies, homos, and head cases. He dosed on LSD, mellowed out with weed, and took God knows what else—he estimated forty or more acid trips. He trained for the ring in a sweatbox gym downtown. He sparred with real fighters who kicked the shit out of him. During one phase, he was a Mexican. He wore a sombrero and talked with a *pachuco* accent.

September 1972: Herbie moved back to Santa Cruz. He rented a room at the Pacific View Apartments. He traded his VW Bug for a fourteen-year-old Chevrolet Nomad station wagon. He told his parents it was time he made something of himself. He began cutting wood. One month later, he left home, telling his mother he was driving to San Francisco to return an overdue library book. He diverted instead into Henry Cowell Park and murdered migrant worker Lawrence White.

Don Lunde spent more than a hundred hours assessing Mullin. Dr. David Marlowe administered an MMPI (Minnesota Multiphasic Personality Inventory), a clinical staple that shrinks use for assessing personality traits and psychopathology. It asks 567 true/false questions along ten scales that cover an array of conditions from hypochondria to social introversion, with possible scores ranging from 1 to 120. A mark of 70 or higher in any of the scales indicates that the subject is whacked. Herbie may have set a record. He scored 70 points or higher in six of the ten.

Inventory of madness:

Herbie claimed his father was a mass murderer. He asked that he be fingerprinted and the prints matched against all unsolved homicides in California and Oregon since 1925. Herbie believed in reincarnation. He maintained that a conspiracy of family members was suppressing him in this life to reduce his authority in the next.

He cited his bisexuality. He said he should have known sooner than his twenties. He blamed Bill for not administering fatherly blow jobs from the age of six. He blamed Jim Gianera for messing his mind up with drugs and hippie "claptrap." Herbie hated hippies. He heard voices directing him to kill. He was born on April 18, 1947. Albert Einstein died on April 18, 1955. Herbie jumped to a cosmic conclusion: confluent birth/death days meant that he was chosen to lead his generation, much like Einstein. April 18, 1906, was the date of the San Francisco earthquake and fire.

Herbie leaped again. He raked pagan thought with Catholic repression and Eastern religion until it was all mucked up with the drug damage in his brain. He patterned his murders around the mystical number 13. He cross-referred death rates with incidents of natural disaster. He claimed that God invoked natural disaster when death rates slowed—Herbie had God massaging actuarial charts. Herbie heard voices demanding human sacrifice to ward off an apocalyptic earthquake that would drop California into the ocean. He killed Lawrence White on Friday the thirteenth, Father Tomei on All Souls' Day. He killed thirteen people. He killed the last of them on February 13, 1973.

May 14 to July 9, 1973: Judge Franich opened a competency hearing. Two shrinks assessed him—Dr. Peschau from Agnews and Dr. Charles Morris from Oakland. Dr. Peschau believed that his lunacy stemmed from bad acid trips. Dr. Morris said Herbie was a paranoid schizophrenic currently in remission. They agreed that he was free of mental defect such that he could assist in his own defense.

Pete Chang underwent an emergency appendectomy, and the trial was delayed. Chang contracted peritonitis and was replaced by Art Danner and Chris Cottle. Chris Cottle crammed for twenty hours a day for a solid week to prepare. The trial began on July 30. Guilt/innocence was determined by a line of prosecution witnesses certifying forensic evidence.

Mullin pled not guilty by reason of insanity. Jim Jackson moved to combine the trials, in effect pinning his entire defense on Herbie's mental state. Herbie wanted to testify. Jackson would have preferred videotapes of his first interview with David Marlowe (he was wackier then), but Judge Franich disallowed the tapes. Jackson settled for live. Either way, he wanted his client's fruitcake mind on display.

Don Lunde spent two days on the stand. He was eloquent but clinical. He said Mullin acted under deluded moral obligation.

Human sacrifice would prevent cataclysm via earthquake; telepathic voices—sometimes those of the victims—impelled him to kill. According to his lunacy, he felt he was doing the right thing. Dr. Lunde wouldn't concede that Mullin could appreciate a social standard that considered his murders unlawful. Chris Cottle brought up John Linley Frazier. He asked Lunde to explain why Frazier was legally sane while Mullin wasn't. Lunde expounded on esoteric distinctions. He lost the jury in jargon.

Cottle brought in his own expert, behavioral analyst from San Francisco, Dr. Joel Fort. Dr. Fort stipulated that Mullin was paranoid schizophrenic but stated that the condition was not inclusive. He said it mixed with patterns of lucidity. Herbert Mullin recognized that murder was wrong by accepted social standards; his delusions overwhelmed any civilized restraint.

The trial ran for five weeks. Herbie testified on August 14. Pete Chang recovered and returned to the prosecution table. Herb wouldn't swear the oath. He stood up in front of the witness chair—wouldn't sit during his testimony. He testified for a day. He spewed gibberish. He maintained that he was a scapegoat destined to "carry the guilt feelings of others to an exaggerated extent." He called his parents "killjoys" who were trying to reduce his reincarnated status in the next life. Under oath, he indicted his father as a mass murderer.

He ticked off points mentioned by Don Lunde. When natural death rates receded, God compensated with natural disasters. Mullin claimed he killed by direction of telepathic voices to prevent devastating earthquakes—the voices alternating between his father, mother, and the victims themselves. The jury saw their dilemma. Herbie was clinically batshit, but no one wanted him loose. M'Naghten resolved the conflict. Herbie calculated crimes, and he covered them up. He killed the Francises because Kathy Francis knew he'd asked about Jim Gianera. He took pains to hide the bodies and pocket the empty cartridge casings. He ran when he was chased. He was able to calculate consquences.

They deliberated for three days. Verdict: Herbert Mullin guilty on two counts of first-degree murder for the Gianera kills—jurors said they were clearly premeditated—and eight counts of second-degree, because those murders were impulsive. Santa Clara charged (and convicted) him for Father Tomei; he wasn't charged for Lawrence White or Mary Guilfoyle. Ballistics nailed him on the other ten; White and Guilfoyle would be harder to prove. Judge Franich sentenced him to concurrent life terms on the first-degree counts, consecutive on the second. Death penalty out: the state supreme court had ruled it cruel and unusual seven months earlier. Virtual LWOP for Herbie, who would not be eligible for parole until he was seventy-three.

At trial's end, jury foreman Kenneth Springer wrote Governor Ronald Reagan, shredding him for closing mental hospitals and blaming him for Herbert Mullin's serial killing spree. Don Lunde claims otherwise. He says Big Ed Kemper turned the verdict. After Kemper, Lunde writes in his book *Die Song* that, "No way would any jury anywhere hand Herb over to the state mental health system."

VII

Big Ed's story:

Born Edmond Emil Kemper III in Burbank on December 18, 1948. His father, E. E. Kemper II had married Clarnell Stage. Ed was the middle child between two sisters. Man-hating Clarnell drove Ed II to divorce by the time Ed III was seven. Clarnell moved to Helena, Montana. Ed reminded Clarnell of his father, big and clumsy. She deflected rage among other ways by belittling her oafish son. Ed grew huge and petrified of females. He showed early. He dismembered his sisters' dolls. He killed pet cats and toyed with their corpses. Clarnell feared for the girls. She made Ed sleep in a locked basement. Ed ran away at thirteen, made his way to Van Nuys, and found his father.

Ed II had remarried a normal woman who didn't debase her husband. He had more children. Ed III gave the new wife migraines. Ed II didn't want memories of his previous dysfunction. Clarnell was sighting in on husband number three. She didn't need Ed in the mix screwing things up. She devised a solution: ship him to his paternal grandparents in North Fork, a tiny town in the central Sierra above Madera.

Ed II had married in the image of his own mother. Maude Kemper was as domineering and distempered as Clarnell. Ed found himself in the sticks with a henpecked grandfather and a grandmother who maybe was worse than his mother. Ed I tried. He bought Ed III a .22 rifle for Christmas and taught him to shoot. Ed III went to school in nearby Tollhouse without outrageous incident. Maude wrote children's adventure stories and unknowingly triggered Ed III.

August 27, 1964: Maude bent over her typewriter table. Big Ed slipped in behind her. He raised his .22 and shot her twice in the head. He suffered from remorse when it dawned on him he had created an issue for Ed I. He said later he didn't want his grandfather to feel bad. When Ed I rolled in from grocery shopping, Ed walked outside to his pickup and clipped him with a head shot. He dialed Clarnell in Helena in tears and confessed. She said to wait in the house while she called the sheriff.

The California Youth Authority (CYA) sent Big Ed to Atascadero, to the hospital for the criminally insane. Big Ed endured puberty in a nuthouse, arresting his already twisted sexual development. Oddly, he thrived. He ingratiated himself to an overburdened staff (sixteen-hundred patients to eight shrinks). He proved adept at tricking testing instruments. He worked as a de facto psychiatric aide. He learned appropriate answers to the MMPI. He learned acceptable interpretations of Rorschach blots.

1969: Big Ed, twenty-one, released from Atascadero as cured. He had managed to camouflage his accelerating sexual sadism.

Atascadero shrinks warned the CYA to keep him away from his mother. Clarnell had taken a job with the new UC in Santa Cruz, in College Five (Porter), as an administrative assistant. CYA bureaucrats read Ed's file only as far as the word *cured*. They kicked him loose, ignoring shrink warnings. They sent him on probation to Santa Cruz. Santa Cruz County probation and parole was overloaded with criminally-inclined pyschotics of their own. Ed tried to report. SCC probation and parole asked if he had problems. He said no. They said they'd get back to him. They never did. They put him in the worst possible place, where his primary social link was his mother.

Big Ed: Past puberty with primal fears of inadequacy. CYA was supposed to transition him with halfway status—let him mix with peers. He had never been on a date and was clueless how to forge a normal alliance. Imagine the icebreaker: "Hi, I'm Ed. I killed my grandparents when I was fifteen. I've spent the past five years in an institution for the criminally insane." Ed found work as a laborer in the East Bay with the highway department. He bought a motorcycle and wrecked it twice. The second time yielded a settlement he used to buy a '69 Ford Galaxie. Ed had been cooped up for half a decade. Motion was anodyne. He spent his spare time roaming back roads and constructing gruesome fantasies. He shared an apartment in Alameda with a coworker. On days off, he gravitated toward Santa Cruz.

Clarnell Stage was a big, homely woman, six-plus feet with glasses, a bird beak, and skinny penguin legs. She was married and divorced three times. She drank. Quality time with Ed never failed to fire up issues. Clarnell obtained a staff parking sticker for Big Ed's Galaxie but told him that UCSC girls were off limits. She knew how to press his buttons. She said he was too much like his father. He wasn't good enough for her UCSC coeds. Ed picked up hitchhiking females for boy-girl contact, working up nerve. His estimate: he'd picked up 150 of them before Anita Luchese and Mary Ann Pesce on Ashby Avenue in Berkeley.

He hung out at a local bar, the Jury Room, across the street from county administration. He popped tequila shots and grooved on guns with off-duty cops. He said he wanted to be a highway patrolman but was too tall. He killed college girls. He didn't rape the first two, Luchese and Pesce. He wasn't impotent, just frightened. He raped Aiko Koo postmortem and followed suit with the rest. He decapped them all, except his mother's friend, Sally Hallet. He buried Cynthia Schall's head in the backyard behind 609A Ord. He swiveled her eyes toward his bedroom.

April 1973: County sheriff responsible for vetting gun-owner applications, filtering out ex-cons, dope addicts, and foreigners. The systems slowed when the serial murders spiked weapons sales. Doug James, scanning dealer records of sales, came across a slip for a Remington .44 Magnum with a six-inch barrel: a Dirty Harry handgun. The name on the card: Edmond Emil Kemper III, age twenty-four, from Aptos. A clerk's note on the card: Edmond E. Kemper had a sealed juvenile file transferred from Madera County.

The case had been heard in Fresno seventh months earlier, on September 15, 1972. Two Fresno shrinks had testified on Big Ed's behalf. Over objection by the Madera County DA, the seal was granted. The only flag in the redacted file was the phrase "Double Homicide. 1964." Doug James wasn't sure if Kemper was entitled to own a gun. He dispatched detectives Michael Aluffi and Don Smythe to 609A Ord in Aptos. He told them to confiscate the weapon until a judge could rule.

At his front door, Ed told the deputies the gun was stored in the trunk of his car. He walked them to the car port and popped the Galaxie's lid. The Mag was wrapped in a gray rag. Ed reached for it. Mickey Aluffi patted his holster to back him off, said he'd remove the weapon himself. Aluffi noticed the trunk had no fabric liner—just flat-black metal coating. Big Ed was spooked. He thought the cops were onto him for the coeds. Shrinks said later that everything from his sisters' dolls to cats to UCSC coeds was dress rehearsal. They said by then Ed was beyond ready for the spotlight act.

April 20, Friday night: Ed fought with Clarnell. She was drunk and denigrating. He snapped. He woke at 4:00 a.m. on Saturday, April 21. He padded into her bedroom with a claw hammer and pounded her skull until she died. He decapped her, pulled out her tongue and larynx, walked into the kitchen and dumped them into a whirring Kelvinator. The disposal coughed them back into the sink. Ironic. Ed got off on his mother's skull—literal head. He perched the skull on the mantle and yelled at it. It couldn't talk back—at last. For diversion, he plunked her dead face with darts.

That afternoon he dialed up his mother's UCSC coworker Sally Hallet, fifty-nine. Ed buying getaway time. He reasoned that Sally Hallet was the only one who might notice or care about Clarnell's absence. He invited her to a surprise dinner for his mother. When Hallet showed, he strangled and raped her. He split for the Jury Room and drank past midnight. He came home and slept with bloody corpses.

Back from Colorado, Big Ed showed Dick Verbrugge and Chuck Sherer where he had disposed of heads and limbs in Alameda County. Scherer, Verbrugge, and Mickey Aluffi took him shackled to the Santa Cruz Mountains on Saturday, April 28. He guided stunned investigators to the rest of his discard sites.

Kemper's trial opened on October 23, 1973, superior court judge Harry E. Brauer presiding. Peter Chang organized the prosecution into sequential phases: (1) *corpus delecti*, the dead bodies proving that crimes had been committed; (2) the establishment of Kemper's guilt through an airing of his taped confessions; and (3) the weighing of legal sanity. Jim Jackson moved to exclude the tapes—no attorney present during the interviews. Motion denied—Big Ed had waived Miranda. That was it; Jackson had no other moves. He couldn't find a psychiatrist willing to work the case. He could pound diminished capacity only during opening and closing statements. In between, he was relegated to cross-examination of Pete's Chang's prosecution.

Big Ed was tranqued for the duration. Five-foot-nine, 160-pound deputy Bruce Colomy ferried him daily from Redwood City. Nobody wanted Gargantua turning apeshit on the car ride or in court. Doctors were puzzled about dosage. It would be like sedating a silverback. Bruce Colomy kept a syringe in his bag. Jim Jackson worked a signal system with Judge Brauer: When Kemper stirred, Jackson flashed a finger sign. Harry Brauer would recess. In an anteroom, Bruce Colomy would spike Big Ed into sedation.

Chang played the confession tapes for a day and a half. Big Ed had a marvelous ability to recall horror. He detailed murders, rapes, beheadings, and dismemberments. The tapes transfixed the jurors. Among the accounts: the hearing in Fresno to seal his juvenile record. Don Lunde's point about the system. Two Central Valley shrinks certified Big Ed's mental health at the same time Aiko Koo's head was stashed in the trunk of his Galaxie in the Fresno Countyn courthouse parking lot.

Dr. Joel Fort closed the deal. He said Big Ed was a sexual sadist who was aware of his actions and thrilled by the notoriety. He was an exhibitionist who grooved on cynosure status. He would kill again if he had the chance. He belonged behind bars or dead. Ed's own statement to SCPD from the Pueblo phone booth tipped it: "I've done something bad."

November 8, 1973: The trial lasted less than three weeks. A six-man, six-woman jury deliberated for five hours and found Edmond Emil Kemper III guilty on eight counts of first-degree murder. Judge Brauer to the jury: "I had some fear you would arrive at a different verdict. I agree with you entirely." Judge Brauer asked Ed about proper punishment. Big Ed: "I should be tortured to death." Big Ed thanked Pete Chang for his "restraint and help" and Judge Brauer for his "help." At Some salamander level, he was relieved. Jurors too: grateful for M'Naghten's clarity—its moral absolution for the duty of putting down a ghoul.

Santa Cruz, 1970–73: Murderville, USA.

Postscript

The California supreme court decision of February 18, 1972, took John Linley Frazier off death row. Frazier was remanded to Mule Creek in Ione after it opened in 1987. In 2009 he hanged himself in his cell. Herbie Mullin was sent to Mule Creek as well. He talks about returning to society and starting a family. He's still delusional: he'll never breathe free air again. Big Ed Kemper knows better than to try. He sits behind the old stone walls of Folsom prison and will until he dies.

CHAPTER 6
BERKELEY: THE SLA/PATTY HEARST

May 17, 1974, Friday: 1466 E. Fifty-Fourth Street, Watts. A dilapidated bungalow west of Compton Avenue. Single-story faded-yellow clapboard, with a covered stone porch, tar-and-gravel roof, and a backyard of dry weeds. Inside: six soldiers from the Symbionese Liberation Army crouched near front windows shielded by mattresses, a sofa, a refrigerator, and an upturned table. Behind them, spread on the floor, an arsenal—a half-dozen M-1 and M-2 automatic rifles, a 30.06, seven sawed-off shotguns, and six pistols, plus pipe bombs, Molotov cocktails, and six thousand rounds of ammo.

Outside, LAPD SWAT buzzed around, decked out in black fatigues, Kevlar vests, and jump boots. They deployed front, rear, and on rooftops armed with Colt .45 model 1911s in shoulder rigs and semiauto AR 15 and 180 carbines. As backup: five FBI snipers, two hundred roaming agents, four hundred uniformed patrolmen, motorcycle cops, CHP cruisers, and robbery-homicide dicks. SWAT and FBI waited for word. LAPD and CHP evacuated citizens from nearby stores and houses, struggling to cordon off thousands of milling rubbernecks.

Anxious TV crews lingered in the perimeter, local and network. On-air reporters gripped hand-mics; video guys shouldered minicams. They dodged electrical cords braiding out from satellite vans. Pioneer stuff—real-time news as it happens.

SWAT held radio contact with LAPD and FBI brass gathered at a temporary command post at Newton Station, 1.78 miles north. Two options: surround and call out or blow the doors.

5:43 p.m.: Local and bureau brass feared violent action escalating past sunset in Watts. They green-lighted choice number 1. The SWAT negotiator thumbed his bullhorn to high volume: "Occupants of 1466 E. 54th Street. This is the Los Angeles Police Department. Come out with your hands up, and leave your weapons in the house." No answer. Five minutes lapsed. SWAT launched gas grenades, shattering windowpanes. The grenades hit the living room floor and swirled from the release of eye-stinging vapor. The SLA, in military-grade pig-snout gas masks, fired full-auto bursts, eleven hundred rounds per minute. SWAT returned fire, semiauto.

6:30 p.m.: A lull. SLA had triggered maybe four thousand shots; SWAT and FBI, roughly five thousand. Zero casualties combined. SWAT poured in another fusillade of tear gas. Gunshots or gas ignited combustible materials—Molotov cocktails or premix used for bottling the cocktails. Didn't take long. Red inferno flames crackled skyward, mixed with pluming black smoke, and rose maniacally into an orange twilight haze.

Primal panic inside. SLA ripped up kitchen floorboards. They dropped into base dirt and support studs. Nancy Ling Perry wriggled toward the rear, trailed by Camilla Hall and Angela Atwood. Nancy Perry forearmed her way through a crawl hole. She exited into weeds while triggering a .30 caliber pistol. Snipers squeezed off kill shots to her spinal cord and one lung. Camilla Hall followed, firing a .45 pistol. An LAPD sharpshooter aced her with a single shot to the forehead.

It ended fast. Angela Atwood pulled the dead Camilla Hall back under the house. Thick smoke *whooshed* into the subflooring, consuming tight-space oxygen. Angela Atwood, Patricia Soltysik, and Willie Wolfe inhaled raw carbon monoxide through their melting masks and asphyxiated. Intense heat exploded bullets in bandoliers. Donald DeFreeze, a.k.a. "Field Marshal Cinque Mtume," held a Browning 9mm to his temple and blew out his brains.

6:45 p.m.: Flames burned through framing studs. Outside walls collapsed; roof joists gave way. 1466 E. Fifty-Fourth Street became a two-foot pile of smoking-hot embers and incinerated urban guerillas.

LA fire department units moved in from neighborhood standby—two task-force vans and two engine trucks, plus seven rescue rigs. SID forensic techs and FBI agents worked overnight with coroner Thomas Noguchi sifting evidence and IDing corpses. LAPD and FBI big shots breathed relief: sanctioned SWAT and bureau action hadn't cremated publishing empire heiress Patricia Hearst, a.k.a. "Tania."

I

Patty Hearst and the SLA, 1974–1976: Epic twentieth-century story 591 days in duration, featured on covers of *Newsweek*, *Time*, and *Rolling Stone*; in headlines of major dailies from Seattle to Miami and Boston to San Diego; and in nightly leads from network anchors. Patty Hearst: rich kid from the San Francisco Peninsula—granddaughter of American publishing colossus William Randolph Hearst. The SLA: nihilistic middle-class white dropouts, mostly female, mixed with a black ex-con, all of them bent on violent insurrection

Monday, February 4, 1974: 2603 Benvenue Avenue, Berkeley; shingle-sided fourplex below College Avenue between Parker and Stuart Streets. Cramped urban patio dividing front and back units. Patty Hearst, nineteen, lived in the right-rear quadrant with boyfriend Steven Weed, twenty-six.

9:20 p.m.: Steve Weed and Patty Hearst spooning chicken noodle soup and watching *The Magician*—a shitty '70s crime show starring Bill Bixby as playboy-philanthropist Anthony Blake solving mysteries via stage magic illusions. Knock at the door. Weed opened a crack, Patty hovering behind, dressed in a blue terrycloth robe, underpants, and fuzzy slippers. An indistinct woman on the stoop, her features lost in a bulky coat, shapeless hat, baggy slacks, and heavy shoes.

She said she was in a car accident and needed help; wondered if she could use the phone. Berkleley: help the sister in need. Steve Weed cracked the door wider. Two men in black woolen watch caps, olive-drab field jackets, and combat boots burst into the living room. One man obviously black, the other maybe. They brandished sawed-off assault rifles on shoulder slings. They ordered Steve Weed to the floor. The woman bear-hugged Patty Hearst. The maybe-black guy kicked Steve Weed in the face, knocking off his glasses and stunning him.

The woman tied Steve Weed's hands. Patty Hearst screamed. The black guy said he'd knock her ass out if she didn't shut up. The woman bound Patty's hands. A neighbor, Steve Suenaga, stepped into the breezeway between the rear apartments. The black guy grabbed Steve Suenaga by the shirt front, yanked him inside, and gun-butted him. His sidekick held a wine bottle by its neck and clubbed Steve Weed.

The sidekick popped Patty on the temple with the stock of his carbine and draped her over his shoulder. Fourplex neighbors heard a commotion. They flicked on porch lights and opened front doors. The black guy triple-tapped .30 caliber slugs into the shingle siding. The neighbors ducked back inside. The kidnappers slammed Patty into the trunk of a Chevy ragtop parked in the driveway, engine running. They backed out onto Benvenue, crimping right. They drove 120 feet to Parker Street and turned toward College Avenue, bracketed by a green Ford station wagon and a blue VW Bug. Clean getaway. Nobody caught a plate.

Charles Bates, San Francisco division SAC (special agent in charge), took a relay call from Berkeley PD. He alerted Washington and dispatched agents to Benvenue. They found a hot clue right away: a box of bullets left behind, cartridge tips spiked with cyanide. Big bell ringing: 90/10 they were dealing with a group of violent Bay Area radicals called the Symbionese Liberation Army. Feds can assimilate kidnap cases only after twenty-four hours. After that time, without clues to the contrary, they are permitted to assume interstate flight. Charles Bates jumped the Hearst abduction (FBI file code, HERNAP) by twenty-three hours, attaching it to the SLA investigation.

Early 1970s: Domestic terrorists splintered into theory and action cells themed around egregious treatment of minorities—Black Panthers, Weather Underground, Black Liberation Army, FALN out of Puerto Rico (Spanish for the "Armed Forces of National Liberation"), the RA (Revolutionary Army) from Berkeley. They worked mostly in cities at cross purposes—New York, Chicago, Boston, San Francisco, Pittsburgh, and Washington. They robbed banks, sniped policemen, raided armories. They black-marketed weapons and issued dark communiqués claiming credit for atrocious crimes.

They drew most of their attention by detonating homemade bombs. In one eighteen-month period in 1971/72, the FBI reported more than twenty-five hundred bombings throughout the US, an average of five a day. President Richard Nixon told FBI director J. Edgar Hoover: "Domestic terrorism now represents the single greatest threat against American Society." The SLA was among them, but different: maybe the most distorted.

November 6, 1973, three months before Patty Hearst was taken, Tuesday night of Election Day: Oakland Unified School District superintendent Marcus Foster leaving a school-board meeting at the district administration building at 1000 Broadway, downtown, with his white assistant, Robert Blackburn. Marcus Foster was the state's first black public-schools super—he had developed a distinguished résumé in Pennsylvania.

From an alley, a small woman in a watch cap and peacoat stepped into the sidewalk. She triggered a shotgun at Foster and Blackburn.

Buckshot tore into Marcus Foster's midsection and spread to Robert Blackburn. From behind, two men in peacoats and watch caps shot Foster with handguns firing cyanide bullets. The shooters fled into the night. They left Foster dead, Blackburn wounded.

Two days later, KPFA, a left-wing radio station in Berkeley, received an audio cassette. They spooled it: an SLA message. Dr. Foster had been murdered as an "execution on a shoot-on-sight warrant issued by the Court of the People" and served by "Malcolm X Combat Unit #4, United Federated Forces of the Symbionese Liberation Army." At issue—violence, truancy, and vandalism in Oakland schools. Nonstudent thugs strolled with impunity onto campuses dealing drugs and inciting fights.

Someone on the school board suggested an ID system—photo cards issued to students worn as badges. Too many Oakland blacks had worn prison numbers or knew or were related to someone who had. SLA interpretation: gestapo tactic designed to identify, isolate, and crush minorities, turning K–12 schools into concentration camps. Dr. Marcus Foster felt the backlash and chilled the idea. The SLA didn't notice; they operated on high-fever paranoia. They believed Marcus Foster and Robert Blackburn were police (even CIA) pig lackeys. Their proof? In Philadelphia, Dr. Foster once had served on the city crime commission.

November 6, 1973 to January 8, 1974: Oakland cops stymied. They had nothing beyond the SLA tapes from KPFA.

2:00 a.m January 9: Concord PD patrol sergeant David Duge cruising the suburbs off the Clayton Road. Duge spotted a van crawling the neighborhood. Duge switched off his headlights. He trailed five blocks before toggling his roof bar. The van stopped. Duge approached from the left. Two men inside. The driver flashed an ID in the name of Robert Scalise; he said he was looking for the Devoto residence on Sutherland Court.

Duge walked back to his unit and called dispatch. Cross-directory checks found no one named Devoto on Sutherland

Court. (In fact, a George and Nancy Devoto had rented the Sutherland address, but the cross-check revealed only landlord names.) Duge ordered the men out. The passenger drew down. Duge backpedaled, crouching behind his open car door, pulling his sidearm. Shots popped both ways. Duge hit the driver in the shoulder. The passenger disappeared into the shrubbery. The van peeled out. Duge radioed Concord PD and Contra Costa County sheriffs. Squad cars screeched in. They cornered the van within three blocks and arrested the driver.

Concord PD sealed the area. Cruisers combed the streets.

5:30 a.m.: A patrol unit spotted a man darting through foliage on Sutherland Court and froze him with a spot beam. One of the cops pumped a Remington. The man surrendered with raised hands. He dropped a .380 Walther PPK. The two suspects were processed at Concord city jail and transported to Contra Costa County. They were ID'ed as Joseph Remiro and Russell Little. Inside the van, cops found SLA leaflets, pipe bombs, hand guns, and bullets. They ran ballistics on the .380. Bingo match: one of the Marcus Foster death weapons.

January 11: Neighbors reported a fire on Sutherland Court and called the Contra Costa County fire department. Neighbors said they saw a man and woman cramming boxes into a white Olds and peeling out, their back bumper scraping the driveway pavement. CCFD cooled the blaze. Concord PD investigators went in. Cursory look: weapons, explosives, and subversive documents. Investigators called for a bomb squad and alerted the FBI.

East Bay agents rushed to Sutherland Court. One bedroom escaped damage and yielded big: books on commie theory; pamphlets on guerrilla warfare based on revolutions in Cuba and Brazil; a device for injecting bullet tips with cyanide; a list of Bay Area fat-cat political targets; various acids and poisons; a book on stagecraft costuming, plus face paint, makeup kits, wigs, and wardrobe changes; high-grade gas masks; and random explosives—pipe-bomb makings.

Discards revealed identities. Someone named Nancy had scratched notes on "The Theory of the Ruling Class." One scrap referred to "Camilla's pad in Oakland." They found Joseph Remiro's notebook listing contacts with the UPU (United Prisoner's Union), VNAW (Vietnam Vets against the War), and Venceremos, a race-related radical group originating from Palo Alto. They found a library card made out to a Gary Atwood and letters from a Clifford "Death Row Jeff" Jefferson at the Vacaville State Prison Medical Facility addressed to a Willie Wolfe at 5939 Chabot Road in Oakland, just off College Avenue.

The authorities stitched it together. The white Olds was found abandoned in Berkeley, registered to a Dr. L. W. Wolfe, an anesthesiologist from Emmaus, Pennsylvania. Dr. Wolfe said his son William had been a UC student since 1971. Sutherland Court neighbors ID'ed a woman whom they knew as "Mrs. Devoto" as Nancy Ling Perry, a former UCB student from Santa Rosa. Her parents hadn't heard from her in months. Russell Little had given an Oakland address during booking: 434 Forty-First Street. Renters of record: Jonathon Salamone and Anna Lindenberg. DMV cross-files revealed them as aliases for Bill and Emily Harris, a married couple who'd recently moved from Indiana and associated with Venceremos and VNAW.

The feds drew warrants. Momentum boiled. Simultaneous raids at the Forty-First Street apartment and the house on Chabot Road. The Harrises had fled, but the property yielded more SLA documents and hit lists, another address book, and evidence of an additional tenant, Angela Atwood from Indiana. The Chabot Road address in fact was a Maoist commune called the Peking Man House (named after a Chinese food pushcart on Telegraph Avenue). Two of its tenants, jazz musician and militant socialist David Gunnell and his artist girlfriend Jean Chan, were affiliated with Vacaville's Black Cultural Association (BCA), a program organized to uplift recidivist blacks.

Investigators combed the BCA visitors' list. Recurrent names: singles Willie Wolfe, Joseph Remiro, and Russell Little, and a married couple, Bill and Emily Harris. They found another Peking Man House radical denied BCA status—Nancy Ling Perry, who was already visiting Death Row Jeff, the putative founder of the SLA—as well as an inmate named Albert Taylor. A new name popped into view: thirty-one-year-old fugitive Donald DeFreeze, a.k.a. Cinque Mtume.

DeFreeze, born in Cleveland, late of Los Angeles, had been in and out of jail since he was a teenager. In 1967, he was sentenced to five to life for armed robbery: two hundred guns from a surplus store. He once had been an LAPD informant and prison snitch. His jacket labeled him prone to violence, an alcoholic fascinated by bombs. Rumor had him hooked on "pruno"—raisin jack that cons ferment in jail-cell shitters. DeFreeze completed a psych-eval tour at Vacaville in December 1972; he was transferred to Soledad coincidental with Soledad reactivating its shut-down south section, a minimum-security wing outside the main walls. DeFreeze qualified for a trusty job in the south unit. He worked graveyard under guard in the boiler room.

March 5, 1973, 12:40 a.m.: The guard left for twenty minutes. DeFreeze took advantage. He climbed over the twelve-foot fence, walked across an open field to a frontage road off Highway 101, and flagged a ride with a Chicano farm laborer. The Chicano lived in Gonzalez, eight miles north. DeFreeze told the Chicano he'd been robbed and beaten. The Chicano took him home, fed him soup, and let him call long distance to Berkeley. An unknown male—maybe Little or Remiro—drove the hundred miles south and hauled him back.

By the end of January 1974, Oakland PD and the FBI had thumbnails on DeFreeze, Perry, the Harrises, Wolfe, and Angela Atwood and had added two more names from Berkeley—Patricia Soltysik and Camilla Hall. The authorities had two soldiers in custody: Remiro and Little on the Marcus Foster murder. They had ferreted the full roster of SLA names but were clueless as to fugitive whereabouts. They had no way to anticipate the SLA's next strike. Truth is, they missed the best clue. At Sutherland Court, on a notebook page, three scrawled lines never registered: "At UC—Daughter of Hearst—that bitch's daughter—junior art student. Patricia Campbell Hearst. On the night of the full moon...Can you make up a teamwork game?"

The next full moon? Monday, February 4, 1974.

II

The Hearst fortune originated with Patty's great-grandfather George, an uneducated storekeeper from Franklin County, Missouri. George Hearst moved west with the gold rush in 1850. He never struck Sutter's Mill pay dirt, but he thrived as a speculator and landowner. He and two partners controlled three of the most productive mines in America: The Anaconda near Butte, Montana, yielding vast lodes of silver and copper; the Homestake in Lead, South Dakota, the largest, deepest gold mine in North America history; and the Ontario silver mine in Utah. George Hearst doubled as a land grabber. He held title to hundreds of thousands of acres in Mexico and California, including the world-famous Hearst Ranch in San Simeon.

George Hearst married Phoebe Apperson in 1862; she was nineteen; he was forty-one. They had their only child, William Randolph, in 1863. George controlled an unprofitable newspaper in San Francisco called the *Examiner*. He obtained a majority interest as collateral for bad loans drawn to keep the paper alive. Democrat George Hearst was a California state senator from 1887 until his death at seventy in 1891. He soapboxed his politics through the *Examiner*'s news and op-ed pages.

His only offstpring had no interest in mining or ranching. The newspaper was another matter. WRH had flunked out of multiple Ivy League colleges, including Harvard, where he had edited the *Lampoon*. In 1887 he asked George for the *Examiner*, and George indulged him. WRH was a media prodigy from the beginning. He hired big-name writing talents Bret Harte, Ambrose Bierce, and Mark Twain. He subtitled his paper the *Monarch of the Dailies*. He pioneered newspaper cartooning. His editorials screamed outrage on behalf of the common man. Truth never was an issue. Sensation was. Hearst papers slanted facts, often invented them, to spike circulation.

William Randolph Hearst leveraged capital to purchase the *New York Journal-American* and from there amalgamated a publishing empire that would peak at twenty-eight big-city newspapers nationally—San Francisco, Los Angeles, Seattle, Chicago, Philadelphia, New York, Atlanta. He published popular magazines—*Cosmopolitan, Good Housekeeping, Harper's Bazaar, Esquire*. He diversified into radio and syndicated comics and, later, into movie news, movies, and television. In his time, WRH controlled the content of a high percentage of the nation's reading, listening, and viewing habits.

He harbored political ambitions that never would materialize—he aspired to the US presidency. He reckoned his rich-guy playboy image wouldn't resononate with American voters. He married showgirl Millicent Willson the day before his fortieth birthday, in 1903. She was twenty-two. Millicent bore him five sons. Patty's father, Randolph Apperson, was a twin, minutes older than Ebert Wilson, the youngest of WRH's issue. Ebert Willson later changed his name to David Whitworth.

Phoebe and only child Willie had spent much of Willie's formative years touring Europe and Asia, marveling over art and antiquities. From that exposure, WRH developed acquisitive impulses that surpassed obsession. He was especially fond of castles. At his peak, his own spending was obscene.

Pre-Depression, he was churning through $15 million a year—more than $200 million at current rates. He ran out of room in his residences to display his purchases. He bought warehouses in the Bronx to store priceless objects he never uncrated. He lived in the top floor of a block-long building on Lexington Avenue in New York City. He would buy a house in Beverly Hills with twenty-nine bedrooms. In a private zoo at San Simeon, he owned the largest private collection of animals on earth—a range of species from Australian giraffes to Madagscar apes.

He expanded George Hearst's Mexican property, Babicora, to a million acres, and San Simeon into 470,000. He bought property in Hawaii. He had a beach house in Santa Monica. He purchased an actual castle, sight unseen: the eight-hundred-year-old Saint Donat's in Wales; he dumped millions into restoration and a million-plus per year on upkeep. He erected monuments to profligate wealth. On direction from his mother, he built Wyntoon, a Gothic stone castle and outbuildings in Trinity County, on inherited Hearst property around a bend of the McCloud River. The living room of Wyntoon's main building itself covered 2,880 square feet. WRH hosted high hats at Wyntoon: among them, Charles and Anne Lindbergh, Clark Gable and Carole Lombard, Joseph P. Kennedy and his son Jack.

WRH began building Hearst Castle in 1919. His father originally had purchased 250,000 acres along fourteen miles of Central California coastline in San Luis Obispo County, midway between Los Angeles and San Francisco. George Hearst had been satisfied with a capacious ranch house on the slopes above the shore. His son had bigger ideas. He retained reknowned architect Julia Morgan to design La Cuesta Encantada.

They laid it out on a virgin hilltop eight miles above the beach at San Simeon. Casa Grande, the big house, occupied sixty thousand ostentatious square feet: more than a hundred bedrooms, sixty-one bathrooms, nineteen sitting rooms, and enough wall and floor space for previously warehoused art objects. The grounds spread over 127 acres and featured fountains and gardens, indoor and outdoor swimming pools, tennis courts, an airfield, a fifty-seat cinema screening room lined with shelves stacked with rare books, and the heavily stocked Hearst private zoo.

WRH died filthy rich at eighty-six in 1951. He couldn't take his fortune with him but did the next-best thing: he controlled it from the grave. He reasoned that none of his sons could absorb the inheritance tax on San Simeon. George Hearst's original ranch was carved out and kept in the family, eighty-six thousand acres. The castle and the remaining 384,000 acres were ceded to the state of California. WRH figured his progeny as individuals or a collective wouldn't be able to handle his fortune. He and his advisors had formed the Hearst Corporation to bury debts in 1937, when the Depression threatened to wipe him out entirely. World War II bailed him out. From after the war to his death, the Hearst Corp. was ridiculously flush.

His personal will ran 128 pages and transposed an estate of $59 million ($560 million current value). It bequeathed his holdings into three trusts: (1) $6 million to his wife (along with $1.5 mil cash); (2) a hundred shares of corporate voting stock for each of his five sons, plus enough preferred stock to guarantee a $150,000 per annum income, in addition to generous salaries and perks from cushy Hearst Corp. executive positions; and (3) a residual fund for charitable and educational purposes—principal beneficiaries the LA Museum of Art and UC Berkeley.

The Hearst name stands huge in left-wing, university-dominated Berkeley. Hearst Avenue in North Berkeley runs west-east from the bayshore marina to the botanical gardens west of Grizzly Peak along the top edge of the Cal campus. In 1903, the year he married, WRH funded construction of the eighty-five-hundred seat UC William Randolph Hearst Greek Amphitheater on Gayley Avenue. In 1907, his mother underwrote the Hearst Mining Building in George's honor, home of the UC materials science and engineering department.

In 1927, WRH donated money in his mother's name to build the Beaux-Arts Phoebe Apperson Hearst gymnasium for women. The student/alumni tennis courts on Bancroft are named for the Hearsts. Patty's mother, Catherine, was appointed a UC regent in 1956 by governor Goodwin J. Knight. In 1971, the twenty-six-member board of regents agreed to invest in Rhodesian (now Zimbabwean) concerns, earning bitter enmity from leftists for endorsing apartheid interests. Catherine Hearst, notably, voted yes.

The SLA snatched Patty Hearst as a symbol of establishment status/arrogance. Like most SLA assumptions, the one concerning the Hearsts' liquid assets was full of crap. Patty's father, Randolph, served as publisher of the *San Francisco Examiner*; he was corporate board chairman; he lived in comfort and could access Hearst Corp. properties in Hawaii, Wyntoon, and San Simeon. But the way the old man rigged it, the family wealth was under foundation control. Each son had a vote, but the corporate board included thirteen members—five from inside the family and eight outside. The Hearst brothers could present a united front (unlikely) on any issue, including Patty's ransom, and still be outvoted eight to five.

Patty's parents were attending a Hearst Foundation conference for youth in Washington, D.C. the night she was snatched. Patty's younger sister Anne answered Berkeley PD phone calls to the family home at ten fifteen Pacific time (one fifteen Eastern). Anne, frantic, dialed Randy and Catherine's suite at the Mayflower. Randy shook himself awake. He manged to reach FBI director Clarence M. Kelley. Kelley told him that the FBI in SF was already active. The Hearsts lifted off from Dulles at 7:00 a.m. on Tuesday, February 5. They touched down at noon. They drove home, 233 W. Inez, Hillsborough, where they found the FBI already bivouacked.

Randy tried icing the news. The feds had trapped all his phones—they wanted to limit crank calls and free the wires for ransom demands. Heavy irony: The *Examiner* sitting on a depth-charge scoop that would have splashed seventy-two-point headlines in every Hearst paper in the country had anyone else been involved. The *Examiner*, the *Chronicle*, and local TV honored the embargo, but William F. Knowland, publisher of the *Oakland Tribune*, wouldn't bend past twelve hours.

SF Chronicle morning headline on Wednesday, February 6: HEARST DAUGHTER ABDUCTED BY 3 ARMED COMMANDOS. Hot story in viral circulation—with only one update. The kidnap vehicle, the white '63 Chevy convertible, which belonged to thirty-one-year-old UC radiation mathematician Peter Benenson.

His story:

The night of February 4, 1974, he bought three bags of groceries at the Berkeley Co-op on Ashby and Telegraph. He exited west on Ashby and north on Grove toward his apartment on Josephine Street in North Berkeley. He didn't notice, but he was followed by a Ford station wagon. At his house, he was pulling a grocery sack from his backseat. Three figures emerged from the Ford wagon, two men and a woman. They grabbed him and dropped his food onto the sidewalk. They bound his hands behind him and shoved him across the tranny hump on the floor. They told him to stay down and shut up, or they'd smoke his ass.

Benenson pressed himself to the floor during the abduction. He heard the bullets the black man fired into the shingled siding. He felt a thump/bang when the SLA threw Patty into the trunk and slammed it shut. Benenson was disoriented. He knew the escape vehicles hadn't driven far. In fact, they had traveled seven blocks: right on Parker, right on College, and left on Derby to exclusive Tanglewood Road, a short, winding lane just below the Claremont Hotel. They stopped next to tall hedges. Benenson heard the trunk open. He heard a voice say, "Look up, and you're dead."

Eventually he peeked and saw no one. They had taken his keys. He walked in shock four miles to his sister's house in North Berkeley, loosening the cords on his hands on the way. Peter Benenson hid at his sister's. A Berkeley PD patrol unit spotted his car near dawn. It had two bags of food in the backseat. They noted the address on his registration. At 1304 Josephine, they saw a grocery bag on the sidewalk mow strip. They didn't find Benenson for another twelve hours.

The FBI bugged phone lines and covered mailboxes. They set up a command post in the Hearsts' library. Nothing eventuated until Thursday, February 7. That day, radio station KPFA received a brown envelope containing a cassette along with a bona fide: half of one of Patty's credit cards. Transcribed, the cassette rambled a full page, with a date of February 4, 1974, and the header:

SYMBIONESE LIBERATION ARMY
WESTERN REGIONAL ADULT UNIT

The tape was theatrical, as though devised by psychotic fifth-graders play-acting something out of *Lord of the Flies*. It called Patty "a prisoner of war"; referred to Randolph Hearst as a "corporate enemy of the people"; referred to a "Warrant Order" calling for "Arrest and protective custody, and if, resistance, execution." It was signed SLA and postscripted, DEATH TO THE FASCIST INSECT THAT PREYS UPON THE LIFE OF THE PEOPLE. Feds puzzled. The message mentioned nothing about ransom.

February 12, 1974, Tuesday, eight days after the kidnapping: KPFA received another cassette. A typed page in the envelope demanded that the transcript be aired verbatim by all media. News this hot—nothing would keep it from the public anyway. Patty's voice, muted, dissociated, filled part of the recording:

> Mom, Dad, I'm okay. I had a few scrapes and stuff, but they washed them up...And I've caught a cold but they are giving me some pills. I am not being starved or beaten or unnecessarily frightened...And I know that the SLA members here are very upset about press distortions...

Cinque kicked in with extortion:

> Each person with one of the following cards is to be given 70 dollars' worth of meats, vegetables, and dairy products: all people with welfare cards, Social Security pension cards, food stamp cards, disabled veteran cards, medical cards, parole or probation papers, and jail or bail-release slips.

Preposterous, something out of Woody Allen's *Bananas*. The demand would pencil out to a distribution of $400 million worth of food to 5.7 million people in California. Randy Hearst could raise only a fraction of that amount; logistics would derail any attempt to comply. The message was stunning. Obvious now: Patty's life was hanging on the whims of murderous fanatics whacked out of their skulls.

III

SLA soldiers Donald DeFreeze, Bill Harris, and Angela Atwood—frumpy female feigning car trouble—had abducted Patty Hearst. On Tanglewood Road they hoisted Patty from the trunk of Peter Benenson's Chevy and stashed across the rear foot wells of the green Ford. They crept at speed-limit pace across the Bay to the Westlake section of Daly City. They pulled into a single-car garage at 37 Northridge, a shoe-box flat-top fifteen miles south of the Hearst family mansion.

They yanked her from the Ford and dumped her into a two-by-six closet smelling of mold, soundproofed by pieces of carpet padding tacked to the walls. They left her trussed, gagged, and blindfolded. The closet was dim, lit by a low-watt bulb over the door. The SLA plugged in a portable radio blaring high-decibel soul music. Donald DeFreeze threatened to beat the shit out of her if she tried turning it down. Patty crimped into a fetal ball. Nothing could have prepped her for the terror she would endure—certainly nothing from her affluent upbringing would.

Patty had lived in Beverly Hills until she was eight. In 1962 the family moved to the San Francisco Peninsula, Hillsborough, twenty miles South of San Francisco, uphill west of El Camino Real, a town of immense wealth not zoned for commercial enterprises. The town is laid out on the eastern slope of the coastal range, on a vine work of narrow winding streets, not a grid. The smallest Hillsborough lot is half an acre; the smallest house, twenty-five-hundred square feet. The Hearst property at 233 W. Santa Inez Avenue sat hidden behind a stucco wall on a 1.21-acre lot. By any scale, it was splendid. Rain-forest landscaping surrounded a three-story house: 9,856 square feet of living space with nine bedrooms, six bathrooms, and tennis courts, plus a pool with cabana.

Randy Hearst had left Harvard in 1937 to apprentice as an assistant to the editor of the Hearst Corporation's *Atlanta Georgian*. In 1938, he married eighteen-year-old Atlanta debutante Catherine Wood Campbell. Their first daughter, Catherine, arrived in 1939; the second, Gina, ten years later. Patty was born in 1954; the younger girls, Anne and Victoria, in 1957 and 1958.

Catherine was a devout Catholic. Episcopalian Randy accepted Catholic Church training for marriage but never converted himself. Raising children in the church was part of the deal, and he didn't object. The five girls learned catechisms, attended Mass, confessed sins, sipped wine for Communion, and dabbed soot on their foreheads for Lent. For his part, Randy slept in on Sundays. Patty exploited the schism.

She attended parochial schools. At age fifteen, she boarded at Santa Catalina on the Monterey Peninsula, a blue-blood alternative to an Eastern prep. Santa Catalina was operated by dour Dominican nuns. Her first week, Patty skipped a benediction service with her best friend from Hillsborough, Trish Tobin. Trish Tobin's family had founded the Hibernian Bank in San Francisco in 1859. The nuns laid on demerits that had to be worked off before any privileges could accrue. Patty felt like a prisoner from the start.

Santa Catalina permitted one home weekend visit a month, but only if students were free of demerits. Randy dropped in one weekend her second year. He wanted to take her to lunch. The nuns said no—Patty had eighty hours' worth of misbehavior to work off. Patty said, "I eat lunch with my father, or I fly home tonight, and you'll never see me again." Patty pushed her displeasure when Randy arrived. Catherine interceded on Patty's side. Her junior year, she registered with the two-hundred-student Crystal Springs Day School for girls in Hillsborough, four minutes from West Inez.

Patty was sixteen with a driver's license. Randy gave her his duck-hunting sled, a '53 Chevy three-speed stick that smoked a quart of oil a day. The Chevy crapped out one night on a dark lane several winding miles from her house. No cellphones then. No

7-Elevens with pay booths uphill from El Camino Real. Patty had to walk home. The next day, Randy bought her a new MGB-GT.

Crystal Springs evaluated her transcript and ruled that she could graduate after one year, in the spring of 1971, when she was seventeen. With two semesters before exit, she knew she could romp. She developed a crush on a rookie math teacher, a recent Princeton graduate originally from Palo Alto, twenty-three-year-old Steven Weed.

Weed was tall and skinny, with long hair, a soupstrainer moustache that overgrew his upper lip, and gold-rimmed glasses. Patty thought he was sophisticated. Weed lived fourteen miles south of Hillsborough, in Menlo Park, a twenty-minute drive. He shared a rundown house on half an acre of underbrush and oak trees in a neighborhood mixed with retired couples, hippies, Chicanos, and Hell's Angels. Patty never was his student, but she rolled in twice a week for tutorials. Patty didn't give a shit about math; she was stalking with hormones. Weed didn't resist.

1970s: teacher/student fraternization frowned upon only by bluenoses and Republicans. Patty and Weed consummated when she was seventeen. Weed could have been jailed for statch rape and contributing to delinquency.

Weed the teacher introduced Patty to weed the narcotic. She had never before smoked dope. Catherine had browbeaten her on the subject. Patty believed the "Reefer Madness" fable. Weed snickered. He had blazed since Princeton. He black-lighted grows in his house. He rolled a joint to share. Patty puffed herself mellow and giggled. Weed orated Bible passages in exaggerated voice, mocking serious scripture. Patty was drawn to his worldly and irreverent ways.

She graduated in June 1971 and enrolled that August in Menlo College, a private junior college in Menlo Park, located near Steve Weed's tumbledown dwelling. Menlo was in its first year as a coed school. Patty was one of twenty women on campus. She was assigned to a dorm room; she shared space with the daughter of the

Iranian minister of agriculture. Patty used the dorm as a mail drop. She moved her stuff to Weed's house, where they lived as a couple.

At the end of the 1971-72 school year, Weed was awarded a fellowship at UC Berkeley, a grant to teach logic and work toward a doctorate in philosophy. Patty told her mother she was moving across the Bay to live with Steve Weed. Her parents were less than thrilled. Catherine was moneyed old South, a conservative UC regent. She despised student protests and leftists.

She wanted Patty secure at proper blazer-and-slacks Stanford, not jumping into the bell-bottomed socialist cesspool of Berkeley. Catherine saw Steve Weed as a left-leaning dilettante. Patty had taken him to San Simeon and Wyntoon—they always arrived in Patty's MGB. Patty was eighteen and determined. Randy's unique paternal spin: ply her with extra money. Patty and Weed settled in, college students in a campus apartment furnished with oak antiques and Persian rugs. Patty detached from her debutante life. Steve Weed rode first class on the Hearst Corp. gravy train.

Widely assumed after February 4, 1974: Patty was taken by militant blacks for political ransom. Investigation revealed that the group had spawned from the Vacaville prison Black Cultural Association. A black fugitive, Cinque, was SLA spokesman. He ended the February 7 tape to KPFA with: "...I'm that nigger you have killed hundreds of my people in vain hope of finding. I am that nigger that is no longer just hunted, robbed, and murdered. I am that nigger that hunts you now...Death to the fascist insect that preys upon the life of the people."

Truth is, the SLA was white middle class assimilating black ghetto rage. They vibed anger. They percolated a bad-ass rap and played with military firearms. The group's big drawback: zero authenticity. They believed that only blacks could lead the struggle for freedom. Whites didn't know the streets; they hadn't suffered enough. Donald DeFreeze had turned political in prison. Muslim mosques in San Quentin, Folsom, Vacaville, and Soledad were inciting racial discontent. DeFreeze was unschooled—some doubt how much he actually read. But groups such as the BCA echoed Eldridge Cleaver (*Soul on Ice*), Malcolm X, and George Jackson (*Blood in my Eye*), and DeFreeze listened.

They tacked on urban-guerrilla tenets and tactics from Regis Debray (*Revolution in the Revolution*), who fought in Bolivia with Che Guevara, and the Afro-Caribbean radical Frantz Fanon. They spouted political platitudes from Lenin, Chairman Mao, and Ho Chi Minh. Cellblock dialogues convinced DeFreeze that he wasn't just some prison punk: he was a victim of fascist-pig oppression.

DeFreeze was the missing link. He mimicked revolutionary rhetoric and called for murder strikes that in fact had originated with the SLA's angry white women. The SLA men—once Remiro and Little had been jugged—were dangerously feeble. Willie Wolfe was a follower no one took seriously. Bill Harris was a weapons-trained Vietnam vet, a small man with esteem issues—his FBI wanted poster specked him at five foot seven, 145 pounds. Cinque strutted in from Soledad; he assumed command over unfulfilled white-bread followers.

Nancy Ling had been a high school cheerleader from Santa Rosa. Her father owned a furniture store. Nancy emulated his politics. She worked on the Barry Goldwater campaign in 1964. She enrolled in Richard Nixon's alma mater, Whittier College, before transferring to Berkeley in 1966. In '67 she married a black jazz musician with an afro named Gilbert Perry, a bad hookup that took six years to disintegrate. Gilbert cheated on her. She took solace in LSD, opium, and pills. She danced topless in San Francisco's North Beach. In 1972, she dated a black man named Chris Thompson, who introduced her to radical jingo. She found truth in the cause of black oppression.

The Harrises had moved from Indiana in 1972 with friends Gary and Angela Atwood. Bill Harris had a masters in urban education. Emily taught middle-school English. The Atwoods were actors looking for their big break. Both couples had been '60s activists at IU and were eager to reaffiliate. They tumbled into the BCA. Radical Hoosiers to Berkeley militants: a serious transition—too heavy for Gary Atwood. He split for Bloomington, leaving his wife and library card for the feds to find.

Patricia Soltysik was from Goleta. She turned down a hometown UCSB scholarship to join the UCB counterculture carnival ride. Straight-A Pat right away was lost in Berkeley's sociopolitical miasma. She lived with a boyfriend who ignored her outside of bed. She mixed with demonstrators in Sproul Plaza. She empathized with the downtrodden. She met Russell Little. She fell for unlovely lesbian Camilla Hall. Camilla Hall wrote dreamy poems about Pat Soltysik. In one, she renamed her "Mizmoon."

Chris Thompson ran soul-food carts around the congested intersection of Telegraph and Bancroft: "Black Market" and "Harlem on My Mind." He met Pat Soltysik, brought her to the Peking Man House, and bopped her. She reacquainted with Russell Little, who introduced her to Joseph Remiro. Russell Little told Chris Thompson he needed a place "that's cool for a friend," code for harboring a fugitive. Chris Thompson passed the task to Patricia Soltysik. Donald DeFreeze blew in from Soledad and said the magic words: "When we starting the muthafucking revolution?"

Mizmoon and Cinque shacked at her Parker Street pad from March to August 1973. They formulated SLA aims and goals. Nancy Ling Perry, on the rebound from a toxic marriage and drug addiction, joined them in August. The three moved to a small apartment on Channing Way. Nancy and Mizmoon collaborated as chief SLA theoreticians. They tried recruiting new soldiers from the black community and were rebuffed. They drew fervor only among fish-belly whites. They gathered in Little, Remiro, Angela Atwood, Willie Wolfe, Camilla Hall, and the two Harrises.

They assembled at the Peking Man House. They screwed gratuitously. They studied Swahili and target-shot assault weapons at the Chabot Hills Gun Club. They sweated their way through military calisthenics. They spread the gospel of Chairman Mao. They plotted terrorist tactics. They adopted melodramatic new names. Donald DeFreeze was "Cinque"; Joseph Remiro, "Bo"; Russell Little, "Osceola; Patricia Soltysik/Mizmoon, "Zoya"; Nancy Ling Perry, "Fahizah"; Camilla Hall, "Gabi"; Willie Wolfe, "Cujo"; Emily Harris, "Yolanda"; Bill Harris, "Teko"; and Angela Atwood, "Gelina."

They wrote loved ones, declaring their intentions to disappear. They burrowed underground as radical narcissists. They assassinated Marcus Foster on November 6, 1973. They snatched Patricia Campbell Hearst on February 4, 1974.

IV

The SLA stayed seven weeks in Daly City. They confined Patty to the closet for the duraton. They threatened her with imminent death, verbally abusing and ridiculing her for her upper-class attitudes. They code-named her "Marie Antoinette." They—mostly Cinque—interrogated her on politics and Hearst-family finances. She knew little about the first and even less about the second. Patty was just twenty and unformed—prime subject for an epic brainwash. She had no conspicuous social awareness; she seldom read a daily paper. She never despaired over the war in Indo-China or living conditions in America's ghettos. She spent Randy's money. She studied art history, baked soufflés, and braided macramé plant slings for her campus pad.

In the closet, Patty separated from herself. Confucian masses in China didn't reform into red commies on their own volition. The Great Helmsman, Chairman Mao, coerced them via an articulated 3-D program: debility, dependence, and dread. The SLA wracked Patty with a crude version of same. Sensory deprivation and malnutrition weakened her. Fear spiked to her marrow and spread through her system. 3-D distorts cognitive processes. Patty dissociated into an SLA construct, never a willing convert. She was sustained only by an atavistic will to live. At some lizard level, ultraresilient Hearst DNA kicked in. She wasn't Patty exactly. Nor was she SLA Tania. She rearranged herself into the existential essence of "Survivor."

The female comrades escorted her to the bathroom and wouldn't shut the door. She bathed, peed, and crapped under watch. Patty grew faint from inactivity. She ate blindfolded. She barely picked at the diet of the noble poor they served on paper plates: mung beans, bland rice, bananas, and peppermint tea. She couldn't manage the toilet trip without them propping her up by the elbows. Bill Harris scorned her as a bourgeois bitch. He said a true political prisoner would engage in isometrics to stay strong. Patty lost weight—she dropped below a hundred pounds. She disoriented. She lost her reasoning skills. She saturated blindfolds with spontaneous tears; her captors fashioned new masks out of kitchen sponges and bedsheet strips. The SLA soldiers—most often Cinque—hunkered outside her closet and rapped urban guerrilla propaganda.

Cinque was a broken record. He mixed D-block profanities with Marxist/Maoist claptrap. He quoted Ho Chi Minh: "Today the locust fights the elephant, but tomorrow the elephant will be disemboweled." They all droned proverbs from Chairman Mao's *Little Red Book*. The group motto: "Dare to struggle; dare to win." Each had favorites, all pretentious and nihilistic. Willie Wolfe, a.k.a. Cujo: "All men must die, but death can vary in significance." Bill Harris, a.k.a. Teko: "A revolution is an insurrection, an act of violence by which one class overpowers another." Donald DeFreeze, a.k.a. Cinque: "Political power grows out of the barrel of a gun." Red radical overkill. Patty drifted into oblivion at the sounds of their voices.

Cinque characterized the SLA as a honeycomb of highly trained military units mobilized into combat, intelligence, and medical teams and supported by revolutionary sympathizers spread strategically across the world. He told her the movement was poised to conduct righteous guerilla warfare against fascist states and that repressive governments all would fall.

He was bullshitting. Excepting Camilla Hall—their outside runner—the entire SLA slept on the floor in the next room. Her fifth day in captivity in Daly City, Cinque had brought a tape rig into the closet and had her read from a script—the first of the KPFA communiqués, the one that demanded $4 million in food at seventy dollars per to 5.7 million oppressed California citizens. Cinque held Randy responsible for controlling a bourgeois media that supported a capitalistic military-corporate fascist state. He held Catherine responsible for her insensitivity to crimes against people as a UC regent.

February 12, 1974: Randy and Catherine held a press conference. Randy countered with a $2 million offer: $500,000 of his own money and $1.5 million from the Hearst Corp. Cinque told Patty that Randy was trying to lowball the deal—that Patty's life was worth less to her father than the overflow of Hearst Corp. cash. Cinque pointed out that Catherine stood by her husband at the press conference wearing a black dress suitable for mourning. Patty, lost in fear, sank deeper.

Nancy Ling Perry, Patricia Soltysik, and Angela Atwood collaborated on the scripts. Donald DeFreeze performed them on tape. They brought in Patty to read her parts. The total combined effect: The SLA terrorized the Hearsts, infuriated the FBI, and spellbound the listening/viewing/reading public.

February 20, 1974: Cinque, in another communiqué:

Greetings to the people...The Hearst Empire has attempted to mislead the people by claiming to put forth a good faith gesture of two million dollars...an act of throwing a few crumbs to the people, forcing them to fight over it amongst themselves...

He prattled on. He cited the Hearst alliance with sources of worldwide wealth from Howard Hughes to the Shah of Iran. He demanded that an additional four million worth of high-grade food be distributed to the poor of San Francisco and Los Angeles over a one-month period beginning in one week. Food was to be given to whoever asked, no ID required. Any attempts to harm Joseph Remiro and Russell Little or rescue Patty and they would execute her.

Randy consulted Hearst Corp. accountants and lawyers. He consulted Ludlow Kramer, secretary of state from Washington State, who had run a relief program for unemployed aerospace workers displaced in Seattle. Lud Kramer's calculation was that two mil worth of food products could feed a hundred thousand people a month for a year. Randy added a couple of bonuses: he would hire his friend, San Francisco attorney William Coblentz, to warranty fair legal treatment for incarcerated SLA soldiers Remiro and Little; the Hearst Corp. would kick in an additional two million worth of food donations beginning in January 1975.

Randy's PIN (People in Need) program stumbled over obstacles. Radical groups distrusted one another. Go figure—the Black Prisoner's Union suspected the American Indian Movement, who couldn't stand the Black Teachers' Caucus. The Black Panthers refused to join at all—they didn't approve of kidnapping on principle. Other groups weren't as proud. Literal tons of food were loaded into rental trucks and ferried to collection points in black neighborhoods from East Oakland to Richmond, from Hunters Point to the Fillmore. Some of it was highjacked and black-marketed. The Black Muslims exploited PIN. They claimed restitution for $150,000 worth of fish and eggs they said had been taken from their warehouses by angry crowds. Kramer let the Muslims Mau-Mau him; he blinked and paid, unwilling to risk disruption to distributions.

Food-giveaway centers were a disorganized mess at first. Thousands crowded the first giveaway site in a black section of Oakland. Riots broke out. Neighborhood punks stole food and scurried off. Some deserving poor stood in line all day and came away with nothing. Randy persevered. He made site visits. He met with radicals and tried to access a world he only knew as a view through top-story windows from his executive suite. Through it all, a good percentage of the food actually made it to the hungry and needy minorities. Not everyone was thrilled. Governor Ronald Reagan was quoted as saying, "Too bad we can't have an epidemic of botulism."

The irony: It didn't matter. The SLA was playing a parallel game. Outside: the PIN program was a grandstand ploy to tweak Randy and the public as punishment for being pigs. Inside: the SLA was prepping for action unrelated to PIN. The SLA—principally Cinque—grew anxious in Daly City. Nancy Ling Perry and Angela Atwood had rented the house masquerading as stewardesses; they dropped implications to neighbors that any clamor would come from partying with pilots. They had stayed far too long for that dodge to hold. The last week in March, they secured a one-bedroom place on the second floor of a three-story brick-faced building at 1827 Golden Gate Avenue, two blocks off Divisadero, the western border of the City's traditionally black Fillmore district.

They staged a dead-of-night getaway. They stuffed Patty into a thirty-three-gallon plastic garbage can and jostled the can into the trunk of a car. The others left in disguise. Angela Atwood had been an actress who had waited tables before joining the SLA. Her thespian career had peaked in 1972 with the second lead in a production of *Hedda Gabler* at the Company Theater in Berkeley. She left behind her dramatic ambitions but managed to retain her backstage skills in makeup and wardrobe. She dressed Cinque in drag and applied blackface to herself and the others. They pulled on afros wigs. They departed in two cars—six coloreds and Aunt Esther.

At Golden Gate, they stashed Patty into a closet more cramped than the one in Daly City. Over the next eight days, they brought her out at intervals for indoctrinations. Patty relented to pressure—perrmitted them to train her like a parrot. She memorized the SLA codes of war. She embraced the SLA logo, the seven-headed black cobra hooded and hissing from a field of red. She learned the

African names for each of the seven heads: Umoja, Kugichaglia, Ujima, Ujamaa, Nia, Kuumba, and Imami. She bought what they sold and vice versa; in her mind, resistance was a death warrant. The group changed her name from "Marie Antoinette" to "Tiny." She breathed relief. She was still alive.

Patty had redacted a huge part of herself. Her wetware worked overtime clicking in new registers as "Survivor." First breakthrough: the communal toothbrush. True revolutionaries share; they don't need personal effects. She tamped disgust and brushed. They explained revolutionary sex. Urban guerillas can't afford bourgeois ties. They screw intramurally—freely offering what is asked. Willie Wolfe entered the closet that night. Patty toggled off revulsion and submitted. Cinque followed a few days later.

April 1, 1974: Cinque led Patty out of the closet to face the others. She had been confined for fifty-seven days. She was psychologically rearranged. Cinque to Patty: "The war council has met and ruled that you can join us or be released and go home." He told her to remove her blindfold. She feared she would be executed if ever she could identify them. She responded according to ordeal. She said, "I want to join you."

Cinque: "You'll be an urban guerrilla and fight for the people."

Patty flashed—they'd never release her alive. She lied: "I want to fight for the people."

Cinque: "I welcome you to the Symbionese Liberation Army." She removed her mask. Her first thought, unspoken: they were repulsive.

She lied again: "You're all so attractive."

Cinque: "All freedom fighters are beautiful people."

They issued her combat boots and an unloaded carbine. They called her "Tania," after Tania Burke, a freedom-fighter comrade of Che Guevara. Willie Wolfe gave her a stone-sculpted talisman of an Olmec monkey. He said it was twenty-five-hundred years old, a twin to one he dangled on a rope necklace he had braided himself.

Two months had passed. April 4, 1974: FBI desperate; time ticking. The most sophisticated domestic law-enforcement agency on earth rendered impotent, forced to realize it couldn't infiltrate, let alone capture, a ragged band of social dropouts plus one erratic ex-con. Heavy irony: The federal building at 450 Golden Gate on the corner of Polk sits fourteen blocks east on the opposite side of the street from the SLA safe house, a ten-minute hop by muni bus. Three-hundred-plus FBI agents rotating in and out of 450 Goldent Gate, stumped.

No inquiry too bizarre. KPFA tapes had been shipped to the science labs in Washington. One sound tech thought he detected ambient noise of croaking frogs. Clarence Kelley opened the bureau wallet. At a meter rate of 50k per hour, the DoD OK'd Lockheed YO-3A Quiet Star spy flights over the Bay Area. The YO-3As were Vietnamera low-altitude stealth planes equipped with night-vision aerial periscopes. They scoped for regional frog ponds...without useful results.

V

April 4, 1974: Everything turned on its head. New tape surfaced on KPFA—a shocker. *LA Times* page-one headline, subhead, and first graph plus quote:

> MISS HEARST SAYS SHE
> HAS JOINED THE SLA
> DENOUNCES FATHER AS 'LIAR' ON TAPE TELLING
> DECISION; PARENTS DON'T BELIEVE STATEMENT
>
> SAN FRANCISCO—Kidnapped newspaper heiress Patricia Hearst, speaking on a dramatic tape recording...said she had decided to join the terrorist Symbionese Liberation Army members who abducted her. She denounced her father as a "liar."

"I have been given the choice of being released...or joining the forces of the Symbionese Liberation Army and fighting for the freedom of all oppressed people..."

The SLA still holed up at 1827 Golden Gate, running low on funds. Cinque occasionally wandered out—he said to attend war councils. He exaggerated. He was rapping on doors trying to recruit blacks from San Francisco's Western Addition neighborhood, bullshitting them about the depth of the movement. He enlisted no new soldiers but did manage to solicit sympathy from a few Muslims. He brought a few in to meet Patty as proof. He pitched black solidarity to a married couple from the building, Retimah X and her husband, Rasheem X. Rasheem X didn't miss much: "I don't see no blacks but you." Cinque talked fast. He said the SLA's war council had commissioned him to lead a white unit; the black squads were underground elsewhere.

Quarters were cramped. Eight of them plus Patty in a fifteen-by-twenty studio with one small bath, a tiny kitchen, and a Murphy bed jutting out from one wall—Cinque's rack, usually shared with Angela Atwood. They subsisted on starchy foods. They ordered Patty to load up on peanut butter and crackers. They broke down weapons and reassembled them. They sweated with prison-cell exercises—deep-knee bends, push-ups, and sit-ups. They plotted to raise cash. The city of San Francisco has mom-and-pops on three corners out of every four in downtown neighborhoods. Bill Harris wanted to heist a mom-and-pop. Cinque scoffed. Risk capture for strong-arming a grocery till for $113, or rake in thousands taking a bank? Bill Harris, Teko, at heart a dipshit. He swooned: "That's why blacks have to lead the revolution. They know these things..."

They picked a Hibernia branch on Twenty-Second and Noriega in the Sunset district in the foggy avenues. Patty freaked. Hibernia Bank had been founded by her best friend's family, the Tobins. She suppressed anxiety.

Cinque had the career criminal's feral cunning, and it showed. The stickup was professionally organized. Comrades reconned the site in disguise. They sketched the branch layout on poster board taped to the wall. They studied street maps and plotted escape routes. They cross-referred bank hours with Sunset district traffic flow. They timed the action. Cinque's plan: a five-man team deployed inside, expropriating pig money in a two-minute raid, abetted by a four-soldier unit in a separate car across the street, engine running, itchy to open fire if cops converged.

Patty resisted inside status—said she was the least experienced. Cinque said she was the star attraction—she had to be filmed by bank cameras. Bill Harris said they should shoot a bank guard and announce the holdup. He said the guard carried a gun; he was an enemy pig. Nancy Ling Perry had seen the guard; he was sixty-six years old on a pension, moonlighting as a bank dick. Probably had no bullets for his gun. Cinque said they would shoot the guard only if provoked.

April 15, 1974: Camilla Hall and Emily Harris had slipped out the day before and rented four different cars from four different agencies using stolen CDLs and credit cards.

9:40 a.m.: They stashed two switch cars, a Ford LTD and a Ford Maverick, ten blocks from the bank, on Lawton between Thirtieth and Thirty-First Avenues.

9:44 a.m.: They approached the Twenty-Second and Noriega intersection in a red AMC Hornet, and a green Ford station wagon. Camilla Hall drove the assault unit in the green station wagon: Cinque, Nancy Ling Perry, Patricia Soltysik, and Patty. Willie Wolfe piloted the rest in the red Hornet: Bill and Emily Harris and Angela Atwood.

The inside team parked on Twenty-Second, at a bus stop across the Noriega intersection. The outside team set up directly across from the bank on Noriega.

10:00 a.m.: Camilla Hall and Patty pushed through the double glass doors, cut-down carbines hidden under thigh-length black coats. Cinque trailed wearing a flop-brim super-fly hat, followed by Perry and Soltysik. The women wore wigs in colors and styles different from their own. Patty walked to the third writing counter in direct line of the overhead camera. She pulled an M-1 from under her coat. The camera caught it all at four hundred frames per minute. DeFreeze: "This is a holdup! The first motherfucker who don't lay down on the floor gets shot in the head."

Frightened customers sank to the tiles. Nancy Ling Perry kicked through them on the run, vaulting the teller's partition, stuffing cash into a drawstring bag. Patty: "This is Tania. Patricia Hearst..." She was told to recite a longer script but choked on the rest. Cinque and Patricia Soltysik drew a bead on customers and staff. Cinque clocked down the seconds out loud.

A gray-haired guy walked in. Nancy Ling Perry ordered him to the ground. He stumbled back toward the doorway. Nancy Perry crouched to a knee and triggered a burst from her .30 caliber carbine. The gray-haired fellow owned a nearby liquor store. He had pushed through the door to deposit overnight receipts. One of Perry's rounds hit him in the leg. A seventy-year-old bystander was walking past the alcove when Perry opened fire. A bullet from her spray hit him in the hip. Both men would survive.

The robbers exited less than 120 seconds after entry. They piled into the station wagon and drove north on Twenty-Second two blocks to Lawton, turning west eight blocks. The red Hornet followed. They switched to the Ford LTD and the Ford Maverick. Patricia Soltysik drove the LTD; Emily Harris, the Maverick. They traveled north on Thirty-First and right on Judah, left on Ninth to Lincoln Way parallel to Golden Gate Park. They wrapped west around Kezar Pavilion to Stanyon, down to Oak and east to Baker and north to Golden Gate. They offloaded the others with the money at the safe house and wheeled into a public parking garage in Japan Town off Geary and Laguna. They abandoned the switch cars. They walked back to the safe house. Upstairs, they joined the others in an ecstatic swag count. The Hibernia take: $10,660.

Fallout: everyone piped in. Public opinion had swayed when Patty announced she was joining the cell. A victim of political kidnapping or a radical convert? The Hibernia bank job tipped it toward convert. The April 16, 1974, *SF Chronicle* headline conceded doubt in sympathy with the Hearsts: SHE MAY HAVE BEEN COERCED. The *SF Examiner* followed the company line that afternoon: WAS PATTY A PUPPET?

Politicians spoke otherwise. San Francisco mayor Joe Alioto: "Killers, extortionists, and third-rate intellectuals. We have indulged them long enough." In Sacramento, attorney general Evelle Younger thought law enforcement was "too timid" out of deference to Patty. Richard Nixon's attorney general, William Saxbe, told the assembled press that Patty was "not a reluctant participant" in the holdup. He called the SLA "common criminals" and said his opinion included Patricia Hearst. Randy H. said Saxbe was making "irresponsible statements." Catherine said that "a person is presumed innocent until proven guilty. I just hope the Attorney General won't make any more prejudicial statements." Randy offered a very public 50k reward for information leading to Patty's safe return.

Cinque ordered a new communiqué. Patty's part of Angela Atwood's script: "Greetings to the people. This is Tania. On April 15, my comrades and I appropriated $10,660.02 from the Sunset Branch of the Hibernia Bank. Casualties could have been avoided had the persons involved kept out of the way and cooperated with the people's forces until after our departure." Patty's copy referred to her father as "Adolf" and her erstwhile family as the "Pig Hearsts."

Bureau dragnet on the SLA. The feds had full jurisdiction over bank holdups. They had twelve hundred stills of bank-cam footage. They issued robbery-arrest warrants on Donald DeFreeze,

Patricia Soltysik, Nancy Ling Perry, and Camilla Hall. They issued a material-witness warrant on Patricia Hearst. They drew warrants on Willie Wolfe, both Harrises, and Angela Atwood for possession of false ID's for the rental cars.

Cinque was convinced that the feds were conducting house-to-house searches in the Fillmore. He feared a rogue Muslim would take a run at Randy H.'s 50k reward. Loyal Muslims moved them out of 1827 Golden Gate to a four-room flat with a back door in Hunter's Point. They packed weapons, ammo, and explosives. They couldn't take everything. They left foodstuffs and decaying kitchen garbage.

They didn't have time to destroy evidence—incriminating notes, diagrams, photographs, and sketches. They piled it all in the bathtub and filled the tub with hot water. They added kitchen condiments, hair dye, Ajax, and a bag of cyanide crystals. They took turns pissing in the stew. They scribbled on the walls. Patty wrote "Patria o Muerte—Venceremos" and signed it "Tania." Bill Harris wrote a note explaining the half pound of cyanide mixed with the clues. He signed off: "Happy Hunting Charles," meaning bureau SAC Bates.

They hid for three nights in three rooms of a rat-hole motel in Hunters Point until the safe house—a duplex thick with cobwebs and dust—on Oakdale Avenue was ready. The Muslims brought in three soiled double mattresses and a cot. Cinque talked nonstop about revolution breaking loose in the summer. He heard police helicopters *whap-whapping* figure eights in the night sky. He saw the spotlights beaming shadows on dilapidated ghetto streets. His paranoia festered.

May 1, 1974, May Day: Law enforcement had cracked the safe house on Golden Gate Avenue. Floor neighbors smelled rotting garbage and saw cockroaches swarming the door sill. They complained to the super, who called the cops. Big news: SLA arrogance on full display—disgusting mess; graffiti taunts on the walls; evidence dump in the tub. Fresh momentum for the feds. Cinque felt the heat and redrew his field plan; he would take his army to LA that day. A Muslim named Brother Ali secured three vans, two VWs, and a Chevy. The SLA slipped into the night, convoying south to Watts.

VI

May 17: Patty and the Harrises watched the firestorm live on TV from a tourist motel across the street from Disneyland. Dipshit Bill Harris caused it.

Sequence:

Cinque looked at South Central LA as home, but he had no remaining contacts. He hadn't lived there for five years. The SLA squatted a few days in a burned-out fourplex on W. Fifty-Third Street. They left the vans at the curb. Street sweepers groaned through the curb lane between two and six every morning. Lamppost signs: parking prohibited between those hours. Traffic cops cited the vans. Nancy Ling Perry secured an abandoned bungalow: 833 W. Eighty-Fourth Street, near the Compton border. She rented it for seventy dollars a month from a large black guy—six foot five and prison-yard ripped—named Prophet Jones. Prophet Jones hated white folks but took the deal only after Nancy Perry pulled an M-16 from a shopping bag and convinced him by gun barrel she was SLA. They parked the vans on the next block, W. Eighty-Third, and took up residence. Same deal with the street sweepers: early-morning prohibition. The SLA racked up more parking citations.

They didn't venture out except for supplies. They covered the windows with ratty blankets. Cinque struck by a fresh fear: alien whites in the blackest hood on the West Coast—sure to draw resident attention. Cinque unhinged a closet door, leaned it against a wall, and traced a cop-size silhouette. Comrades carried six-inch survival knives sheathed and hooked onto web belts—Retimah X had bought them from a military-surplus store in San Francisco.

Cinque ordered knife-throwing practice. He was ghetto, adept at blade work. The whities clanked the silhouette more often than not.

In their downtime, the soldiers sat in the dark like bats, cupping cigarettes to shield the glow. They ate field rations mixed with canned spinach and okra flavored with mackerel chunks. They worked up cabin fever. Cinque revved messianic. One night, buzzed on plum wine, he placed the soldiers in a circle. He commanded them to sit straight. He lit a candle and stared at the flame. He told them in ritual solemnity that he was a prophet who had been placed on the earth to lead the people. He said he would write a book to spread his word. The people needed to know.

He intensified exercises and weapons drills. He plotted ultimate urban-guerilla combat action. Outline: search and destroy pigs. Roam the streets and ambush patrolmen on foot or in squad cars. Strike fast with heavy firepower. Recede into shadows and invade civilian homes. Commandeer civilians through the following day, sleeping and standing guard in shifts, before moving on. Civilians would see that the SLA only killed pigs. Civilians would sense the truth and convert, just like Tania did. Pig kills would accelerate revolution. Patty cramped from anxiety. She bled at irregular intervals. Cinque was out of his mind. Her life was in his hands.

May 16, 1974: Cinque considered escape to the Mojave. He had organized the army into three divisions of three soldiers. He placed Patty with the Harrises. Bill Harris commanded the trio as general Teko. Patty despised both Harrises but faked otherwise. Cinque assigned them a buying trip to secure a stock of long johns, wool socks, heavy coats, and denim jeans. Patty pulled on an afro wig and wore blue horn-rimmed glasses with oversize lenses. They took the red and white VW.

Emily Harris drove west on Manchester. At the intersection of Crenshaw Boulevard, they looked up the street and spotted a sign for Mel's Sporting Goods. They parked in a lot on the opposite side of the boulevard. Bill Harris told Patty to stay in the van with the weapons. He and Emily jay-ran across Crenshaw. Twenty minutes later, Patty saw Bill Harris on the sidewalk with one hand cuffed, scuffling with two store employees. At checkout, Harris had palmed a bandolier stitch-pocketed for shotgun shells. Emily was in front of him purchasing thirty-one dollars' worth of outdoor gear.

Harris slipped the bandolier under the sleeve of his red wool camping shirt. Twenty-year-old college student Anthony Shepard worked security and noticed. When the Harrises exited, Shepard grabbed Bill Harris by the arm and snapped a cuff around one wrist. The store manager, Bill Reuhl, joined them. Anthony Shepard slammed Harris facedown, grappling with his loose arm while trying to cuff the other hand. A two-inch Colt .38 wiggled out from Bill Harris's waistband and clattered to the sidewalk.

Patty— "Survivor"—reacted according to the SLA codes of war. She grabbed the first weapon off the weapons stack in the van, a sawed-off M-16 with a thirty-round clip. She aimed high according to protocol: overhead burst to distract. The heavy rifle recoiled downward. Patty hosed twenty-seven rounds into Mel's front window. Plate glass shattered. Civilians dove for cover. Bill Harris broke free. He and Emily bolted through boulevard traffic. Patty picked up an M-1 and fired three shots in an overhead volley. Bill Harris jumped in the shotgun seat. Emily wheeled the VW from the lot. Tony Shepard grabbed the .38 on the sidewalk. He fired three shots toward the van.

Emily Harris vectored southwest to the Lennox district between the 405 and the 105. She braked when she spotted a gray Pontiac trying to parallel park. Bill Harris slammed a fresh clip into the M-16. He braced the Pontiac's driver. He pointed the carbine at him and said, "We're the SLA. We're taking your car." Patty collected ordnance from the VW. The driver bolted. Emily wedged into the driver's seat—Bill had lost his glasses in the struggle at Mel's: Mister Magoo as urban guerilla.

Patty piled in back with the weapons. The Pontiac crapped out in an intersection in Hawthorne three blocks later. Bill Harris jumped out and headed toward a blue Chevy Nova parked from which a Mexican was off-loading a lawn mower. Bill Harris pointed the M-16. He had his lines down: "We're the SLA. We need your car." The Mexican flipped him the keys. Bill Harris interpreted it as solidarity for the cause: a minority showing contempt for oppression. Harris didn't seem to credit Chairman Mao's barrel-of-the gun's ability to influence.

The backup plan in case of trouble: everyone would reconnoiter at midnight at the Century drive-in theater in Inglewood. Until then: evasive action. They bopped through El Camino Junior College and a small shopping center nearby. They drove back up Manchester and South into Lynwood. Emily Harris spotted a Ford Econoline with a For Sale sign on a parked on a residential street. The sign included an address. They drove a few blocks. Emily Harris left on foot for the Econoline address. Ten minutes later she was back, test-driving the van, the teen age owner riding along. She stopped. Bearded Bill Harris climbed in the van cradling his M-16. Patty followed. The kid, Tom Matthews, a high school senior, seemed excited for adventure more than scared.

They stopped at a hardware store to buy a hacksaw. After dark, they pulled into the drive-in, which was featuring *The Sting*. Henry Gondorf scammed Doyle Lonnegan on the big screen. Tom Matthews sawed off Bill Harris's handcuff in the panel van. They waited until the exit lights turned on: comrade no-show. They slinked out, drove past the safe house and saw nothing stirring. They headed to the Hollywood hills to crash overnight. By daybreak they couldn't risk more time in Tom Matthews's Econoline. Emily and Patty walked to the bottom of hill and pretended to thumb a ride. A building contractor named Frank Sutter drove within view in a year-old Ford LTD. Two chicks. His lucky day. He pulled over and waved them in.

Patty slid in front. Emily Harris climbed in back; she pointed her handgun at his neck. Not his lucky day. She ordered him over the seat back onto the floor. She took the wheel and drove up the slope where Bill Harris was waiting in the van. They transferred their arsenal into the LTD and told Tom Matthews he was free. They warned him against snitching, said they knew where he lived. They draped a blanket over Frank Sutter on the floorboard and sped off.

May 17, 1974, 8:00 a.m.: Frank Sutter still a prisoner. Bill Harris bored him with a filibuster on the evils of the capitalist ruling class and the glories of revolution. Occasional radio feeds broke into his rap. Newscasters reported that SLA capture was near—because Bill Harris shoplifted a forty-nine-cent pair of sweat socks. Bill Harris was incensed. The newscasts trivialized him and the cause. Sweat socks and a leather bandolier? News reports couldn't distinguish between a derelict warming his feet and a freedom fighter stocking for battle.

Cops found the abandoned VW. It was registered to Brother Ali from the Fillmore District in San Francisco. Among the evidence left behind: an empty gun case with a parking ticket stuffed inside. It had been written two days earlier, citing a W. Eighty-Third Street address. LAPD ran the .38 Colt through weapons registry. Gotcha: Emily Harris had purchased the Colt at a gun show in Oakland. The search for the SLA beaconed into Watts.

Part of Cinque's overwrought planning: establish dead drops over parts of Compton and Inglewood. Patty and the Harrises still had Frank Sutter kidnapped in his own car—on the floorboard under a blanket. They spent the day trying to buy another car and be-bopping from one dead drop to another. They checked the underside of a lavatory sink in a twenty-four-hour coffee shop, the underside of a mailbox outside a post office, and under curbside return boxes at public libraries.

They taped coded notes in all five drops and found nothing in return. They scanned want ads and managed to buy a rattletrap

Corvair for $300 cash from an Ecuadorian woman somewhere in South Central. They convoyed to Griffith Park. Patty drove the LTD; Bill rode shotgun—he still couldn't see. Emily followed in the Corvair. They left Frank Sutter by the observatory. They drove his car down the hill. They told him they wouldn't kill him because he was a civilian.

May 17, 1974, 4:00 p.m.: None of them knew LA. Emily had wrong-turned between Watts and Burbank and was lost for an hour on the drive to Griffith Park. Emily Harris had worked Disneyland for a summer. She said they could blend into mouse-eared bustle. They drove thirty freeway miles to Orange County. They found a vacancy across from the park. Patty hid under a blanket. Bill and Emily checked in as a couple. They snuck in Patty and flipped on the TV.

May 16, 1974: The day before the shootout. Cinque and the others listened to reports on the debacle at Mel's. They knew they were hot. They loaded the other two vans after dark and headed for a rendezvous at the drive-in. They stayed until lights flicked on at movie's end. Same with Teko's trio: comrade no-show. Explanation: one unit or the other drove to the wrong theater. Back on the street post-midnight, they roamed South Central.

May 17, 1974, 4:00 a.m.: They circled the area around W. Fifty-Third where they had squatted two weeks earlier. They eyeballed the burned-out fourplex. The next block south, they spotted house lights. 1466 E. Fifty-Fourth, a small clapboard dump with a porch. They returned to the charred fourplex and pulled into the weeds on the side yard. They walked through backyards to E. Fifty-Fourth. Cinque rapped on the door. Inside, two fast young ladies, Minnie Lewis and Christine Johnson, soaring on drugs. Cinque bought a room from the girls for $100.

May 17, 1974, midmorning. They occupied the whole house. A neighbor kid named Brenda bopped in. Cinque slipped her twenty bucks and sent her to the nearest store for food, beer, and Camels.

Cinque checked windows. He noticed too many white guys walking along the streets. He called a war council. Two conclusions: risky to leave before nightfall; they needed to prep for combat. Cinque sent Camilla Hall for the arsenal. She dragged in five guitar cases stuffed with arms and ammo. Broad daylight; Camilla Hall, blond, fat, white, standing out. An albino in an Aloha shirt might attract less attention. SLA security defunct. SLA: all but done.

May 17, 1974, afternoon: The hunt was on. Intel crackled through radio waves on the parking citation from Eighty-Third Street. Law enforcement canvassed the neighborhood. Not hard to pinpoint the shack on Eighty-Fourth where white folks hung out. Rumors flew through the streets. Residents pinned it. TV crews blundered in. Cops hit the house—piped in gas grenades and blew the doors. Empty. SLA a step ahead. For now.

Minnie Lewis's mother, Mary Carr, lived near W. Fifty-Fourth. She was baby-sitting Minnie's children. Mary Carr had run into Brenda at the corner store. Mary Carr was horrified by the kid's strange tale of white folks with weapons at her daughter's crib. She ran for help. She waved down a patrol car. The uniforms called it in. Mary Carr barged into 1466 and pulled out her spaced-out daughter and Christine Johnson. LAPD and FBI converged. TV followed. Cops found the two vans in the fourplex yard on Fifty-Third. A quick scan: SLA detritus inside the vehicles. Go time for SWAT.

VII

SLA had cut the Hibernia swag into ninths. Each of the comrades held his/her own shares. The Harrises and Patty shaken, on the run in Orange County. Funds dwindling fast. Two thirds of their army fried. Law enforcement breathing down the backs of their necks. LA County DA Joseph P. Busch charged them with nineteen felonies from the Mel's debacle, ranging from assault with a deadly weapon (ADW), car theft, and kidnapping. Bill Harris had lifted $250 from Ralph Sutter. The Corvair cost

$300. Food cost money. New wigs, hair dye, and fresh clothes for new disguises cost money. New glasses for Bill cost money. The Disneyland motels charged in-season rates; a long stay would breach security. They rented a cheap room in Costa Mesa. They reached a no-shit conclusion: Cinque had blundered taking them to So-Cal.

May 31, 1974: They mixed with Memorial Day traffic and chugged the Corvair to San Francisco. The Harrises aged themselves via disguise. Patty rode the rear foot well under a blanket. At roadblocks or traffic stops, they figured pigs would be looking for three people, not a middle-age married couple in a crappy car. They reached San Francisco without incident. The Corvair conked out in the Panhandle of Golden Gate Park; they pushed it into a Chevron station. They off-loaded a duffel full of weapons. They had less than $200 combined. Emily used the Chevron phone booth. She reserved a motel room on Lombard Street. They took muni into the Marina.

The Harrises squabbled over money and hideouts. Patty had no say and dummied up. Feds in full force. Patty and the Harrises under their radar. Feds had budgets, manpower, and science but couldn't break the case.

Three reasons:

(1) They tracked down twenty-five thousand false leads involving fifty-nine field offices and eighty-five hundred agents nationwide; too much of their time was wasted chasing crank tips.
(2) They never developed reliable informants. The feds drove four-door G-rides and traveled in pairs. They wore suits, white shirts, ties, and fedoras. In hoods where Patty might be hiding, FBI agents stuck out like Mormons on fat-tire bikes spreading the gospel of the angel Moroni. FBI counterintelligence take from young radicals: zero. The feds

were ultimate pigs. No one in the '70s counterculture would talk to them.
(3) The SLA, fanatic fools in so many ways, had developed an expert ability to disguise themselves. They had cased the Hibernia holdup undetected. Willie Wolfe in a junior-exec three-piece suit. Nancy Perry as a sixty-year-old woman in a gray wig and support hose, cheeks packed with cotton, a black shawl wrapped around her shoulders. Angela Atwood, a pillow stuffed under a tented muumuu, lumbering when she walked like an exhausted housewife seven months pregnant. The Harrises dressed as yokels with landmark maps and cameras. They pointed at bridges and cable cars. They snapped Polaroid images of bank branches.

May 17, 1974 to September 18, 1975: Patty and the Harrises sank from sight. FBI burned big-budget dollars failing to find them. The feds felt stomach-acid dread that a random hick in a straw hat, a town constable's badge pinned to his overalls, would apprehend their fugitives in a Midwestern haystack.

Protracted underground itinerary:

Emily Harris approached contacts. She procured minor money but mostly ran into slammed doors. Black activists wanted no part of the SLA. Most never reconciled to Marcus Foster; others saw SLA affiliation as a death wish. Emily rented a small apartment near Mills College in the Oakland Hills. A smattering of fringe white radicals backlashed from the conflagration in Watts and joined them.

Angela Atwood's best friend, Kathleen Soliah, spoke at a memorial to the SLA in Willard Park in Berkeley—nicknamed Ho Chi Minh Park. Emily Harris met with her. Kathleen Soliah conscripted her younger sister Josephine and younger brother Steve. Steve Soliah and two friends, Jim Kilgore and Michael Bortin, supported themselves painting houses in the Bay Area. They were politically left of left. Michael Bortin was friends with Joseph Remiro. He was on parole for a 1972 weapons-and-explosives bust. The Soliahs, Jim

Kilgore, and Michael Bortin joined Patty and the Harrises as the new, pure-white SLA.

Kathy Soliah connected with sports activist Jack Scott. They convened at a North Berkeley pad that Steve Soliah was house-sitting. Jack Scott arrived in a blindfold—a Bill Harris security measure—escorted by Jim Kilgore. Jack Scott: radical author and sportswriter espousing the cause of black athletes. He was the former athletic director at Oberlin College. In 1974, he directed a one-man shop in New York called the ISSS (Institute for the Study of Sports and Society). Jack Scott and his wife, Micki, had rented an abandoned farm in the foothills of the Poconos. He offered the farm as a hideout until things cooled out on the West Coast. He said he'd ferry Patty and the Harrises across the country. He would support them financially and supply a nanny to run errands so that the fugitives could remain in hiding.

Patty and Jack left the next night. They rode in the backseat of a Ford LTD driven by John and Lydia Scott, Jack's parents, motel managers in Las Vegas. Long-distance drive: conversations rambled. One subject was Jack's brother Walter, an alcoholic who spun fantasies about his CIA and FBI connections. The elder Scotts said they could never tell Walter what they were doing. Jack seconded the motion. Another subject: Jack's ulterior motive. He wanted to write the SLA book.

Emily was transported by a hippie college professor in a Ford Pinto. Emily liked the plan and the driver; she humped her prof at every stop across America. Jack Scott deferred moving Bill Harris. Field Marshal General Teko was so obnoxious that nobody cared he was left behind except his wife. She thrived on their love-hate horseshit. Eventually Jack Scott flew back to the coast. He drove Bill Harris to Pennsylvania in a rented ride. It was that or listen to Emily whine.

They stayed in the Poconos for a month. The babysitter was Berkeley resident and fugitive bomb thrower Wendy Yoshimura. In 1972, Berkeley PD had uncovered an explosives workshop in a garage rented to Yoshimura. They staked it out. They nabbed Wendy Yoshimura's boyfriend, Willie Brandt, a UC student radical, the head of a group called the Revolutionary Army. The RA was tied to Bay Area bombings of banks, police cars, and nuclear labs. Arrested with Brandt: Michael Bortin. Wendy had heard the bust on a police scanner. She fled.

Mid-September 1974: They moved to a farm in the Catskills in upstate New York. The New SLA had grown sick of open-air confinement and of one another. They were bored with picturesque barns and dense trees with leaves that changed color. Bill Harris drove everyone nuts. He insisted on long-distance runs and military calisthenics. He insisted on daily self-help criticism sessions, where heaviest disapproval always deflected off him and fell on Patty, Wendy Yoshimura, and his wife.

Wendy Yoshimura hated Bill Harris. She challenged his him relentlessly. Patty and Emily Harris walked around with black eyes from similar challenges. One day, Wendy Yoshimura back-talked him. He started to slug her. She said she'd gut him with a knife while he slept. He backed off fast. They managed to agree on only one point: time to go.

October 1974: Temperatures dropping in the Catskills. The Harrises rode back on Amtrak, ages disguised with gray hair and old-people duds. Jack Scott rented a van to move stuff from his New York apartment. Patty rode in back. They laid over for a time in Portland, Oregon, staying with NBA star and deadhead hippie Bill Walton. Jack Scott dropped Patty off at a Las Vegas motel. Jim Kilgore came in by bus with two return tickets. They sat in rear seats on the gray dog to Sacramento.

Kathy Soliah rented a tumbledown duplex on W Street in downtown Sacramento. Kathy and Josephine Soliah took jobs in San Francisco as waitress and bank teller. Mike Bortin, Jim Kilgore, and Steve Soliah resumed their Bay Area housepainting. The fugitives lay low in Sac; the others burned gas on I-80 running back and forth. The new SLA had trouble making expenses. They supplemented by shoplifting food and dipping wallets from pants and purses draped over bench backs at public gyms and tennis courts.

February 24, 1975: One year, twenty days since Patty was snatched. She had turned twenty-one. New SLA desperate for funds. Mike Bortin, Jim Kilgore, and Steve Soliah robbed the Guild S&L on Arden Lane. Mike Bortin and Jim Kilgore went inside in masks. Jim Kilgore pulled a shotgun from under the folds of a long coat. He racked it, holding staff and customers at bay. Mike Bortin pulled a .45 auto and forced the tellers to hand over cash. Steve Soliah drove a getaway car. Kathy Soliah observed from a coffee shop across the street. The take: $3,700, most of it spent on fresh ordinance in splurge-shopping at a Sacramento gun show.

April 21, 1975: New SLA cased banks for two months. They settled on Crocker National in suburban Carmichael. Chronic dispute in Teko's regime: loud bickering over roles. Emily Harris wanted a bigger part. Bill Harris took command. He deferred to his obstreperous wife. She led the four-person assault team disguised in clown faces. Mike Bortin entered the bank.

He hustled to the cash counters, pulling his .45. Jim Kilgore followed, Kathy Soliah right behind. They pointed cut-down carbines and ordered everyone to drop. Mike Bortin directed the tellers to stuff cash into his drawstring bag. Emily cradled a shotgun by the door. Steve Soliah sat in an idling getaway car around the corner. Patty Hearst and Wendy Yoshimura parked blocks away in stolen switch cars with mismatched plates lifted from UC Davis parking lots.

A Seventh Day Adventist named Myrna Opsahl entered the bank to deposit funds from a church benefit. She walked in behind Kathy Soliah, to the side of Emily Harris. Emily Harris had been jittery with her shotgun during pre-heist practice. She twitched nerves with her finger on the trigger. The shotgun roared and jumped. Myrna Opsahl, forty-two, a doctor's wife with four kids, took a load of buckshot to the midsection and died. The robbers/killers fled the bank with $15,000 in cash. News reports said it was an "SLA-style" holdup.

May 1975: Sacramento too hot to stay. The new SLA moved back to the Bay Area. The others had jobs as credible cover. Patty wore a red wig and makeup freckles. Wendy Yoshimura could do nothing about looking Japanese. The Harrises could disguise themselves into multiple variations of average. They all had fake ID's. They juggled safe houses in obscure parts of town.

September 18, 1975: The FBI finally caught a break. John and Lydia Scott blabbed to weird son Walter. Walter snitched off the Pennsylvania farmhouse. The new SLA had wiped the premises, but Wendy Yoshimura's prints showed on newspaper padding a hole in a mattress. The feds ran known associates and came up with the Soliahs through Willie Brandt and Mike Bortin. They braced the Soliahs' father, Martin, in Palmdale.

They alarmed him with threats of long prison terms. They suggested he reach out to his children. Martin drove to San Francisco under a FBI tail, a Judas goat. Martin took Kathy, Josephine, and Steve to dinner. Feds followed the Soliahs. They lived in the Crocker-Amazon in South San Francisco near Daly City but frequented two other low-rent addresses: 288 Precita Street in the outer Mission and 625 Morse Avenue in Bernal Heights, less than a mile away. The feds black-bagged Precita and confirmed ID's—the Harrises. They hit both addresses. They took down Bill and Emily Harris at one in the afternoon as they were returning from a jog.

An hour and fifteen minutes later, in the backyard of 625 Morse, FBI agent Tom Padden and SFPD inspector Timothy Casey scaled rickety back stairs to a Dutch door on the second-story landing. Through the open top half, he saw Patty Hearst and Wendy Yoshimura. Tom Padden, service revolver drawn: "Freeze or I'll shoot." Patty threw up her hands, pissed her pants, and waited for the bullet that didn't come.

Tom Padden rolled his G-ride to the federal building on Golden Gate and Polk—fourteen blocks from the safe house of her captivity. He slowed at the curb cut into the tunnel under the building. The media swarmed. Reporters knocked on windows. Photographers jumped on the hood popping flashbulbs for dim-light close ups. Wendy Yoshimura sat glum. Patty clasped her cuffed hands in a two-handed salute and broke into a broad grin. She was out-of-body euphoric and had no idea why. Tom Padden inched the duty car toward a gang of marshals waiting near the interior elevator.

Upstairs she heard her rights. The feds grilled her in waves. Leftist attorney Terrance Hallinan, nicknamed "Kayo" (he'd been a boxer in college at UCB), managed to wiggle his way in as SLA counsel. Marshals escorted her into a courtroom. Federal magistrate Owen Woodruff arraigned her on the charge of armed bank robbery.

The FBI has no jails. The SF Federal Building only had wire-mesh detention cells. Security was the overriding concern. The marshals whisked her, Emily Harris, and Wendy Yoshimura to the San Mateo County high-risk lockup in Redwood City. News pix caught her in the backseat of the marshals' car, smiling stupidly, pressed in with the other defendants. The processing deputy at SMC asked Patty her occupation. The question puzzled her. She didn't have an occupation. She blurted: "urban guerilla."

VIII

February 4, 1976: Two years to the day of her abduction. Patty on trial for Hibernia. Verdict of guilt inevitable. The average American was sick of violent '70s radicals and suspicious that the Hearst Corp. could juice a release. Public opinion bought the Tania act: pampered heiress turned pampered SLA enlistee. Field polls ran 68/32 against leniency. Public opinion saw Patty mocking authority by saluting her cuffed hands upon her arrest and stating her occupation as urban guerilla.

Patty had spoken on air in tapes in which she announced her fidelity to SLA. The final communiqué—the eulogy tape—was damning. The Harrises wrote it from Oakland after returning from Southern California. It was cloying and smug, glorifying violence and dripping disdain for core America. Steve Soliah drove the finished product to an attorney friend of Jim Kilgore's in Santa Barbara, an ex-classmate from UCSB. The attorney stuck it in a pile of rubbish outside radio station KPFK in North Hollywood, a KPFA sister station. Bill Harris wanted the pigs to think the fugitives still were in LA. The attorney phone-tipped KPFK. It hit the air in minutes. Excerpts:

> Bill Harris: To those who would bear the hopes and futures of our people, let the voices of their guns express the words of freedom…On Friday, May 17, a CIA-directed force of FBI agents, Los Angeles City, County and California state pigs…encircled elements of the Malcolm X Combat Unit of the Symbionese Liberation Army. The result of the encirclement was that the people witnessed on live television the burning to death of six of their most beautiful and courageous freedom fighters by cowardly fascist insects…

> Patty: This is Tania. I want to talk about the way I knew our six murdered comrades because the fascist pig media has, of course, been painting a typical distorted picture of these beautiful sisters and brothers…Cujo [Willie Wolfe] was the gentlest, most beautiful man I have ever known. He taught me truth and he learned it from the beautiful brothers in California's concentration camps. We loved each other so much, and his love for the people was so deep that he

was willing to give his life for them...Neither Cujo or I had ever loved an individual the way we loved each other...I was ripped off by the pigs when they murdered Cujo, ripped off in the same way that thousands of sisters and brothers in this fascist country have been ripped off of people they love. We mourn together and the sound of gunfire becomes sweeter.

US attorney James R. Browning and his second chair, David Bancroft, felt obligated to prosecute fully. Judge Oliver Carter resisted any suggestion of Hearst influence. "You can't be in public life and not know Randy Hearst," he said, "...but I've got people, forbearers, buried at just as many places he has."

Randy shopped legal talent. He brushed off the local Hallinans and went for the big name—F. Lee Bailey, from Boston. Bailey and his corpulent assistant, Albert Johnson, agreed to take the case for book rights. Bailey was famous for earlier acquittals. He sprung Dr. Sam Sheppard on appeal. Sheppard was the Ohio doctor convicted of killing his wife in 1954, inspiration for the TV series *The Fugitive*. Ernest Medina was a US Army sergeant in Vietnam. In 1971, he was court-martialed for ordering a massacre of civilians in My Lai village. Bailey argued successfully that Medina's men had shot women and children on their own volition.

Turns out, Bailey was past his prime and stretched too thin. Patty's case overwhelmed him. He commuted too often to Boston. He held controlling interest in a helicopter company, Enstrom's, in upper Michigan, that required attention. During Patty's proceedings, he was moderating evening seminars for trial lawyers in Las Vegas. After court each day, he'd fly to Vegas and return late that night. He was pimping book deals. He drank with lunch, at cocktail hour, with dinner, and after. Vincent Hallinan, legendary left-wing Bay Area attorney, Kayo's father, said, postverdict: "No amount of mischance, negligence, stupidity, or idiocy could have loused up this case worse than it was loused up."

F. Lee Bailey pushed diminished capacity. Patty endured more than one hundred hours of psychoanalysis by three egghead shrinks for the defense: Dr. Louis Joloyn West, chairman of the UCLA Department of Psychiatry; Dr. Margaret Singer, a clinical psychiatrist from UC Berkeley; and Dr. Martin Orne, a psychiatrist and psychologist from the University of Pennsylvania.

Court-appointed shrinks had diagnosed her as legally sane. At bar, F. Lee Bailey opened with Patty on the stand. He flubbed it. James Browning asked her why she never escaped. His questions pinpointed opportunities during the underground year and during the episode at Mel's, when she was alone in the van with the weapons. Bailey hadn't accounted for the trap: Patty talks about Mel's, and she incriminates herself on 19 felonies. Bailey objected and was overruled. He was stuck. He couldn't allow her to answer. He signaled her forty-two times to take the Fifth. Effect on his case: ruinous. Impression on the jury: beyond negative.

Bailey brought on the experts. By the time they finished abstruse explanations of Patty's frames of mind, Judge Carter was asleep, and jurors wanted to pound their ears with the flats of their hands to pop the jargon out of their skulls. Dr. Margaret Singer scored the only lucid point. She said her tests revealed that Patty's IQ had dropped from 130 (at Santa Catalina) to 90 at the time of her arrest. The jurors were desperate for a flash of clarity. James Browning called a rebuttal expert, Dr. Joel Fort, behavioral analyst, neither a psychologist nor a psychiatrist. Flash forthcoming.

Dr. Fort had testified for the prosecution in the Santa Cruz slayers cases of John Linley Frazier and Herbert Mullin. They had killed eighteen people between them, and Dr. Fort held them legally sane.

Jim Browning: "...in your opinion was the defendant a private in an Army of generals?"

Joel Fort: "No, in my opinion she was a queen in their Army. She brought them international recognition. It was an exciting thing for her and for them that the media responded... the way it did."

Bailey compounded the damage. He battled Joel Fort on cross. He attacked his credentials and his conclusions. He asked for Fort's explanation of Patty's mental state at every interval following her abduction. Bailey claimed Joel Fort was a witness for hire and a mountebank. He snarled rambling questions; Fort growled adversarial answers. Sample: "Doctor, would you comment, please, on the effect of the defendant's pre-kidnapping personality on the attitude change after her kidnapping?"

Fort: "Yes, she had been a strong, willful, bored, and dissatisfied person in poor contact with her family, disliking them to some extent, dissatisfied with Weed after their three years together, missing a sense of purpose in life."

Sample: Bailey: "Doctor, what can you tell us, from a psychiatric standpoint, with respect to the claim that she fired the gun at Mel's almost voluntarily, or spontaneously?"

Fort: "I find it unbelievable."

The jury ate it up.

Bombastic Lee Bailey called for a mistrial. He claimed Joel Fort was directing the jury about what to believe. Motion denied. A pit bull against a mastiff in a high-profile dogfight trial, leashes held tight by judge Carter. Bailey browbeat Joel Fort on the stand for a full week. Fort never cracked. Bailey lost the jury.

Patty's judicial fate: Occam's razor—the obvious answer is the truth. She said she was SLA on tape. Bailey couldn't convince the jury of the simple contradiction at the core of her defense: she was terrorized by the SLA and brainwashed into behavior outside her own initiative. She had been abducted, threatened, and tormented; she had endured sensory deprivation and extreme confinement.

How do those facts build voluntary conversion? James R. Browning sealed the state's case with a totem. LAPD had recovered Willie Wolfe's Olmec monkey in the rubble on W. Fifty-Fourth. Browning produced it in court. Patty had testified that Willie Wolfe had raped her. She said the eulogy tape was scripted by the Harrises. She claimed she couldn't stand Willie Wolfe.

Patty still had the monkey when she was arrested. Browning wondered why she would keep a gift from a person she hated. Bailey hadn't seen it coming. Patty's answer was weak. She said she was an art history major; the Olmec monkey was priceless. James Browning said the talisman was for sale by the gross at any roadside trinket shack in Latin America. Patty had no idea Willie Wolfe had lied about its worth.

Al Johnson reassured her. Bailey would rescue her with closing arguments. Said the boss was known for his closings.

Thursday, March 18, 1976: James Browning wrapped up his case with a stiff recitation of facts. Bailey was up after lunch. He was pathetic. He lasted less than forty-five minutes, most of the time moaning about the difficulties of the case. He babbled digressions. He sounded incoherent. He gestured across the podium and toppled over a water glass. Water sloshed the midsection of his navy-blue suit. Looked like he'd peed his pants. Patty thought he might be drunk.

Friday, March 19, 1976: Judge Carter instructed the jury; he handed over the case at 10:48 a.m. Less than twenty-four hours later, they came back with a guilty verdict. Judge Carter sentenced Patty to thirty-five years: a formality. The reviewing judicial authority would slice it back to seven years. F. Lee Bailey flew back to Boston.

Randy H. kept Bailey on record as counsel for charges in LA, but Patty demanded he hire another lawyer for her appeals. Her bodyguard, Clay Shaw, recommended George C. Martinez from Oakland. Randy hired him. The Harrises plea-bargained their parts in the shootout at Mel's and subsequent kidnappings. They took three-year sentences. Patty had to stand trial for Mel's. Lee Bailey argued the case. The judge gave her time served and probation, mindful of the seven-year sentence she had received for Hibernia. Alameda County DA Lowell Jensen filed on the Harrises for her kidnapping. Patty was listed as a witness. The Harrises pled again: eleven more years.

Patty served her time at the federal lockup in Santa Rita, outside of Oakland. Her sisters organized "Free Patty" initiatives. George Martinez filed writs and motions. Public opinion mellowed and swayed back. A cross section of influences lobbied for her release: congressman Leo Ryan, later killed by fanatics while investigating Jonestown; forty-eight members of the House of Representatives; former California governor Ronald Reagan; state senator S. I. Hayakawa; lieutenant governor Mervin Dymally; labor organizer Cesar Chavez; seventy-five San Francisco policemen prompted by Clay Shaw; and, notably, San Francisco FBI SAC Charles Bates.

Patty served as a model prisoner for a year and a half at FCI Santa Rita and was sprung on a commutation of sentence issued by President Jimmy Carter. She was released on February 1, 1979. She married bodyguard Clay Shaw and moved to Connecticut. In 2001, Bill Clinton issued an unconditional presidential pardon.

True terror runs deep and stays long. Patty was "Survivor". She endured SLA thought coercion. She was abducted and brainwashed. How could she be criminally complicit for anything that followed? From the White House press release announcing President Carter's order of executive clemency, January 29, 1979: "...but for the extraordinary criminal and degrading experiences that the petitioner suffered [at the hands of the SLA] ...she would not have become a participant in the criminal acts for which she stands convicted and sentenced..."

No shit.

Postscript

Spring 1999: *America's Most Wanted* aired a special on Kathleen Soliah, still at large on a bombing warrant from 1976. Someone recognized her as Sarah Jane Olson, wife of a Minnesota doctor, and called it in. Events followed fast. Soliah as Olson was convicted on the bombing charge and sent to the Chowchilla prison for women in Central California. New ballistics techniques had linked physical evidence from the Crocker National Bank job to the new SLA. Patty, Wendy Yoshimura, and Steve Soliah agreed to testify against Soliah/Olson under immunity.

The feds charged her in Chowchilla. They dragged the rest of the new SLA from their midlife white-bread nests. Michael Bortin had married Josephine Soliah and was working as a flooring contractor in Portland, Oregon. Emily Harris was a computer tech in LA, sharing her life with a woman in Altadena. Bill Harris was an investigator in Oakland who was working for one of his previous lawyers. He was remarried, the father of two boys. The feds took him down at his boys' soccer practice. Jim Kilgore, a.k.a. John Pape, was a researcher on international labor at Cape Town University in South Africa, married to an economics professor. He was extradited on bomb-related charges.

November 2002: All of the new SLA defendants were arraigned for the first-degree murder of Myrna Opsahl. Each bargained for sentences ranging from six to eight years.

The SLA in the 1970s: Arrogant nihilists deluded into believing they could remake the world. Anarchic fools oblivious to sense and consequence, way too willing to extinguish innocent lives in the vain pursuit of their hopeless cause.

CHAPTER 7

BRENTWOOD: O. J. SIMPSON

June 17, 1994: Friday-evening freeway traffic northbound from Orange County. Hot crime by rush-hour carnival. Gridlock fully dissolved: 1994 white Ford Bronco pushing up I-5 dumping into 91 W at thirty-five mph, trailed by a twenty-four-car cortege of police and CHP cruisers, grills and tails strobing halogen hazard lights, roof bars throbbing red and blue. The Bronco merged into the 405 N past LAX, Culver City, and the I-10 interchange, poking along at school-zone speeds. All six lanes cleared to Sepulveda Pass. Way beyond weird.

A man named Al Cowlings (AC) driving the Bronco. His childhood friend O.J. Simpson, age forty-seven, slumped in the backseat, wigged out, gripping a loaded .357. Five days earlier, June 12, 1994, just past ten at night, an unknown assailant murdered Simpson's ex-wife, Nicole, on the front steps of her condo at 875 S. Bundy Drive in Brentwood. Brutal assault—a dozen frenzied stab wounds, Nicole's throat slit through the jugular veins and carotid arteries down to the C-3 vertebra. Twenty-six-year-old Ron Goldman, Nicole's friend, was slashed as well, stabbed thirty-three times. Goldman was a male model, an aspiring actor, a waiter at the trendy Mezzaluna restaurant on San Vicente and Montana, half a mile from Nicole's townhouse.

Nicole had dined at Mezzaluna that night with her children, parents, and sisters following a dance recital at Paul Revere middle school featuring her seven-year-old daughter by OJ, Sydney. Nicole's mother had left a pair of eyeglasses at the restaurant. She didn't notice until she was home in Dana Point, fifty-seven miles south in Orange County. She called Nicole. Nicole rang the restaurant. Nice guy Ron Goldman offered to return them to Nicole in person. Figure Ron Goldman a wrong-time/wrong-place victim; figure Nicole Brown Simpson the object of deep personal rage.

The chief suspect was an ex-husband with a protected history of wife-beating. Blood evidence slam-dunked it. Drops from Bundy matched OJ's type and resumed at his estate at N. Rockingham Avenue less than a mile away. Size-12 footprints (OJ's size) traced blood out to the pathway. The driver's-side carpet of OJ's own white Bronco revealed a size-12 outline of blood. The driver's-side door had a blood spot under the handle. Bloody dress socks lay on his bedroom floor. OJ had a flimsy alibi.

Only in LA. No takedown for celebrities. The DA had issued an arrest warrant—possible death penalty bounce. OJ's lawyers promised delivery downtown by 11:00 a.m. on June 17. OJ instead split with Al Cowlings. Nicole had been interred the day before at the Ascension Cemetery in Lake Forest, Orange County, between Mission Viejo and El Toro Marine Base. OJ, popping prescription opiates, slurring his words and thought processes, said he wanted to visit her grave. He was suicidal. He told AC Cowlings that he wanted to pull the trigger at Nicole's headstone. On approach, he saw cops and rubbernecks near the iron gates. He told Cowlings to flip a U.

Things went viral two decades before YouTube. AC dialed 911. He told dispatch, "I have OJ in the car. He's still alive, but he has a gun to his head." LAPD pinged his location. Media scanners picked up the story. TV, CHP, LASD, and LAPD sent up choppers.

Satellite vans followed. Live-report minicams rolled footage. Ninety-five million viewers tuned in. NBC split the screen with game-five coverage of the NBA finals, New York Knicks versus the Houston Rockets. OJ in AC's white Bronco dominated the split. Gawkers lined 405 overpasses, many with signs: "Go OJ Go"; "Run, Juice, Run"; "We love you OJ."

Homicide special detective-III Tom Lange dialed OJ's cell. OJ said he couldn't go on, said he deserved to die. Lange implored him to throw his .357 out the window. Al Cowlings drove into West LA and circled off at Sunset. He headed into Brentwood and turned north onto Rockingham Ave. He pulled through *Day of the Locust* frenzy into Simpson's gated estate. Police had barricaded the entries. SWAT was geared up and ready. Sharpshooters sat in tree limbs with AR-15s. Cop, media, and onlooker vehicles jammed the streets. Raucous pedestrians clogged traffic.

OJ's eighteen-year-old son Jason by his first wife, Marguerite, burst toward the Bronco in tears, gesticulating. Al Cowlings shivered him the fuck away. Cops grabbed Jason. OJ didn't budge. Tense minutes passed before he put down the gun and pulled himself the Bronco. Cops wary. They let him swig a glass of orange juice and call his mother in San Francisco before they snapped on cuffs and hauled him downtown.

Events screamed guilt. None of OJ's celebrity buffers could possibly help—USC all-America; NFL Hall of Fame; *Monday Night Football*; Hollywood movies; Hertz commercials. Even in LA, he couldn't skate.

I

Beginnings: Post-WWII San Francisco, 906 Connecticut Avenue. The projects. Cinder-block barracks housing tiered into the south slope of Portrero Hill, a dead-end ghetto of two-story rectangles radiating zero hope. Orenthal James Simpson, third of four children, was born in 1947 and raised on the Hill in welfare conditions. His mother's sister, Jonnie Durton, pinned him with the first name Orenthal, after an obscure French actor. Nobody on the Hill had ever heard of the actor or gave a shit about French cinema. No one believed it was a cool tag for a kid. OJ abbreviated to his initials sixty years before personal branding became a concept.

Portrero Hill overlooks freight tracks, shipping cranes, and warehouses of San Francisco's industrial waterfront south of China Basin. One of the City's worst areas but boasting some of its best weather—coastal fog and wind blocked by Twin Peaks to the west. OJ's father, Jimmy, left home when OJ was five but stayed in the projects. Jimmy ahead of his time, an out-of-the-closet gay man. Eunice supported the family as an orderly in the psychiatric ward of SF General Hospital on Portrero Avenue. She worked nights to monitor her kids during the day. Jimmie was a swing-shift custodian at the Federal Reserve Bank on Market Street.

At nine months, OJ developed a calcium deficiency, a condition akin to rickets. He was a fat, pigeon-toed kid with spindly legs beginning to bow. Eunice couldn't afford prosthetics. She innovated. She made him wear his shoes on the wrong feet and braced them with a scrap-metal bar. Hill kids noticed, as kids will. They ridiculed his crude correction rig and his skinny legs—called him "Pencil Pins." OJ had a big dome; the kids turned him into "Waterhead" and "Headquarters." They nicknamed his father as well: "Sweet Jimmy" and "Mother Simpson."

OJ compensated with physical assets. His legs stayed thin, but he grew big, strong, and fast. The juvenile order in the Portrero Hill projects pecked according to athletic ability. OJ's superior skills elevated him to alpha status. Eunice's work routine kept him in check when he was younger, but it left him on his own after dark as a teenager.

Ghetto life fosters gangs, and not the types prevalent today. OJ's crews didn't tag walls, murder over turf incursions, push drugs, pimp women, or collect armories of assault weapons. They fought with fists and feet. They grew up rough, sporting satin jackets with gang logos silk-screened in script on the back. OJ was a "Gladiator' in grade school; fourteen kids from the Hill, roaming after dark, drinking, smoking, throwing rocks at moving trains and warehouse windows, shoplifting from corner mom-and-pops.

The SF school system in those days had three grades of junior high (seventh through ninth), followed by sophomore, junior, and senior years at one of the SF unified high school district's seven campuses. OJ attended Edwards JH, He was ticketed for Mission High on Eighteenth and Church, in a downscale neighborhood mixed largely with Hispanics and blacks. OJ had joined a fighting gang at Edwards, the "Persian Warriors," a citywide band, mostly from the Fillmore. In high school, he was a "Superior."

His gangs played sports. They moved around. They could reach any corner of San Francisco's seven-by-seven-mile radius with fares and transfers on muni buses or trolley cars. They snuck into SF Giants games at Seals Stadium on Sixteenth and Bryant and later at Candlestick Park on the windy southwest point of the Bay. They scammed 49ers tickets at Kezar Stadium on Stanyon Street off Haight-Ashbury, scalped them for money, and snuck into the games. Postgame, they hustled seat cushions for concessionaires and redeemed them at a nickel apiece.

They fished for perch on Pier 90 across Army Street, bringing some home and selling the rest to neighbors. They brawled with kids from other gangs. They skipped school. They threw parties in industrial parking lots. They stocked their bashes with beer and wine shoplifted from Third Street liquor stores and cold cuts boosted from Butchertown packing plants. They avoided the pitfalls of the psychedelic '60s. They were badass black jocks from the Hill—ghetto bred juvenile delinquents—not longhaired hippie dropouts and dope fiends flooding into the Haight.

Strong women on the Hill raised their kids and others based on strict Southern Baptist doctrines, routinely swatting other mothers' kids for transgressions. From the third grade on, Al Cowlings was as much a part of OJ's family structure as OJ's brother and sisters. Jimmy stayed close enough to interject occasional discipline, but the hood enforced its own will. Eunice saw the boys running wild in junior high and feared what high school would bring. OJ was mostly a baseball player then, a catcher with big-league dreams playing with older kids in youth leagues; later with men's teams stocked from shipyard workers out of Hunter's Point.

Eunice despaired. Mission High profiled the same demography that was sinking her kid into unchecked delinquency. OJ's junior-high baseball coach assisted football at Jesuit Saint Ignatius, a parochial prep powerhouse located in the middle-class Sunset district. The coach hinted at a Saint Ignatius (SI) scholarship. Eunice breathed hope for a future off the Hill, but OJ scuttled it. He had discovered girls by then. He skipped baseball practice one day to attend the first spring dance at the rec center. Rigid Jesuits—redundant—couldn't countenance his impulsive expression of free choice, the temptation of the flesh over ball-field sweat and sacrifice. The coach kicked him off the baseball team and jerked his offer of scholarship.

Eunice, the ultimate mother, was persistent. SFUHSD boundary rules were subject to appeal. Eunice knocked on doors. No one recalls how, but she managed to place OJ, AC, and another projects kid, Josiah Bell, into Galileo High in the Marina district off Van Ness and Bay at the north bottom of Russian Hill. OJ's new demography was less than an hour away from his house: one-minute walk to Seventeenth Street; thirteen minutes on the 22 line to Sixteenth and Mission before transfer to the 49 for a thirty-six minute ride to North Point and Van Ness. From there, a three-minute walk to school. At Galileo, OJ and his buddies blended with North Beach Italians, Chinatown Asians, Fillmore blacks, and Presidio of San Francisco Army dependents.

1962, fall, first day of JV football practice: OJ at five foot ten, 170 pounds, and Al Cowlings, even bigger, dwarfed tough Asian kids playing O and D lines at five foot six, 145 pounds. JV coach Jack McBride scoped the size and placed OJ and AC at tackle. Jack McBride: "The first time we saw him move, we thought we might have made a mistake." They shifted him to fullback. Big Al Cowlings stayed in the trenches. Best friend, AC: perpetual sidekick for the charismatic Juice.

Early signs of OJ exuding narcissism: Always about OJ. On a game day that first year, Jack McBride caught him, AC, and Joe Bell shooting craps in the boys' bathroom. Jack McBride escorted them to the office. The dean of boys brought them inside. Sugar-tongued OJ told the dean he was helping Coach McBride deliver the others—he wasn't rolling dice himself. The dean bought the lie. AC and Joe Bell never spilled. The dean suspended both for a week. OJ played that day.

Fall semester, senior year: Joe Bell, already eighteen, floundering. He'd been kicked out of football. He was lost in school. He hooked a buyer for two joints. OJ and AC passed—they had football practice. The buyer, a teacher, narced for the cops. Joe Bell already was on juvenile probation for beating up a muni bus driver. The drug bust violated him; he went to prison for two years.

AC found a girlfriend—a black Catholic chick from the middle-class Western Addition named Marguerite Whitley. She lived at 1947 Golden Gate Avenue, three miles from school and one block west from 1827, where the SLA would stash kidnapped heiress Patricia Hearst a dozen years later. OJ was styling—driving a new red Mustang on loan from a college recruiter. He chauffeured AC to Marguerite's house in his borrowed sled. One thing led to another. Marguerite dumped AC and became OJ's girl, later his first wife.

Earlier that football season, Galileo was sporting a string of nineteen straight losses. Gal had hired a new assistant, Larry McInerney, formerly of Saint Ignatius, to help head coach George Poppin. Galileo faced SI the third game. SI a city prep powerhouse; Gal a doormat. Should have been a mismatch. George Poppin through Larry McInerney told the team that if it didn't win, he was sitting the seniors. OJ was a lazy student disinterested in education and avoiding core academics. He thought shop classes were too tough—home economics was his most demanding course. Sports only kept him in school. He was motivated by the threat. He scored three TDs that day, one a sixty-yard run after he stripped the ball from an SI running back. Galileo won 31–26.

Galileo won five of its last six. OJ was attracting attention. College recruiters peeked in. He made All-City as the third back behind Wayne McConico from Lincoln High and Nate Kirtman from Washington.

Senior year of football ended. Al Cowlings dropped out of school. Eunice demanded OJ stick through it until the spring and graduate. The Superiors were throwing a party. They needed booze. They'd charged admission in advance. They had money; they reasoned they'd have more money if they didn't pay for the hooch. OJ and three Superiors pulled a heist on a Third Street liquor store. OJ and two others were caught and arrested. OJ was still seventeen. He pulled a week at juvenile hall on Woodside Avenue on the west slope of Twin Peaks.

OJ home from his juvie week maybe ten minutes. Knock on the door. OJ bouncing in from the kitchen. The great Willie Mays standing in his living room. OJ was floored. Willie Mays was a god. The San Francisco Giants had moved from New York in time for the 1958 season, when OJ was in the sixth grade. OJ and his crew gate-crashed Seals Stadium. Willie Mays was more famous to Hill kids than President Kennedy.

Someone from the rec center, prompted by Eunice, had set it up. Willie Mays: "C'mon kid, take a ride?"

Hang with the greatest Giant ever? Purely rhetorical. Willie Mays squired the big-eyed delinquent on errands in his Chrysler 500 and took him home to the thick white rugs and high ceilings of exclusive Forest Hills.

Willie Mays was a product of Jim Crow Alabama. If they worked at all, Birmingham blacks from his era toiled in textile factories for low wages. They worshiped at unpainted Baptist churches on the shady side of town, refrained from glancing at white women, and drank from coloreds-only faucets. Baseball genius transported him. Mays didn't preach; he told OJ, "Your ability can get you over. Don't screw it up, man."

OJ picked it up clear. He was raised on urban-ghetto economics: 70 percent welfare. Profitable career paths: pusher, pimp, or thief. Mothers in charge; fathers too often absent. Fiscal alternatives: public assistance or street crime. Every bump in pay at SF General would alter Eunice's welfare eligibility. Higher wages reduced her allowance. Benefits shrank by formula: if she made more money, she needed less in assistance. More than once, she packed her family and moved them to a smaller unit in the Terrace.

OJ saw magic in Forest Hills: African-American superstar busting the block, living large, accepted by bigots who otherwise denigrated blacks. He saw luxury square footage, expensive furniture, big-ass console TV and hi-fi cabinets, and closets full of slick threads. He fixed on Willie Mays's spiral staircase—he'd never seen anything like it. He caught it in Technicolor: sports, the E ticket off the Hill. Dream stuff.

His transcript snagged him. The PAC-8 was in a state of reform after '50s recruiting scandals. No point in wasting breath on admissions auditors from the big schools in California, Oregon, and Washington. Even Arizona State, then an independent, couldn't reconcile his academics. He talked about enlisting in the marines.

What he knew about the military came from watching Audie Murphy movies in Market Street theaters. Jack McBride said the service was just another form of welfare. Southeast Asia was heating up. The Gulf of Tonkin attacks had sparked the Vietnam conflict the summer before. Nightly news brought it home: *whap-whapping* Hueys hovering over jungle clearings kicking stiff winds into infantry grunts in OD wife-beaters and cargo pants loading body bags. Hollywood heroics vs. live carnage. War hero Audie Murphy suffered from undiagnosed PTSO. He slept with a shotgun; he drank hard and was hooked on sleeping pills. A Hill kid, Joe Patterson, a year ahead of OJ in school, returned from Vietnam minus a leg. OJ rethought his prospects as a first-to-fight jarhead. Selective Service loomed. Options shrinking.

II

Fall, 1965, Sunnyside district in San Francisco, a fog belt off Ocean Avenue, four miles south and west of Portrero Hill. One day before the start school, OJ enrolled in San Francisco City College, securing an SS deferment in the process. SFCC running backs from town had been challenging him. They said he could play defense. The Rams lost his first game against LA Valley College with him at cornerback. A car wreck sidelined a couple of offensive starters. OJ was moved to tailback for game two against Foothill College. He scored four TDs. SF City didn't lose again that year. Mark it: football history on the move under overcast skies in JC obscurity.

His numbers were ridiculous. He averaged eleven yards/rush his first season. A game against San Jose City College settled the conference championship: OJ gained 304 yards and scored six TDs. He set state records—fifty-four career touchdowns and 2,552 yards from scrimmage. CCSF ended 1965 in the Prune Bowl in San Jose against defending national JC champion Long Beach. CCSF fell behind by 20 points but won 42–20. OJ scored three TDs. Recruiters noticed. OJ now a big-time NCAA D-1 prospect.

His CCSF teams went 18–2 over two seasons—the Rams lost his first and last games. After a year, he still was short of credits for PAC-8 transfer. He needed twenty-four transferable with a minimum 2.0 GPA. One more semester at least. Three years earlier, he had watched USC defeat Wisconsin in the Rose Bowl, 42–37, on TV. The pageantry hooked him. Dance and cheer squads kicked long legs in short skirts, flashing pompons, jiggling large jugs. A sword-wielding mascot in a Ben-Hur rig galloped Traveler, a white Arabian, up the sidelines after every score; the Trojan marching band banged out the SC fight Song, "Conquest."

OJ had a monster '66 season at CCSF. He completed his credits in the fall. Fifty four-year colleges pounded him with offers. He resisted all in favor of USC.

Spring, 1967: O. J. Simpson a USC Trojan. Mixed with spring football, he joined the track team; even at his size—six foot two, 204 pounds—he could run a 9.4 hundred. USC won the NCAA track and field title at the championship meet held in Provo, Utah. OJ contributed points, placing sixth in the hundred-yard dash. He ran third leg on the 440-relay team that blistered the field with a time of 38.6, setting a world record. Everything happening for him: high-profile track and football pyrotechnics in an era of convulsions in America favorable to his fortune.

Backstory, beginning December 28, 1958: OJ nine at the time. Forty-five million viewers watching the "Greatest Game Ever" on black-and-white Barney Rubble oval TV screens. NBC airing the NFL championship from Yankee Stadium. Baltimore Colts vs. New York Giants. Game tied at 17 at the end of the fourth quarter. Sudden death: first championship overtime in NFL history.

Colts QB John Unitas subsumed his particular genius into epic TV drama, calling all his own plays on the winning drive, taking the Colts eighty yards in thirteen plays, several on out patterns to split end Raymond Berry (twelve receptions for 178 yards in the game). Sharp sideline throws: the hardest to complete, the easiest to pick for a TD return. Unitas drove the Colts to the six; fullback Alan "the Horse" Ameche burst off-tackle for a 23–17 victory.

The 1958 game coalesced television with the NFL. Pro football's attraction escalated beyond anyone's imagination. The decade of the 1960s deepened the equation—it was now possible to reimagine regional bias. TV gave marketers the entire nation. General

Motors: "See the USA in your Chevrolet." Georgia-based Royal Crown Cola could expand beyond its KKK "RC and Moonpie, the Workingman's Lunch" limitations.

Things converging. Big money from advertising. Companies could reach all of America. Two professional football leagues, NFL and AFL, had merged. Potential bubbling for historic inclusion: national enterprise soliciting endorsement from famous American athletes. For the first time, African Americans were moved toward the front. No longer Jackie Robinson alone pitching Chock Full O' Nuts. In the age of Super Fly, the Blank Panthers, and Martin Luther King Jr., a new market direction: TV spots featuring blacks flakking for minority money without wrinkling gray flannel suits.

O. J. Simpson picked USC for more reasons than big-boob cheerleaders and a white horse. He caught how USC featured tailbacks, black or white. Mike Garrett, a projects kid from Aliso Village in Boyle Heights, won USC's first Heisman Trophy, in 1965. Nobody wins the Heisman without aggressive PR campaigning, especially 1960s blacks, when other parts of the country still called African Americans *coloreds* and used Uncle Tom modifiers such as "negro halfback." OJ at the threshold of a brave new world.

January 28, 1969, Belmont Plaza Hotel, New York; final year of the common NFL/AFL draft before the official merger of 1970: "With the first pick of the 1969 draft...the Buffalo Bills select O. J. Simpson, running back from the University of Southern California." Deflating reward for the best college football player in the country: exile to the worst team in either league, banishment to Rust Belt Buffalo.

OJ had had two super-stellar years at USC. Two-time all-America; national champion his first year; Heisman Trophy his second; two Rose Bowls. In only two seasons, he set an all-time Trojan rushing record with 3,423 yards. He was voted college football's player-of-the-decade for the 1960s. No question he would be chosen number one in the draft. He was West Coast; he grew up watching the San Francisco 49ers and had adopted the LA Rams. He made it obvious: he wanted to play pro ball in California. Bills owner Ralph Wilson didn't care what OJ wanted. Wilson had a crappy team from an industrial town enduring economic recession. He needed transcending star power.

OJ's consolation was big money. He hired thirty-eight-year-old Chuck Barnes (USC '53) as his agent. Chuck Barnes's idea: leverage OJ's fame for sheltered investment cash; sign with a significant few for max dollars. He said O. J. Simpson had a chance to make more money than any professional athlete ever had. His talks with Ralph Wilson paralleled endorsement deals. OJ inked a three-year deal with Chevrolet for a quarter of a million plus a Corvette for himself, a Chevelle for Marguerite, and a Caprice for Eunice. He negotiated a book deal with McMillan ghosted by Pete Axthelm, *OJ: The Education of a Rich Rookie*. ABC signed him for $35,000 for guest shots and sports reporting. He signed with RC Cola for $120,000 over three years. Off-field take: $650,000 (4.3 mil in today's dollars).

He was on his way. He bought Eunice a new house in San Francisco. He broke ground on a thirty-seven-hundred-square-foot home with a pool on a third of an acre in the hills west of the 405 above Brentwood—two and a half blocks south of the Bel Air Presbyterian Church, where Ronald and Nancy Reagan worshipped and where former UCLA all-America center/linebacker Donn Moomaw was pastor. Rev. Moomaw delivered invocations and benedictions at Reagan's '81 and '85 inaugurations. Distance from 906 Connecticut Street, Portrero Hill, to 3005 Elvill, West LA: 374 miles but a galaxy removed. The hills off Mullholland were populated perhaps with more honky Republicans per capita than anywhere on earth.

March 1969: Chuck Barnes's first offer to the Bills, outrageous by 1969 standards: $600,000 for a five-year no-cut contract plus a $500,000 loan at 5 percent for stock investments. Wilson countered with $350,000 for four years and no loan. Ralph Wilson was rich. He owned a trucking company, a TV station, an insurance firm, and a stable of thoroughbreds. He said that even with his assets he couldn't obtain a 5 percent loan.

Endorsements hinged on identity as an NFL superstar. Hard to star as a holdout. Talks dragged through spring and into the summer. Mid-July, the Bills reported for training camp at Niagara University—OJ a no-show.

August 11, 1969: Four weeks into camp; marathon contract talks in a San Diego hotel room. Both sides gave a little, and the impasse was broken. OJ signed for $250,000 spread over four years, a retirement annuity maturing at age fifty, and a $150,000 loan.

He played eleven years in the NFL: nine with Buffalo, and two with the San Francisco 49ers. In 1985 he was inducted into the Pro Football Hall of Fame—a career honor that could not have been predicted by the way it began.

Buffalo was coming off a 1–12–1 season. The Bills had a new coach, John Rauch, who believed in moving the ball through the air. John Rauch broke into NFL coaching under Al Davis, who obsessed over the vertical stretch. An I-back with thirty to forty carries a game: not Rauch's style. He viewed OJ as a pass blocker and swing receiver. OJ came to camp late and wasn't in great shape. He was distracted by commercial shootings orchestrated by Chuck Barnes. He felt stifled by Rauch's offense. He played sparingly through the preseason. The Bills went on the road for their final exhibition game—to the LA Coliseum, against the Rams in front of seventy thousand people. Buffalo lost 50–20. The local hero gained a minuscule nineteen yards.

OJ would post Hall-of-Fame numbers with the Bills but never truly synced with Buffalo, the town. His daughter Arnelle was born in LA on December 4, 1968. OJ was three time zones away at the time, accepting his Heisman in New York City; son Jason was born in April 1970, also in LA. OJ rented an apartment in

Buffalo the first season. His second year, he bought a Tudor house in Woodstream Farms, Amherst, on the border of Erie County. Marguerite followed him at first, but as the children grew, she stayed in LA year-round. OJ was posted in Buffalo for football only—he lifted off for LAX after the final game each season, usually with snow on the tarmac.

In LA, he was a rich celebrity draped in jet-set privilege, sipping Courvoisier behind red-velvet ropes at restaurant openings. In Buffalo, he was a rich celebrity slugging Genesee Cream Ale at a joint called Mulligan's. LA high rollers wore silk sport coats and designer dark glasses in winter months. Buffalo big shots sported fur-lined Elmer hats, Gore-Tex parkas, and galoshes. OJ's first three seasons were as miserable as the climate. He averaged 622 yards from scrimmage from 1969 through 1971: dead-end marks for a super star. The team was no better: 4–10; 3–10–1; 1–13.

1971: Ralph Wilson dumped John Rauch for interim Harvey Johnson and replaced Johnson in '72 with peripatetic Lou Saban. Saban had coached the Bills before; he had led them to consecutive AFL championships in 1964 and 1965. Lou Saban played under Paul Brown in the '40s and 50s. He understood run/pass balance.

Saban promised the Bills that he would find an NFL-caliber quarterback and grow an offensive line. Sid Gillman in San Diego tried to slide injured QB Jack Kemp through waivers, and Saban picked his pocket for the $100 signing fee. He hired ex–Green Bay Packer immortal Jim Ringo to coach the offensive line.

Success followed fast.

1972: OJ gained 1,251 yards.

1973: He shattered Jim Brown's season rushing record (1,863, set in 1963). He became the first ever to rush for more than two thousand yards in a season (2,003). Lou Saban coached the Bills from '72 to '76. In that five-year span, OJ averaged 1,540 yards a season. He was electric, the best in the game, arcing toward Jim Brown's career record of 12,312 yards.

O. J. Simpson was always shrewd, and as an athlete, recognized the inevitable—NFL running backs rarely excel into their thirties. His long-range ambition was acting—nothing he could actuate in the Queen City of Lake Erie. OJ's aspirations outstripped his talent. He would peak as pratfalling Nordberg, the bumbling detective in the *Naked Gun* series starring Leslie Neilson as lieutenant Frank Drebbin. He would make his money off football and endorsements. He collected sponsors: Tree Sweet orange juice, Spot-Bilt shoes, Dingo boots, Ray-Ban sunglasses, Swiss Army products, Bugle Boy jeans, Reebok shoes. He had ditched Chuck Barnes—believed he could negotiate his own deals.

OJ seemed to transcend racial divides; he strutted into white enclaves too famous to be restricted. He rushed rich white-guy outlets, tennis, golf, and backgammon. In 1970, he met Robert Kardashian on the private tennis court of a Benedict Canyon mansion owned by a pair of playboy brothers, Harry and Pete Rothschild. He was introduced by East Coast expat Joe Stellini—OJ nicknamed him "Stiff"—maître d' of the Luau restaurant on Rodeo Drive. The Rothschilds hung out at the Luau; so did OJ and AC.

Robert Kardashian was in transition from practicing law to innovation in the music industry. He founded and served as CEO of Movie Tunes, Inc., a company that fed songs into theaters for performance between features. Kardashian's young children all referred to his friend as "Uncle OJ." Kardashian ceded his Brentwood office at 11661 San Vicente Boulevard and his secretary, Cathy Randa, to OJ.

OJ established Orenthal Enterprises and staffed it with USC grads who could protect his image and make his money make money: business advisor LeRoy "Skip" Taft and entertainment attorney Howard Weitzman. Skip Taft handled his income. Cathy Randa served as gatekeeper—his personal assistant/appointments manager.

OJ added Orenthal Productions in '78, designed to control any made-for-television acting gigs. He retained Jack Gilardi—husband of original Mouseketeer and former beach-party movie star Annette Funicello—as his agent for film and television roles. In 1990, on recommendation from Marcus Allen, he would hire Mike Gilbert as a sleaze agent—pimping autographs, appearances, and memorabilia. His whole world was trending not as much white as wealth.

III

1976: His Bills deal lapsed. He implored Ralph Wilson to trade him, citing strains on his marriage and family. Marguerite would no longer take the children out of school for half a year. Ralph Wilson wouldn't budge. He countered with the NFL's richest offer to date, a three-year deal for $2.5 million. OJ snapped it up, figuring it would be his last.

1977: Seismic changes. OJ had slicked Ralph Wilson. His marriage was on the rocks but not from distance. Bo Diddley, the "Originator," released this number in 1965:

Bo Diddley done had a farm
On that farm he had some women
Women here, women there, women everywhere…

OJ harvested women like Bo Diddley. Most of his conquests stayed private. Pre–social media, it was possible then. Some didn't. He had met Maud Adams in '76 on the set of *Killer Force* and launched an open affair. Beyond beautiful and white, he had only two filters—anyone and everywhere. His staff worked overtime to keep his philandering secret from gossip rags and Protestant sponsors.

He couldn't hide his flings from Marguerite. He barhopped West Hollywood and Beverly Hills hot spots. She stayed home with the children. They fought. OJ, easily provoked and occasionally violent, tended to settle disputes with F-bombs and fists. Marguerite often wore dark glasses indoors and at night. Their marriage was all but over when Marguerite delivered a scoop: she was pregnant with their third child.

OJ stunned, feeling trapped, claimed Marguerite broke a promise of contraception. He would have opted for abortion, but devout Catholic Marguerite drew the line. They looked to relocate; maybe a new house would help. His '76 contract could finance a dramatic upgrade. They had custom specs: gated estate, northern exposure—Marguerite painted as a hobby—lighted tennis courts, and a pool. (She loved to swim; OJ never learned how.) Celebrity realtor Elaine Young—fourth wife of actor Gig Young—cut a Hollywood deal.

360 N. Rockingham Avenue was not on the market. Two previous tenants, Tony Orlando and Carly Simon, both made offers; the owner refused. Elaine Young knew the house. She heard OJ was looking. She thought the place would be perfect. She hustled OJ's phone number from Jack Gilardi. The Rockingham owner was a huge football fan. Selling to O. J. Simpson would confer status. OJ wrote a check for $650,000. All spring he and Marguerite supervised a remodel—occupancy set for late May. Among the design touches: a life-size statue of OJ in uniform, number 32, bare-headed, holding his helmet in his right hand and a pair of cleats in his left, set on a stone plinth near the pool.

OJ's social circle spun into Beverly Hills with golf and tennis buddies—movie people, TV people, restaurateurs, business and garment industry bigwigs. They ate and drank at places where Frank Sinatra or Gregory Peck would frequent, at the Luau and La Scala. They often ate lunch at the Daisy, a Rodeo Drive discotheque invented by Jack Hanson, an LA original.

The Daisy had opened in 1963 as a Hollywood hot spot to accommodate changing times. Notorious '40s and '50s nightspots on the Strip either were closing— Ciro's, the Mocambo, the Trocadero—or were giving way to the jagged energy of the baby boom, go-go clubs, and the British Invasion. Jack Hanson had been a triple-A shortstop for the PCL LA Angels in the 1940s, playing at Wrigley Field on Forty-Second and Avalon. Jack Hanson had a fashion designer's eye with an obsession for beauty. He sketched women's sportswear on long road trips when still a player. He used baseball money to start a small women's-wear shop on Balboa Island and struck the mother lode. He had a seminal idea. He (and his wife Sally) scored millions creating styles that glorified the female ass—specifically Jax slacks—created for size 8 and 10 socialites, stars, and starlets. Jax slacks zipped up the back, had no pockets, and clung to contours.

Marilyn Monroe wore Jax slacks; so did Marlene Dietrich, Audrey Hepburn, a young Joan Collins, and Natalie Wood. Jack Hanson drove an immaculate '34 Roller. He lived in a white mansion with a large pool and lighted tennis courts on Beverly Drive once owned by silents star Pola Negri and later by studio boss Hal Roach. Hanson franchised Jax stores in New York, Chicago, Palm Beach, and San Francisco. The main store was located on the corner of Wilshire and Bedford, two blocks from the Beverly Wilshire Hotel. Nancy Sinatra Jr. and her sister Tina worked at Jax as salesgirls.

Hanson branched into café society. He bought a building two blocks from Jax, 326 N. Rodeo, former location of Prince Mike Romanoff's restaurant. He turned it into a members-only meet-and-mingle place where A-listers could rock the Watusi, swim, and frug on a parquet dance floor, drink under dim bar lights, shoot eight-ball or play backgammon in a game room, or dine outdoors behind a low brick wall on the street-front patio. O. J. Simpson, A. C. Cowlings, and Robert Kardashian were regulars at Jack Hanson's mansion for tennis, regulars at the Daisy for long lunches.

May 20, 1977, sixty-nine miles southwest of Beverly Hills at Dana Point, on the southernmost tip of Laguna Beach: Nicole Brown, one day past her eighteenth birthday, finalizing a decision. High school graduation still two weeks away; she held few firm ideas about her future, only that she wouldn't find her destiny among hodads idling around the Seventeenth Street pier in Huntington Beach. She had no college aspirations. Her older sister by two years, Denise, was an Eileen Ford model in New York, tripping off to glamour shoots in exotic locales in Europe, the Mediterranean, and the Caribbean. Nicole thought she might want to study photography.

Nicole was half German. Her mother, Judi (Juditha Baur), had been raised in Frankfurt. Judi was twenty-three in 1954, a secretary for the fiscal director of the US military's *Stars and Stripes* newspaper. Ladies' man and Texan Lou Brown, with a wife and three children back in the United States, was circulation director. Romance with the German Juditha snuffed Lou's marriage vows. He divorced the wife and married Judi, and they had four daughters.

The Browns moved to Gardena. Lou invested in a string of car washes. They moved to Laguna when the older two girls were in high school. Like Denise before her, Nicole was homecoming princess at Dana Hills High. She was a stunner. She had bikini-perfect looks—blond hair, smooth tan skin, straight teeth, and a leggy athletic frame. She turned heads like the Girl from Ipanema.

A male friend from Laguna, David LeBon, eight years older, had graduated from the Brooks Institute in Santa Barbara. He photographed cars for magazine ads in LA. Nicole called him "Pinky"—he had unfortunate skin tones for a beach kid. Pinky LeBon lived in a broken-down one-bedroom apartment on First and Virgil downtown between Wilshire Boulevard and the Hollywood freeway. He offered and Nicole accepted: move to LA and stay with him. Their relationship was purely platonic. She took the bed; he racked on the floor in a sleeping bag. The first week of June she found work as a salesgirl at Jax. Jack Hanson himself hired her. After two weeks, he thought she might be more useful serving food at the Daisy.

June 26, 1977: Nicole was drawing oglers, O. J. Simpson included. He ladled on his legendary charm. She knew nothing about football, but she flirted back. OJ showed up daily. Hs never broached the subject of his pregnant wife and two children. Within a week, she agreed to a date. He picked her up at Pinky's in his black '69 Silver Cloud carrying the vanity plate, "JUICE." She wore tight denims and a loose top. She returned to First and Virgil at 2:00 a.m. with her jeans ripped at the zipper near the button hole. Pinky thought the worst. She said, no, the evening was that good—they did it in the backseat at a Cahuenga Pass overlook. Said OJ went wild climbing into her pants.

Three weeks to training camp in Niagara Falls for the '77 season. OJ was already possessive. He could live as husband and father with Marguerite and the kids but couldn't stand the thought of Nicole in a house with another man. He set her up in an apartment in Westwood, an easier commute between domiciles than downtown LA. Marguerite kept busy with her pregnancy and the move from Elvill to Rockingham. OJ finally spilled his situation to Nicole. He rationalized: his marriage had been over for years; separation was imminent; Marguerite's pregnancy a deliberate trap. Nicole in love: she bought the pitch.

OJ made her quit the Daisy. He didn't want her hanging in such a tempting milieu. OJ was picking up all tabs. He could afford it. He was starting the second of his three-year $2.5-million deal with the Bills. He had jumped ABC and signed a more lucrative five-year deal with NBC. He moved her to a slicker apartment, on Bedford and Charleville in Beverly Hills, South of Wilshire.

July 9, 1977, OJ's thirtieth birthday: He spent it with his concubine, not his family. The next week, OJ, Nicole, and A. C. Cowlings took a Caribbean vacation.

July 22: He left for camp.

August 27: He flew back to LA for the birth of his new daughter, Aaren. Nicole returned with him to Buffalo for the season.

The end of his NFL life was in view. Lou Saban had resigned after five game in '76. Jim Ringo took over, and the Bills didn't win another game that year. OJ led the league in rushing with 1,540 yards, the flash before the fizzle. In '77, he hurt his knee in game seven, requiring season-ending surgery. His heavy contract wasn't looking like such a hot deal for the Bills.

Sidebar: In March 1977, the DeBartolo Corp. (a megamillion-dollar shopping-mall-construction firm from Youngstown, Ohio) acquired the San Francisco 49ers from the estate of the original owners, Tony and Vic Morabito. Edward DeBartolo Sr. had purchased the club for his son, Eddie Jr., thirty-three years old. The '76 49ers had posted an 8–6 record under Josephine Morabito (Tony's widow), general manager Lou Spadia, and head coach Monte Clark.

Rookie owner Edward D. Sr. sought industry advice from his cross-Bay neighbor, Oakland Raiders managing general partner Al Davis. He was naive. Al Davis's interests ran counter to Mr. D.'s. Al Davis was triple-OG AFL with the business ethics of an octopus. He was reluctant to share the Bay Area spotlight with the enemy. For a generous finder's fee, he recruited from the Minnesota Vikings a top executive for the Niners, former Miami Dolphins and Baltimore Colts GM, Joe Thomas.

With that maneuver Al Davis set back the 49ers for half a decade. Al Davis neglected to point out that Joe Thomas was as whacked as Captain Queeg. Thomas replaced Monte Clark—popular with press and fans—with a yes man named Ken Meyer. Joe Thomas bragged that he had a special gift for spotting talent, both players and coaches. Ken Meyer proved a dud. Thomas fired him after a 5–9 season and hired Pete McCulley for 1978, a no-name assistant off the staff of the Washington Redskins. Thomas claimed Pete McCulley had been his first choice all along.

McCulley was quirky. He kept his watch and his body clock set to East Coast time. He started his days at three in the morning;

worse, he couldn't coach. The 49ers lost eight of their first nine games. Joe Thomas dumped McCulley after game nine, elevating offensive coordinator Fred O'Connor, another hack, who had served as Thomas's locker-room spy under McCulley.

Joe Thomas had had grandiose plans for 1978. In the first round, he drafted tight end Ken McAfee from Notre Dame, alma mater of Eddie Debartolo Jr., now fully vested as team owner. Joe Thomas had the same idea as Lou Saban—run to pass. He had his all-America tight end for sealing the edge. He needed a marquee running back. Ralph Wilson saw a way to recoup a bad investment. New head coach Chuck Knox jumped all over it. The Bills traded OJ to San Francisco for five future draft picks over the next three years—two firsts, two seconds, and a third—quite possibly the worst-ever NFL trade.

Simpson was shot by then, not fully recovered from his surgery. His knees ached from arthritis, his joints showing wear from nine three-hundred-carry NFL seasons and more than eleven thousand hard-rushing yards. Ken McAfee proved a stiff, too slow to block NFL linebackers. OJ, for his part, didn't work too hard learning the playbook. The 49ers posted a league-worst 2–14 record and scored a league-low 219 points but led the NFL with sixty-three turnovers. They would have had the first pick for the '79 draft if Joe Thomas hadn't traded it (and four other high choices) for damaged OJ. Eddie D. had seen enough. He fired Joe Thomas and hired Bill Walsh. O.J. hung on for another unspectacular year. Cocaine use was rampant in the NFL in the late 70s and early 80s. Rumors floated about drug among the 49ers. The rumors didn't exclude OJ....

May 19, 1978: Nicole and OJ together for nearly a year. Nicole spending her nineteenth birthday with her parents in Laguna. OJ still married. Marguerite would file separation papers (divorce final in June 1980). She stayed at Rockingham with the children and OJ's statue while lawyers argued terms. OJ bought a condo in San Francisco for his first season with the 49ers.

He kept Nicole in the Bedford Drive love nest and leased a house on Deep Canyon Drive off Benedict Canyon. OJ drove to Dana Point, AC in a trail car. He was delivering her birthday present, a new black Porsche 914 with an ostentatious red bow taped to the bonnet. Nicole was thrilled; Lou and Judi and the two younger sisters, Tanya and Dominque, all wowed. They didn't notice the purple mouse under Nicole's right eye peeking through her makeup.

During eleven months with OJ, she had become proficient at cover-ups.

IV

June 13 through 17, 1994: Nation captivated. Ghastly slaying of Nicole Brown Simpson headlined in every paper in the nation. It was the nightly lead on all cable and network newscasts; feature story on *CNN, Larry King, Nightline, Hard Copy,* and *Geraldo Rivera.* Early accounts alibied OJ. He had jetted to Chicago on a June 12 red-eye. He was scheduled to tee off the next day with Hertz Corp. high rollers. He was checked into the O'Hare Plaza Hotel by 6:15 a.m. central daylight time on June 13.

West LAPD homicide detective Ron Phillips reached him an hour later. Arnelle had told the cops that OJ was in Chicago—Cathy Randa would have details. Arnelle woke Randa; Randa relayed OJ's itinerary. Phillips dialed and ID'ed himself, said he had bad news—his wife had been killed. OJ, howling: "Oh, my God? Nicole is killed. Oh, my God, is she dead? I'll leave for LA on the first available flight." Phillips told him his two young children were safe at the WLA station house. He said Arnelle could pick them up (Arnelle would call AC to help). Phillips found it odd: OJ hadn't asked any routine *when, how,* or *where* questions related to the murders. *He knew?*

OJ packed in a frenzy. He rushed the front desk, demanded a taxi and a bandage for a cut on his left knuckle. He waited in the carriage entrance for a cab. Dave Kilduff, Hertz sales VP, drifted in with a load of golfers. Kilduff saw him. OJ commandeered a lift to O'Hare International for the nine fifteen nonstop to LAX.

He fidgeted in first class next to a copyright attorney named Mark Partridge. OJ told Partridge that his wife and another man had been found murdered in the garden at the front of her condo. Ron Phillips had never used the word *murder*, never mentioned a second victim or the location of the crime.

11:20 a.m. PDT, touchdown at LAX: Skip Taft and Cathy Randa picked him up at arrivals; he had called ahead, told Randa to find Howard Weitzman. Weitzman had repped him on a spousal battery, New Year's Eve, 1989—he had beat the shit out of Nicole that night. She rang 911, one of nine police callouts during their stormy time together. OJ skipped out in his Bentley before the cops could detain him. The city attorney filed—misdemeanor spousal battery. OJ pled no contest. A judge ordered a $700 fine plus 120 hours of community service and counseling. OJ paid the fine, shined the counseling, and worked his community service with appearances at Ronald McDonald houses. Howard Weitzman had a gift for damage control.

A WLA uniform guarded the Rockingham entrance, a big black guy named Don Thompson. His orders were to let no one else in and detain OJ when he showed. Skip Taft braked the caddy at the gate and cut the ignition. OJ climbed out the passenger side. Skip Taft followed, saying he was OJ's attorney. Thompson said OJ's attorney was already inside—he opened for OJ only. Two steps in, he cuffed him.

Homicide special from the robbery-homicide division at Parker Center had taken over at 5:00 a.m.; case lead Phillip Vannatter had driven to Rockingham from Bundy fifteen minutes before Taft and OJ arrived. Robert Kardashian had hustled in from Encino. Said he was OJ's best friend. Don Thompson blocked him too. Inside the bars, Howard Weitzman was talking to Phil Vannatter.

OJ stood around looking disconnected. Howard Weitzman saw him manacled. To Vannatter: "Is that necessary?" Vannatter: "Of course not," and unlocked him. Vannatter buying time. He had forty-eight hours after formal arrest to file a case with the DA or he'd have to cut him loose. Blood, hair, and fiber clues would take longer than forty-eight to process.

1:00 p.m.: Vannatter wanted OJ downtown. OJ rode with him to Parker Center—cops called it the "Glass House"—150 N. Los Angeles Street. Skip Taft and Howard Weitzman followed in Skip Taft's Caddy. They met in R-H headquarters on the third floor. OJ said he didn't need the attorneys—insisted it would make him appear guilty. Weitzman conceded. He asked Vannatter to tape the interview and read OJ his rights. He and Taft left for lunch—lunch is big in LA. Vannatter's partner Tom Lange wheeled in from Bundy. Vannatter and Langer were stunned—they couldn't believe a lawyer in a capital case was handing them a free shot. They steered OJ into a cubicle.

Howard Weitzman had represented celebrity automaker John DeLorean in 1983. He repped Michael Jackson on perv complaints. DeLorean had been busted for trafficking cocaine. He was caught in an FBI sting documented with an undercover videotape. Weitzman sprung him with an entrapment defense. In eleven years, he had grown rusty. He violated rule number one of criminal representation: never leave the client alone with the cops. In the I-room, Vannatter read off a Miranda card. OJ waived counsel.

Techs hadn't typed crime-scene blood yet but would by week's end. DNA would take months. In the meantime, OJ had multiple cuts on his left hand, the largest a deep gash on his middle knuckle. His interview with Vannatter and Lange left them convinced that he was the killer—maybe more accurately, unconvinced that he wasn't.

They interviewed OJ for ninety minutes. His answers were nonresponsive at best. About any physical difficulties with Nicole: "We had a big fight, uh, about six years ago, on New Year's...Then we had an altercation about a year ago. It wasn't physical—you know, I kicked her door or something..."

About the white Bronco, his whereabouts on the night of the murders, the cut on his left knuckle: "I don't know...at the house I was just running around." Said he'd reopened a cut when he broke a drinking glass in the bathroom after taking the call from detective Phillips. He contradicted himself later—said he'd cut it Sunday night at Rockingham while pulling his cellphone—changed later to phone charger—from the Bronco before leaving for Chicago.

They recycled the abuse issue. "Did you ever hit her, OJ?"

"That one night, we had a fight. Hey, she hit me..."

They asked if he would submit to a polygraph. OJ, stumbling, "No. I mean. I'm sure eventually I'll do it. But it's like, hey, I've got weird thoughts now. And I've had weird thoughts—you know, you've been with a person for seventeen years, you think everything..."

They took him to the second floor for a print spread. They took him up to the fourth floor so a police photographer could snap color stills of the wounds on his hand. They took him to the dispensary around the back of the Glass House. The duty nurse, a sickly old Greek named Thanos Paratis, drew a vial of reference blood. He eyeballed it and asked Vannatter if it was enough. Vannatter didn't care—he would have taken a full eyedropper. Paratis capped the tube and sealed it in an evidence envelope.

3:30 p.m.: OJ left with Taft and Weitzman for Orenthal Enterprises, 11661 San Vicente in Brentwood. Robert Kardashian was waiting with anxious Cathy Randa. Vannatter slogged west through I-10 rush-hour traffic. He needed to deliver the blood sample to criminalist Dennis Fung at Rockingham.

The case was drawing manic interest. Cathy Randa had been taking calls from Roger King of Kingworld Productions, creators of the TV tabloid *Inside Edition* and daytime *Oprah*. If OJ were charged, the cost for his defense would run wild. King offered to pay. Tacit thought: he'd be repaid with inside scoops. He said OJ needs the best—he stumped for Century City slickster Robert Shapiro. Implication: Howard Weitzman useful for PR, not legal defense of a superstar slasher.

Monday, June 14: TV reporting OJ the prime suspect. LAPD neither confirming nor denying. OJ depressed. Howard Weitzman spinning rosy platitudes—it'll all work out. 360 N. Rockingham overrun by media and citizen gawkers, a madhouse of distractions. OJ packed a bag—he would bunk at Kardashian's house in the Encino hills. Robert Kardashian drove them to OJ's office. OJ, gripping the implications, said they should take up Roger King's offer. Skip Taft agreed.

They reached Shapiro on speakerphone from Skip Taft's office. Shapiro drove from Century City and took command. He talked about assembling high-priced experts and treating them first-class. He regarded Kardashian as the ideal go-between, a lawyer with a lapsed practice. Shapiro told him to renew his law license—he'd ummunize himself from incriminating knowledge with attorney-client privilege.

3:00 p.m.: Shapiro called OJ in Encino, told him he had an ultrasecret three-thirty appointment at the mid-Wilshire office of a man named Edward Gelb. Gelb ran a private polygraph service. OJ and Kardashian met Shapiro and Taft at Gelb's office. Gelb was in Spain; his associate Dennis Nellany would run OJ through the drill.

Polygraphs work off relativity. The box is wired with sensors—Velcro finger wraps, blood-pressure cuff, respirator band, and a butt pad. The sensors blip impulses to needles scratching lines on a graph-paper readout. The examiner establishes a baseline with harmless yes/no questions: "Do you live at 360 N. Rockingham? Do you drive a Bentley? Were you born on July 9, 1947?" He sprinkles in questions relating to the target subject; the needles graph a pattern relative to the baseline. Parallel: he's probably telling the truth. Sharp spikes: he's lying. OJ's exam took thirty minutes and registered like stalactites on a ceiling in Carlsbad Caverns. Dennis Nellany told Shapiro his client scored a minus 22, the lowest possible. He failed every target question.

Thursday, June 16: Nicole's funeral and burial in Orange County. OJ was overheard mumbling into the casket, "I'm sorry...I loved you too much." Overtones of Shakespeare. Othello snuffed out Desdemona and talked of himself as "...a man that loved not wisely but too well." Eerie parallel on the day the serology test results were delivered. Bombshell news. Less than one-half of one percent of the population shared enzymes in the combination of O. J. Simpson and the killer. Phil Vannatter filed with deputy DA Marcia Clark. Her boss, Los Angeles County DA Gil Garcetti, endorsed it. Marcia Clark called Robert Shapiro. Shapiro promised Clark he'd deliver OJ the next day, Friday, June 17, by 11:00 a.m.

June 17, 11:30 a.m, thirty minutes past the deadline: Shapiro called homicide special commander Will Gartland, begging for more time. Shapiro said OJ was talking to his children and making out a will. Shapiro put Beverly Hills shrink Dr. Saul Faerstein on the horn. Faerstein explained that OJ was under his care and suicidal. Faerstein expected compassion. Captain Gartland didn't give a fuck about OJ or his feelings. He rang off with a sharp order to deliver the suspect.

Time passing. 11:45 a.m., another phone call: Shapiro saying OJ won't budge, quoting OJ: "I won't be getting out. What's the hurry getting in?" Gartland to Shapiro: "Get him in now, or we're coming to get him."

12:45 p.m.: Gartland called again; Saul Faerstein picked up. Gartland demanded the location. Faerstein waffled. Gartland threatened harboring charges. Faerstein copped to Kardashian's address. Gartland contacted the West Valley Division day-watch commander in Encino. He ordered dispatch of two sector cars and a supervisor.

1:45 p.m.: WVD cops arrived. OJ already in the wind. BOLO on OJ and AC. Valley cops hung with occupants—Kardashian, Shapiro, Faerstein, and OJ's post-Nicole squeeze, Paula Barbieri. Phone rang. Kardashian's office assistant, Nicole Pulvers, answered. She told Kardashian his "sister" was on the line. Sister OJ told Kardashian he was in the parking lot of Bel Air Presbyterian church, near his first house on Elvill. OJ dispirited, said he held the .357 to his temple and pulled the trigger, but the gun misfired.

Kardashian had deep Bible-thumper convictions; he told OJ that God meant for him to live. OJ was deranged from a mix of his own complicit angst and Dr. Faerstein's prescription downers. He had left a sealed envelope for Kardashian. He told him to read it "when it was time." Kardashian said the cops were on hand in Encino to arrest him. OJ said he had no intention of turning himself in—figured he'd be dead anyway.

The Bronco on the move, heading South on Sepulveda. OJ called Lou Brown. Lou Brown said he was sorting through Nicole's stuff at her condo. OJ said he'd drop by. Lou Brown called the cops. AC motored down to Sunset and over to Bundy. He spotted squad cars at the condo. OJ said drive to the Ascension Cemetery in Lake Forest; he wanted to end it at Nicole's grave.

5:00 p.m.: Shapiro called a press conference at his Century City office. He and Kardashian assumed OJ was dead. Kardashian took the mic and read OJ's hand-scrawled Othellian note. Excerpts:

> "...I had nothing to do with Nicole's murder..."
> "If we had a problem it's because I loved her so much..."
> "Don't feel sorry for me, I've had a great life..."
> "Please think of the real OJ and not this lost person."

He signed: "Peace and Love, OJ"—a happy face scrawled in the O of his brand.

6:10 p.m.: OJ in the Bronco talking with his multimillionaire mentor, USC alum Wayne Hughes. Wayne Hughes reading him the Forty-First Psalm: "...Mine enemies speak evil of me...Against me do they devise my hurt." OJ asked Wayne Hughes to look after his kids' money. Kardashian had left Century City for Rockingham to minister to Arnelle and Jason, all three holding back shock and anticipating bad news. TV in the background: NBA finals game five, Rockets/Knicks. News cut-in: white Bronco rolling on 91 W. The slow-speed chase was on...OJ still alive.

...June 17, 1994, 8:30 p.m.: OJ giving up in the Rockingham driveway to SWAT negotiator Pete Weiterer. Cops hooked him up inside, away from the media swarm. Pete Weiterer and three R-H dicks drove him to Parker Center in an unmarked police-issue Plymouth. At Rockingham, cops arrested Al Cowlings—$275,000 bail. Wayne Hughes posted bond. Cops and prosecutors interpreted the Bronco sequence as a "consciousness of guilt." They noted the letter's subtext: all about OJ—zero attention dedicated to slaughtered Nicole; total lament over burden of being OJ.

V

Tuesday, June 21, 1994: OJ on keep-away status, off suicide watch, housed in the isolation wing, third floor of the Men's Central Jail. The only other prisoner in his unit was parricidal Lyle Menendez. Legal proceedings running hot. DA's office seeking a grand-jury indictment. Smart move—GJ prevents the DA from exposing his case to the defense, postponing discovery. Defense attorneys are barred from grand-jury proceedings; witnesses appear under subpoena and cannot be cross-examined; transcripts are sealed. GJ makeup determined by population. An indictment requires a two-thirds vote. LA County seats the maximum number of jurors in California: twenty-three. The DA's challenge is to convince sixteen panelists to hand down a true bill. Marcia Clark served as lead counsel for the hearing.

Should have been simple. Clark brimmed with overconfidence, but she was blindsided by epic convolution overrunning every phase of the trial. Clark called Jill Shively, one of sixteen witnesses. Shively had contacted LAPD on June 14. Phil Vannatter vetted her. Her story, if true, would be devastating for OJ. Shively, thirty-two, lived with her young daughter in a one-bedroom apartment in Santa Monica. She'd been sick for days but was regaining her appetite.

Ten forty-five Sunday night, June 12: She was driving her beater VW Bug east on San Vicente Boulevard, headed for the Westward Ho in Brentwood Village. A white Bronco boiled up from Bundy (her right), blew a red light, and forced her to swerve. Some college-age dude in a westbound gray Nissan approached the careening Bronco from the inside lane. All three vehicles slid to stops. The Bronco's driver stuck out his head, spewing venom at the Nissan guy. Shively recognized the Bronco driver: O. J. Simpson. She thought he must be drunk.

Marcia Clark ready to light the victory cigar. Blood evidence at Bundy and Rockingham plus a witness placing agitated, erratic OJ three blocks from the murder minutes after the crime had been committed.

Stunning reversal: Jill Shively appeared on *Hard Copy* that night, telling the same tale to a national audience. She had sold her story to King World for five grand.

Thursday, June 23: Clark re-called Shively to the stand. No law against paid TV appearances. Shively claimed the DA's witness coordinator Patty Jo Fairbanks approved.

Marcia Clark grandstanding. She excused Shively, instructing the panel to disregard her testimony. Clark said it wasn't for *Hard*

Copy but from a contradiction under oath on Tuesday. Clark had asked whom she had told about the June 12 incident. She said only her mother. Turns out she had blabbed to coworkers about her upcoming TV spot. Nothing then or later contradicted the facts of the near-collision. Phil Vannatter believed she should be retained. Vince Bugliosi echoed the same in *Outrage: The Five Reasons Why O. J. Simpson Got Away with Murder*. Marcia Clark said no.

OJ's and Nicole's friends were split 50–50 over OJ's guilt. Robert Kardashian, Skip Taft, Cathy Randa, Mike Gilbert, Joe Stellini, his golfing and tennis buddies, his black brothers—AC and Marcus Allen—all held out for the "SOG" explanation: Some other guy. Nicole's gal pals—her sister Denise, Khris Kardashian Jenner, CiCi Shahian, Cora Fischman, Cindy Garvey, and Faye Resnick—knew too much to disbelieve. They'd heard seventeen years of anguish spilling into snippets of girl talk over margaritas and white wine, telling an ugly tale of obsession, infidelity, and battery.

Nicole had moved into Rockingham after Marguerite left in May 1980. They fought, often violently. Early in their marriage, they were vacationing in a suite on the Las Vegas Strip. Show-biz party that night. They mixed with stars including Frank Sinatra. OJ was drunk or coked out, furious. Nicole had said something he interpreted as demeaning. Back in their suite, he screamed that she had belittled him in front of Sinatra. She was undressing, wearing only panties. He went off. He grabbed her by the hair, punched her repeatedly, threw her into the corridor, and locked the door. The suite was situated in a blocked-off wing. She curled into a fetal ball and cried. Hours lapsed. A hotel security guy happened by eventually and keyed her in. OJ was passed out, snoring.

She'd had two abortions before their wedding on February 2, 1985. The ceremony was conducted at Rockingham. Sydney was born less than a year later, in 1986. Justin was born in 1988. OJ abused Nicole verbally and emotionally both times she was pregnant—castigated her for gaining weight and called her a "fat pig."

May '87: Nicole found a jewelry box in the drawer near his side of the bed. She opened it—diamond stud earrings. She assumed they were a birthday present.

May 19: OJ gave her a present but not the earrings. Nicole heard that actress Tawney Kitean was showing off a pair of diamond studs. She confronted OJ. Inevitable argument escalated into violent assault. OJ ended it by locking her in the closet. Nicole rated it her worst-ever beating.

Nicole was all alone with her misery. She was reluctant to open up fully to friends; most were OJ's friends too. She couldn't confide in her parents. They were riding the OJ gravy train; she could only screw it up. OJ rigged it for Lou to manage the Hertz desk at the Ritz-Carlton in Monarch Bay, Laguna. He set up Judi as a travel agent. He hired Judi's nephew Rolf Baur to manage his Pioneer Chicken shops in South Central LA. He fronted college tuition for Nicole's two younger sisters. They went to better schools than their parents could afford. Hertz was ready to dump him after the New Year's Eve beating. OJ sweet-talked Nicole into calling Hertz and taking the blame.

1990: He insisted on a boob job for Nicole—his human Heisman needed bigger jugs. She resisted, then relented. OJ diddled other women, bareback always; it terrified her. AIDs was rampant in America—she had no idea who he was with. She wanted no more children; she feared more for any growing fetuses than for herself. She aborted four more times. Their marriage was a sham; it couldn't hold. They divorced—final decree was October 15, 1992. Sick obsession drew them back.

May 1993: Trial reconciliation. They agreed to give it a year. The notion was doomed. In their time apart, Nicole had found wild freedom. She drove a white Ferrari through the fast lane of West LA nightlife. She had a lavish settlement, better than Marguerite's. She could fly to New York for a restaurant opening, to Aspen for New Year's Eve, or Cabo San Lucas for a week in the sun. She was active. OJ had controlled her since she was eighteen.

She had broken his hold for the first time as an adult. She had flings with ritzy guys, a hairdresser named Joseph Perrulli; a waiter named Marcello; a legal intern, Brent Shaves, who worked for her divorce attorney; an actor named Grant Kramer, the Son of Terry Moore and Howard Hughes; the manager of the Mezzaluna chain, Keith Zlomsowitch; and…Marcus Allen.

OJ typically followed his beatings with an ostentatious gift and a vow of monogamy.

1992: OJ took a step. He and tomcat buddies Marcus Allen and Tom Kardashian, Robert's brother, sought help from Reverend Donn Moomaw at Bel Air Presbyterian. Rev. Moomaw led them in Bible study. No way of knowing the text of their dialogues. Assume it was scripture plus frank, maybe graphic, recall of their lapses. The lessons boomeranged. OJ, Marcus, and Tom Kardashian still chased skirts. Reverend Moomaw was defrocked on February 4, 1993, by the Presbytery of the Pacific for ministering between the sheets to five different female parishioners.

OJ replaced Nicole with Paula Barbieri but couldn't let go. He stalked her. He peeped from foliage through a window of her condo while she was honking Keith Zlomsowitch. He showed up at the same restaurant as Nicole and a date too often for coincidence. He confronted her and Keith Z. at a restaurant about the blow job on the couch when his kids were asleep upstairs. He stank-eyed Marcello at another restaurant until Marcello skulked out the back door. He drank heavily and hoovered coke.

He was most bothered by Marcus Allen. Nicole told Faye Resnick and Khris Kardashian Jenner that she was in love. Faye Resnick claims Nicole told her that OJ threatened to kill her if he found her with Marcus. Marcus was a USC Heisman winner thirteen years younger than OJ, still an NFL superstar, with Super Bowl rings from the Oakland/Los Angeles Raiders.

OJ was afflicted with Othello's insecurity: Marcus as Cassio, a younger version of himself poaching his prize. OJ felt threatened to his marrow.

Mid-May 1994: One-year deadline approaching. Nicole, drained from spousal insanity, kicked him loose. Three weeks later, she was dead. Faye Resnick and Mike Gilbert both insist in their tell-all books they saw Marcus Allen's car parked near Nicole's condo the afternoon of June 12.

June 22 to October 25, 1994: The city attorney's office caved to media pressure. Under the California Public Records Act, the CA released transcripts from Nicole's frantic 911 call—the second of two within one minute—from the time when OJ was beating on the door of her rental on Gretna Green Avenue. Excerpt:

> Can you get someone over here...?
> He's back, please...
> He broke down the back door to get in...
> He's O. J. Simpson. I think you know his record. Could you just send someone over here?
> He's going fucking nuts...

Nicole's terror radiated. Audible in the background: OJ's raspy baritone spewing barely intelligible profane rage.

Robert Shapiro had assembled most of his so-called dream team by then: his friend from Florida, F. Lee Bailey (courtroom tactics); University of Santa Clara Law School dean Gerald Eulman (California codes); and Alan Dershowitz from Boston (constitutional law/appeals). Shapiro also brought in reputable experts: Dr. Michael Baden, former New York City medical examiner who had autopsied JFK, and Dr. Henry Lee, reknowned state of Connecticut criminalist. Eulman and Shapiro scrambled to file responses to the Gretna Green tapes.

June 24: Superior court presiding judge Cecil Mills thanked the grand jurors and recused them, citing widespread publicity from the 911 tapes and concern for the "integrity" of the grand jury process. He scheduled a preliminary hearing for June 30. Game on—beginning of the end for the prosecution.

June 30 to July 6: Six days of prelim. Prosecutors laid out the skeleton of their case; timelines, blood evidence, and OJ's shameful history of spousal abuse. They elided the classics—motive, means, and opportunity. They were a bit weak in those areas. Defense countered with questions about police procedure and innuendo of racial bias. Robert Shapiro told the media, "Race is not an issue here." Johnnie Cochran told him in private that he was naive. That or dead-ass wrong. Race is always an issue in black-on-white LA crime. Evidence of same still was smoldering citywide from two years earlier.

March 31, 1991: CHP chasing an '87 Hyundai Excel west on the 210: high-speed pursuit with lights and sirens. Twenty-six-year-old black guy driving, Rodney King, with two black passengers, all three drunk or lit on PCP. King screeched off the freeway. He hit speeds up to eighty mph on surface streets into Lake View Terrace north of Sylmar. LAPD squad cars road-blocked him at the intersection of Foothill and Osborne. Officers pulled the three occupants from the car. CHP backed off. LAPD uniforms assumed tactical command. They tasered the suspects and whacked them with staccato baton bursts—what LA Police Academy trainers call "power strokes."

A citizen named George Holliday videoed the brutal takedown from his second-story balcony. Holliday handed the tape to TV station KTLA. The footage caught pure excess! too graphic to deny and too ugly to whitewash. Four white cops charged with assault with a deadly weapon and excessive force. DA Ira Reiner cited adverse publicity; he changed the venue to Simi Valley in Ventura County.

April 29, 1992: The jury, ten/twelve white, acquitted the four white cops, and black LA exploded into six days of riots. Statistics: fifty-three dead, 2,383 injured, seven thousand fires, more than a billion dollars in damages. Mayor Richard Riordan called in US Marines and the Army National Guard. Rodney King nicked the city of LA for $3.8 mil in civil damages, another $1.7 for attorney's fees.

July 19, 1994: Urban League headquarters on Crenshaw Boulevard. Gil Garcetti met with distinguished LA blacks on the issue of fairness in the O. J. Simpson case. Among them, Reverend Cecil Murray of the First African Methodist Church; John Mack, president of the Los Angeles Urban League; Joseph Duff of the NAACP...and a prominent black attorney who had made millions civil-suing the LAPD for wrongful arrests and excessive force, Johnnie Cochran. Garcetti against the wall and apprehensive about another riot, promised a racially mixed jury.

Nicole and Ron were murdered in Brentwood. The superior court of LA County moved the trial from the nearest division, Santa Monica, into the Criminal Courts Building downtown. The superior court cited damage to the Santa Monica courthouse from the '89 earthquake and better security at the CCB. All but guaranteed: the jury, when selected, would be three-quarters black. The same day: *LA Times* reported that O.J. Simpson was offering a $250,000 reward for information leading to the arrest and conviction of the "real killer."

VI

January 29 to October 3, 1995: The *People of the State of California v. Orenthal James Simpson*, the most riveting, overpublicized courtroom reality saop opera in history. The day of the verdict, water usage plummeted nationwide: pre-TiVo, ninety-five million viewers distended their bladders fearful of missing the moment. Long-distance call volume declined by 41 percent. Trade volume on the NYSE dropped. Estimated one-day loss in US productivity: $450 million.

Johnnie Cochran was the most responsible for flipping the verdict toward the defense. Summer, 1994. Cochran earned good money during the pretrial phase as a talking head for daily overkill from CNN, CNBC, *Geraldo, Hard Copy,* and *Larry King Live.* Cochran wanted the case for this firm but wouldn't stoop to soliciting. He was the obvious choice for cocounsel, but pride told him he had to be invited. OJ called him personally from jail—that was all it took. Cochran signed in on July 15, 1994, four days prior to Gil Garcetti's meeting with black leaders, in time for OJ's second arraignment. (California criminal procedures require two arraignments: once upon arrest, the second following the preliminary hearing.)

July 22: Cecil Mills presided. Two orders of business. Judge Mills named Lance Ito as trial judge, and he asked the defendant for his plea.

OJ responded, "Absolutely, one hundred percent not guilty." A Johnnie Cochran prompt: play to *Court TV.* Cochran moved fast. He brought in juror consultant Jo-Ellan Dimitrius. Cochran knew her from the riots. She consulted for the defense on the jury that acquitted the cops who battered Rodney King; and for the defense of the Four 8-Trey Gangster Crips who nearly killed truck driver Reginald Denny at the intersection of Florence Avenue and Normandie the night of April 29, 1992. Denny was crossing into Inglewood with a twenty-seven-ton load of sand. His retro truck had no radio—he had no idea Watts had detonated. The LA-Four jerked him from his cab and beat the snot out of him. The trial ended with a hung jury.

For Cochran, Dimitrius ran telephone surveys, mock trials, focus groups, and shadow juries using downtown and South Central LA demography. Some amazing feedback. Sample: 50 percent of poll respondents didn't *want* to believe OJ guilty—he was typecast. Respondents couldn't reconcile atavistic butchery with the magnetic black football hero—their hero—who scampered through their living rooms in Hertz commercials. The superstar in a Rent-a-Car couldn't be Freddy Krueger.

More Demitrius: Middle-aged, divorced black woman of some education vilified Nicole, a twist on normal psychology. Blonde, sexy Nicole had seduced one of their own. She was living the life that should have been theirs. Respondents distrusted LAPD and the court system. They hated Marcia Clark—thought she was a honky bitch conniving to destroy a black icon. The huge irony: the prototypical juror for the defense resembled Marguerite Whitely Simpson.

Guilt seemed foreordained anyway. Blood drops paralleled shoe prints at Bundy. OJ contradicted explanations of the gash on his left knuckle. His hair matched strands from a knit cap found next to Ron Goldman's dead body. Cops bagged a bloody left glove lying on patio foliage between Nicole's and Ron's corpses. They picked up a matching right glove with Ron's blood behind Kato Kaelin's guesthouse at Rockingham. Size-12 footprints, slightly pigeon-toed, were stamped in the victims' blood at Bundy and in the carpet of OJ's Bronco. Pigeon-toed OJ was among 9 percent of the US population with size-12 shoes. The blood in the Bronco mixed his DNA with Nicole's and Ron's. His blood type dripped up the Rockingham driveway. Bronco carpet fibers showed at Bundy.

Blood-typing from June 16, 1994 pinned OJ as the killer 200 to 1. DNA probabilities drove the numbers into the stratosphere. Dr. Robin Cotton of Cellmark ran DNA tests for the prosecution.

May 10, 1995: Dr. Cotton took the stand and recited incredible figures: seventeen million to one against the blood on the sock from OJ's bedroom coming from anyone else; 9.7 billion to one for the drops paralleling the size-12 Bruno Magli shoeprints at Bundy, in the Bronco carpet, and up the Rockingham driveway. How could the prosecution lose?

Backtrack to the scene of the crime, June 12, 1994, midnight: A Brentwood couple, Sukru Boztepe and Bettina Rasmussen, flagged down a WLA black-and-white. They approached patrolmen Robert Riske and Miguel Terrazas. They had a stray dog with them—Nicole's white Akita, Kato. Kato's wailing had drawn the couple to the entry gate of Nicole's condo. The couple said they thought they saw a body on the ground. Riske and Terrazas beamed two corpses steeping in pools of blood. A blonde female in a black nightgown in a fetal curl on her front steps; a dark-haired man steps away, wedged between a tree stump and an iron fence, half sitting on his right side.

Riske radioed for an ambulance and backup. Sector cars sped in, lights, no sirens. Watch commander David Rossi showed. Uniform cops yellow-taped the perimeter to the intersection of Bundy and Dorothy, sealing off the block to the north. Cops searched the house: nothing ransacked, no signs of home invasion or burglary. Cops found sleeping children: a girl and a boy. No indication that the kids had seen or heard anything. Cops wrapped them in blankets and carried them out through the garage. A male-female patrol unit ferried them to the WLA station house at 1633 Butler Street. The older one, a girl, Sydney, close to tears, said, "Where's my mommy...I want my mommy."

Robert Riske saw a framed lithograph of OJ in the hallway. He saw an envelope with a Rockingham return address. He figured the connection and dialed WLA homicide coordinator Ron Phillips. Phillips checked the duty roster.

1:05 a.m.: Homicide detective Mark Fuhrman on call, home asleep in Redondo Beach. Fuhrman met Phillips at Butler Street. They took a car and a homicide kit. They logged in at Bundy at 2:10 a.m., the sixteenth and seventeenth police officers to enter the crime scene.

Lieutenant Rossi placed Phillips and Fuhrman with officer Riske. The three surveyed the cramped courtyard. Riske flashed his Magna-Lite at clues—a single glove, a watch cap, and track of bloody shoeprints, with parallel drops on the left leading out the back gate. Riske lit up the gate: a bloody smudge on the latch—possible case turner. German Mark Furhrman took precise notes—he listed seventeen items.

4:30 a.m.: Vannatter's partner, Tom Lange, checked in. He relayed a message from above: notify OJ so he can arrange child care.

Vannatter asked where OJ lived. Furhrman knew: he'd answered a 911 domestic disturbance call in the mid-'80s—OJ whacking his wife's car with a golf club. Vanatter, Lange, and Phillips were all detective-IIIs. Furhrman was a D-II. 360 N. Rockingham was less than two miles west. Vannatter figured ten minutes breaking bad news to OJ, five to set up a return visit for background on his ex-wife. WLA was out of the case. He'd leave Phillips and Fuhrman to arrange pickup for OJ's children. He thought he'd be back to Bundy by 5:00 a.m.

At Rockingham, they saw a white '94 Bronco parked with its ass end sticking into the street. Vannatter buzzed the intercom. No answer. They noticed a light burning in the house; a Bentley and a Saab in the driveway. Phillips thumbed the button. Fuhrman strayed to the Bronco. He noticed a red spot the size of a dime under the door handle. He called to Vannatter.

5:45 a.m.: Vannatter claimed exigent circumstance—the fear that OJ and/or his live-in maid might be inside under threat. All four detectives circled the property to the back fence. Furhrman scaled it—he was the tallest and youngest—and unlatched it for the other three. They pounded on the front door. Nobody home.

They gathered Kato Kaelin from one bungalow and Arnelle Simpson from another. They repaired to the sunroom off the back entrance of the main house. Kato reported hearing a thumping noise in back at 11:00 p.m., maybe as early as 10:45 p.m. Fuhrman left to check. Vannatter talked to Kato and Arnelle. Phillips phoned OJ in Chicago; Lange called the Browns in Dana Point. Denise Brown's reaction: "I knew he'd do it...OJ did it...OJ killed her...I knew the son-of-a-bitch was going to do it..." Fuhrman returned. He said, "You gotta see what I just found..." He brought them to a leafy area in back of Kato's guesthouse. He pointed to a bloody right glove. Rockingham now a crime scene. Vannatter left to draw up search warrants for the house.

Nobody knew it at the time—it would take fifteen months to play out—but the prosecution had just lost the case. Fuhrman could have been the star. His case notes included the smudge on the back gate at Bundy. He handed the notes to Vannatter, but Vannatter never read them. The gate was cleaned before SID could lift any prints. A bloody thumbprint on the Bundy gate? If it was Simpson's thumb, he is guilty, and Fuhrman's a hero. As it was, Fuhrman's discovery of the left glove at Rockingham gave the defense the one element it needed to manipulate the trial: an LAPD patsy.

January 23, 1995: Pretrial motion. Johnnie Cochran vs. Chris Darden: Cochran moved for permission to question Fuhrman whether he'd used the word *nigger* in the last ten years. Darden argued that the prejudicial nature of the word outweighed any relevance to the murders. Fuhrman had been a target since the preliminary hearing the previous June. Robert Shapiro's investigator, ex-LAPD Bill Pavlevic, had dug up potentially damaging intel on Fuhrman.

Lance Ito weighed the merits. Ito had permitted TV coverage. He loved attention and played to the cameras. He feared reversible error. If OJ were convicted, appellate motions would peck at the flaws in his transcript. Upheld appeals would make him look like an all-time judicial asshole. He turned the race card face up—he overrode precedent and ruled to admit Fuhrman's racist past. Green light for Johnnie Cochran.

February 12, 1995: Jury field trip to the crime scenes. Arnelle and Cathy Randa staged Rockingham. OJ wanted fires in the hearths and the American flag furled up the pole. The ladies brought in $1,000 worth of flowers. They removed a nude picture of Paula Barbieri from his bedroom. They removed pix of all the white women and of OJ in golf foursomes with rich white guys. They placed a picture of Eunice in a silver frame on his bedside table. They borrowed from Robert Shapiro's office a framed lithograph of Norman Rockwell's 1963 classic, *The Problem We All Live With*: little black girl in braids escorted to a Little Rock school by federal marshals—like OJ ever gave a fuck about *Brown v. The Board of Education.*

March 15 to June 13, 1995: Fuhrman on the stand now for six days. Lee Bailey probed exhibits collected by police during the early hours of June 13, 1994, insinuating evidence plants and sneaking up on the key question. Has Furhrman uttered the N-word anytime in the past ten years? Whipsaw. He says yes, and he's labelled as a racist cop, a career ender. He says no, and Bailey mousetraps him into perjury. Marcia Clark objected. Judge Ito sustained the objection. Even Lance Ito recognized that Bailey was grilling Fuhrman on evidence not yet presented.

June 15, 1995: Pivotal trial moment. Cochran goaded Chris Darden into asking Simpson to try on the Bundy glove. Darden bit. The defense was prepped. OJ met daily in MCJ with his entourage and lawyers. He couldn't handle being alone. Kardashian had assigned his assistant, Nicole Pulvers, to babysit him at twenty-five dollars an hour. Someone always with him. Mike Gilbert came and went—they were netting a fortune off autographs'dated during incarceration. Mike Gilbert asked him what would happen if he stopping taking his arthritis meds. OJ said his knuckle joints would swell. Lightbulb. At trial, OJ couldn't make the Bundy glove fit. He tried Rockingham. Same. OJ, later: "I knew they wouldn't fit…they're not my size…I've got really big hands…"

August 15, 1995: The defense had subpoenaed thirteen hours of tape, Mark Fuhrman interviewed by aspiring screenwriter Laura Hart McKinny. McKinney had retained Fuhrman for technical advice on a project she had envisioned about women cops. In the tapes, played to the jury and the television audience, Fuhrman uttered different declensions of the word *nigger* forty-two times. Worse, he bragged about his role in the OJ case: "I am the key witness in the biggest case of the century. And if I go down, they lose the case. The glove is everything. Without the glove—bye-bye." Fuhrman ruined.

September 6, 1995: Fuhrman back on the stand staring at a perjury rap. Gerry Eulmen cross-examining, replacing Bailey—no one trusted Bailey anymore; he was drinking heavily and leaking backstage info to the media. Fuhrman took the only path available. He invoked. The Fifth Amendment is a blanket—defendant cannot merely answer select questions. Eulman: "Detective Fuhrman, did you plant or manufacture any evidence in this case?" Fuhrman, dead in the water: "I assert my fifth amendment privilege." Jurors didn't hear the words for their precise legal meaning—that he was not admitting guilt. They heard, "I refuse to answer because I put the 'nigger' in the frame."

DNA couldn't save the case. In fact, DNA backfired. The concept was still fairly new—first used to convict a criminal in England in 1988, a murderer/rapist named Colin Pitchfork. Dr. Robin Cotton recited incomprehensible numbers indicting OJ. DNA lawyer Barry Scheck countered with gobbledygook about different methods producing different numbers. Sheck was New York edgy—he snarled when he cross-examined witnesses. He poured it on with spurious attacks on the LAPD crime lab.

Microbiologist Dr. John Gerdes examined the lab for the defense. He said it was "a cesspool of contamination." Criminalist Dr. Henry Lee testified. He was a scientist who spoke in accented Charlie Chan aphorisms. The jury loved him. He was theatrical. He alluded to corruption. He talked about "Dumping the whole pot when you find cockroaches in the spaghetti." Barry Sheck raised a question of moisture in one of the blood swatch transfers. Dr. Lee: "Something wrong." Neither Sheck, Lee, nor Gerdes ever said the DNA results were invalid.

The jury never got it. Degraded blood still retains its DNA properties. If OJ's DNA was present at Bundy, if his blood was mixed with Nicole's and Ron's on the glove, it still was OJ's blood—degraded or full octane. It doesn't re-form its molecular properties. Months of scientific testimony coalesced through technical exposition into one big yawn. The jurors reverted to human nature. They dismissed the things they didn't understand.

They reverted to bias—they were unsure about intricacies of genetic science but certain about racist cops and systemic LAPD abuse of minorities.

In closing arguments, Johnnie Cochran compared Mark Fuhrman to Hitler, referring to Fuhrman and Phil Vannatter as "twins of deception"—coconspirators bagging an innocent black, accusing Vannatter of targeting OJ and Furman of planting evidence.

The notion falls apart from two facts and two rhetorical questions. Facts: (1) under California law, framing a suspect in a capital case is in itself a capital offense. (2) Fuhrman and Vannatter had never met until that morning and didn't exactly click.

Questions: (1) How could Fuhrman know he would be ordered to Rockingham? (2) If he found the right glove at Bundy and dropped it at Rockingham, how could he possibly have known whose blood was on it?

Johnnie Cochran was preaching to Southern Baptists from South Central LA. He wasn't leading with logic. Logic could never sustain the syllogism: Mark Fuhrman says "nigger"; Mark Fuhrman therefore planted the Rockingham glove. Pastor Johnnie C. was speaking in revival cadence, alluding to blue-eyed Satans and colored corpses a la Billie Holiday, Harlem, 1939:

> Blood on the leaves
> Blood at the root
> Black bodies swing in the Southern breeze
> Strange fruit hanging from the poplar trees...

The same jurors had had living room access to exclusion their entire lives. White lives mattered in network sitcoms. Blacks hadn't evolved that far from the minstrel diversion of Amos 'n Andy. Check out Rerun's rainbow suspenders and red beret; Steve Urkel's nerd glasses, high-water pants, and falsetto pitch. Historic chance for jury nullification. For once, the white devil doesn't get to lynch the black brother. Johnnie Cochran closed with a reference to the bloody glove: "If it doesn't fit, you must acquit." Nine months of trial: jury out for four hours. Verdict, unanimous: Fuck you, Whitey.

Twelve to zero: OJ not guilty.

Across America, ninety-five million toilets flushed.

VII
Aftermath, Part I

OJ was desperate to resume life as before. Wouldn't happen. NOW organized a boycott; pickets outside any business dealing with him. Neighbors posted signs assailing him as a murderer. The Riviera Country Club nudged him out—a message through Skip Taft that he was no longer welcome. His sponsors cut him loose—even if innocent of murder, who'd want a product associated with a wife-beater? Paula Barbieri dumped him. Hero to pariah. He sold Rockingham. He tried another LA neighborhood before moving to Florida with his children and living off his NFL pension.

Everybody else scored. Johnnie Cochran: $4-mil book deal with Ballantine, 25–30k per speaking engagement. Robert Shapiro: $1.5 million from Warner Books. Marcia Clark: $4.2 from Viking/Penguin. Chris Darden, $1.3. Books contracts for Vannatter and Lange, Allan Dershowitz and OJ jurors. Nicole's closest confidante the last two years of her life, Faye Resnick, had published an expose during the trial, ghosted by a *National Enquirer* editor. Her account was a shocker—she had all the dirt on OJ's serial spousal abuse, but the timing of the book DQ'd her as a witness.

July 1996: Fred Goldman, Ron's father, obsessing, crushed by grief, outraged that his slaughtered son was merely a footnote to OJ's celebrity. Someone told him about a possible remedy—civil action. Fred shark-hunted for an attorney. He settled on a successful West LA business lawyer named Daniel Petrocelli—a UCLA guy. Petrocelli had never tried a wrongful-death case, let alone one as centripetal. He overrode his inexperience with commitment and guile. He was tireless, unrelenting, and clever. He matched Fred Goldman's capacity for obsession and shared Goldman's sense of injustice. The results proved he was the right man.

The trial was held in the Santa Monica division of the superior court, the district of the original crime. Significant: OJ's dream-team attorneys had scattered. He was represented in the civil action by LA guy Bob Baker. Jury makeup followed the local demographic—nine whites, a Jamaican, a black, and a Mexican.

Civil suits play by different rules. Discovery is exclusive—access to the opponent's material is made available, but only upon specific request. Double jeopardy doesn't apply. Defendants cannot invoke against self-incrimination—they face no criminal penalty, only financial. Plaintiffs may subpoena the defendant as a witness and for pretrial deposition. If defendants fail to appear for either/both, they default judgement.

In strategy sessions for the criminal trial, OJ clamored to take the stand; he had a fool's faith in his ability to schmooze a jury. His lawyers (except Lee Bailey) nixed the idea. Johnnie Cochran's female assistant, Shawn Chapman, worried about OJ's pheromones if he were cross-examined by Marcia Clark. OJ was incorrigible. She feared he would lose the jury playing cozy with a female prosecutor. For a small fee plus expenses, Cochran flew defense attorney Cristina Arguedas from Emeryville, near Oakland. Arguedas grilled him as a surrogate DA.

OJ opened on cue with charm and smiles. He was met with mirthless stares. Arguedas asked him about the domestic abuse. He smiled. She asked if he thought beating his wife was funny. He fidgeted. Arguedas swept his magnetism off the table.

Sample Q&A:

"What about your wife's 911 call?"
"We were just scuffling…"

"How is it she had bruises on her?"

"Well, you know, I think we were in the mud, and she fell, oh, she fell, down."

"How did she fall down?"

Shawn Chapman called it off. Arguedas went at him the next day. Robert Kardashian watched with the dream teamers. Doubts crept in. His friend vibed guilt. He voted with Cochran, Shapiro, and Barry Sheck. He told OJ: "She kicked your ass…"

The civil trial ran for forty-one days: 101 witnesses. OJ was his own worst advocate, as bad as when he was cornered by Cris Arguedas. Petrocelli deposed him for thirteen days and called him as a witness. Investigators in the murder investigation had cracked Nicole's safety-deposit box. The contents never came up in the criminal trial: Judge Ito ruled them "inadmissible hearsay." Pages from Nicole's diary trembled:

> I just don't think everybody goes through this…
> "You're a fat pig," "you're disgusting," "you're a slob …"
> "I want you out of my f–ing house."
> "I want you to have an abortion…"
> "I have a gun in my hand right now."
> "Get the f–out of here."

Box contents also included a letter from OJ to Nicole in 1989 promising to cancel the prenups if he ever hit her again.

Petrocelli's paralegal clicked on the ELMO—the courtroom projector—showing pix of battered Nicole from the 1989 New Year's Eve beating. Under Petrocelli's relentless cross, OJ dissembled double-talk. He claimed responsibility for the fight but wouldn't admit he'd ever laid a hand on her.

Petrocelli asked about the 1989 beating, referring to the "physical confrontation."

OJ: "I wouldn't describe it as that, but we probably touched... But I wouldn't describe it as 'physical.'"
Dan Petrocelli: "...and you heard the testimony that Nicole told the [responding] officers that you punched her and pulled her hair, right?"
OJ: "Yes."
DP: "And those were true statements by Nicole, were they not?"
OJ: "No."

The jury listened to OJ and watched battered Nicole on ELMO. Her bruises spoke decibels louder than his lies. He was cooked.

In deposition, Petrocelli had asked about the Bruno Magli shoes. FBI shoe expert William Bodziak had testified at trial that the killer was pigeon-toed and wore size-12 shoes, a high-end Bruno Magli "Lorenzo" style with a distinctive Silga Gomma outsole. Exclusive footwear—only 299 pairs purchased in the United States in '91/'92. The shoes, like the murder weapon, never surfaced.

Petrocelli showed him a recent photo in the *National Enquirer*—full-frame and date-stamped: September 26, 1993—never produced for the criminal trial. An AP stringer named Harry Scull had shot it: OJ wearing Bruno Maglis before a Bills/Dolphins game. Harry Scull had found it in his files and sold it to the *Enquirer*. OJ denied its authenticity: admitted it was his face but not his shoes, said the picture was faked. He said, "I wouldn't own those ugly-ass shoes." Defense figured it was an easy sell. Who'd believe anything from a supermarket checkstand rag that published stories about Elvis and JFK being miraculously alive and sharing a desert island?

December 18, 1996: The *Enquirer* picture came up at trial. Bob Baker called a photo authenticator named Robert Groden. Groden said 90/10, the photo had been doctored. Petrocelli's cocounsel Peter Gelbrum rose. He showed Groden a spread of pictures snapped by another Buffalo photographer named E. J. Flammer Jr.

Flammer's spread was time-stamped the same day as the Scull photo. OJ had been chatting with Flammer Sr. among a group of middle-aged boosters. Gelblum had received sample pix and negatives days earlier. Under civil codes of discovery, OJ's attorneys would have had to request copies. They couldn't—they were unaware that the Flammer pictures existed. Gelblum shattered Groden as a witness. No way around it: OJ owned ugly-ass murder shoes. The original of Scull's *Enquirer* snap showed impressions in still-wet bright-white end-zone paint: Silga Gomma sole.

February 5, 1997, 3:45 p.m.: The jury returned from five days of deliberation. Unanimous verdict on both counts: O. J. Simpson willfully and wrongfully caused the deaths of Ronald Goldman and Nicole Brown. Award: $8.5 million, split among Fred and Kim Goldman, Sharon Rufo, and Nicole's two children by OJ, Sydney and Justin. OJ no-showed the subsequent hearing on punitive damages. Bob Baker pled poverty. The jurors weren't moved. They hit OJ with an additional $25 million, for a $33.5-million total.

Aftermath, Part II

Ten years later, September 7, 2007: OJ rapping with Al Cowlings by phone from Florida. He was telling AC about his stash of possessions purposefully held back from the civil-suit creditors: game balls; autographed photos; the "lucky" suit he had worn during the criminal trial; three thousand signed copies of *I Want to Tell You*, OJ's self-serving book published from jail and ghosted by Lawrence Shiller. Mike Gilbert had stored the stuff in a commercial storage unit in Hanford, his San Joaquin Valley hometown.

The unit had been cleaned out, OJ said, by a guy named Bruce Fromong—former Gilbert associate—and Fromong's partner, Alfred Beardsley. Fromong was attempting a quick sale of OJ's goods through a Las Vegas auctioneer named Thomas Riccio. Riccio smelled triple-cross profits. He tipped OJ and suggested a burn. OJ jumped all over it. Riccio told Fromong he knew of some heavyweight collectors eager to buy his entire haul. The thing was set. OJ told AC: "Got me a couple guys. We going to Vegas and jack those motherfuckers."

AC: "you can't do that—you're OJ the Juice."

OJ: "That's what I'm saying."

September 13, 2007: OJ on a long drop in status from golf and tennis Hollywood buddies. Riccio led him and four throwdown thugs into suite 1203 in the Palace Station Hotel on Sahara Boulevard, a mile north of the Strip. Riccio was wired for audio. He was stinging OJ for Vegas cops under an immunity guarantee. OJ's crew pushed in, one of them rolling his own microcassette from a coat pocket, another pointing a .45 Ruger—OJ's idea. He wanted them to look tough for the caper.

OJ: "You think you can take my shit and sell it, muthafuckers…?" To the punk with the Ruger: "Don't let nobody out of this room." Ruger dude positioned Fromong, Riccio, and Beardsley, gesturing them toward the other side of the room with his gun barrel. Forced movement, even an inch: kidnapping under the law. OJ's crew stuffed cartons and split. The heist clocked six minutes. Fat-guy Fromong keeled over with a nonfatal coronary. Riccio dialed two numbers: TMZ to barter his tape, and 911, in that order.

OJ and his boys were arrested three days later, on September 16, 2007. His boys cut deals. Loyalty to OJ—an outdated concept, a habit for honky chumps from his former life. OJ was arraigned on twelve counts of armed robbery, kidnapping, and conspiracy. He was tried on all twelve: nothing dealt down. No credible defense to offset his voice on tape. Verdict was delivered on October 3, 2008, thirteen years to the day that he was acquitted for slashing Nicole Brown Simpson and Ron Goldman. Different this time: twelve-to-zero guilty.

Nevada District Court Judge Jackie Glass was unimpressed by OJ's celebrity aura and charm. She noted his multiple motives:

strong-arm robbery of property that had been hidden from the plaintiffs in defiance of the civil judgment. She said she didn't know whether he was criminally arrogant or criminally greedy. She decided it was both. She gaveled down the max: thirty-three years in the state prison at Lovelock. He would be eligible for parole after nine years, in 2017.

Upshot: O. J. Simpson skated in California on double murder but was imprisoned in Nevada for stealing back his own stuff. A Hollywood plot line twisting with irony, spinning toward a denouement of hard noir truth.

The postman always rings twice.

EPILOGUE
MERCED

The great Central Valley of California stretches 450 longitudinal miles through eighteen rural counties from the Cascade Range to the Tehachapi. The Valley comprises precisely 13.7 percent of California's land mass and approximately 0 percent of its glamor.

Forty-one miles north of the midpoint of the state, the city of Merced features blistering-hot summers, tule-fog winters, and a typical Central Valley agrarian profile: big profits from almonds, tomatoes, cotton, and dairy; epidemic allergies from airborne histamines; disportionate dependency on welfare—39–42 percent of the population on some form of public assistance. Merced is small (population twenty-six thousand in 1975), nondescript, and dull, a stereotypical "good place to raise kids." Like most Valley towns, nothing ever happens in or near Merced...except when it does, as in the Steven Stayner kidnapping, 1972; his older brother Cary beheading female tourists in Yosemite Park, 1999; the Chowchilla school-bus kidnapping, 1976; and a crime in 1975 that never made a headline, the murder of nineteen-year-old Denise Lynette Catlin, an underpublicized episode with ramifications rippling across four Western states.

FBI case file RENROB (Reno robbery): early June 1974, Reno, Nevada. Federal fugitive Curtis Ray Mickelson, thirty-five, escapee from McNeil Island in Tacoma, Washington, paused in the lobby of the First National Bank of Nevada on Second and Virginia Streets. He entered an open car of an elevator bank serving the basement through five upper floors. He punched B. The door whooshed open, revealing double glass doors across the hall rimmed in brass and accessing the main vault. Mickelson didn't leave the car. He hit L, rose to street level, and exited onto Virginia Street.

Mickelson added vault facts to what he already knew. The First National stood steps away from the largest downtown casinos—Cal-Neva, Harold's, Harrah's, the Comstock, the Silver Slipper. Post-closing any Friday, it had to be fat with gambling jack. Mickelson began formulating a plan.

Fifty-four-year-old parolee Ed Malone flew in from Los Angeles on June 22, the day of the annual Rodeo Parade. Mickelson and Malone dipped into the entry alcove that separated the building lobby from the elevator stand. They rode down. Nobody in the vault. Malone stood guard. Mickelson pulled a pick set from a gym bag. Within seconds he'd sprung the lock and opened the door—he had mastered locksmithing in prison from a Bell Saw Institute correspondence course. He unscrewed doorplate bolts and replaced the lock assembly with a dummy—five minutes.

They walked a few blocks west to a room at the Fireside Motel. Mickelson spread his kit on the table. The lock was old; the tumblers fell loosely into his hand. Exact reassembly was impossible. Mickelson improvised. He left in two tumblers, trashed the other three. He imprinted a blank and filed serrations—easier with two tumblers. He replaced the cylinder, tightened the spanners, and inserted his new key. The lock clicked open. Short stroll back to FNB to reinstall the lock.

September 27, 1974: They had added an accomplice, another parolee, thirty-four-year-old hard case Floyd Clayton Forsberg, from Oregon. They hit the bank at 6:10 p.m., coinciding with a Shriners parade along Virginia Street. Mickelson had boosted an E-plate van in Sacramento from the California DMV. They parked in a garage in the alley behind the bank. They dressed in painters' overalls and desert boots, with adjustable gray gimme caps and sunglasses. Mickelson had a miniature police scanner in the breast pocket of his coveralls, wired with an earbud. He carried two large green duffel bags. Forsberg lugged a blue duffel; his held handcuffs and leather thongs. They wedged .357s inside the waist belts under their coveralls.

They slipped on old-woman Halloween masks. They took the lobby elevator to the basement. Mickelson keyed them through the glass doors. They drew guns. They herded nine shocked bank employees into the vault. They cuffed the employees' hands, tied their ankles with the thongs, and ordered them facedown on the floor. Thirty minutes later, the DMV van blended into traffic toward Sparks, loaded with $1,000,044 of FDIC money. At the time, it was the largest cash bank holdup in US history.

Bound bank employees wriggled on the ground. One of them worked free and hit the alarm. Cops and feds converged, lights, sirens, and confusion. The feds assumed command—bank robbery a federal crime. Local agents John Norris and Tom Dempsey took statements from shaken employees. They collated facts. They speculated inside job. The bandits had entered the vault area through a locked door; a manager pointed to cash-drawer keys without resistance. No one was harmed. The feds strapped all nine bank workers to polygraphs. All nine needled truth. The feds scratched the insider angle. Division HQ in Las Vegas dispatched a bank squad: twenty agents working on leads. "With all that brass, our biggest job was trying not to look stupid," said Tom Dempsey.

September 29, Monday night: Norris answered the ringing phone. An agent from Portland, Oregon, named Regis Boyles calling from a vacation in Cleveland. Boyles: "Tell me about the holdup,

I think I know who pulled it." Norris recited MO facts: time of day, method of entry, handcuffing and binding of employees, stashing employees in the vault—everything down to the desert boots and Dodge van. Boyles said: "Yeah, that's him. Curtis Mickelson. He crashed out of McNeil 18 months ago—he was doing 22 years. We're looking for him for two vault jobs I know goddam well he pulled. Someone else you need to look up: Floyd Clayton Forsberg. He was at McNeil with Mickelson—they were weightlifters. He's on parole out of Oregon. We think he helped Mickelson escape. We think his girlfriend, Deetta Schulze, harbored him."

Tom Dempsey, after Norris rang off: "He's here. He's been spotted. We got a flash on that guy, the one Boyles is talking about, Mickelson." Dempsey dug into a stack of file folders. He fished out a note. Curtis Ray Mickelson, alias Curt Mickelson, Curtis Ray Nickerson, Butch Mickelson, Mike Mickelson. Thirty-five/blond/green/five foot eleven/150 pounds. Several months earlier, an informant recognized the driver of a Mercury Cougar stopped at a red light, a Korean woman named Kim. The informant knew her from the casinos and clubs—a card dealer. He locked in on her passenger. He recognized him: Butch Mickelson. He called in the plate.

Agents ran Kim's Cougar and came up with a Rizzo Street address in Sparks. They canvassed the area. Rizzo Street neighbors ID'd Mickelson's mug shots. They knew him as Michael Ronnigen. The feds rented a nearby apartment. They watched 2137 Rizzo through a high-powered telescope and came up empty.

They worked Mickelson's known associates and came up with Ed Malone. Malone was gray-haired and wore rimless glasses. He looked like Dennis the Menace's next-door neighbor, Mr. Wilson. As a young man, Malone was bounced from a Catholic seminary for fag proclivities. He turned to a career in bank robbery. In 1968 he was sentenced to McNeil for holding up a So-Cal S&L. Malone file note—Malone to one of his POs: "I look at a bank, and I start thinking how I'm going to rob it." Malone had been paroled in the spring of '74 but broke contact with his PO.

September 29: Federal agents in Portland spotted Forsberg. They lurked in his shadows, tailed him close, and marked his whereabouts. They monitored his mail and spending patterns. They interviewed relatives and associates. Forsberg had hired a Portland lawyer, Terence McCauley. McCauley wanted no part of him; he tipped agents. Forsberg had retained him on a $5,000 cash payment, all in five-dollar bills.

October 24: Feds met with Forsberg and Deetta in McCauley's office. Forsberg said that on Thursday September 26, they had driven her Plymouth Valiant from Portland to Seaside, Oregon. He said they camped near Seaside that night; he couldn't recall precicesly where. He said the following day, Friday, September 27 (the day of the heist), they went to Lincoln City. They ate dinner in a café. That night, they headed north fifty miles and camped at Netarts. He said that on Saturday, September 28, they pushed south from Netarts and developed car trouble—problem with the electrical system.

He said they tried visiting Deetta's daughter, Mary Schulze, in Eugene. Mary wasn't home, but they talked to her landlord. Forsberg said he tried the car again. It seemed to run fine. They returned north along coastal Highway 101, where 101 intersects the Sunset Highway. He said the electrical problem happened again. He said he hitchhiked to Portland, rented a car, and returned to the Valiant. He said they kicked the Valiant back to life and they brought both cars back in tandem. He said he had the Valiant in for repairs on Monday, September 30.

Interrogating agents knew Floyed and Deetta were lying—story too elaborate, vague at key points, dotted by witnesses not trained to pay attention. Deetta's employment records said that she hadn't worked from September 26 to September 30. A car-rental receipt showed that Floyd had rented an Avis car on September 28,

Saturday night, and kept it for one day and sixteen hours. Service records confirmed that Floyd and Deetta had taken the Valiant in for repairs. The service manager at Roy Burnett Motors said they took in the car but were unable to wait. The service manager voided the ticket.

Forsberg and Deetta dropped from sight, but agents stayed busy. They watched Forsberg's lawyer and Deetta's relatives. Near Christmas, they flipped Deetta's son-in-law, Bob Youngs. Classic bureau double play. They threatened Youngs with prosecution for harboring but offered him $2,500 to snitch. Some choice: Youngs opted for the money. He said Floyd and Deetta had been in New York for five weeks.

He said they were moving around, laying cash on Deetta's relatives to hide them. He said they had given him a large sum of money to put down on a remote piece of property near Amboy, Washington, in Cowlitz County near the Oregon border. He said that Deetta bought a Ford Bronco in the name of Janet Craig.

January 3, 1975: under a pounding rain at five in the afternoon, Floyd and Deetta drove a Ford Bronco to the post office in Amboy. Surveilling FBI agent Thomas Manning watched them leave with a handful of envelopes. He tailed them loose to two-lane road 503. He radioed the Cowlitz County sheriff's department in Kelso who patched it to patrol deputies. A two-man unit fell in behind the Bronco just east of Woodland. Forsberg's rear-view mirror filled with pulsating red light.

Mickelson and Malone were already in custody. They had left Sparks on Saturday night, September 28, in a blue Chevrolet. In Las Vegas, they separated: Malone flew to LA, and Mickelson stayed in Nevada. After a week in Vegas and a few days in Phoenix, Mickelson went home to LA. He abandoned the blue Chevy in long-term parking at LAX. He paid $30,000 cash to an Orange County car dealer named Bill Rennick for two '75 Chevy Monte Carlos. The feds knew of the Mickelson-Rennick connection. They had been running a mobile stakeout of Rennick's house, 1807 Irvine, Newport Beach.

On November 22, agents spotted a '75 Monte Carlo in front. They saw a man stroll out and wave to another man, who remained on the porch. They saw an old guy in glasses at the wheel of the car. They double-checked headshots in their file folder. Positive: Rennick at the door, Mickelson headed to the curb, and Malone the driver.

They screeched their duty car sideways within inches of Malone's Chevy with. Mickelson tensed on the balls of his feet. His hands dropped. The agents drew down, yelling "FBI," telling him to throw up his hands.

The car dealer had stepped down from the porch and was scudding left across the lawn toward a hedge between his and the house next door. Agent commands stopped him where he stood. One agent moved toward the driver's side of the Monte Carlo. He cocked his .38, held it tight in both hands and pointed it at Ed Malone's left temple. The other rushed Mickelson. Mickelson's hand snaked toward his right hip. The fed hammered back his revolver and drew a bead. Mickelson gave it up.

Spring, 1975: The jailbreak had been anticipated for three months. Floyd Forsberg had laundered bank money through a Santa Ana attorney, a bent ex-police captain named Frederick Hopper. Forsberg found Hopper through another member of the McNeil Island weightlifters clique, a big dude named Lawrence "Giant" Graham.

Graham had been paroled from McNeil in March 1975. He returned to So-Cal to mule for Hopper. Hopper knew Forsberg had been captured. He knew about RENROB. He had ideas about the bank money. Hopper flew to Reno and used his lawyer credentials to visit Forsberg at Washoe County jail. He convinced Forsberg to retain him offically. Hopper told Graham to recruit a goon for a crashout. Graham tapped a San Diego County ex-con, a drug runner named Clark Timmons.

They gathered at Graham's house, 312 Garner Street in Santa Ana. Timmons termed it "discussing things pertaining to helping Mr. Forsberg" and working a scheme for laundering money that Hopper said "came from a bank job in Reno." Hopper offered preposterous escape alternatives in meets held over a period of two weeks.

Hopper said he could put Timmons inside the jail with bogus attorney papers (attorneys are not subject to search). He said that Curtis Mickelson and Ed Malone were the only witnesses who could place Forsberg in Reno the night of September 27, 1974. Hopper said that he had smuggled LSD to Forsberg in WCJ. He said they could lace acid with strychnine. Forsberg could feed it to Mickelson and Malone. With them dead, the case against him would disappear. Alternative scheme: Hopper would pay Timmons $5,000 to snipe Mickelson and Malone as they were transported from the jail to the courthouse across Riverside Street. Timmons rejected the first as flaky, the other as way beyond risky. Hopper tabled the issue.

April 23, 1975: Timmons at Graham's Garnsey Street house for another meet. Timmons arrived with a young blonde, "Denise, from Merced." Hopper was cold to her presence. He told her to wait in a bedroom. When she padded away, he produced a canary-yellow legal pad. Three pages of the pad outlined in Floyd Forsberg's handwriting another escape scheme. Hopper and Timmons alternated reading. They liked it. They green-lighted a breakout for three days later.

Denise's last name was Catlin. She was nineteen and naive: a '70s kid desperate to belong, thrilled to be the girlfriend of a big-time dealer. Timmons carried a CDL and social security card in the name of Dennis Crowley. A drug dealer in Escondido named Baba told him that federal officers were asking about a "Dennis."

He figured the Crowley ID was blown. He had called his parole officer. The PO told him the feds had issued warrants—parole violation and suspicion of narcotics trafficking. He couldn't afford to be stopped. He told Hopper that Denise was his driver. Hopper seized it. He suggested that Denise wheel the jail break.

They called her in. They spelled it out, told her it would involve criminal activity. Denise Catlin stepped across a fatal line. In the seventies, drug guys were cool. "The man" was the enemy, hers and everyone else's under the age of thirty. Dennis would take care of her. No thinking took place. Millions like her in America. Most of them survived the era into adulthood. She was one who didn't. She signed on.

April 24: They spent the night in Merced with Timmons's friend, Hubert "Huck" Hunwardsen, an ex-con who ran a body-and-fender shop on the Yosemite Highway and lived nearby. Denise was friends with Hunwardsen's wife, Pokey. Denise had met Timmons when Pokey had introduced them at a party.

They were in Reno the next night, April 25, a Friday. They checked in to the six-story Riverside Hotel, 17 South Virginia Street. The Riverside stands six feet from the building next door—the Washoe County jail. Clark Timmons registered as Leroy Gaines. Gaines was a So-Cal biker who had burned Timmons in a drug deal the previous January. Timmons figured any investigation would involve hotel cards. He figured records checks could cause trouble for Gaines, maybe flush him from hiding. Timmons asked for room 633. It was available.

April 26, midnight: Graveyard-shift change at WCJ. Timmons and Denise had been watching John Wayne in *The Green Berets* on television. Timmons dressed in black pants, a thick black sweater, and a black watch cap. He wore laced-up black high-top tennis shoes with white trim. He slipped black socks over his tennis shoes—no white showing. He wriggled his fingers into black handball gloves. Room 633 was on the southeast corner of the hotel building, on the side closest to the jail. Room 633 had a view from the window that spanned the jail's rooftop and the street entrance below.

Early that day, Timmons had purchased an aluminum extension ladder from a Sears-Roebuck in Sparks. He had taken it to the roof through the back stairs. He stepped lightly now into the hallway. He carried a stuff sack packed with coveralls, a coil of rope, a 9mm Browning, extra ammo, and a sack of tools. He pushed through the fire-escape door, into the stairwell, and through the door to the roof. He was blasted from the cold. Whistling winds dropped the mercury below twenty degrees. Timmons laid the ladder flat across the gulf between the hotel and the jail buildings. He slung the tool sack around his neck. He went across on his hands and knees. The tools clanged on the ladder rungs.

Forsberg figured to make his run at ten on Saturday morning, two hours before the lunchtime head count. Forsberg knew the system would be shut down for repairs on April 26. Without hot or cold air rushing through, the ductwork was a tunnel. He would enter through a shower-room ceiling grate and crawl to the rooftop chiller that Timmons was unbolting. Timmons needed four and a half hours. His fingertips went numb in the 17-below wind chill. He squirted the bolts with Liquid Wrench. He took each one a turn at a time. He was wary of making noise or setting off an alarm.

He was in the shower in their hotel room by 4:30 a.m. At eight Timmons was downstairs in the garage, packing the Mercedes. Denise sat behind the wheel, nerve ends jangling. He told her to pull across from the jail and park with the engine running. He said, "When you see people come off the roof, pull up to the Island Street entrance." He returned to room 633 to wait for Forsberg.

Forsberg wasn't reported as missing until the noon meal roll call. By that time, he was in California traveling Gold Country back roads, headed toward Merced in Timmon's Mercedes piloted by Denise Catlin. Federal agents backtracked to room 633 at the Riverside. The name Leroy Gaines dead-ended. But a parking stub from the garage yielded the license number of Clark Gable Timmons currently residing in El Cajon, California. John Norris went to work on the Timmons ID. He checked that Timmons had done time at McNeil with Forsberg and Mickelson.

He ran down his list of Timmons KAs and settled on Lawrence Field Hart, nicknamed "Tangle-Eye," currently on parole, a Gypsy Joker biker-gang guy. Hart operated a B&F in Santa Cruz. He lived in the mountains west of Highway 1, in in a rundown house lost among the redwoods near Boulder Creek.

Hart and Timmons drove to Portland to pick up Deetta Schulze. Denise stayed in Merced with Forsberg. Hart and Timmons drove all night down Interstate 5, rotating shifts at the wheel. They drove down the straight spine of Oregon, past Eugene, Corvallis, Roseburg, Grants Pass, and Medford. They crossed the Cascades into California and drove past Redding and Red Bluff, Sacramento and Stockton.

They arrived midmorning on April 28, a Monday, at the Murrieta Motel in Merced. Clark Timmons unlocked the door to room 50. Floyd clean-shaven. The last time Deetta had seen him he had a beard. His black hair had been dyed blonde. Deetta scoped the young girl in the room. Denise Catlin was thirty-four years her junior, alone in a motel room, paying fond attention to her husband. Deetta was a scorpion. Denise was a Central Valley innocent halfway to dead.

Wednesday, April 30: John Norris teletyped the special agent in charge of the San Francisco division, Charles Bates, who'd been the SAC conducting for the Patty Hearst investigation. Bates ordered a team of agents from the Santa Cruz field office to stake out Hart's place in Boulder Creek.

Hart lived on Fern Avenue, where Fern dead-ended in an unpaved turnout. A two-man team eased into the turnout. Hart's house was a tin-roofed, batt-and-board shack with a scatter of cars parked off to the side: white '74 Mercury Monarch, red '67 Mercury, dented black VW Beetle, and an old green-and-cream Dodge pickup.

The agents saw the white Mercury heading down the driveway. At the bottom, it pulled out onto the macadam coming their way, turning in front of them, moving down the hill at an even pace. The agents eyeballed: driver didn't fit the description of Floyd Forsberg or Larry Hart. The white Mercury turned right on 236, heading toward Santa Cruz. The agents held back. The red Mercury bounced toward them. This driver: bearded face drooped by scars on his brow. Tangle-Eye, Larry Hart.

Agents followed the action. The white Merc had doubled back on 236. Red and white met on the shoulder facing opposite directions. Both drivers spotted the agents. Red spun gravel and screeched toward town. White's driver bolted from the car, dashed to the woods, and disappeared into the trees. The feds broadslid next to the white Merc. They scoped the registration: a rental from Merced. They pulled the agreement from the glove box—from a Hertz office in Merced, Walsh and Ramirez, dated Monday, April 28, 1975, charged to Dennis Crowley.

Clark Timmons, a.k.a. Dennis Crowley, jogged through rough forest terrain eleven miles to Felton. He was breathing hard and sweating, adrenalin pumping. He bought a pair of running shoes at a Western Auto store on Main Street. He laced them on and dumped his $150 dress boots. He jogged to Larry Hart's shop in Santa Cruz. Denise was standing in Hart's shabby office. She updated: the feds had returned to Hart's house and had grilled her and Larry Hart's common-law wife, Jackie Perry.

Denise said she showed the feds her driver's license and said she was a friend of Jackie's who was visiting from Atwater. She said they didn't seem too interested. She said they kept asking about "Larry and Floyd and Floyd's wife." Hart gave Timmons money, several thousand. Timmons told Denise to round up the Forsbergs and move them fast. He peeled off a few hundred and told her to buy a junker in her own name. Timmons left on foot. He ran across town to a Mercedes garage he knew. He bagged a mechanic's shirt with an oval name tag sewn onto the pocket. He hustled from the garage to the house of a friend, Ray Bubblets. He hid two days with Bubblets.

Denise Catlin moved with fugitive fear. She bought a '65 Chevy Bel Air off a lot. She had left the Forsbergs at Jaye's Timberlane Resort in Ben Lomond off Highway 9, two miles north of Felton. Denise yanked them out so fast she didn't bother to pack her belongings or Timmons's—even replace the cap on an open jar of mustard. She transported them to the Hitching Post motel in Santa Cruz. They hid in the Hitching Post for three days. She hooked up with Timmons through Larry Hart via pay phone.

Friday, May 2: RENROB hit the Valley from two pieces of information, the Merced rental receipt from the white Merc and a Larry Hart KA, a local punk named Hubert "Huck" Hunwardsen. Fifty-year-old Tom Walsh was the senior resident agent in Merced. He worked with four agents: Mel Shannon, Jerry Hicks, Herb Davis, and Denny Hughes. Jerry Hicks had taken the call from the assistant special agent in charge (ASAC) in Sacramento. The facts were sketchy: six days earlier, Floyd Clayton Forsberg had escaped from the Washoe County jail with the help of two accomplices, a man and a woman. The woman was thought to be Forsberg's fifty-six-year-old wife, Deetta, who had jumped bond in Oregon three days earlier. The man was thought to be a So-Cal ex-con named Clark Gable Timmons. The ASAC said, lean on Hundwardsen.

Hunwardsen lived outside the city limits on the Yosemite Highway, off the corner of Moomjean and 140. Tom Walsh knew the area. It consisted of one street three blocks long a mile or two east of town on the Yosemite Highway, a downscale cluster of stucco shanties with tar-paper roofs. Moomjean had no curbs or gutters. Front yards were overrun by scrap autos and brown weeds. Hunwardsen's occupation fit. Walsh tagged it a bandit neighborhood. He said, "They all come out of the joint as body and fender men."

They hit the place at 2:00 a.m. on May 3. Bureau protocol, late-night raids—late nights caught suspects off guard—had to do with sagging biorhythms. Both federal cars formed a vee in the weeds of Hunwardsen's front yard. Lights blazed inside. A man answered the door. Jerry Hicks stood off to one side cradling a 12 gauge. Mel Shannon flanked him on the other side. Tom Walsh held his leather badge case to the light from the door. He said, "Hubert Hunwardsen? Huck Hunwardsen? FBI." Herb Davis and Denny Hughes covered either side of the house in back. Walsh entered; Hicks and his shotgun trailed him inside. Mel Shannon hung back.

Walsh scoped him: Five foot ten, 180 pounds, black beard, a mat of long black hair, no shirt, jailbird ink sleeving arms. Hunwardsen wasn't surprised he was rousted. *He's tough,* Walsh thought. Hunwardsen volunteered nothing. He stared at Hicks and mumbled monosyllables to Tom Walsh's questions. He knew the drill. "If they don't pull out handcuffs and Miranda cards, they got nothing." He knew Larry Hart but hadn't seen him lately. He'd never heard of Clark Timmons. He remembered a Dennis Crowley as someone he'd seen around town. He didn't know what Crowley did for a living. He'd heard of Floyd Forsberg but had never met him. Didn't know Deetta. Hunwardsen's wife—Walsh thought her name was Linda at first—sat in a chair. She offered nothing. "Huck told you how it is," she said. Walsh asked her name again. It was "Linday."

Tom Walsh had Catlin's name and description along with information Sacramento had relayed from Santa Cruz. Catlin's CDL listed an address in Atwater, a small Air Force town, population ten thousand in 1975, six miles northeast of Merced, home of since-decommissioned Castle Air Base.

Walsh investigated the Hertz rental lot at the Arco station on Twenty-Third and G. Nothing. He drove out to Atwater. The Catlins lived in a middle-income tract near the air base. Walsh found their corner house on Caliente Court. Master sergeant Franklin Catlin was nervous. Walsh ID'ed himself and showed his badge. Catlin figured the subject was Denise. He said neither he nor his wife had seen Denise for two weeks. Denise had her own place, a duplex on West Twentieth in Merced. "She's a good girl, you understand," he offered. "She's never been in trouble, run away, or given us any reason to distrust her." Denise had phoned long distance; she wouldn't say from where. She evaded questions. Denise's mother spoke in a British accent.

She said Denise hung up abruptly before answering any real questions. She said her tone was nearly incoherent. "She seemed to want to tell us she loved us, not for that I don't think, but like it was important for her to know we loved her." Frank Catlin said he considered calling the police, but he thought his story would sound foolish.

Tom Walsh profiled Denise Catlin as a lonely girl easily led. Her parents had moved from Virginia just after she'd graduated high school. Tough time to relocate. He asked about friends. Frank Catlin said she'd met people through jobs. She worked at a peach cannery. She worked at an earring stand at the mall. She had a friend named Anna. She roomed with a girl named Sandy. He didn't know last names. He added, "There's another girl who called when Denise was still living at home. Pokey. What's her real name?"

The mother: "Linda, I think. No…Linday."

Walsh: "What about boyfriends?"

The mother: "There's this fellow she sees from San Diego. Dennis."

Saturday, May 3: Denise and the Forsbergs drove the Chevy into a roadside rest stop on Highway 17 in the Santa Cruz Mountains.

They met Timmons and Ray Bubblets driving a 1969 Ford camper. Bubblets had purchased the camper for $2,200. Timmons and Bubblets had stopped at Jaye's to retrieve Timmons's and Denise's luggage. They switched rides. Ray Bubblets drove the Bel Air junker to the Hitching Post. Denise gave him a letter for mailing to her parents in Atwater with instructions to retrieve the car. Denise took the driver's seat of the camper. Timmons rode shotgun. They stashed the Forsbergs in the shell. They headed north on 17 to 101, up the California coast to Willits and disappeared for nearly two months.

The Merced investigation seesawed between Hunwardsen's house, his shop, and the Catlin residence. Walsh fed the Catlin interview back through the system. The feds revised their view. Denise was looking more like the jailbreak accomplice. Walsh vacillated. He built sympathy for Denise. He said, "Everyone on our side was assuming now she was a street-smart chippie who knew straight up what she was doing. They penciled her in with Forsberg, Deetta, Timmons, and Hart. I wasn't so sure. The more I talked to those poor parents, the less sure I was…I got nine kids. I felt what those people must be going through…"

Monday, May 12: Walsh ran the plates of a Mercedes parked among the crates at Hunwardsen's shop. Return hit: Clark Timmons. Tom Walsh called it probable cause. He obtained a warrant from the local US magistrate—in Merced, a lawyer working for the government part-time out of his office. The charge was escape and rescue. Walsh rounded up his agents and every deputy the sheriff could spare. They swarmed the B&F Quonset. They arrested Hunwardsen and Hart and impounded the Mercedes. The charges would never stand. Walsh didn't care. He wanted the hoods in custody bartering information for freedom.

Hunwardsen refused to deal. Walsh confronted Pokey. She said: "He's got me and the little boy. We're afraid of what Forsberg and them would do." Hunwardsen was peripheral and knew it. He stonewalled the federal charge. Larry Hart was cagey. He was sure the escape-and-rescue charge would bounce. He wanted freedom plus a pass as an accessory. "I got enough trouble for this already," he said. "And I don't want no more. I didn't rob no bank and didn't break nobody out of jail. I don't need the bullshit that's coming down on this." He agreed to talk but would never testify. "That has to be understood…" He said Forsberg was a killer: "You can't hide from a guy like that. He'd have you wasted in jail or wait till you got out and waste you then."

Monday, May 14: Walsh brought Larry Hart before the magistrate for a bail reduction amounting to an OR release. Outside, Hart delivered his first installment of information: "You know, they're going to off that little girl, Denise Catlin. They gave me the contract. It was that guy Hopper's order. His mule, Giant, Larry Graham, asked me if I wanted $5,000 to clip Clark's girlfriend. I told him no. I told Clark I wouldn't and he's in a crack over this thing. I hated to see it. I liked that little girl."

Forsberg, Timmons, Deetta, and Catlin had vanished. Agents spun wheels in two states. Merced showed slim promise because of Larry Hart. "We didn't have a hell of a lot of active investigation here," Walsh said, "except I wanted to keep the pot stirred. I was hoping to turn the wife, Mrs. Hunwardsen, Pokey, but that just went from bad to worse. She was scared of her husband, and he was scared of Forsberg."

Walsh watched Larry Hart place daily calls from a pay booth next to a supermarket on 140. Walsh guessed Hart was in contact with Forsberg. He guessed Hart knew he was being watched. "I think he was telling me in his own stupid way, 'Go ahead. Here's how you get them.'" Walsh implored Sacramento division headquarters for permission to tap the supermarket phone on 140.

Under federal law at the time, wiretapping was not illegal, but dissemination of wiretapped information was. Under California state law, wiretapping was illegal, plus it constituted trespassing to set up the wire. Post-Hoover, legal wiretaps were all judicial scrutiny and red tape. Even with bureau sanction, Walsh would have to obtain a court order under title 3 of the Omnibus Crime Act. The court order involves a chain of affidavits and judicial approvals. Walsh asked often. Sacramento refused every time. "They told me to take it up with the Department of Justice." The timing was all wrong.

Walsh said, "It was just after Hoover died…They worried about image. We'd carried on illegal wiretaps for years, until the late 1960s, and everyone wanted it swept under the rug. They were worried about the disclosures. Henry Kissinger and Alexander Haig had authorized taps on government employees suspected of leaking information to the press. Watergate was still hot. Daniel Ellsberg was still hot. They were worried about everything. They were scared shitless."

Walsh struck out wherever he went. He drove to Atwater. The Catlin parents said Denise had called them collect from Santa Cruz early in May, two days before Walsh had visited the first time. Mrs. Catlin elaborated. Denise had said, "Mom, I swear I didn't do anything wrong, but there's going to be policemen asking questions, and I didn't know…" Mrs Catlin: "It was just this strange message: 'Don't tell them anything, I can lay low for a while.' I don't think she knew about—what is that, 'statute of limitations.' She told [me], 'After a couple years, it'll be all right.'"

The case went dormant in Merced. Tom Walsh felt shackled. "I thought I could do something for her if they'd only turn me loose. I wanted to get those guys, Hart and Hunwardsen. I wanted to take them out back and kick their asses—to where they'd tell me what I wanted to know, or I'd break their goddammed fingers."

Timmons, Denise, and the Forsbergs had traveled north to Willits on Saturday, May 3. They stayed in a motel in Willits for two days. They cut to Fort Bragg on the coast and rented a house from an absentee landlord. Forsberg and Timmons tripped into Washington to dig up $45,000 in buried bank money.

Timmons and Denise left the Forsbergs in Fort Bragg. They slipped down to Santa Ana and cleaned the money through Timmons's Baja-to-Southern-California washateria. They changed the '69 Ford for a '71 International Travelall. Rent was about to expire on the Fort Bragg house. Fred Hopper took a call from Deetta Forsberg. Deetta said Catlin wanted to split. Timmons picked up an extension. Hopper asked him if Catlin would talk if she were arrested. Timmons said she might. Hopper said he wanted Catlin taken care of. Timmons balked. He offered to take her to Mexico. The situation hung fire. Timmons and Denise round-tripped to Fort Bragg, hauling the Forsbergs back.

Hopper stashed them in Romoland, in a rundown house his girlfriend Joanne Jost had purchased with a down payment of laundered RENROB money. Romoland is a Mexican migrant shantytown southeast of Riverside, population fourteen hundred. The fugitives holed up among blood-orange groves and desert dust. Forsberg grew restless. He was running out of money. He suggested hitting a bank in Oregon, Timmons and Catlin helping. Timmons didn't like the idea. Moods snarled.

Timmons didn't want to rob anything with Forsberg. Graham told him that he was responsible for the Forsbergs. Graham told him that if he couldn't take care of the Forsberg/Catlin thing, Graham would take care of him. They stayed in Romoland for two weeks. Graham came to the house one day and said the FBI was close. He said they could trace the Romoland house to Hopper and Jost. Graham told Timmons to move the Forsbergs to Oregon. Timmons repeated his Mexico option. He resisted ferrying the Forsbergs to Oregon. Graham asked him whom he liked best, Catlin or his El Cajon squeeze, Bobbette Lane. Timmons caved.

Timmons had been in contact with Bobbette Lane. The feds knew it and flipped her. She gave them the Riverside Hotel in Bend,

Oregon. Agents from Portland swooped down and took Forsberg, Deetta, and Timmons without incident. Denise Catlin was missing. The Forsbergs said she had split a fews earlier by bus. They couldn't explain she had left her suitcase and clothes in their motel room.

July 19: US marshals transported Clark Timmons from Portland to Reno. Federal agents John Norris and Alf Stousland interrogated him in jail off and on for two and a half months. Timmons was looking at escape charges, harboring charges, weapons charges. He was looking at first-degree murder. He was scared of Forsberg. Scylla and Charybdis—hard choices. Ultimately, he yielded to honor among thieves.

He rolled on Graham, Hopper, and the Forsbergs. He said Catlin was dead. He said Forsberg clipped her and buried her in a spot where he was planning to hide bank money, seven miles below Bend, near the Snake River turnoff from Highway 97 in the Deschutes National Forest. Portland agents found Denise Catlin's body exactly where Timmons said they would. They uncovered her remains on October 1, 1975, thirteen days after FBI agent Tom Padden and SFPD inspector Tim Casey had captured Patty Hearst in San Francisco. Hearst and Catlin: Two '70s kids with time frame, criminal complicity, and age in common but nothing else. One a high-society heiress to a conglomerate fortune, her story an international headline for nineteen months, the other a nobody from a nothing town who warranted no more than a page-six blip in the *Merced Sun-Star*.

Timmons claimed he knew the location because Forsberg had showed him where he intended to bury bank money from the Oregon heist. Timmons said he was hiking in the hills near Bend when Forsberg took out Catlin. Timmons feigned surprise that Catlin was missing. Timmons lied: he was on hand when Floyd Forsberg shot her in the back of her head. She trusted Timmons, a Judas goat who led her to slaughter.

Tom Walsh says he never felt right about what happened with Denise Catlin. When he retired from the bureau in 1978, he palmed a copy of Timmons's confession. He said he hoped one day he could use it to tell her story.

That day, finally, is at hand.

Postscript: Adjudication for Expedience

Deetta Schulze Forsberg was draped with charges: bank robbery in Phoenix with Curtis Ray Mickelson; parole violation; violations of the 1934 National Firearms Act; perjury; escape and rescue; accessory after the fact; receiving and concealing; unlawful fight to avoid prosecution; possession of dangerous drugs; harboring. The feds reduced Deetta to violation of title 18, bond default, and put her away for five years.

Prosecutors couldn't place Ed Malone inside the Reno bank. The US attorney severed Malone and Mickelson. Malone wouldn't testify against Mickelson, and Mickelson wouldn't testify against Malone. Forsberg, at large at the time, couldn't testify against either. Malone walked. Mickelson dealt a reduction-plus-protection by returning substanial sums of bank swag. He confessed to RENROB, implicating Forsberg.

Forsberg was tried by the feds in Nevada for parole violation, bank robbery, and escape—twenty-five years for the bank and twelve for the escape. He was looking at Leavenworth or Atlanta until he was seventy-three, when Deetta would be in her nineties. Oregon indicted him for murdering Denise Catlin. Forsberg knew the drill. He was a big-shot recidivist, at home in the Oregon system. State time over federal: Timmons's testimony would nail him either way. He plea-bargained for assurance that he'd serve life in Oregon. He was sentenced in June 1976.

PSS: Giant Graham wasn't charged; neither was Larry Hart or Huck Hunwardsen. The feds raised Hopper's prints from RENROB banknotes uncovered in Romoland. Timmons' confession fingered him as well. Hopper was convicted for abetting a jailbreak and money laundering. He was disbarred and served a year and a half. He was paroled to Orange County and found work as a legman for a shyster attorney.

Timmons received immunity on murder. He served a short stint in Nevada for his role in the jailbreak. The feds witness-protected him. In 1978, still with the bureau, Tom Walsh ran Timmon's DOB through the system. Still a goon, Timmons had been arrested under the alias Terry Clark Wilson six times since Denise's murder—for robbery, conspiracy, burglary, weapons and five counts of ADW.

Denise Catlin died before she had a chance to live because she couldn't discern Timmons and his crew for what they were: unrepentant crows among a murder of crows. Predatory creatures on the make, heedless of anyone else's lives but their own.

www.ingramcontent.com/pod-product-compliance
Lightning Source LLC
Chambersburg PA
CBHW071944110426
42744CB00030B/253